ANTHROPOLOGY AND CONTEMPORARY HUMAN PROBLEMS

ANTHROPOLOGY AND CONTEMPORARY HUMAN PROBLEMS

Fifth Edition

JOHN H. BODLEY

ALTAMIRA PRESS
A Division of Rowman & Littlefield Publishers, Inc.
Lanham • New York • Toronto • Plymouth, UK

ALTAMIRA PRESS
A division of Rowman & Littlefield Publishers, Inc.
A wholly owned subsidiary of The Rowman & Littlefield Publishing Group, Inc.
4501 Forbes Boulevard, Suite 200
Lanham, MD 20706
www.altamirapress.com

Estover Road
Plymouth PL6 7PY
United Kingdom

British Library Cataloguing in Publication Information Available

Library of Congress Cataloging-in-Publication Data

Bodley, John H.
    Anthropology and contemporary human problems / John H. Bodley. — 5th ed.
    p. cm.
    Includes bibliographical references and index.
    ISBN-13: 978-0-7591-1138-7 (pbk. : alk. paper)
    ISBN-10: 0-7591-1138-3 (pbk. : alk. paper)
    1. Ethnology. 2. Civilization, Modern—1950– 3. Human ecology. 4. Social
problems. 5. Social prediction. I. Title.

    GN320.B62 2008
    306—dc22   2007025062

Printed in the United States of America

∞™ The paper used in this publication meets the minimum requirements of American National Standard for Information Sciences—Permanence of Paper for Printed Library Materials, ANSI/NISO Z39.48-1992.

CONTENTS

List of Figures and Tables

List of Figures

List of Tables

Preface and Acknowledgments

THIS BOOK EXPLORES the development of humanity and our global prospects for the future. It explicitly links social and environmental problems, viewing them from a distinctive anthropological perspective on culture scale and the distribution of social power, considering the full range of cultural diversity in time and space. The focus is the global megaproblem of unsustainable growth in production and consumption that is readily apparent in the well-known contemporary convergence of resource depletion, ecosystem degradation, global warming, escalating energy costs, poverty, and conflict that now threatens the well-being of humans everywhere. Anthropology makes it possible to find solutions to these global problems by examining prehistoric and modern tribal societies alongside ancient imperial societies and contemporary commercial societies. *Anthropology and Contemporary Human Problems* is for readers interested in social science and history, environmental studies, globalization, and political economy. It will also be attractive as a supplemental reading in anthropology and sociology courses on globalization, cultural ecology, social class and inequality, social justice, the environment, sustainability, and development.

Much has changed in the world in the eight years since the fourth edition of this book was completed in 1999. This edition sorts the great diversity of cultures into three distinctive cultural worlds: tribal, imperial, and commercial, according to the size of the largest social units in each and the way social power is distributed. The tribal world is organized by small-scale societies with leaders who are actually public servants. The ancient imperial world was composed of chiefdoms, kingdoms, empires, slaves, and peasantries ruled by chiefs, kings, and emperors. The commercial world encompasses the entire globe within a vast and complex market-based society that is directed by a relatively small network of commercial and political rulers who disproportionately benefit from economic growth.

This analytic framework draws on the author's book *The Power of Scale: A Global History Approach* (2003), as well the most recent edition of *Cultural Anthropology: Tribes, States, and the Global System* (2005). This new edition stresses that global problems can be solved, but the major cultural changes that will be needed are now much clearer. Throughout it will be shown that scale changes in social organization can make it possible to distribute social power more equitably, reduce poverty, and reduce the energy costs of production and distribution. An important new focus is on the causes of global warming from a culture scale and social power perspective, linking it to poverty and misdirected growth. Much new material has been added on sustainable development, energy, oil depletion, food, and population, including helpful new concepts and methods such as the ecological footprint, and various development indices, including the UN's new Millennium Goals. The crucial role of the United States in the global system is also examined. Chapter 8 is heavily revised to include a discussion of several new global futurist models developed for major corporations, government agencies, the UN, and non-governmental organizations (NGOs).

There are many advantages to the culture scale approach, but most importantly it means that contemporary problems are related to particular cultural processes, especially the centralization and concentration of political and economic power. The decision-making role of the transnational global elite is addressed directly. The culture scale perspective emphasizes the long-term survival value of local and regional autonomy, the satisfaction of basic human needs, sustainable resource management, and social equality—all primary goals of tribal and small-scale societies—because these values are often undermined by politically organized large-scale states and global-scale commercial interests. The focus on culture scale suggests that many solutions to contemporary problems may be found by developing local communities supported by regional markets and ecosystems, rather than by making the continuous accumulation of financial capital the dominant cultural process throughout the world.

Acknowledgments

Earlier editions benefited from the helpful materials and ideas offered by the following students and colleagues at Washington State University: Fekri Hassan, Barry Hewlett, Tim Kohler, Bill Lipe, Frank Myka, John Prater,

Margaret Reed, Jim Rotholz, and William A. Warren. I also want to thank Audrey R. Chapman, Ricardo Falla, Thomas Headland, Daniel Salcedo, and Alan E. Wittbecker. The following reviewers commented on previous editions, even though I did not always follow their suggestions: Diane E. Barbolla, San Diego Mesa College; Daniel L. Boxberger, Western Washington University; Michael Chibnik, University of Iowa; Norbert Dannhauser, Texas A&M; Kathleen S. Fine-Dare, Fort Lewis College; Mary Kay Gilliland, Pima Community College; Robert H. Lavenda, St. Cloud State University; Robert Lawless, Wichita State University; Michael Merrifield, Saddleback College; Richard H. Moore, Ohio State University; Francis A. O'Connor, Lehigh University; Emily A. Schultz, St. Cloud State University; and Dianne Smith, Santa Rosa Junior College. I am also grateful to the reviewers of the fourth edition: Kathleen Fine-Dare, Fort Lewis College; Richard Reed, Trinity University; Nicola Tannenbaum, Lehigh University; and George Westermark, Santa Clara University. I gratefully acknowledge the guidance of my former Mayfield editor Jan Beatty, and the work of the production staff at Mayfield who helped shape the second through fourth editions, especially April Wells-Hayes and Lynn Rabin Bauer. Mary Roybal deserves special thanks for her thoughtful editing of the fourth edition manuscript. Some of the research incorporated in the fourth edition was supported by a sabbatical leave from Washington State University during the 1998–1999 academic year and by research grants from the Edward R. Meyer Fund at Washington State University in 1996–1997 and 1998–1999. I would also like to thank George Guilmet, Chris Harris, Gary Huckleberry, and Steve Mikesell for providing very helpful new material and suggestions.

The inspiration for preparing this fifth edition came from Rowman & Littlefield executive editor Alan McClare. Much of the research was carried out with support from an Edward R. Meyer Distinguished Professorship 2001–2003, and in 2006 with support from a sabbatical leave and a Meyer Project from Washington State University. I have benefited from the materials, suggestions, and stimulating discussions with my current and recent graduate students Kerensa Allison, Christa Herrygers, Troy Wilson, Xianghong Feng, Ben Colombi, Brad Wazaney, and Ming Kuo Wu. I am grateful for the continuing support that my home university and the College of Liberal Arts has extended to me. My wife, Kathleen, helped me think through too many of the world's problems, and I am more than grateful for her insights and endless patience. I dedicate this book to our children, Brett and Antonie, and our grandchildren, Lili and Ramona.

Anthropological Perspectives on Contemporary Human Problems

1

A knowledge of anthropology enables us to look with greater freedom at the problems confronting our civilization.

—FRANZ BOAS, *ANTHROPOLOGY AND MODERN LIFE*[1]

CULTURAL EVOLUTION, through processes that many would label progress, has brought humanity to major turning points many times: the adoption of upright posture, the first use of tools, the development of language, culture as an adaptive strategy, food sharing, village life, food production, social stratification, urbanization, state organization, and now the emergence of an industrially based global commercial economy. All of these changes have been decisive ones—crucial developments with critical implications for the future. However, at this point the outlook is suddenly different because orders-of-magnitude increases in the scale of societies, global population, resource consumption rates, and the concentration of wealth and power associated with growth in the commercial economy have dramatically intensified the problems created by earlier developments and significantly reduced the resiliency of both human and natural systems. The UN estimated that in 2003 there were more than a billion people living in "abject poverty."[2] The World Wide Fund for Nature estimated that since 1985 human consumption of food, fiber, and energy has exceeded the annual biological productive capacity of the world.[3] Now we also face a suddenly threatened global environment due to global warming.[4] This has only been possible because of our use of fossil fuel energy. It is difficult to imagine a continuation of present trends without the global socio-cultural system either breaking down or transforming in any of several ways. In that sense, the world's societies are at a crisis point. Drastic cultural changes will occur—the questions are what these changes will be, how they will be directed, and whose interests they will serve.

It is now clear that many of our most serious contemporary problems of global warming, resource depletion, ecosystem degradation, poverty, and conflict are inherent in the basic cultural patterns of our global-scale commercial civilization. These were not overwhelming problems in the small-scale tribal world, and they did not threaten all of humanity and the global environment until the dramatic scale increases in the twentieth century. Contemporary human problems are generated by the scale and complexity of commercially dominated human society. These are social organizational and cultural perception problems that will not be solved by further technological intensification. Growth itself has become the mega-problem because we are exceeding crucial size thresholds that define the practical limits of manageable social systems, given the moral frailties of human beings.

In many respects this book is volume two of my earlier work, *Victims of Progress*, which deals with the destruction of small-scale, domestically organized tribal cultures by much larger and more powerful commercially organized societies. Tribal people designed their cultural world around small-scale social groups. They remained small, segmenting and dispersing rather than creating hierarchies, and therefore managed to avoid the most destabilizing problems that now threaten contemporary civilization. The crucial point is that tribal societies were small enough that people could effectively monitor each other and restrain potentially dangerous anti-social or maladaptive behaviors by powerful leaders. This made it difficult for leaders to become rulers, and it reduced incentives for anyone to promote growth in the scale and complexity of society, or to maximize the flow of energy and materials. What we are now witnessing is perhaps the final irony of cultural evolution—the latecomer, global-scale commercial society, has suddenly become a cultural dominant, overwhelming all other socio-cultural systems at least in the short term. It has conquered the earlier tribal world, which was a proven long-term success. However, we now seem to be victims of our own "progress."

In order to improve our future prospects it will be helpful to take a very broad anthropological view of our present predicament. This will help us find new organizational and cultural solutions to contemporary problems that take into account our basic human nature and our biological limits. This is perhaps anthropology's most critical role. Anthropologists have the best understanding of the social and cultural forms that satisfied basic human needs for at least 100,000 years in the tribal world. It is worth considering why tribal peoples did not develop the social and technological capacity to destroy humanity. They had our brains, our personalities, and the same human nature, yet tribal people did not produce totalitarian societies that killed millions of people, and unlike the contemporary commercial world, they did not appropriate 30 to 40 percent of global biological productivity, and they did not cause global warming by excessively burning fossil fuels.

In order to restore social and environmental sustainability we need to reorganize to create more democratic societies, redistribute social power, and reduce the cultural incentives that promote unsustainable growth. This is not going back to the Stone Age; it is about reclaiming our future and making our lives better and more secure. Everyone needs to be engaged in social and cultural development. We cannot afford to allow a self-interested elite few to make the crucial decisions that shape everyone's future. All people must now take deliberate control over the socio-cultural systems that sustain their households and communities. This anthropological scale and power approach suggests that many solutions to contemporary problems may be found by developing local communities supported by regional markets and ecosystems rather than by making the continuous accumulation of financial capital the dominant cultural process.

Nature and Scope of the Problems

We face a global crisis of environmental degradation, poverty, and conflict. The human use of fossil fuels, electricity, and nuclear energy, which all converged in 1945, has multiplied our power over other people, society, and nature so dramatically that the future of humanity is at risk for the first time since the appearance of the first hominids some 4 million years ago. From an anthropological perspective we can conclude that the global crisis is an unintended outcome of many socio-cultural transformations directed by individuals who have used culture as a tool to increase the scale and scope of their personal power. These sudden changes have expanded the scale of human society and our individual powers far beyond the adaptive capacity of our basic human nature that evolved over millions of years. Individuals will advance their self-interest, as they perceive it, to the limits of their powers. Other people must counter those efforts when they become destructive, but this becomes more difficult as the scale of society increases.

The rapidity of the cultural transformations that created the present global crisis is astounding. Most of the major technological innovations that created the material infrastructure of the twentieth century[5] (electric lights, telephones, electric motors, electric generators, steel-framed skyscrapers, automobiles, airplanes, radio broadcasts, synthetic ammonia fertilizer, and typewriters) were developed between 1867 and 1914. The technological transformations in the post–World War II era—such as international air travel, the completion of the interstate highway system in the United States, television, antibiotics, computers, and the Internet—have simply expanded the technological foundation that was already in place by 1914. Although the adoption of these technologies has dramatically altered our ways of life and transformed the environment, they should nevertheless not be viewed as independent forces, because these technologies were called into existence and directed by individual investors, business leaders, and politicians with a common interest in promoting economic growth. Technology is a tool; what matters is how it is employed and to what ends. The most profound socio-cultural changes since 1950 have been in the scale of society, in our institutions, and most importantly in the great concentrations of private wealth and income, and of commercial and political power. Modern business corporations, with their ability to expand forever, are the most obvious human-directed growth machines, but corporations and the financial capital that they produce exist primarily as cultural ideas that give a few people immense power over many other people.

For most of human history and prehistory the scale of human societies, global population, and material production have increased only very slowly, or not at all. Growth itself was not a human objective. The Paleolithic era lasted perhaps 2.5 million years, during which there were at best only incremental intensifications in material culture and no dramatic elaboration of non-material culture until the last few millennia during the Upper Paleolithic, beginning some 50,000 years ago. Paleolithic peoples and their immediate hominid ancestors remained hunter-gatherers, foraging in the small, thinly scattered bands that produced small-scale, domestically organized societies and physically modern humans through a process that could be called *humanization*. This most crucial biocultural evolutionary process involves the production and maintenance of human beings as biological organisms, as well as the production and maintenance of the societies and cultures that sustain human beings. Culture is the learned and shared symbolic information and way of life and thought that people use to improve their own and their children's survival. The focus of humanization is necessarily to promote the well-being of the household, the fundamental domestic unit in which the primary functions of human biological reproduction and maintenance occur and through which much of culture can be transmitted to our children. Successful humanization also requires a human society of at least 500 people to sustain a mating network, to provide material and emotional support to households, and to collectively create, store, and reproduce vital cultural information through a common spoken language.

The humanization process helped people optimize their well-being by minimizing the cost of social activity while maximizing long-term sustainability. Today's human problems have arisen not from the cultural processes that make us human, but because humanization has been superseded by two more recent cultural processes—politicization and commercialization—that have undermined the well-being of most households while bestowing enormous advantages on a few. Furthermore, these new cultural processes have dramatically raised the cost of social activity and thereby have threatened both social and environmental sustainability. The most problematic aspect of the politicization and commercialization processes is that both give individual rulers and leaders cultural incentives to promote perpetual growth to enhance their personal power. This creates a vicious cycle in which growth gives leaders power to produce more growth until the system collapses.

The transition through the Epipaleolithic or Mesolithic period to food production in the Neolithic and to the brink of political centralization by the end of the Neolithic period was a rather gradual transformation that required perhaps 8,000 years. It occurred as part of the Paleolithic environmental crisis of global warming and sea level rise at the end of the last glacial period. In most of the world tribal peoples adapted to this natural environmental change by either downscaling their societies to fit smaller territories and fewer resources, or by intensifying their food production, becoming village farmers, herders, and gardeners. In a few regions tribal peoples allowed aggrandizing individuals to become divine rulers who used their political powers to promote growth, and within a few millennia succeeded in directing the establishment of the first cities, kingdoms, and empires, thereby creating the imperial world. Politically centralized imperial societies repeatedly grew to their limits and collapsed in seemingly endless cycles, until about AD 1350 when the entire imperial world seemed to simultaneously reach a global crisis of imperialism. This time economic elites, allied with political rulers, deposed divine monarchs, concentrated their economic powers, and created the commercial world in which perpetually expanding market transactions became the new dominant cultural means of concentrating social power. The institutional, ideological, and technological growth-machines produced by alliances between commercial and political elites have brought the entire globe to the brink of disaster in barely two centuries.

The present generation is experiencing humanity's most profound crises. Whereas earlier crises, such as the Neolithic transition, were certainly revolutionary in giving people a more dominant ecological role in the world, this change would have been virtually imperceptible to the individuals involved because they occurred over millennia, and their outcomes in particular communities would not have been obvious for hundreds or even thousands of years. Tribal people were generally able to adjust their sociocultural institutions to prevent their leaders from promoting runaway growth, but today we seem totally unprepared to deal with the complexity of a sudden new global crisis with many interconnected growth-related problems. Not only has the pace of culture change increased, but its scope has dramatically widened. The early evolution of human beings was not initially a global event. Humans have occupied all of both hemispheres for perhaps only 15,000 to 30,000 years, barely 0.005 percent of humanity's existence. The Neolithic global warming crisis unfolded very slowly. The first truly global-scale socio-cultural system was not securely in place until near the end of the eighteenth century when a relative handful of European elites successfully fashioned the cultural and institutional infrastructures that allowed them to create a growth-based political economy that spanned, but did not totally control, the entire world. The fully effective commercial world, capable of rapid growth, required electronic communication and fossil fuels to gain truly global cultural domination. As recently as 200 years ago, perhaps 50 million people continued to live in politically autonomous domestic-scale tribal societies. These independent tribal communities still controlled vast areas of the globe and were only marginally affected by either governments or commercial business enterprises. Now, however, commercialization has become a global process that has destroyed or transformed virtually all previous cultural adaptations, and has given a few thousand political and economic decision makers overwhelming power over virtually all of humanity, as well as the ability to speed the extinction of many other species, and to alter the earth's basic biological and geological processes on an unimaginable scale.

The most critical qualitative difference in the organization of contemporary cultural change is that change is now primarily commercially driven, directed by influential elites who control vast capital accumulations and powerful organizations and institutional structures. New technologies, information, and other cultural products that affect the daily lives of billions of people are produced by corporate business enterprises controlled by very few people. This commercialization process has produced a global-scale society that is staggeringly different from anything preceding it. Its impact on the biosphere, the process of cultural evolution, and humanity itself is impossible to predict because it is so unprecedented. If the commercially driven global society were to disappear overnight, it would leave an impoverished planet; in contrast, the extinction of humans during the Paleolithic era would have been of no more global significance than the passing of the woolly mammoth. The human impact of the present crisis is also far greater than any previous crisis because far more people are now alive than at any time in the past. The 8 or 10 million people who may have populated the world by the end of the Paleolithic represent only 0.1 percent of the 6 billion people living in 2000.

We are presently confronted with crises on the global, national, community, and household levels. Globally, the biosphere's capacity to absorb human insults is reaching a tipping point beyond which major discontinuities could occur, and critical world resources such as clean water, fossil fuels, and biological diversity are rapidly declining. Individual national governments must meet these crises while at the same time confronting a multitude of domestic threats in the form of political instabilities and social and economic distress. Many countries are now hard pressed to merely continue satisfying minimal human needs for food, shelter, health, and education, and seem totally incapable of meeting rising demands for increased levels of material consumption. Individuals may temporarily ignore certain global- and national-level crises, but at the community and household levels, where daily needs must be met, we are now confronted with health, family, and value crises of unprecedented frequency, scope, and complexity.

World Scientists' Warning to Humanity, 1992

> If not checked, many of our current practices put at serious risk the future that we wish for human society and the plant and animal kingdoms, and may so alter the living world that it will be unable to sustain life in the manner that we know. Fundamental changes are urgent if we are to avoid the collision our present course will bring about. . . . The greatest peril is to become trapped in spirals of environmental decline, poverty, and unrest, leading to social, economic, and environmental collapse. (Union of Concerned Scientists 1992)[6]

In 1992 the Union of Concerned Scientists issued one of the strongest global crisis statements of the century, the "World Scientists' Warning to Humanity." This unprecedented statement was signed by some 1,700 of the world's leading senior scientists, including five anthropologists, most of the living Nobel laureates in science, and the president of the American Association for the Advancement of Science. They warned that human actions were on a "collision course" with the global environment that threatened to make human life as we know it less sustainable and placed the future of humanity at risk. They predicted an increase in destructive conflicts, destabilizing mass migrations, and vast human misery unless effective corrective action was undertaken quickly. The greatest danger, as noted above, is that humanity will "become trapped in spirals of environmental decline, poverty, and unrest, leading to social, economic, and environmental collapse." Their warning covered specific threats to the atmosphere, water, oceans, soil, forests, biodiversity, and climate change that were leading to irreparable damage to global environmental systems. They felt that if action was not taken to halt these trends within ten to twenty years, the prospects for humanity would be "immeasurably diminished."

The Union of Concerned Scientists recognized that the world problems they identified required social and cultural responses to bring humanity within global limits. They called for a halt to environmentally damaging activities, to over-consumption by developed nations, and to unrestrained population growth. Recognizing the interconnected socio-cultural nature of these problems, they also called for the reduction or elimination of poverty, for gender equity, and for a "new ethic" to support the radical changes that would be needed. They also advocated a reduction in the use of fossil fuels and their replacement by less polluting, renewable energy sources.

A group of MIT scientists concerned over government misuse of science and technology formed the Union of Concerned Scientists in 1969. Throughout the 1970s and 1980s the group issued various statements against the arms race and poorly regulated nuclear facilities. In 1990 they began a campaign against global warming signed by seven hundred members of the National Academy of Sciences. It is significant that these scientific perceptions of crisis frame world problems in very broad terms. Scientists—whether physical, biological, or social—who view human problems from the broadest perspective recognize that they are socially and culturally determined and require radical social and cultural solutions, not simple technological fixes.

The UN Millennium Goals

The UN General Assembly's Millennium Declaration,[7] adopted in 2000, was a remarkable document that acknowledged some problematic realities about the contemporary commercial world. In its "Values and Principles" section the declaration stated that the "central challenge" facing the world was the reality that the costs and benefits of globalization were not being equitably distributed; many people were paying costs but not benefiting. Furthermore, the UN acknowledged that current patterns of production and consumption were environmentally unsustainable. The international system was not meeting its obligations to humanity. The declaration noted that a billion people were living in "abject and dehumanizing poverty." This is a mind-numbing number and actually equivalent to the total population of the world in 1820, suggesting that global development is indeed producing an odd sort of progress. Since 1820 the global economy increased more than fifty-fold, and per capita GDP (gross domestic product) grew nearly tenfold,[8] yet more people are absolutely and relatively impoverished now than were alive at that time. Certainly many of the billion people in high-income countries are doing very well, but more than half of the world is not. This global imbalance of social power is inhumane and dysfunctional, and creates fertile ground for disorder and conflict. This observation suggests that poverty can be viewed as a distribution problem, rather than a production problem, especially given the ongoing negative environmental consequences of further increasing economic growth and production. It seems unlikely that we will ever be able to produce our way out of this problem. The UN General Assembly committed world leaders to the goal of freeing the entire human race from want, but it spoke somewhat vaguely of achieving that by creating an environment "conducive" to development and the elimination of poverty. These UN objectives and other specific goals demonstrate the persistence of very serious global problems more than fifty years after the founding of the United Nations.

The seriousness of these human problems is also indicated by some of the specific goals that were agreed upon in the Millennium Declaration. Member nations resolved to reduce by half the *proportion* of humanity in extreme poverty, defined as living on less than a dollar a day, as well as the proportion that is hungry or without access to safe drinking water by 2015. They also wanted boys and girls equally to be able to complete a primary education by 2015, and they wanted maternal mortality reduced by 75 percent, and infant (children under five) mortality by two-thirds (table 1.1).

Another ranking of global problems was produced in 2004 by a team of some thirty-five distinguished economists working with the Danish statistician Bjørn Lomborg at the Copenhagen Consensus Center.[9] Their work seems much narrower and more cautious than the warnings of either the Concerned Scientists or the UN delegates in 2000. Like economists

Table 1.1.   Millennium Goals

By 2015
- Reduce by half the percentage of people living in extreme poverty, suffering from hunger, or with no access to safe drinking water
- Ensure that boys and girls have equal opportunity to complete primary education
- Reduce maternal mortality by 75 percent
- Halt and reduce spread of HIV/AIDS and malaria, assist AIDS orphans

By 2020
- Improve lives of 100 million slum dwellers

General Resolve
- Promote gender equality and empowerment of women
- Stimulate "truly sustainable" development
- Give young people "a real chance to find decent and productive work"
- Ensure that benefits of new technology are available to everyone
- Make essential drugs available
- Make sure the planet is not "irredeemably spoilt by human activities," and that resources be available for our children and grandchildren

generally, these business-focused economists consider economic growth to be the solution, not a problem. However, the Copenhagen Consensus is particularly significant because it demonstrates that the business community is taking global problems seriously. Lomborg is widely published in the business press and has been recognized by *Business Week* as one of the "50 stars of Europe" and one of nine European "agenda setters." Because the Copenhagen Consensus represents the view of economists, their 2004 ranking was directed toward the most "cost-effective" way to solve global problems. They considered ten world problems: climate change, conflicts, communicable diseases, education, financial instability, corruption, migration, malnutrition and hunger, trade barriers, and access to water. The inclusion of trade barriers in the list shows that these economists considered economic growth and trade expansion to be important solutions to global problems. They ranked seventeen projects to solve these problems, placing disease, malnutrition, and trade barriers and subsidies as the highest-priority problem-solving projects, and placing three projects to reduce global warming at the bottom as lowest-priority "bad projects." By 2006 the Copenhagen Consensus added UN ambassadors and experts to the panel of economists. This time they ranked forty "Challenges," adding sanitation, water, and education to the top five along with disease, malnutrition, and hunger, whereas subsidies and trade barriers were dropped to ninth place. "Corruption" appeared for the first time in the middle of the ranking, and one climate change solution, the Kyoto Protocol, now ranked twenty-seventh. Poverty and resource depletion did not rank as readily solvable problems.

Crisis Awareness and Response

The emergence of the global market economy has intensified many pre-existing problems and has touched off a variety of new crises. Qualitatively unique social problems, international political problems, and an environmental crisis have all suddenly materialized in rapid succession since the Industrial Revolution began in the eighteenth century and have now widened to include the entire globe. People perceive and respond to crises in many different ways, but in view of the pace and scope of the present multiple crises, our social capacity to adjust quickly enough is clearly in doubt. As the commercial world has progressed into its present crisis, many individuals and institutions have sounded the alarm to activate the initial negative feedback mechanisms, but the corrective response has been painfully slow and inadequate.

Certainly the earliest and most persistent resisters against the global commercial system have been the tribal peoples who have become forced participants, but they have not been alone or unsupported in their resistance. During the height of colonial expansion in the late nineteenth and early twentieth centuries, a very active group of British anti-imperialists[10] condemned the entire colonial adventure that was then feeding the expanding global economy and called for reduced industrial output. However, the relatively few very powerful political and economic rulers, whose decisions were directing the early stages of colonial expansion, easily swept aside these scattered protests.

Throughout the nineteenth century the enormous social upheavals produced by the early development of industrial capitalism were widely perceived as a social crisis by workers, religious leaders, political revolutionaries, and social philosophers in Europe and North America even as the vast cultural transformations were applauded as progress by their prime beneficiaries—the emerging captains of industry and finance. The dramatic changes in ownership and production accompanying the Industrial Revolution served to concentrate ownership and control in a few hands and increase profits, producing even more social power for the elite. This same industrialization process disempowered millions, driving formerly self-sufficient rural peoples to a precarious and dependent existence in the cities. The path taken by the leaders of industrial capitalism proved to be so disruptive and damaging to the social order that it spawned an almost instant outpouring of social criticism, dire predictions, outright rebellion, religious revitalization movements, and proposals for alternative development. Beginning in 1811, on the eve of the Industrial Revolution, unemployed English textile workers who were losing their jobs to mechanization attempted to halt the entire process by attacking the machines and the factory system directly. These early resistors, called Luddites, were not opposed to new technology as such, rather they opposed the way it was being organized and directed, and the ends to which it was being employed.[11]

Even before the 1848 edition of the revolutionary *Communist Manifesto* of Karl Marx and Friedrich Engels, social theorists and political activists put forth many novel proposals for alternative forms of society in response to the escalating social crisis produced by industrial capitalism. For example, English philosopher William Godwin (1756–1836), in his *Enquiry Concerning Political Justice* (1793), argued that economic justice and individual freedom would make oppressive government unnecessary and eliminate poverty, sickness, war, crime, political turmoil, and even overpopulation.[12] Godwin advocated a new form of "free" society based on small, democratically based independent communities in which goods and labor requirements would be equitably distributed. This of course was the essence of tribal society, and Godwin was absolutely right to identify social scale as a critical ingredient of a just society. Robert Owen (1756–1836) in Scotland, as well as Charles Fourier (1772–1837) and Henri de Saint-Simon (1760–1825) in France, advocated social association and cooperation based on different organizations of industrial production and property ownership as a replacement for competition and monopoly. Contemporary co-ops of various sorts are the heritage of these social theorists.

Marx and Engels not only wanted workers to unite in a class struggle against the capitalists but also predicted the eventual demise of capitalism due to its internal contradictions. Many of the more flagrant human costs of rapid capitalist development in Europe and North America that might have led to such collapse were partially ameliorated during the twentieth century by laws setting minimum wages, providing social welfare, and prescribing work conditions, allowing workers to organize, and attempting to regulate corporate economic power. The belatedness of such efforts is apparent in the fact that in the United States there were no laws prohibiting child labor in mines and factories until after 1900.

At the level of international political organization (thanks to the new industrial tools of war and the new demand for resources), the growing potential for destructive military conflict met with equally slow response even though many individuals perceived the threat. Ironically, on the eve of the Russian Revolution the Russian czar urged world leaders to ban the use of aircraft in warfare. Immediately thereafter nearly 13 million soldiers were killed during World War I. Thirteen million is an astounding casualty figure, more than the entire population of the tribal world before the rise of the imperial world 9,000 years ago, but there were only tentative efforts to regulate international order. It was not until 30 million people died during World War II that more effective international regulatory organizations, including the United Nations, were established.

Commercial society's impact on the environment has been a subtler crisis, and its full potential for catastrophe has only recently become widely recognized. The general feeling that a rapidly evolving technology could overcome any problems seems to have blinded most economists and government planners to the need to acknowledge environmental limits until those limits became undeniably obvious. In the United States a group of scientists representing the American Association for the Advancement of Science petitioned Congress as early as 1873 for resource conservation measures. But the first forest reserve was not established until 1891, nearly twenty years later;[13] not until Earth Day in 1970, almost a century later, did Americans generally begin to acknowledge that industrial progress might not be fully compatible with nature.

A general pattern in the responses to crises by modern nations has evolved. Once the factors that will lead to a crisis are set in motion, considerable time passes before anyone perceives the potential problem. There are further delays before the problem is widely perceived and still further delays before corrective action is taken. For example, DDT, "discovered" in 1934, was being used as an insecticide by 1943, was known to be killing birds by the late 1950s and fish by the early 1960s, and was found to be contaminating milk in 1963. Yet it was not even partially banned until 1972. In this case, nearly thirty years' lag time was required before a biologically disastrous technology was regulated, even though its harmful aspects were apparent to many scientists for some two decades.

The Significance of Culture Scale

We have defined the general nature of global problems and suggested some of the possible dangers and difficulties inherent in slow response. Now we must demonstrate that anthropology has something important to say about these issues. The problem-solving advantages of anthropology's eclectic combination of holistic, cross-cultural, and evolutionary approaches emerge most clearly when these approaches are used to sort societies by their dominant organizational forms into three distinctive cultural worlds: tribal, imperial, and commercial. These cultural worlds represent increasing levels of social scale and cultural complexity, and greater concentration of social power. The underlying assumption is that growth in scale occurs because individual elites seek to increase their social power, in other words, their ability to get other people to do things for them. Every household needs sufficient social power for successful maintenance and reproduction, but if power becomes too concentrated in a few elite households, overall social and cultural resiliency and sustainability may be threatened. Each major increase in social scale beyond established thresholds requires new social institutions, technologies, and ideologies in order to overcome the natural and cultural limits to growth. A greater concentration of social power requires growth in population, greater production and consumption, and greater wealth accumulation. Growth in all of these dimensions can generate social and environmental sustainability crises. Larger-scale societies may lose their resiliency and become increasingly difficult to sustain. This perspective suggests that throughout history and prehistory the persistent human problems of environmental crises, hunger, overpopulation, poverty, and conflict all involved—and continue to be either produced by or amplified by—increases in social scale and the concentration of social power. We will treat all the contemporary human problems examined in this book as aspects of this maladaptive long-term trend toward increases in social scale and social inequality.

Small-scale tribal societies are anthropology's traditional specialty. They represent humanity's way of life in the tribal world before aggrandizing elites were able to centralize political power in their own family lines to produce chiefdoms, urban civilizations and kingdoms beginning some 7,000 years ago. Tribal societies are the only societies with an archaeologically demonstrated record of sustained adaptive success. They have existed since the dawn of human culture, some 2 million years ago, measured by the earliest stone tools, or some 100,000 years ago, measured by the earliest spoken language. Speech very quickly allowed humans to become dominant life forms on the planet, next to bacteria[14] and social insects such as ants.[15] Human cultural adaptation to the natural environment was so successful that adapting to other people in the social environment quickly became the greatest human problem.[16] There is strong evidence that the evolution of the human brain and culture was driven by the selective advantage to individuals of "social intelligence."[17] This is the intellectual balancing act of using the mind to deceive and out-maneuver others for access to resources while still maintaining the benefits of membership in social networks. People were able to do this for tens of thousands of years in the tribal world, satisfying human needs in a remarkably egalitarian way, without high levels of energy consumption, or costly and risky technology. Politically autonomous tribal societies still occupied much of the world, alongside ancient regional civilizations, until approximately AD 1800, when globally organized commercial societies began to dominate the world. Today, few if any independent tribal worlds exist, but many tribal societies operate within the commercial world.

Anthropology's most striking and relevant generalization about the tribal societies that existed in the tribal world is that they were totally different from both our own commercial societies and the ancient civilizations in the imperial world that immediately preceded the commercial world. We can better understand the sources of contemporary problems by carefully comparing our own situation with related aspects of tribal societies. Such a comparison is one of this book's primary objectives. Scale itself may prove to be a key to the success of the tribal world, and by selectively reorganizing to gain the advantages of scale, we may be able to solve our problems and retain the human benefits of accumulated knowledge and advanced technologies. The secret of tribal success is almost certainly related to the small absolute scale of their populations and the relative simplicity of their technology.

The Uniqueness of Tribal Societies and Cultures

The term *tribal*, as used here, refers to small-scale societies of 500 to 2,500 people integrated by shared language, culture, and identity who were originally politically and economically independent. Tribal societies are composed of households clustered in bands and villages, cross-cut by kinship and marriage connections. Beyond their immediate households, people in tribal societies interact face-to-face with the 30 to 50 persons in their small residential bands, or hamlets, or with 100 to 200 persons in larger villages, or dispersed kinship groups. This means that on average an individual's total personal network will be about 150 persons, and is unlikely to exceed 200 people.[18] Small groups of this size limit the total social power potentially available to any single person and make it easy to monitor everyone's behavior, because everyone knows everyone else personally. Under these social circumstances leaders are truly public servants and decision making is likely to be fully democratic. The tribal world was a decentralized social network connecting individuals in different tribal societies through intermarriage, ritual, trade, and conflict. The entire tribal world functioned to maintain social groups at their optimum sizes and resisted any tendencies for social groups to grow larger. The crucial point is that throughout the tribal world social power was widely diffused, and polities, production, and consumption were so decentralized that there was no cultural incentive for anyone to promote destabilizing growth. Tribal societies are highly suited to human nature and to the satisfaction of basic human needs for maintenance and reproduction. Households are the primary units in tribal societies, and because they are highly self-sufficient and autonomous, individuals can enjoy maximum human freedom.

Tribal societies and cultures evolved simultaneously with physically modern humans and language, appearing fully developed in the religion, art, ornamentation, and almost certainly, in kinship and marriage systems in the Upper Paleolithic archaeological record 40,000 years ago. The size-related qualities of small-scale "tribal" social structures that regulate social power and meet human needs are highly adaptive and in the contemporary world may be combined with advanced technologies to sustain humanity more effectively than the very large-scale social structures that presently dominate the commercial world. Small-scale, local, and regional societies that have no present connection with the tribal world enjoy many of the human advantages of tribal societies because of their small size, and may be referred to as "domestic-scale" societies when the welfare of individuals and households is a primary social objective.

Contemporary descendants of conquered tribal societies often identify themselves as "indigenous peoples" to call attention to their attachment to their ancestral land and cultural heritage. Indigenous peoples are often small-scale societies culturally organized around the basic principles of self-reliance, autonomy, kinship, social justice, and family that made the tribal world so successful. In many places in North and South America indigenous peoples also refer to their societies as tribes. Some anthropologists avoid the term "tribal," or claim that "tribes" do not exist, because before state governments intervened, tribes were not permanently fixed entities with centralized leaders. Nevertheless, the size-related social and cultural qualities that made the tribal world sustainable are the very qualities that can help us solve contemporary human problems.

The tribal world offers remarkable contrasts with the pre-industrial states and ancient empires that ranged in size from about 50,000 to more than 100 million people, whose well-being depended on decisions made by ruling elites in often remote capital cities. The overwhelming power of ruling elites in the ancient imperial world is well illustrated by the recorded statements of Empress Dowager Tz'u-hsi, who ruled the Ch'ing dynasty Chinese Empire from 1861 to 1908. She declared, "I am the cleverest woman who ever lived. . . . Now look at me, I have 400 million people all dependent on my judgment."[19] Today, in a similar way, the daily lives and future prospects of virtually all of the world's 6 billion people are shaped by the political and economic decisions made by a relative handful of people who command trillions of dollars in financial capital and overwhelmingly powerful armed forces.

Scale shapes the distribution of wealth, power, and opportunity in the tribal, imperial, and commercial worlds. In the tribal world social status was determined primarily by a person's gender, age, and personal qualities. All tribal individuals and households were generally "rich" in that they enjoyed access to the natural resources, food, shelter, and basic services needed to maintain and reproduce themselves and their culture. Misfortune occasionally made a few poor, but tribal society was basically the reverse of the steeply sloped social pyramids that characterize ancient imperial worlds and the contemporary commercial world. Ancient imperial civilizations displayed great individual differences in material wealth and political power based on inherited rank and social class, but because they relied so heavily on human labor the ruling elite had a vested interest in meeting the minimal subsistence needs of all households, even when there was a slave class. In the commercial world millions lack access to safe drinking water and basic nutrition, as the UN Millennium Declaration notes, and even in the rich United States many people are too impoverished to successfully raise a family. Such poverty conditions would be considered inhumane and incomprehensible by anyone from the tribal world, and would also seem odd to the rulers of ancient empires.

The extreme contrasts between forms of production and distribution in the tribal and commercial worlds also help explain the different impacts of these cultural systems on the natural environment. Most significant is the fact that tribal economies tend to be locally self-sufficient, subsistence-based systems characterized by reciprocal exchanges and few cultural incentives for growth. The global market economy, as presently constituted, thrives on high levels of local specialization and interdependence in which local communities generally do not consume the products they produce, and market exchanges occur with individual profit as the primary motive. The goods and services that sustain life have become commodities that are not freely available. In tribal systems production stops when everyone has goods and services sufficient for their needs. At the same time, because all production is locally and domestically controlled, people can respond immediately to detrimental impacts on their resources. The globally organized commercial system requires continuous expansion of production and consumption and shifts to new, totally different resources and territories in response to depletion or reduced profits. Tribal societies minimize these problems, because they are small enough to make decisions by consensus, and they can make the well-being of households, community, and local ecosystems their primary objective.

The culture-scale perspective identifies certain size-related cultural features as important defining features of the tribal world but does not assume that tribal cultures, or any cultures for that matter, are changeless entities. Culture is a tool that people use and modify to meet their needs. It is socially shared symbolic information that guides human behavior. Cultural differences do affect the way different societies create or solve human problems. Anthropologists have recognized many of the advantages of small-scale tribal societies since the 1960s, as the following section shows.

The "Original Affluent Society"

Seventy-five anthropologists assembled in Chicago in 1965 for the Wenner-Gren-sponsored symposium "Man the Hunter." They examined the latest research findings on the world's last remaining tribal foragers, or hunting and gathering peoples, who were being forced to abandon their independent way of life. The result[20] was a new description of life in these technologically simplest of ethnographically known societies, showing their existence to be stable, satisfying, and ecologically sound. It was found that when they remained in control of their resources, tribal foragers seemed to enjoy relatively good health and long lives, while they had the good sense to maintain their wants at levels that could be fully and continuously satisfied without jeopardizing their environment. Marshall Sahlins even suggested that this culture was, after all, the original "affluent society." Other researchers have since challenged and revised some aspects of Sahlin's original interpretation of forager affluence,[21] but the general conclusion that a low-density, domestically organized forager lifestyle offered many human advantages not easily obtained by urbanized politically or commercially organized societies seems valid.

Most significantly, when the symposium discussions ended, the participants concluded that the hunting way of life, which had dominated perhaps 99 percent of humanity's cultural lifespan, had been "the most successful and persistent adaptation man has ever achieved."[22] In comparison, newly arrived industrial civilization was in a precarious situation given the "exceedingly complex and unstable ecological conditions" it had created. At least one distinguished participant even felt that we should study why hunters were so successful and thought that our civilization might actually learn something from them. These conclusions referred to tribal foragers, but they apply equally well to tribal villagers and herders. In the following chapters I will deliberately emphasize certain aspects of tribal societies where they can highlight the problems that our own commercial-scale culture has created and point to solutions.

Understanding Commercial Societies and Cultures

> This theory of the global system, then, revolves around the perceived necessity for global capitalism to continually increase production and international trade, to guarantee the political conditions for this to occur uninterruptedly all over the world, and to create in people the need to want to consume all the products that are available, on a permanent basis. (Sklair 1991: 54)[23]

The global scale of the contemporary commercial society and the significance of its unique cultural organization must be carefully considered before contemporary problems can be productively understood. The entire world is now driven by a dominant cultural process that can be called commercialization. This process makes perpetual capital accumulation the primary objective, producing great inequalities of wealth and power. In this system the economy is in a sense disembodied from the rest of the culture, symbolically becoming an autonomous entity whose growth is considered essential for human well-being. This reverses the cultural order that defined the tribal world, where the humanization process dominated and goods and services were produced to meet basic human needs while promoting long-term survival.

The world's 6.5 billion people are now combined into a single commercial network ultimately dependent on computerized financial transactions that take place in a few organized markets in the richest countries. Money, government and corporate bonds, shares in corporations, and contracts for the future sale of food, fiber, and other commodities change hands daily, and vast quantities of raw materials and manufactured goods move physically between markets as investors seek commercial profit. The purpose of all this activity is to keep the global "economy" growing, as measured by the steady accumulation of financial capital and increases in GNP. Some curious things about all of this are that it is directed and controlled by relatively few people, the outcome need have no bearing on basic human needs, and the actual risks and rewards are very unevenly distributed. In reality, costs are systematically shifted downward to those least able to pay, while rewards flow disproportionately to the wealthiest and most influential corporations and individuals, and from poor to rich countries. Just as the earlier politicization process made the needs of governments more important than the interests of households and villages, the commercialization process now makes the needs of giant corporations and anonymous investors more important than the well-being of either governments or communities. Indeed, it could be argued that governments now exist primarily to make the world safe for large-scale commercial enterprise. Individuals with no direct investment in the global economy are important only as consumers of commercial goods and services or as minimum-wage laborers.

Analysts of the contemporary world commonly speak of governments, corporations, or civil society as decision makers who shape the world. Sociologist Leslie Sklair[24] observes that it is no longer very helpful to focus on the activities of nation-states, because the primary agents in the world system are all transnational. Sklair lists three groups and industries as the most important transnational agents: (1) transnational corporations (TNCs), (2) the transnational capitalist class (TCC), and (3) the transnational mass media and advertising. Sklair aligns these agents with three analytical spheres of the global system: the economic, political, and cultural-ideological spheres, respectively, and functionally distinguishes each agent by its particular set of transnational practices (table 1.2). The economic sphere is dominated by the TNCs and the special institutions that support them, such as the World Bank, the International Monetary Fund, the United Nations, the World Trade Organization (WTO), and the various stock markets and commodity exchanges. This is a useful framework for examining the

Table 1.2.   Transnational Agents in the Global System, According to Leslie Sklair (1991)

Sphere	Primary Agents	Transnational Practices (TNP)
Economic	Transnational Corporations (TNCs)	Commodities production and marketing services Job creation and destruction
Political	Transnational Capitalist Class (TCC)	Political support for marketing and international trade
Cultural-Ideological	Transnational mass media and advertising	Consumerism

unique cultural structure of the commercial world, and for conceptualizing it as a functionally interconnected system.

Although Sklair refers to the corporations, the capitalist class, the media, and related global institutions as "agents," it is crucial to recognize that they are directed by individual human agents who compete fiercely with one another and may individually reap enormous benefits from their personal roles in the global-scale commercialization process. Their individual households may flourish, even as millions of others may be impoverished by their decisions to shift vast financial resources from one part of the world to another in an effort to gain a higher rate of return on their investments. The transnational capitalist class is composed of the corporate managers, politicians, and other elites that make the system work. Their nationality is irrelevant. Making the global system work requires maintaining dominant influence, or cultural hegemony, over billions of people. The concept of cultural hegemony was originally developed by the Italian Marxist Antonio Gramsci (1891–1937), who argued that the ruling elites define the dominant symbols and thoughts of a people. When the elites do this successfully, people internalize the ideals of the culture and behave appropriately. In the global system the cultural hegemony function is most effectively carried out by the transnational mass media and advertising, which maintain consumerism as the dominant cultural value. In striking contrast to the tribal world, where human well-being is the dominant value, the commercial world makes increasing consumption of commercial goods and services the ultimate meaning of life. This commercial priority deceptively makes one of the means to human happiness an end in itself, and in effect subordinates human relationships and social values to the economy.

The absolute power of transnational corporations and the capitalist class of owners and managers is indicated by the fact that the world's 500 largest publicly traded companies had combined revenues of $19 trillion in U.S. dollars in 2005. This was an astounding 43 percent of the $44 trillion in global GDP in 2005,[25] and equivalent to the combined GDPs of 170 countries with 4.3 billion people. The $363 billion revenues of ExxonMobil, the world's largest company by revenue, were larger than the GDPs of all but 21 countries, yet it had fewer than 84,000 employees. Extraordinary benefits flowed directly from the company to a tiny number of people. Seven corporate officers and board members each held shares worth from $7 million to over $100 million. ExxonMobil's largest shareholders and corporate officers were richly rewarded by dividend payments, salaries, and retirement benefits. For example, ExxonMobil CEO Lee R. Raymond received $386 million in 2005, his final year, including a lump sum $98 million retirement package and the value of stock options.[26] Global warming is a cost of ExxonMobil's principal products, petroleum and natural gas. The company has waged a long campaign to convince the public that global warming was first not real, then not caused by human activities, then too costly to do anything about. Between 1998 and 2004 ExxonMobil spent nearly $60 million in lobbying the federal government on energy policy,[27] some $12 million on various advocacy organizations that support its interests,[28] and over a million dollars in political donations in 2002.[29]

The ExxonMobil example represents a widespread and long-standing pattern of concentrated power. Corporate stock ownership is widely dispersed, but a surprisingly small group of interconnected people controls these powerful TNCs as board members and chief executives. For example, the 1993–1994 boards of directors of a sample of eleven of the largest Fortune 500 American companies yielded 137 people, who also helped control 155 other Fortune 500 companies. Collectively these companies controlled roughly half of the total assets or sales of the Fortune 500 in thirteen major sectors of the American economy. These same individuals were also associated with many other companies, foundations, universities, commissions, government agencies, and civic organizations where they could promote their corporate interests. The top ten individuals were linked to thirty-seven companies whose combined assets represented 10 percent of the global GNP in 1991. In an exhaustive study of the American institutional elite in the early 1980s, Thomas R. Dye found that just 5,778 individuals "ran" the giant corporations, the federal government, the news media, and the primary cultural institutions in the country as a whole.[30]

No analysis of contemporary problems and solutions would be complete without consideration of the cultural organization of wealth and power in the world, because our problems are cultural problems. They are not problems of human nature, and they will not be solved by a narrow technological approach. Solving contemporary human problems requires a careful assessment of the way the world is culturally organized in relation to the full range of cultural possibilities. The following chapters will explore particular types of problems and solutions while devoting special attention to the role of human decision makers in: (1) corporate business enterprises, (2) governments, and (3) local communities. An anthropological perspective suggests that solving human problems requires designing cultural systems that establish a more humane balance among the three cultural processes that shape our lives: (1) humanization, (2) politicization, and (3) commercialization.

Notes

1. Boas, Franz. 1928. *Anthropology and Modern Life*. New York: Norton.

2. UNDP. United Nations Development Programme. 2005. "Human Development Report 2005: International Cooperation at a Crossroads. Aid, Trade and Security in an Unequal World." New York: UNDP. hdr.undp.org

3. Loh, Jonathan, and Mathis Wackernagel. 2004. *Living Planet Report 2004*. Gland, Switzerland: World Wide Fund for Nature.

4. Prominent environmentalist James Lovelock prefers the stronger phrase global heating, rather than global warming. Lovelock, James. 2006. *The Revenge of Gaia: Earth's Climate Crisis and the Fate of Humanity*. New York: Basic Books.

5. Smil, Vaclav. 2005. *Creating the Twentieth Century: Technical Innovations of 1867–1914 and Their Lasting Impact*. Oxford and New York: Oxford University Press.

6. Union of Concerned Scientists. 1992. "World Scientists' Warning to Humanity." www.ucsusa.org/ucs/about/1992-world-scientists-warning-to-humanity.html

7. Office of the United Nations High Commissioner for Human Rights. "United Nations Millennium Declaration." General Assembly resolution 55/2 of September 8, 2000. www.ohchr.org/english/law/millennium.htm

8. Maddison, Angus. 2003. *The World Economy: Historical Statistics*. Paris: OECD Development Centre Studies.

9. Lomborg, Bjørn, ed. 2004. *Global Crises, Global Solutions*. Cambridge and New York: Cambridge University Press. See also Lomborg, Bjørn. 2001. *The Skeptical Environmentalist: Measuring the Real State of the World*. Cambridge and New York: Cambridge University Press.

10. Porter, Bernard. 1968. *Critics of Empire*. London: Macmillan.

11. Noble, David F. 1993. *Progress Without People: In Defense of Luddism*. Chicago: Charles H. Kerr; Sale, Kirkpatrick. 1996b. *Rebels Against the Future: The Luddites and Their War on the Industrial Revolution: Lessons for the Computer Age*. Reading, MA: Addison-Wesley.

12. Marshall, Peter, ed. 1986. *The Anarchist Writings of William Godwin*. London: Freedom Press.

13. Gustafson, A. E., C. H. Guise, W. J. Hamilton Jr., and H. Ries. 1939. *Conservation in the United States*. Ithaca, NY: Comstock, 7.

14. On the dominance of bacteria see Gould, Stephen Jay. 1996. *Full House: The Spread of Excellence from Plato to Darwin*. New York: Three Rivers Press, Crown Publishers, 176–78, 186–95.

15. On the dominance of ants see Bert Hölldobler and Edward O. Wilson. 1990. *The Ants*. Cambridge, MA: Belknap Press of Harvard University Press.

16. Alexander, Richard D. 1990. *How Did Humans Evolve?: Reflections on the Uniquely Unique Species*. Ann Arbor: Museum of Zoology, the University of Michigan Special Publication No. 1.

17. Humphrey, Nicholas K. 1976. "The Social Function of Intellect." In *Growing Points in Ethology*, 303–17. Based on a conference sponsored by St. John's College

and King's College, Cambridge. Edited by P. P. G. Bateson and R. A. Hinde, Cambridge and New York: Cambridge University Press; Dunbar, R. I. M. 1993. "Coevolution of Neocortical Size, Group Size and Language in Humans." *Behavioral and Brain Sciences* 16(4): 681–735.

18. Dunbar, "Coevolution of Neocortical Size," 681–735.

19. Warner, Marina. 1972. *The Dragon Empress: The Life and Times of Tz'U-Hsi Empress Dowager of China 1835–1908.* New York: Macmillan, 7.

20. Lee, Richard B., and Irven De Vore. 1968. *Man the Hunter.* Chicago: Aldine.

21. Bird-David, Nurit. 1992. "Beyond 'The Original Affluent Society': A Culturalist Reformulation." *Current Anthropology* 33(l): 25–47; Burch, Ernest S., and Linda J. Ellanna, eds. 1994. *Key Issues in Hunter-Gatherer Research.* Oxford: Berg; Headland, Thomas N. 1997. "Revisionism in Ecological Anthropology." *Current Anthropology* 38(4): 605–30; Smith, Eric Alden. 1991. "The Current State of Hunter-Gatherer Studies." *Current Anthropology* 32: 72–75.

22. Sahlins, Marshall. 1968. "Notes on the Original Affluent Society." In *Man the Hunter*, edited by Richard B. Lee and Irven DeVore, 85–89. Chicago: Aldine.

23. Sklair, Leslie. 1991. *Sociology of the Global System.* Baltimore, MD: Johns Hopkins University Press.

24. Sklair, *Sociology of the Global System.*

25. *Fortune Magazine*, Global 500 (July 24, 2006); World Bank. 2006. *World Development Indicators.* devdata.worldbank.org/data-query/

26. Mouawad, Jad. 2006. "For Leading Exxon to Its Riches, $144,573 a Day." *New York Times* (April 15, 2006), Business/Financial Desk.

27. The Center for Public Integrity, "Lobby Watch: How Private Interests Influence Public Policy." www.publicintegrity.org/lobby/ (October 7, 2006).

28. Greenpeace International. www.exxonsecrets.org (2006).

29. Center for Responsive Politics. Opensecrets. www.opensecrets.org/index.asp (October 2006).

30. Dye, Thomas R. 1983. *Who's Running America?: The Reagan Years.* Englewood Cliffs, NJ: Prentice-Hall.

Scale, Adaptation, and the Environmental Crisis

2

> *Nor are those cultures that we might consider higher in general evolutionary standing necessarily more perfectly adapted to their environments than lower. Many great civilizations have fallen in the last 2,000 years, even in the midst of material plenty, while the Eskimos tenaciously maintained themselves in an incomparably more difficult habitat. The race is not to the swift, nor the battle to the strong.*

—MARSHALL SAHLINS AND ELMAN R. SERVICE, EDS.,
EVOLUTION AND CULTURE[1]

MANY GENERAL CONCLUSIONS OF DIRECT RELEVANCE to the contemporary environmental crises of resource depletion, loss of biodiversity, and ecosystem degradation emerge from a careful analysis of cultural ecological data in the anthropological record from a culture-scale perspective. The most striking conclusion is that the speed and scale of resource depletion and environmental degradation accelerate with increases in the scale of culture and the concentration of social power. People living in tribal societies may often have depleted their natural resources, and they certainly modified their environments. However, it is not idealizing them as "ecologically noble" to point out that small-scale, self-sufficient societies with locally controlled economies have been better able to maintain long-term, relatively resilient relationships between human populations and the natural environment than peoples living in larger-scale societies. Scale itself and the cultural organization of social power are crucial issues that we cannot ignore in attempting to understand

and alleviate environmental problems. This generalization may seem obvious, even trivial, but the policy implications of the scale and power perspective are profound. Furthermore, the importance of scale and resiliency may be obscured by the difficulty of operationalizing crucial ecological concepts such as adaptation, conservation, carrying capacity, equilibrium, resource management, and sustainability. Resiliency in this context refers to the ability of systems to avoid collapse and retain their shape and scale in the face of various stresses or shocks. Resiliency emphasizes the dynamic aspects of human and natural systems and is a more useful concept than balance or equilibrium alone. This chapter explores some of the many reasons why culture growth amplifies environmental problems and why small-scale systems offer important human advantages.

Newer ways of thinking about cultural evolution that take into account the significance of human agency, cultural transmission, and scale theory can make our understanding of evolutionary processes more relevant to contemporary human problems. We explore these perspectives in the next two sections.

Cultural Transmission and Maladaptation

Biocultural evolutionary theory helps explain why cultural evolution can become a maladaptive process undermining the resilience of both natural and human systems. Biocultural evolutionists see genes and culture playing similar roles in the evolutionary process. Culture, conceptualized as the shared symbolic information of a people, directs human behavior in the same way that genes contain the encoded instructions that create the human body. Biocultural evolution involves changes through time in the frequency of either genes or cultural information in human societies. Like biological reproduction and genetic transmission, cultural transmission is the most basic evolutionary process that produces changes in the frequency of the basic cultural ideas that help produce human behavior. In addition to undergoing the processes of natural selection, mutation, and drift that change gene frequencies in a population, individuals can simply acquire new cultural traits. Individuals can produce and transmit novel cultural ideas through rational calculation according to certain criteria, or they can selectively borrow and transmit ideas from a variety of sources.[2] Much cultural transmission occurs in the household as a social inheritance from parents to children,[3] but cultural transmission is frequently biased. People often accept cultural ideas that are thought to be shared by the majority. More important, people emulate the beliefs and behavior of individuals that appear to be most successful. Emulation, though often easier and more efficient than trial and error, can lead to maladaptive processes, such as runaway economic growth when people emulate power aggrandizement, conspicuous consumption, or wealth accumulation.

There is a striking connection among culture scale, cultural transmission, and the process of cultural evolution. In small tribal societies, cultural transmission is primarily through enculturation within the household. At this level each household is in effect a cultural experiment, discovering and transmitting to the next generation the behaviors that will sustain households under very specific local conditions. Seriously maladaptive behavior will be quickly punished, and the "right" behavior will be rewarded and transmitted. In such small, domestically organized societies, cultural creativity and emulation are biased toward behavior that promotes the humanization process—that is, the successful production and maintenance of human beings. French anthropologist Claude Levi-Strauss[4] pointed out that virtually all the important domestic technologies—including tool making, farming, herding, weaving, basketry, ceramics, and food preparation techniques such as brewing and bread making—were developed by Neolithic tribal societies for household use. Levi-Strauss called it paradoxical that people in the Neolithic era did not go on to develop more elaborate technologies such as metallurgy, wheeled vehicles, and writing, because they clearly had the intellectual capability. However, these "higher" technologies were not needed by self-sufficient households living in a relatively egalitarian world. Rather, they were later used by elites to support the concentration of social power in larger, politically organized societies with large, dense populations, urban centers, and standing armies.

Beyond the level of domestic-scale culture, cultural evolution is fundamentally a political process.[5] This means that its direction can be determined by an elite subset of a population or even by a single ruler. For example in ancient Mesopotamia, Ur-Nammu and his son Shulgi instituted a series of cultural changes that created the first multi-national empire.[6] Ancient empires based on a state religion enforced by a written legal code, sacred texts, census records, formal schooling, temples, calendrical ritual, and military power easily overpowered cultural transmission occurring at the household level. The crucial difference with regard to politically directed cultural transmission is that it is primarily elite-directed for elite benefit. Any benefits to lower-ranked people would be a secondary outcome. Elite-directed evolutionary change might prove maladaptive for humanity as a whole. Such change might also be short-lived, especially if it alienates too many people or reduces cultural diversity. Until the most recent centuries cultural evolution produced increased human diversity, but European colonialism and global capitalism have radically reduced cultural diversity.[7] The global mass communication technologies directed by contemporary commercial elites for power-concentrating commercial purposes overwhelm both household and political cultural transmission processes that maintain diversity. This makes it possible for a few people to decide what information billions of people should receive. Cultural homogeneity fostered by commercial-scale culture could be maladaptive because diversity is the basis of cultural evolution.

Scale and Cultural Evolution

Culture scale is naturally related to evolution and adaptation in other important ways. Size itself is a crucial variable in nature. For example, small animals have an adaptive advantage over large animals in the event of environmental fluctuations such as drought. Because smaller animals can survive on fewer resources and reproduce more rapidly, populations of small animals can recover more quickly.[8] It is no surprise that bacteria are the most successful organisms on earth and perhaps in the universe, considering their total number of individuals, diversity of species, total biomass, overall adaptability, and breadth of environmental niches.[9] The same scale principle applies to human societies. Small societies can be highly responsive to changes in the environment, can adapt quickly, and can reproduce quickly. They can also practice democratic decision making in ways that would be extremely difficult in larger societies.

Gravity, the laws of geometry, and the functional connections between dimensions in systems tell us that as things grow larger, counter-intuitive changes may occur. For example, grasshoppers can jump distances a hundred times their length, and ants can lift objects ten times their weight. A tenfold increase in the length of a cube results in a hundred-fold increase in surface area and a thousand-fold increase in its volume or mass. Likewise, a larger society is not physically the same as a smaller society, and this affects social structure, function, and adaptation. Disproportions in the size of different parts of an organism as growth occurs are such mathematically regular phenomena that they can be described in allometric equations.[10] Social power will naturally be disproportionately concentrated at the top of a social hierarchy as societies grow larger, unless people take specific counter-measures.[11]

Just as the size and shape of organisms are limited by physical laws within relatively narrow ranges, the size and form of human societies must also be limited. The size of everything in the cosmos can be compre hended within forty powers of ten, ranging from the smallest subatomic particles (10^{-16} meters) to a segment of the universe 1 billion light-years across (10^{25} meters). The largest living things, giant sequoias, are just over 100 meters in length, just two powers of ten (10^2 meters). The size of tribal societies typically varies within a narrow range of from 200 to 2,000 people. The shift from a few hundred to thousands is an order of magnitude difference of only one power of ten (from 10^2 to 10^3), multiplied by two. Politically organized chiefdoms, city-states, and agrarian empires ranged from 2,000 to 200 million (from three to eight powers of 10, multiplied by two). Commercial organization produced a global society unlikely to exceed ten powers of ten (tens of billions).

Cross-cultural research reveals that human settlements show scale effects that are not intuitively obvious but that have adaptive consequences. For example, Roland Fletcher[12] found that population density declines as settlements become larger. This means that larger societies with larger settlements will cover a relatively larger area per person at lower density than smaller societies with smaller settlements, and will place disproportionately more human stress on regional ecosystems. Fletcher uses a geometric law to explain this phenomenon. The number of social interactions that a person will potentially experience increases exponentially as settlement size grows, following a simple mathematical equation. A tenfold increase in population produces a hundred-fold increase in potential social interactions. Fletcher argues that such increases would quickly exceed the human capacity for information processing and become intolerably costly. Therefore, people could be expected to reduce density as settlement size increases in order to compensate for the stress of interaction. Fletcher[13] found that the total surface area of urban settlements—regardless of population density—and the rate of urban growth are limited by the technology of interpersonal communication rather than by food supply. The earliest preliterate urban centers, where communication was by word of mouth, did not exceed 100 hectares and grew at a rate of only 0.5 hectare per century. The development of writing in the ancient agrarian civilizations permitted a hundred-fold increase in the area of cities and a thousand-fold increase in the area's growth rate. Electronic communication and mechanized printing permitted another hundred-fold increase in the size of cities and a second thousand-fold increase in growth rate.

Cultural Evolution and Adaptation

Among the popular misconceptions regarding cultural evolution and adaptation is the view that evolutionary progress has meant greater security, greater freedom from environmental limitations, and greater efficiency of energy use. In many minds, higher levels of evolutionary development have also been equated with greater adaptive success. However, as anthropologist Roy Rappaport[14] points out, the increasingly hierarchical structures of more complex cultural systems tend to become maladaptive. Higher-level decision makers are likely to be inadequately aware of the local impacts of their actions. If theories of cultural evolution are to be harmonized with what is known about the obvious ability of domestic-scale societies to avoid environmental catastrophes, then these theories and their interpretations must be examined more closely.

The principal pioneer of modern cultural evolutionary theory, Leslie A. White,[15] defines evolutionary progress largely in relation to per capita rates of energy utilization. A culture that consumed more energy per capita was by definition more highly evolved. Other writers[16] have elaborated on this theory, arguing that two kinds of cultural evolution were involved, general and specific. General evolution was concerned with levels of evolutionary progress, the more "advanced" forms that interested White. These "higher" forms were defined by higher energy consumption, greater organizational complexity, and the ability to exploit a wider range of environments and to replace cultures at "lower" levels. This kind of evolutionary development corresponds closely to the concept of culture scale used in this book, such that tribal, imperial, and commercial-scale societies represent increasing levels of organizational complexity. Paradoxically, as we are now seeing, general evolutionary cultural progress of this sort may actually reduce security, diversity, and energy efficiency, and dramatically increase the likelihood of environmental crisis. Furthermore, such progress may increase the workload and reduce the life chances of many individuals. Specific evolution means adaptation to local environments, which is what tribal societies excel at. It is clear that small-scale societies at lower levels of evolutionary progress, as defined above, are far more efficient in energy input-output ratios, and far more stable and successfully adapted to their environments than more "advanced" cultures.

Many of these points were previously disregarded by anthropologists who were particularly impressed with the undeniable material accomplishments of industrial civilization and who did not pay close attention to the differences between general and specific evolution. For example, in an attempt to describe general levels of cultural evolution using adaptation, Yehudi Cohen[17] states that at each stage of technological progress (he uses hunting-gathering, cultivation, industrialism), people became better adapted for survival, more secure, freer from the environment, and more energy efficient. In Cohen's view, cultural evolution has been achieved because people have sought to gain mastery over nature, and it has been inhibited in certain areas through ignorance of basic technologies. Other research on crucial evolutionary advances such as food production and state organization suggests that the role of invention and discovery was greatly overemphasized by earlier theorists. It is more likely that cultural evolution occurred because power-seeking elites developed and promoted the cultural innovations that would produce larger societies by overcoming the natural and cultural limits to scale. The non-elite majority was forced to adjust to the problems produced by increases in scale. Growth-encouraging innovations included more energy-intensive forms of material production, changes in belief systems to make hierarchy appear natural, institutional changes to organize larger production and distribution systems, and changes in the construction and design of urban places to promote larger populations in larger settled areas by expanding communication and reducing the intensity of social interaction. This is a very different view of cultural evolution—it suggests that increased scale actually increased adaptive risks and therefore was not eagerly sought by most people. Also, in this view, it seems likely that the limits to scale that had to be overcome were primarily cultural, not natural, although larger-scale societies ultimately place a greater burden on ecosystems and natural resources.

The doubtful advantages of scale increases can be illustrated by the successive declines in the apparent durability of each of the three cultural worlds. Viewed globally, the tribal, politically centralized imperial, and commercial socio-cultural systems that people successively developed over the past 100,000 years represent system transformations across thresholds to greater complexity, as well as successively higher levels of resource and energy use, but each world proved less durable. The more than 50,000-year duration of the tribal world was an order of magnitude longer than the 6,000-year duration of the pre-capitalist imperial world. The commercial world has lasted only a few centuries, but in the past 150 years it has caused unprecedented biosphere degradation.[18] The direct human cost of the commercial world has been staggering. During the twentieth century some 200 million people died in catastrophic wars and political violence,[19] and by 2001 more than 800 million people did not have enough food to meet their daily energy needs.[20] This is not a progressive trend for humanity.

Progress, measured as greater technological complexity, has indeed allowed people to exploit more natural resources, but such progress does not mean that we have escaped the limits of nature. Cohen devoted considerable attention to the argument that progress means "freedom from environmental limitations," and reached some surprisingly shortsighted conclusions that directly conflict with more realistic assessments of the adaptive shortcomings of global-scale markets and advanced technologies. He argued, for example, that increasing mastery over nature leads to an increasingly secure food supply, and he points to supermarkets and the ability to eat fresh fruit out of season as great triumphs over nature. Strawberries at Christmastime are, in this regard, "perhaps one of man's greatest achievements."[21] However, viewed from a wider perspective, we have supermarkets and Christmas strawberries because they produce greater profits in the global economy—but they carry hidden cultural and environmental costs that must be measured if sustainability is important. As will be discussed in chapters 4 and 5, global-scale food systems are more costly and more vulnerable, and they generate more social inequality than local and regional systems.

Many earlier writers confidently measured the "higher" adaptive success of industrial societies by their apparent reproductive success and their ability to displace and destroy "lower, less effective" societies and cultures. Reproductive success refers both to growth in human population and to the propagation of culture itself. In this respect, industrial capitalism has been enormously successful. What such assessments overlook, however, is the time factor. History shows that growth beyond scale thresholds is accompanied by a new phase of even more rapid growth, followed by a prompt buildup of new stress, decline, and collapse as the next scale threshold is reached. Both stability and growth beyond scale limits are uncommon events. Natural and cultural systems are inherently dynamic, and stability in either can only be viewed as a relative concept. Cultural stability achieved at a level too close to a scale limit could force people to adapt to very stressful conditions, but on the other hand a breakthrough beyond the threshold to another growth cycle only postpones the adaptation problem. Traditional views of growth as evolutionary progress are entrenched in the popular culture, but they overlook the often cyclical, wave-like nature of growth, and they overemphasize the role of technology in only temporarily overcoming the purely physical limits to growth.

As Sahlins points out in the quotation introducing this chapter, real adaptive success can only be measured by survival—over the long run. This is genuine sustainability. If we insist on considering the global proliferation of the high-consumption culture to be an indication of adaptive achievement, then we may push our growth to the ultimate physical limits of the globe, leaving no room for nature. A new law of cultural evolution could then be formulated to measure such progress in purely physical terms, namely that culture evolves as the global biomass becomes increasingly converted to the human sector.

Certainly, a clear trend in cultural evolution to date has been toward a remarkable increase in the human sector of the global biomass (humans and domestic plants and animals) and a corresponding reduction in the earth's natural biomass of wild plants and animals. This reduction in the nonhuman sector is necessary because of the simple ecological fact that a fixed amount of solar energy fuels the planet's primary producers (green plants); consequently, there are absolute limits to how many consumers can exist. As human consumers increase, natural consumers must decrease. The ultimate pinnacle of human evolutionary achievement, then, would be the point at which every gram of living material on earth had been transferred to the human sector and every natural "competitor" had been eliminated. In 1971, biochemist and science fiction writer Isaac Asimov[22] cautiously estimated that at the then-present rate we could reach such a point by AD 2436, less than five hundred years.

Unless the negative effects of global warming intervene, humanity might succeed in conquering nature much sooner than Asimov suggested. Global plant biomass may now be half what it was 10,000 years ago.[23] Human conversion of forests into cropland causes a net loss of global biomass because per hectare agricultural biomass is much lower than forest biomass. Ninety-seven percent of vertebrate biomass is now in the form of humans and their domesticated animals, whereas as recently as 1900 the biomass of wild mammals may have equaled the human biomass.[24] Peter Vitousek[25] and others estimate that by 1980 humans were already appropriating nearly 40 percent of potential global terrestrial net primary biological product. Energy consumption of this magnitude by a top consumer is astounding and would seemingly place humans outside of nature, because such consumption would be truly unsustainable in a natural ecosystem. When fossil fuel consumption is accounted for, people are now taking the biological equivalent of more than the earth produces.[26] These rates of human energy appropriation reduce sustainability in three ways: (1) They necessarily reduce biodiversity and degrade ecosystems, because the number of species in an ecosystem is a function of total available energy; (2) They require a subsidy in the form of non-renewable fossil fuels, which contribute to global warming; and (3) They may depend on poverty-generating unequal market exchanges, which exacerbate social competition and conflicts.

Nature and Scope of the Environmental Crisis

In its most basic sense, the environmental crisis is a deterioration of environmental quality with a corresponding reduction in carrying capacity due to human intervention in natural processes. At the present, given the existing global social order, we are clearly running up against basic limits to the earth's ability to supply the resources we consume and at the same time to absorb our industrial by-products. Later chapters will treat the specific environmental problems of food, energy, population, and resources in more detail, but first it may be useful to consider the general implications of our intervention in the biosphere. In this context it is important to stress that people will experience the environmental crisis as social, political, ideological, and economic stress. The environmental crisis is not new. It has developed as general cultural evolution by increasing the scale of regional and global societies, has given us greater ability to influence nature, has increased population and per capita consumption rates, and has altered distribution patterns. Tribal hunters created grasslands; pastoral nomads overgrazed their lands; peasant farmers caused deforestation and erosion. From archaeological evidence it is clear that tribal societies and early civilizations at times faced their own local environmental crises as their resources declined relative to demand and they were forced to abandon certain regions or drastically alter their cultures. However, the scope and quality of the changes that the global commercialization process has set in motion over the past 200 years make these earlier problems seem quite insignificant. We now have the potential to disrupt basic life support processes and may already be inadvertently reducing our own prospects for survival. The following examples should make this clear.

Biodiversity and the Death of the Tropical Rain Forests

In an article published in *Scientific American* in 1973, Paul W. Richards, then one of the world's leading authorities on tropical rain forests, very calmly and objectively, with only a slight trace of bitterness, made the following announcement: "It appears likely that all of the world's tropical rain forests, with the exception of a few small, conserved relics, will be destroyed in the next 20 to 30 years. This destruction will inevitably have important consequences for life on the earth, although the nature and magnitude of these consequences cannot be foreseen with precision."[27]

Tropical deforestation is an excellent example of the difficulty of understanding and responding to contemporary environmental issues. Tropical rain forests are the oldest and biologically richest ecosystems in the world. They have existed continuously for some 60 million years, and typically have tenfold more species per square kilometer than temperate forests.

A single hectare (2.5 acres) of Brazilian forest contained 425 species of trees.[28] I personally found eight species of palm trees in a 10-by-10-meter forest plot in the Peruvian Amazon. More than half of the world's plant and animal species are found in the tropical rain forests, even though 6,000 years ago they covered only 10 percent of the world's land area. Destroying or degrading these forests dramatically reduces biological diversity and eliminates the numerous natural services they provide. With considerable justification, environmental scientist Norman Myers[29] called tropical forests "the primary source" of human benefits. Because of their high biomass, tropical rain forests are major reservoirs of global carbon, and deforestation contributes carbon dioxide to the atmosphere, enhancing the greenhouse effect and global warming. The loss of tropical rain forests causes regional flooding, decreased rainfall, and degradation of soils, placing many communities at risk. Rainforest plants are also a major source of pharmaceuticals, vegetable waxes and oils, and cosmetics, as well as hardwoods and edible fruits and nuts. The broad patterns of deforestation are clear, but not everyone agrees on the causes, or what action should be taken, because different groups have very different interests in the forest and different degrees of influence with national and international decision makers.

It is always risky to draw public attention to environmental crises such as global deforestation, because these are complex matters with many variables that are often difficult to measure precisely. For example, we now know that Richards, cited above, was wrong about the world's rain forests being destroyed by the year 2000, but he was right about the magnitude and urgency of the threat. As with global warming, even when experts disagree on specifics, it would be imprudent for skeptics to brush aside warnings by citing conflicting opinions, or arguing that specific predictions have not come true. There is a consensus among ecologists and foresters about the broad trend of global deforestation, supported by a multitude of studies using a variety of methods. Six thousand years ago there were some 65 million km^2 (square kilometers) of forest (tropical, temperate, and boreal) in the world, based on climate and biogeographic potential.[30] Estimates based on aerial surveys and remote sensing satellites suggest that by 1975 global forests had declined to about 58 million km^2, with most of this decline occurring since 1650.[31] The 2005 Global Forest Resources assessment by the UN Food and Agriculture Organization[32] confirms that a precipitous decline began in the second half of the twentieth century. Only about 40 million km^2 of forest remained in the world by 2005, including degraded forests and tree farms. More importantly, only 13 million km^2 was undisturbed, primary forest, with centuries-old trees and minimal human impact. It is the primary forests that provide the most crucial ecosystem services that humans depend on. These figures suggest that the world has completely lost 40 percent of its forests, largely in the past 350 years with the expansion of the commercial world, and nearly 80 percent of our primary forests are gone.

Many foresters consider deforestation to be part of an unfolding global forest transition process[33] in which: (1) natural forests first shrink in area, and then expand in the form of managed forests and tree plantations; (2) forest managers shift from a sole focus on wood production to ecosystem management, recognizing the importance of all the benefits that forests provide people and nature; (3) forests are embedded in a single globalized commercial system. In effect, all of this means that forests are being domesticated, or converted from nature to culture. This accurately describes what is happening to forests, but it is an incomplete account. It also does not specify who will make the primary decisions, and how costs and benefits will be distributed. This kind of forest transition is part of a logical global-scale economic growth and intensification process, but it is not inevitable, and it may not be sustainable. It allows a few people to expand the scale of human control over nature in order to extract more immediate human benefits, but it also concentrates both decision-making power and benefits, as well as shifts enormous long-run costs to humanity as a whole, many of which may be unforeseeable and difficult to control.

Richards' projection of the virtual disappearance of tropical rain forests by 1996–2006 was a general warning of the consequences of this ecosystem transformation, not a precise prediction, because there was still considerable uncertainty about how much tropical forest existed and how fast it was actually disappearing. Even now there is considerable variation in how tropical forest is classified in different countries, and many details are incomplete. However, Richards' projection was reasonable given what was known at the time. Deforestation rates were widely believed to be directly linked to global population growth, which was then still hovering around the historic peak of 2 percent a year. Taking the widely accepted global figure of 9.7 million km^2 of tropical rain forest in 1970,[34] declining at a fixed rate of 0.2 million km^2 per year,[35] (a high estimate for the time), about 75 percent of the remaining primary forest would indeed have disappeared by 2005, taking thousands of species with it. If deforestation increased at 2 percent a year, like population, the forest would have been totally converted to other uses by 2004. The average rate of destruction was 1.8 percent per year, suggesting only another fifty-five years or so before Richards' prediction would be fulfilled if the trend continued. In reality, the rate of tropical deforestation was highly variable, because deforestation is not an inevitable force of nature. It is primarily a result of high-level decision making by political leaders, corporate heads, investors, and bankers, whose decisions also affect poverty levels and population growth rates.

The Amazon has more than half of the world's tropical rain forest, and 60 percent of that is located in Brazil. This makes Brazil a good proxy for *global* rainforest deforestation. According to ecologist Philip M. Fearnside, the original Brazilian Amazon forest was some 4 million km², which is approximately the area of Western Europe. Over the 500 years prior to 1970 an area only just larger than Portugal (92,000 km²) was deforested, which was only 2 percent of the original forest. By 1998 the total deforested area exceeded the size of France, a reduction of 16 percent of the original forest.[36] The highest recorded annual rate of deforestation in Brazil was over 29,000 km² per year in 1995.[37] This was the approximate equivalent of an area the size of Belgium lost in a single year. When Richards issued his warning in 1973, approximately 20,000 km² were being cleared annually. This alarming increase over historic rates reflected a sudden shift in Brazilian policy to build the Trans-Amazon highway and convert the Amazon from forest to cattle pastures, colonization, industrial agriculture, and logging for the global market. The close correspondence between the world market price of soybeans and the pace of deforestation on the Brazilian agricultural frontier in 2001–2003[38] suggests that those who direct the global economy also control the future of the rain forest. In this commercialization process primary rain forest is replaced by secondary forest, tree plantations, croplands, and pasture, all of which store less carbon and support fewer species, but bring a higher return on financial investment. The extra carbon released into the atmosphere by deforestation increased Brazil's total carbon emissions fivefold in 2002, moving it from the ninth-largest carbon emitter to the fourth-largest after the United States, China, and Russia.[39] The reduction in total biomass energy flow caused by Amazonian deforestation and the transfer of biomass energy to human uses means less wildlife, because biodiversity is directly related to available energy in an ecosystem.[40]

Michael Williams[41] attributes modern deforestation to "the emergence of an integrated world economy from the late fifteenth century onward" and estimates that the "developing world" has lost half of its forests since 1900. The global economic boom that began in 1980 was particularly destructive. The Worldwatch Institute estimated that between 1980 and 1995 as many as 2 million km² of forest were lost worldwide.[42] Economic growth-related deforestation is a problem not just in the tropics. Analysis of satellite images of the American Pacific Northwest showed that between 1972 and 1996 regional forest cover declined by 37 percent, from 664,000 hectares to 421,000 hectares in the Puget Sound region centered on the Seattle metropolitan area.[43] Actual rates and the specific causes of deforestation vary from country to country and from year to year, but from a long-term perspective there can be little doubt that, globally, all forests, including tropical forests, are undergoing a drastic decline due to human intervention. This is true even though reforestation means that there may now actually be more trees (small trees) in many regions than there were in the recent past. Simply replanting trees does not automatically restore complex forest ecosystems and the services they provide.

Scattered populations of tribal farmers, hunters, and fishermen have lived successfully in Amazonia for several thousand years by relying on small-scale shifting cultivation.[44] Their adaptation rested on their ability to maintain fallow periods of sufficient length to allow regrowth of the primary forest before replanting. Large-scale, commercially driven permanent farming or ranching systems have destroyed the forest, leaving rain-leached, impoverished, rock-hard soils and degraded scrub thorn forests in their place. Small-scale, "shifted farmers" have sometimes been considered the most important cause of tropical deforestation, rather than commercial logging or ranching.[45] Shifted farmers, as distinguished from indigenous shirting cultivators, are the dispossessed rural poor who do not have the political or economic power to control enough high-quality farmland to support themselves, and are forced to open undeveloped forest lands. In the Brazilian Amazon the poor account for about one-third of deforestation, but much of what they clear ends up in the hands of medium and large ranchers, who own nearly 90 percent of the privately held land in the Amazon.[46] Thus, while establishing forest reserves and curbing commercial logging play an important role in safeguarding the forests,[47] the cultural conditions that make it impossible for rural people to make a living also need to be changed.

Ecocide Soviet Style

When historians finally conduct an autopsy on the Soviet Union and Soviet Communism, they may reach the verdict of death by ecocide. . . . No other great industrial civilization so systematically and so long poisoned its land, air, water and people. None so loudly proclaiming its efforts to improve public health and protect nature so degraded both. (Feshbach and Friendly Jr., 1992, 1)[48]

Both free-market capitalism and centrally planned socialist systems have created environmental problems. Concentrated economic power and poorly regulated economic growth, regardless of political ideology, can damage the environment and undermine human health. The former Soviet Union offers a frightening, science fiction-like, worst-case scenario of the consequences of decades of misguided economic development. The 1986 explosion of the nuclear reactor at Chernobyl near the Ukrainian city of Kiev spread radioactive fallout over the western Soviet Union and east and central Europe, and as far north as Sweden. It was an environmental disaster that could not be hidden from the world or from Soviet citizens. The smoldering shell of the reactor inspired public demonstrations against decades of failed environmental policies. Antipollution rallies turned into mass political rallies in which the individual Soviet republics pressed for full autonomy. Even before the Soviet Union dissolved itself in 1991, Gorbachev's policy of *glasnost*, or openness, began to lift the veil of secrecy that had covered the almost unbelievable extent of military and industrial pollution in the country. While the full details can never be known because even secret official records were often systematically falsified, it is becoming clear that all of the now-independent states of the former Soviet Union face severe environmental crises.

Murray Feshbach, a specialist on Soviet health, and environmental reporter Alfred Friendly Jr. chronicled some of the damage in their book *Ecocide in the USSR*.[49] In order to increase agricultural output, the Soviets poured vast quantities of toxic chemicals on their farmland, while soil fertility actually declined and foodstuffs were often badly contaminated. Deadly pesticides were misapplied to crops by poorly trained workers in order to meet government quotas. Dioxin, one of the most toxic synthetic substances known and which is linked to cancer and birth defects, was used on crops freely for more than twenty years. DDT continued to be used secretly long after it was publicly banned. Poorly planned irrigation projects led to erosion, flooding, and salinization. Raw chemical waste from government-owned industrial factories left three-fourths of the country's surface waters dangerously polluted, while industrial smokestacks spewed pollutants into the air at levels five times or more above minimum air-quality standards for 70 million people in 103 cities. The air in one city showed benzopyrene levels nearly 600 times acceptable levels. The soil in many industrial centers became so badly contaminated with zinc, lead, molybdenum, and chromium that it was unsafe for children to play in their sandboxes.

One of the most visible Soviet ecological disasters was the drying up of the Aral Sea, formerly the fourth-largest lake in the world. Soviet agricultural planners recklessly diverted most of the water from the two major rivers that fed the Aral Sea in order to irrigate newly opened monocrop cotton and rice fields in the Central Asian desert. Between 1960 and 1990 the area of the Aral was reduced by 44 percent and converted into two small, 47-foot-lower saline lakes that left the fishing port of Muynak forty miles inland from the retreating shoreline. Windstorms carried toxic dust and salt from the dried lake bed over the adjacent land to mix with the toxic agricultural chemicals. The local climate was disrupted, agricultural soils waterlogged, wells contaminated, and the regional economy devastated. Soviet geographer Arkady Levintanus[50] included the Aral region among the world's ecological disasters of the twentieth century and proposed an ambitious twenty-year restoration plan, but it had to be tabled during the political turmoil resulting from the collapse of the Soviet Union. As it shrank the Aral broke into two smaller seas, and in 2003 there were predictions that the larger southern Aral in Uzbekistan would be almost completely dry by 2020.[51] Since then Kazakhstan has constructed a new dam that is stabilizing the smaller north Aral.[52]

Perhaps the clearest measure of Soviet ecocide is its impact on human health. Even though Soviet statistics were notoriously unreliable, it is now apparent that an unprecedented public health crisis is under way. While for a time the Soviet Union made enormous strides in improving living standards in the country, the government's emphasis on industrial development at all costs eventually poisoned the environment while simultaneously undermining the healthcare system. The economic, social, and political turmoil that followed the rapid conversion of the communist system to corporate capitalism after 1991 amplified the ongoing environmental crisis. The result can be plainly seen in shocking rates of birth defects, malnutrition, cancer, respiratory problems, and infectious disease, leading to reduced life expectancy and elevated infant mortality rates. Nationwide in 1999 life expectancy for Russian men was just fifty-nine years, and infant mortality was 23 per 1,000. Figures of 60 and 21, respectively, show only slight improvement by 2003.[53] In Uzbekistan, under the impact of the Aral Sea disaster, infant mortality rates soared to 72 per 1,000. Comparable rates in the United States were seventy-three years for American men and 6.3 deaths per 1,000 for infants. Officially only thirty-two people were killed by radiation from the Chernobyl disaster. The real figure will never be known, but the World Health Organization estimated that 4.9 million people were exposed to dangerous levels of radiation.[54] The disaster led to the resettlement of 200,000 people, and 50,000 square miles were contaminated. Thousands continue to live in unsafe areas, and cases of radiation-related illness seem to be increasing.

The Soviet system proved exceptionally damaging because highly centralized controls and high levels of secrecy made it difficult for local communities to respond to environmental problems as they arose. The powerful central government imposed its own development program and then did not effectively enforce environmental safeguards. The diffuse nature of most pollution problems made it difficult if not impossible to link specific deaths to specific pollution problems even when broad trends became clear with the publication of general statistics. The Soviet experience gives us a glimpse of what could happen anywhere and demonstrates the obvious: Uncontrolled industrial expansion is dangerous to health—whether directed by a central government, or when commercial developers are given a free hand. The challenge for epidemiologists is to establish safe levels for industrial pollutants; for community development planners, the challenge is to reduce the need for dangerous contaminants.

Environmental Crisis and Cultural Change

Environmental crisis has been a factor in cultural change throughout human history and prehistory. However, the present environmental crisis is very different from any in the past, not only because of its scale and scope but also because it is being accelerated by cultural features that never existed in the past. In the broadest sense, an environmental crisis exists when human demands, or indirect impacts, exceed what the environment can produce. Such a crisis could be initiated by a natural climatic fluctuation that caused a reduction in available resources. More likely, it could be related to changes in cultural scale and the associated increases in aggregate resource consumption.

The environmental changes associated with tribal cultures tend to unfold gradually and are much more likely to lead to a new, relatively stable relationship between society and environment. In contrast, large-scale politically organized and commercial societies are associated with rapid environmental transformations that arise more and more frequently, and impact ever-larger areas. Prehistoric Europe provides an example of gradual change introduced by tribal cultures. Neolithic shifting cultivators began to move into Europe some 8,500 years ago from Southwest Asia and gradually reached the limits of their subsistence adaptation within 4,000 years or so. Forest fallow periods were steadily shortened as population density increased and domestic grazing animals further inhibited the regeneration of forests. Eventually, permanent open country and heath lands appeared over large areas of what had been a vast expanse of virtually unbroken forest that hunting peoples had kept intact for tens of thousands of years.[55] As a result of this gradually unfolding environmental crisis, shifting cultivation eventually became all but impossible, the natural fertility of the forest soils was being exhausted, and a period of population movement, warfare, and dramatic culture change ensued. When conditions finally stabilized, it was at a higher population density on a different ecological basis and level of cultural complexity. Tribes were replaced by politically centralized chiefdoms, and settlements became more permanent. The shift to political-scale culture is reflected archaeologically in megalithic burials and the use of metal.

Numerous examples of environmental degradation and cultural changes in societies can be cited.[56] However, a careful inspection of the archaeological record does not show any clear cases of societies outstripping their resources and collapsing as a direct result. The situation is invariably much more complex, and may often be attributed to bad decision making by elites and extreme climate events.[57] More complex societies are, however, more costly to maintain, and they are more vulnerable to collapse than tribal societies. There is clear evidence that intensive agricultural practices in ancient Mesopotamia, where irrigation caused the gradual accumulation of salts in the soil, were also contributing factors in the fall of Sumerian civilization after 2000 BC,[58] although climatic fluctuation may also have played a part. In the New World, it was long assumed that the collapse of lowland classic Mayan civilization in the ninth century AD may have been caused by increased demographic pressures on a limited resource base and that some kind of environmental crisis either occurred or was developing.[59] However, more recent archaeological research and deciphered Mayan glyphs suggest that chronic warfare between rival kings was a major factor in the collapse.[60] It appears that the Mayan kings developed intensive agricultural systems that proved unsustainable during times of political conflict. Thus, cultures under the influence of the politicization process ultimately made it more difficult for people to maintain a viable relationship with their resource base. The most important question is, are there scale thresholds that set limits to growth, beyond which human well-being and security may be reduced?

Beyond "The Limits to Growth"

> We can thus say with some confidence that, under the assumption of no major change in the present system, population and industrial growth will certainly stop within the next century, at the latest. (Meadows et al., 1972)[61]

The basic behavior mode of the world system is exponential growth of population and capital, followed by collapse. . . . [T]his behavior mode occurs if we assume no change in the present system or if we assume any number of technological changes in the system. (Meadows et al., 1972).[62]

This discussion of "the limits to growth" must be prefaced with the reminder that although the focus here is on energy and material limits to growth, the most ultimately important human problems are social and cultural, and they concern distribution rather than production. The problem is not "running out" of global resources, it is rather that we will face shortfalls, rising costs, and social and environmental damage that will become ever more difficult to overcome if exponential growth trends are not curbed. All limits, whether physical, social, or cultural, must be considered. Even though there are global aspects to many environmental problems, the environmental "crisis" will largely be felt by particular nations, societies, and local and regional communities as they experience their own specific problems of gradually increasing resource shortages, pollution, conflict, and social and environmental costs.

In 1798, early in the Industrial Revolution, English economist Thomas R. Malthus (1766–1834) warned of population's potential for exponential growth and pointed out that, if unchecked, population would outstrip the ability of a country or the world to produce food. He revised and refined his basic argument several times in the face of a barrage of criticism that held that there was no such tendency or that the potential of the earth was virtually limitless. Many critics, particularly economists and social planners, argued that population growth was essential for industrial growth and that together these would assure continued happiness and prosperity for humanity. This growth concept is a dominant ideology of the commercial global-scale culture, and perpetual expansion, whether in population or consumption, is in fact one of the distinguishing features of capitalist economic systems. However, Malthus was not alone in his pessimism regarding growth. Other early economists, including Adam Smith (1723–1790) and David Ricardo (1772–1823), also felt that continual economic growth would not be possible forever because of ultimate limits and inevitable diminishing returns from a dwindling resource base. However, any stabilization of the industrial economic system was thought to be so far in the future that no one need worry about planning for it. Only in recent years have significant numbers of scientists begun to doubt that continual growth can be sustained by a finite planet long into the foreseeable future.

In 1864 American scholar and pioneer conservationist George P. Marsh (1801–1882) published *Man and Nature*, a massive indictment of the deterioration of the natural environments of Europe and America that had already occurred because of human intervention. He boldly warned that a "shattered" earth and the extinction of the species might result from further human "crimes" against nature. This warning was perhaps the first round of a continuing struggle between environmentalists and growth advocates. Unfortunately, much of this debate was clouded by the framing of the issue in a way that set humans apart from nature, suggesting to some that the goal of conservation was the restoration of a pristine nature.

For the next hundred years after these early warnings, government planners and investors largely ignored the hazards of constant economic growth in a finite world, thanks to the dramatic achievements of science and technology in increasing production. Few people seemed to worry that a sudden switch to nonrenewable new energy sources (coal and oil) and the imperialist expansion of Europeans into Africa and Asia might only increase the disequilibrium and temporarily delay a stabilization while greatly raising the cost of readjustment and heightening the potential danger.

In 1954, as the great effort to achieve global economic development gained momentum, the combined problems of population growth, industrial expansion, and the limitations of the world in supporting such developments were posed as serious threats to the future survival of humanity in a provocative book by journalist Harrison Brown (1917–1986), *The Challenge of Man's Future*.[63] Brown suggested that the most likely outcome would be the irreversible collapse of industrial civilization due to its own instabilities and the destruction of its resource base through inadequately regulated exploitation. The only other likely outcome Brown could imagine that would permit the limited survival of industrial civilization was careful planning and rigid restriction of individual freedom by authoritarian governments. In effect, new mechanisms of social integration would need to evolve. Similar pessimism and warnings were expressed in 1974 by economist Robert L. Heilbroner (1919–2005),[64] who a short time earlier had been an optimistic champion of worldwide industrialization.

One of the most ambitious and authoritative early attempts to examine the implications of the instability of the commercial world was the Club of Rome's *The Limits to Growth*, published in 1972.[65] This pioneer study was the result of some two years of research by a seventeen-member international team of experts working with a computer model of the global system devised by systems theorist Jay Forrester of the Massachusetts Institute of Technology. Starting from certain basic assumptions about the interrelat-

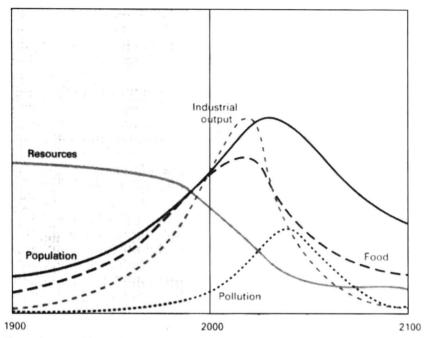

Figure 2.1.   World Model, Standard Run.
The "standard" world model run assumes no major change in the physical, economic, or social relationships that have historically governed the development of the world system. All variables plotted here follow historical values from 1900 to 1970. Food, industrial output, and population grow exponentially until the rapidly diminishing resource base forces a slowdown in industrial growth. Because of natural delays in the system, both population and pollution continue to increase for some time after the peak of industrialization. Population growth is finally halted by a rise in the death rate due to decreased medical services. Meadows et al., *Beyond the Limits*, 133. Reprinted with permission from the author.

edness of exponential growth in population, agricultural production, resource depletion, industrial production, and pollution, the team set out to estimate how these factors might interact to set limits on the future expansion of industrial civilization. The results of this research were surprising to many people and distressing to everyone. According to the model, no matter how the variables are manipulated (that is, by technological solutions, assuming twice as many natural resources, solving the problem of pollution, and so on), the system collapses before AD 2100 because of basic environmental limits. Figure 2.1 illustrates how a collapse could occur if then-present trends were to continue. Stabilizing population extends the system somewhat, but collapse still occurs because production and consumption are too high. According to these projections, the only feasible solution for maintaining the commercial world as a viable adaptation is to stabilize both population and industrial production as quickly as possible.

The Limits to Growth was enormously successful in calling attention to global limits, but was soon ridiculed, scorned, ignored, and later copied. It appeared in thirty languages and reportedly sold 30 million copies.[66] *Limits* prompted severe criticism from technological optimists who argued that the long-run limits are still far in the future and indefinable.[67] Others stressed that limiting growth would be immoral because it would hurt the poor,[68] or that given human ingenuity and the operation of market incentives, resources should really be considered infinite.[69] The world model was variously criticized as imprecise, too complex for wide understanding, and oversimplified. Critics suggested that it might be dangerous to attempt to bring economic growth to a halt, and proponents of stability were accused of being elitists who wished only to maintain the status quo in their favor.

In 1992, twenty years after *The Limits to Growth*, the original authors issued a sober restudy, *Beyond the Limits: Confronting Global Collapse, Envisioning a Sustainable Future*, reaffirming their original findings and proposing solutions.[70] This work responded to the critics by stressing that sustainability, not fixing a doomsday date, is the issue. Yet the authors concluded that resource consumption and pollution had already exceeded sustainable rates in many countries. Their updated computer projections continued to show that global declines in per capita economic production will eventually occur unless we choose to design a world order that maximizes "sustainability, sufficiency, equity, and efficiency." The implication is that we must plan ahead and decide what kind of future we want. A second update of *Limits* was published in 2004,[71] this time citing global warming as the clearest evidence that the global system was exceeding carrying capacity. As evidence of overshoot steadily accumulated, the reality of limits became harder for skeptics to ignore. In 2000, Matthew R. Simmon, founder and chair of Simmons & Company International, an independent investment bank specializing in the energy industry, examined the original *Limits* book, and concluded that "all the original conclusions are precisely on track," and "The Club of Rome turned out to be right. We simply wasted 30 important years by ignoring this work."[72]

Assuming that the relationships among trends shown in the world model are valid, many anthropologists are reevaluating their own positions on the desirability of economic growth and the meaning of development. In the past anthropologists actively promoted economic growth throughout the world, without always considering the real distribution of costs and benefits or the long-term prospect of continued growth. It is becoming more apparent that development emphasizing sustainability with social equity is a more desirable goal.

Environmental Commissions: *Global 2000* and Our Common Future

The most knowledgeable professional analysts in the executive branch of the U.S. Government have reported to the President that, if public policies around the world continue unchanged through the end of the century, a number of serious world problems will become worse, not better . . . the world in 2000 will be more crowded, more polluted, less stable ecologically, and more vulnerable to disruption. . . . Serious stresses involving population, resources, and environment are clearly visible ahead . . . the world's people will be poorer. (Barney, *The Global 2000 Report to the President of the United States*)[73]

In 1977 American president Jimmy Carter commissioned a special study of global trends in population, resources, and environment up to the year 2000 to facilitate long-range planning by U.S. government agencies. *The Global 2000 Report to the President of the United States* was over two years in preparation and ultimately involved a budget of nearly $1 million, thirteen government agencies, and scores of advisors and researchers. In general this study was similar to *The Limits to Growth* in its attempt to project the future outcome of present trends at a global level. However, *Global 2000* was much more cautious than *The Limits to Growth* in that some of the subsections of the study, such as food production, did not always take into account losses caused by activities in other sections, such as industrial pollution. Furthermore, the *Global 2000* study looked only to the year 2000, whereas *The Limits to Growth* looked much farther ahead. The *Global 2000* study was also quite conservative; it assumed continued technological progress, no major political upheavals, and a continuation of the existing world political system. In view of all these conservative elements, it is significant that the conclusions of *Global 2000* still contained ominous warnings of serious problems in the near future, as indicated in the summary quote cited above. The Carter Commission did not predict a catastrophic collapse of the world system, but it correctly warned of population increases, serious water shortages, major deforestation, deterioration of agricultural lands, and increased desertification, together with more poverty, human suffering, and international tension. What it failed to predict, of course, was the end of the Cold War.

The issues raised by these studies, and the increasingly visible evidence of worldwide environmental deterioration, had finally become so undeniable that by 1983 the United Nations General Assembly passed a resolution setting up a World Commission on Environment and Development (WCED). Fears over the state of the environment were officially recognized as a legitimate problem by the highest levels of the global culture. The UN commission, which became known as the Brundtland Commission, after its chairman, Norwegian prime minister Gro Harlem Brundtland, issued its landmark report in 1987.[74] It acknowledged that environmental deterioration and human impoverishment were indeed a threat to the future of humanity. The commission cautiously recommended that development should be sustainable. This was not a very remarkable conclusion given the overwhelming evidence already amassed, but from a global perspective the commission was perhaps the highest-level group to reach such a conclusion, and it understandably commanded international attention. The Brundtland Commission's principal contribution was to redefine development in reference to sustainability and basic human needs rather than strictly in regard to increasing GDP. The commission gave priority to the needs of the world's poor and defined sustainable development as "development that meets the needs of the present without compromising the ability of future generations to meet their own needs."[75]

The UN responded surprisingly quickly following the Brundtland Commission's report. In 1989 the General Assembly called for a major world conference, the United Nations Conference on Environment and Development (UNCED), "to devise strategies to halt and reverse the effects of environmental degradation in the context of increased national and international efforts to promote sustainable and environmentally sound development in all countries." UNCED met in Rio de Janeiro in June 1992 and adopted Agenda 21 as its formal action plan to deal with environmental issues into the twenty-first century. The conservative consensus these commissions and conferences reached was that further economic growth would be needed to reduce environmental deterioration and poverty. World leaders were not yet ready to imagine that major changes in the structure of global society might be needed to achieve sustainability. The World Summit on Sustainable Development, the Rio+10 Earth Summit, held in Johannesburg, South Africa, in 2002 again endorsed sustainable development and the UN Millennium Goals with solemn pledges, but the proceedings were effectively boycotted by the United States, and no dramatic actions were taken.

Positive steps occurred in 2001 when UN Secretary-General Kofi Annan commissioned a special analysis of global ecosystems, *The Millennium*

Ecosystem Assessment,[76] to guide various UN programs concerned with sustainable development. The $25 million project involved some 1,360 experts and produced a multi-volume report in 2005 with six technical volumes and six synthesis reports. The assessment was a detailed worldwide accounting of the status of nature, and of nature's ability to provide services such as nutrient cycling; soil formation; biological production of food, fiber, and fuel; provision of fresh water; and regulation of climate, watersheds, and disease. Again, the trends that the pioneer *Limits to Growth* study described were dramatically verified. The *Assessment* board, which represented a cross-section of UN agencies, business interests, and organizations including the International Union for the Conservation of Nature (IUCN) and the World Resources Institute, as well as indigenous peoples, issued its conclusions in a separate volume *Living Beyond Our Means,* with a "stark warning" that "Human activity is putting such strain on the natural functions of Earth that the ability of the planet's ecosystems to sustain future generations can no longer be taken for granted."[77] They found that nearly two-thirds of natural services were in decline worldwide, and that we were "on the edge of a massive wave of species extinctions." All of this would make it harder to meet human needs.

At this point it will be useful to examine some of the explanations that have been offered for our present environmental difficulties before considering the insights that can be gained from domestic-scale societies and cultures.

Roots of the Environmental Crisis

The basic cause of the environmental crisis is humans making too many demands on nature. The obvious problem is that resources, whether measured globally, nationally, or locally, are being consumed at a rate greater than they are being produced by natural biological or geological processes, and wastes are being created that disrupt natural cycles. This is a problem of per capita consumption as amplified by total population. Over-consumption may be defined as consumption in a given area that exceeds the rate of natural resource production, which reduces social sustainability. Every society has the potential to over-consume, and this potential could be realized by a simple increase in population over local carrying capacity. However, such over-consumption is less likely in domestic-scale societies because negative feedback systems are activated to reduce population or because cultural mechanisms to promote better distribution are used. Unusual increases in per capita consumption rates could also initiate over-consumption, but again such an outcome is normally prevented by negative feedback mechanisms. Unfortunately, the global commercial culture has short-circuited the normal cultural feedback mechanisms that prevent over-consumption in at least four critical ways: (1) dependence on nonrenewable resources, (2) dependence on imports, (3) urbanization, and (4) institutionalized inequality.

Perhaps the most critical turning point in the development of the global culture was its shift away from renewable resources to overwhelming dependence on fossil fuels, which have become substitutes for both solar energy and natural products such as fibers. These resources are stored solar energy that has been "banked" in the earth over millions of years, yet they are now being used to temporarily support consumption far beyond what could ever be supported by local renewable resources. The danger in this case is that by the time these stored resources have become significantly depleted we may well have "overshot" our renewable resource base. The problem is amplified because fossil fuels have made it easy to deplete water, soil, forests, and fisheries. These renewable resources can be completely destroyed or drawn down to the extent that they cannot recover quickly enough for human demand. A society that relied largely on local renewable resources would quickly recognize an impending shortage and could take corrective action, either by intensifying its productive technology or, more wisely, by reducing its demand.

A second critical way in which commercially organized societies have temporarily escaped environmental limits has been through their enormous reliance on large-scale global trade. For example, Ecological Footprint analysis shows that trade, especially imports, made it possible for the United States to consume nearly double its biocapacity (everything that nature produces in a particular region) in 2001.[78] Consuming everything would leave nothing for wildlife, would not be "balanced with nature," and would hardly be sustainable, but consuming double requires a vast external subsidy. Intergroup resource exchange is a cultural universal, and it sometimes follows the economic principle of "comparative advantage," in which different regions exchange items that each produces most efficiently. In the tribal world trade was often limited to a narrow range of raw materials such as salt, obsidian, and ochre that spread widely along decentralized, reciprocal exchange networks. Often the primary purpose of trade was maintaining friendly relations and encouraging intermarriage between groups that might otherwise be hostile. Commercial trade involving highly concentrated economic power allows resources extracted from poor areas to be wastefully consumed in rich territories. Reliance on imported resources to support growth and consumption could easily become unsustainable.

Urbanization creates a similar problem because urban populations must be supported by internal "imports" from rural areas. For example in 1997, Hong Kong, a city of nearly 7 million people living on a land area of 1,100 square kilometers, was drawing the equivalent of the biological product from an area 400 times greater.[79] Likewise, in 2000 Londoners were drawing the biological equivalent of an area 293 times the size of its geographical area.[80] Urban consumers are far removed from their resources and are unlikely to become immediately aware of impending shortages or of any other environmental impact of their consumption patterns.

Institutionalized inequality is socially defined by differential consumption patterns and serves to promote over-consumption at the top of the social hierarchy, and under-consumption at the bottom, while diverting much of its adverse impact onto "lower" classes. Inequality operates between and within nations. Prices in the global market thus do not always accurately reflect the true costs of commercial products. This inequality diverts and delays the mechanisms that would otherwise maintain consumption within environmental limits.

In addition to fostering over-consumption, the global commercial culture has greatly increased the probability that it will cause environmental crises by disrupting natural cycles and simplifying ecosystems on a vast scale. Natural cycles have been disrupted by the introduction of new synthetic materials such as plastics and organochlorine pesticides, which have been used to support over-consumption by replacing depleted natural products but cannot be readily broken down by nature into their constituent parts for reuse. Pollution is a cultural product that does not exist in nature because all natural materials are continuously recycled. Furthermore, commercially generated "natural" organic wastes such as sewage and feedlot wastes have been created and concentrated in ways that block their effective recycling and degrade ecosystems. In this regard we have consistently violated what ecologist Barry Commoner[81] called the basic laws of ecology. Simplification of ecosystems is best exemplified by the industrial factory farm that attempts to remove all but one or two "desirable" species. This process greatly lowers the biological productivity and stability of an ecosystem and can be maintained only at enormous cost in imported energy and by increased use of pesticides and synthetic fertilizers, which in turn deplete nonrenewable resources and disrupt natural cycles.

Thus, our present environmental crisis is the direct result of over-consumption, disruption of natural cycles, and simplification of ecosystems. Since all cultures seem to have the potential for degrading their environment by such means, it remains to be explained why politically centralized

societies—and commercially organized societies in particular—have been
much greater culprits in this regard than tribal societies. Some analysts point
to a single basic cause, arguing that if we can simply develop better technology, achieve zero population growth, or invent a new value system, our
environmental problems will be over. We will examine the population and
technology arguments later, but the values argument may profitably be examined here.

Capitalism and Ideological Roots

If we define culture as the information in people's minds that directs their
behavior, then ideas, beliefs, and values must in some way be responsible
for how people relate to the natural environment. Unraveling the connections between belief and environmental practice is not a simple exercise
because the environmentally most important beliefs may be more fundamental beliefs about human society rather than beliefs about the environment. During the 1960s an influential article in *Science*, written by historian
Lynn White Jr.[82] initiated widespread discussion about the significance of
religion with regard to human use of the environment. White attributed
environmental problems to Christian beliefs, pointing out that in the book
of Genesis God gave man dominion over nature, thereby initiating our
seemingly victorious battle against nature. White concluded that, "since
the roots of our trouble are so largely religious, the remedy must also be
essentially religious." Some environmentally concerned Christians rejected
this interpretation, instead interpreting "dominion" to mean "stewardship,"
and saw no conflict between people and nature. On the other hand, some
environmentalists assumed that tribal animism, which seemingly makes
people part of nature, would prevent the conflict and thus avoid the environmental crisis. This latter viewpoint has had broad appeal for many environmental activists who advocate a "deep ecology" environmental ethic
of reverence toward nature. Some environmentalists envision a spiritual
"oneness" between people and nature, blending an idealized view of tribal
beliefs with European paganism and in some interpretations portraying the
earth itself as a living thing named after the ancient Greek creator Earth
Mother Gaea.[83] Critics of deep ecology dismiss it as escapist mysticism,[84]
or misguided romanticism of fanciful ecologically noble savages.[85]

Anthropologist Marshall Sahlins[86] places Christianity within a broader
European cosmology that assumes that people are naturally evil and selfish,
condemned to perpetual economic scarcity within societies controlled by
hierarchical power structures and coercive governments. These fundamen-

tal beliefs justify social inequality, the quest for increased social power, and technological progress, all of which are thought to be natural and inevitable. These ideas are also fundamental to the belief that economic growth driven by free-market capitalism and free trade will naturally benefit society. The connection between ideology and environmental problems is that ideologies can help motivate people to sustain particular social power structures that in turn promote unsustainable increases in the scale of society.

Although many anthropologists take a cultural materialist position and argue that economic practices are determined primarily by material conditions, ideas do "have consequences."[87] The beliefs underlying capitalism are the most important ideological cause of contemporary adverse environmental changes because capitalism drives the scale changes that have most intensified human pressures on the environment. For sociologist Max Weber (1881–1961) "the spirit of capitalism" was the idea that making money is the ultimate purpose and highest virtue of life.[88] This spirit is well represented by the familiar capitalist dictums "time is money" and "money makes money." Weber argued that the capitalist spirit became a moral imperative and motivating force and was a more important determinant of what people did than the specifics of nationality, technology, or resources. He distinguished this "absolutely irrational" idea of perpetually growing money from the natural human impulse of greed for material acquisition to satisfy needs. "Traditional" non-capitalist peoples stop working when their needs are met. Capitalism is irrational in that the drive to accumulate money goes beyond human needs and thus recognizes no natural limits. Evolutionary anthropologists would explain this as rational emulation of indirect measures of reproductive success.

Although Weber thought that the ideas behind capitalism were irrational, he argued that the hallmark of modern industrial capitalism was the highly rational way in which capitalists organized economic exchanges for the pursuit of profit. Under capitalism, markets for money, labor, and commodities, along with business enterprises, were all organized in a highly rational, calculated way to make money grow. Historically, Weber attributed these capitalist ideas to the work ethic that grew out of the Protestant Reformation, represented by the Calvinist and Puritan concepts of predestination, personal salvation, and work as a divine "calling." Protestant Christians became capitalists because they believed that luxury and wasting time were sinful and because economic success demonstrated that one had been elected for salvation. Weber felt that after capitalism had become the dominant political economy in much of the world the original religious ideology that produced capitalist economic practice was no longer needed. Modern people were bound to their jobs by the economic and material conditions of industrial production. By 1905, when he completed *The Protestant Ethic and the Spirit of Capitalism*, Weber felt that under capitalism the way we must obtain material goods had become an inescapable "iron cage." He directly linked industrial capitalism to unsustainable levels of resource consumption, concluding that capitalism had become an "irresistible force" that would perhaps continue to determine everyone's life "until the last ton of fossilized coal is burnt."[89]

Unregulated Self-Interest and the Tragedy of the Commons

Some environmentalists find the roots of environmental problems in acquisitive individuals seeking their self-interest in the absence of coercive cultural controls to protect publicly owned, or "open access" natural resources. At least one influential writer, biologist Garrett Hardin (1915–2003),[90] called this phenomenon the "tragedy of the commons." For Hardin, the crisis was the inevitable outgrowth of individuals seeking their own self-interest in combination with a failure of appeals to conscience and social responsibility. This implied a repudiation of Adam Smith's belief that an "invisible hand" operated in the market economy such that self-seeking individuals "without intending it, without knowing it, advance the interests of society."[91] Hardin called for mutually agreed on coercive restraints to maintain population and pollution within safe limits and suggested that these problems, strictly speaking, had no technical solutions. Like Lynn White Jr. he felt that a change in values was required, but he added the important qualification that political regulations must be strengthened.

What the "tragedy of the commons" overlooks is that the need for formal controls is determined by the scale of the social system and the way decision-making power is distributed. The problem is not with human nature as such, or whether resources are public or private. Hardin was right that in some situations social restraints on individual behavior are necessary, but he did not describe how such restraints often operate in small-scale societies. Societies must, in effect, define "maximum good" and then adjust demand to what their specific environments can supply. What is "good" is a socio-cultural decision. Hardin argued that no cultural group had solved the "tragic commons" problem because no prosperous population had ever managed to stabilize its population. However, small-scale societies promote resilience or sustainability by defining "maximum good" at attainable levels. Tribal societies achieved "affluence" without at the same time perpetually elevating consumption, and they widely distributed decision making and access. They were thus able to avoid the coercive restraints that Hardin felt would be needed to control the dangers inherent in the pursuit of self-interest. Even very small nation-states, such as Denmark, that maximize social equality, and endorse "low" material expectations, may still enjoy the highest levels of life satisfaction in Europe.[92] Denmark's population was growing at only 0.24 percent a year in 2005, whereas the United States' population was growing at more than 1 percent.[93]

Hardin[94] later observed that "shame" rather than physical coercion could operate to inhibit destructive overuse of resources in small, face-to-face communities. In the tribal world, the absence of commercial incentives for over-production is of course also important. Under the right cultural conditions there need be no inherent conflict between individual self-interest and the interests of society as a whole. Based on his survey of small, domestically organized farming systems throughout the world, cultural ecologist Robert McC. Netting[95] observed, "Communities of smallholders have the demonstrated capacity for cooperative management of environmental resources without the untrammeled individual competition that brings on a 'tragedy of the commons.'"

Hardin illustrated the "tragic commons" by suggesting that in a traditional herding society individual herdsmen would add extra animals to their own herds even beyond the point at which environmental damage would result from overgrazing, because they would receive full advantage for each additional animal, whereas the costs of overgrazing would be shared by all herders. In his view each herdsman was thus caught in a conflict between social responsibility and personal self-interest, and only coercive force would make it obviously in his best interest to refrain from expanding his herd. This was a misleading oversimplification. In reality, in many herding societies grazing is territorially regulated, and not an open-access resource. On arid lands animal populations are often regulated by frequent devastating droughts, as well as warfare, raiding, and disease. In such highly variable environments, the standard concept of carrying capacity may be virtually irrelevant.[96]

There is no necessary conflict between individual self-interest and social responsibility in herding societies. Where self-sufficient individual households or small household groups must depend on herd animals for their primary subsistence, maximum herd size is determined by the number of animals a given herder can safely handle, quality of pasture, and daily grazing requirements of the animals, in addition to sociopolitical considerations such as the size of local kin groups and the vulnerability of herds to raiders. A large herd of large animals in an area of poor pastures would quickly become impractical because the herd would need to move so rapidly to get enough to eat that productivity would decline.[97] It is clearly feasible for a group to successfully manage a resource without resorting to coercive measures.[98] Private access to grazing land may not be a superior alternative, as demonstrated by the experience of commercial ranching systems. Commercial systems, which are designed to maximize the number of animals sold in order to secure a profit, can increase herd size by drawing on fossil-fuel energy subsidies and imported feed. Thus, with commercial herds there are few, if any, cultural limits to herd size.

The successful adaptation of herding societies is clearly illustrated by the traditional herders of East Africa, Southwest Asia, and the Middle East. Nomadic pastoralism emerged in these regions as a means of exploiting the vast steppe areas that were created by climatic changes beginning some 10,000 years ago. Given the particular mix of poor rainfall, poor soil, and rugged topography, these regions are unsuitable for any form of permanent agriculture but can support herds of grazing animals such as sheep and goats. Using ground surveys together with satellite pictures, researchers collected basic ecological data on herders during a two-year study conducted in Afghanistan before the civil strife that followed Soviet intervention in 1980.[99] Their research showed convincingly that traditional herders do not necessarily overgraze their pastures under normal climatic conditions. The researchers measured the biological productivity of all major plant communities in the region and calculated the food requirements of the animals. They found that, during the study, the herders were using only 23 to 32 percent of the available sustained-yield forage production of the natural pastures.

Some researchers[100] have used game theory to demonstrate why it is a predictable adaptive strategy for individual East African cattle herders to restrict their use of common grazing resources near their homesteads during the dry season. Others have used dynamic mathematical models to explore the relationship among soil moisture, grass and shrub biomass, and grazing pressure in the semiarid savannas of South and East Africa.[101] Their work suggests that traditional cattle herders maintained a very resilient mix of grassland and shrubs because their grazing system was "irregular and opportunistic" and the human population remained relatively low. Under these conditions the natural pastures tolerated even intense grazing because it was only periodic. Herd productivity was also relatively low but perfectly adequate for domestic needs in a nonmarket, subsistence economy. Animals that appear to be unproductive and of poor quality by commercial standards may actually be well suited to poor grazing and frequent drought.[102] Traditional herders thus actually favored the growth of a wide variety of grass types, and these wild pastures became more productive. However, settled peasant farmers and commercial ranchers replaced many of the tribesmen after 1900, when the colonial period began, and introduced a much less variable grazing system that has proved less stable. The result is that now there is often serious overgrazing, leading to reduction in the water-absorbing capacity of the topsoil and a replacement of grass by less-productive woody shrubs. Overall, when outsiders have intervened the ability of the natural pastures to support grazing animals over the long term may be reduced.

On marginal grazing lands in many parts of the world, overgrazing may be encouraged when outside energy sources are introduced, making it possible to concentrate animals by drilling wells and hauling feed, and when animals are raised primarily for the market rather than for direct subsistence. Many such developments, often including settlement schemes, have been promoted by governments interested in increasing the productivity of pastoral nomads. Under these conditions self-interest may come into conflict with social responsibility.

Land Degradation in the Mediterranean Region

In 1992, the European Union initiated a large international research project on the land degradation problem in the Mediterranean region of southern Europe. Desertification is a particularly serious problem in Spain, southern Italy, and Greece that threatens to disrupt the lives of millions of people throughout the European Mediterranean. Known as ARCHAEOMEDES, the project was directed by the European Commission's Section DG-XII on Climatology and Natural Hazards. The European Union coordinates economic and social policy among twenty-seven European nations through the Council of Ministers, the European Parliament, the European Court of Justice, and the European Commission, which proposes legislation on environment, trade, social policy, and regional development.

The ARCHAEOMEDES project was a unique interdisciplinary effort involving more than a dozen research institutions and incorporating both social and natural scientists, including geologists, geographers, biologists, archaeologists, and social anthropologists. The researchers' integrated crosscultural, evolutionary, human ecodynamics approach treated humans and the environment as part of an interacting system.[103] The project examined environmental changes on different spatial and temporal scales in eight regions in Portugal, Spain, France, Italy, Croatia, and Greece. Social and environmental transformations were viewed over five time scales: hundreds of millennia, tens of millennia, millennia, centuries, and decades. Land degradation includes the natural dynamic processes of tectonic uplift, erosion, and climate change, changes that often operate on a much longer time scale than human activities. It was found that for tens of thousands of years during the Paleolithic era, as long as humans remained mobile or semi-mobile, the human impact on the Mediterranean landscape was very small. Local erosion increased measurably during the Neolithic when people settled in farming villages and began clearing land and introducing grazing. Human disturbances eventually became the dominant landscape process, but it was initially a very gradual process. After the Paleolithic, human pressure on the environment began to result in progressively shorter cycles of growth and collapse of the social cultural system, with each cycle covering a larger area and accompanied by more severe land degradation, leaving a less-resilient landscape. Historically the Mediterranean landscape has always been shaped by political and economic forces involving social power and scale.

ARCHAEOMEDES researchers found that half of the erosion during the past 10,000 years in the Vera basin of southwestern Spain occurred during the past 500 years, even though the region was occupied by villagers for 5,000 years. Furthermore, over the past 150 years the pace of erosion accelerated. During the seven centuries of the Roman period, from 100 BC to AD 600, the Romans introduced an intensive production system based on individual property holdings, a large-scale irrigation grid, terracing, and drainage in the Rhone valley of southern France. Landscape degradation patterns in the Rhone came to reflect influences from the Roman world political economy rather than local conditions. The Roman system soon reached a critical threshold at which the entire system became vulnerable. By the second century AD widespread collapse occurred in the Rhone because the Roman drainage system proved unable to deal with extreme natural fluctuations in runoff. When researchers examined 1,000 Roman settlements, they found that 70 to 80 percent did not survive more than 200 years and many disappeared within 100 years. The final Roman collapse was a complex social and political problem rather than an environmental crisis, but it left behind a degraded landscape.

Project researchers found that striking changes began in many areas in the 1850s with the introduction of railroads and capitalist commercialization, producing a new and rapid cycle of socioeconomic transformation and landscape degradation. These changes in productive technology led to abandonment of many peripheral areas, the intensification of agriculture in a few areas, and dependence on global markets. In many areas local populations viewed the abandonment of rural areas as landscape degradation because dense brush and trees overwhelmed once-productive small farms and pastures. In the Argolid region in the Greek Peloponnesus during the decades between 1945 and 1995 a prosperous and diverse farming area was desiccated, degraded, and economically devastated by conversion to irrigated fruit-tree monoculture based on deep wells and motorized pumps. These changes, subsidized by the government, were intended to make the region more competitive in the global market. The unintended consequences were rapid drying up of local marshes, a falling water table, devastating orchard epidemics, salinization of soil and groundwater, frost problems, and falling profits. The Romans created similar problems, but over centuries.

This review of the evidence of thirty millennia of cultural evolution makes it clear that the human and natural systems in the European Mediterranean have become less resilient and less sustainable. It would be hard to argue that the cultural systems have become more adaptive as they have grown larger. A report on phase two of the ARCHAEOMEDES project concludes that economic growth is "frequently at odds with social health and well being."[104] Large-scale monocrop agriculture has reduced social and ecological diversity and resilience to change.

Extinctions and Biodiversity:
Human Nature or Culture Scale Crisis?

Biodiversity is declining worldwide at an alarming rate. According to the *Red List of Threatened Species*, prepared by the Species Survival Commission of the IUCN–World Conservation Union in 2006,[105] 40 percent of the world's known terrestrial vertebrates, 64 percent of fish, 95 percent of marine invertebrates, and 87 percent of vascular plants are either extinct, endangered, vulnerable, near threatened, or their survival is dependent on active conservation measures. Some 22 percent of the world's nearly 10,000 bird species whose status is known are in trouble. Forty percent of mammals, 50 percent of amphibians, and 77 percent of reptiles are in the same marginal status. Within historic times, 213 mammal and bird species have become extinct or survive only in captivity. Among mammals, 40 percent of carnivores, nearly 50 percent of bats, 60 percent of primates, 70 percent of whales, nearly 75 percent of even-toed mammals (hippos, pigs, camels, deer, giraffes, cattle), and all manatees and elephants are in trouble.

The known species represent only a small proportion of the planet's life forms, which may number from 5 to 30 million, including invertebrates, plants, and microorganisms. Since 1970 indices of abundance for all animal species have been in decline.[106] This matters because, as the UN's Millennium Ecosystem Assessment points out, extinction rates are now orders of magnitude greater than in the distant past as recorded in the fossil record, yet biodiversity is the basis of the ecosystem services on which human well-being depends.

Many writers suggest that this is not a new problem but is rooted in a voracious human nature, as presumably demonstrated by extinctions caused by tribal peoples. The implication is that we cannot prevent "natural" extinctions, but this conclusion would be a misinterpretation of the anthropological record. There has been much discussion about whether any people ever practiced sustainable hunting and about whether tribal people were intentional conservationists, or whether or not tribal conservation, if it existed at all, was an epiphenomenon. My general conclusion is that subsistence hunting by people in self-sufficient tribal cultures was a highly resilient adaptation. Subsistence hunting endured for millennia through changes in climate, vegetation, fauna, technology, and ethnic identity. Low density and low demand produced cultural resiliency without intentional conservation, and these systems were resilient enough to endure in spite of episodes of over-hunting. There is no need to appeal to a mythical "perfect balance" between predator and prey to recognize the adaptive advantages of small-scale cultures. Likewise, arguments that tribal hunters were no different in their use of resources from larger-scale societies can be misleading. For example, Shepard Krech III[107] effectively demonstrated that Native Americans were not always conservationists, but his discussion included trappers involved in the commercial fur trade and farming peoples living in large permanent villages, along with very low-density Paleolithic hunters. Geoscience researcher Paul S. Martin[108] took the extreme view that within the last 15,000 years tribal hunters over-hunted and destroyed hundreds of species, especially large mammals. He concluded: "The thought that prehistoric hunters . . . exterminated far more large animals than has modern man with modern weapons and advanced technology is certainly provocative and perhaps even deeply disturbing."[109]

The "Pleistocene overkill" or "blitzkrieg" argument is certainly dramatic and must temper our view of tribal societies and their relationship to the environment. The implications of this problem are certainly serious enough to merit careful examination. The undisputed facts are briefly as follows: Throughout the world over a 50,000-year period during the late Pleistocene period, some 200 genera disappeared. These extinctions involved many large animals, such as the mastodon and mammoth, giant birds, giant kangaroos, and other "mega" forms. These animals were not replaced by related species. Although the chronology of these extinctions is not precise, early human populations were colonizing new portions of the globe and improving their hunting technologies during roughly the same time period. However, some researchers[110] stress that, at least for North America there is no archaeological or paleontological evidence for the Pleistocene Overkill hypothesis. There are only fourteen known sites where Clovis hunters occur together with mammoths and mastodons, and these are the only extinct animals found with Clovis sites. In fact, only fifteen of the thirty-five genera that disappeared lasted beyond 12,000 years ago. Looking at the entire sweep of megafaunal extinctions in North America, they conclude, "Large mammal extinctions occurred at the end of the Pleistocene with or without Clovis, with or without the presence of human predators."[111]

When Martin first presented his argument, it was based largely on circumstantial evidence and the absence of equally plausible counter evidence. Later research challenged some of Martin's basic assumptions and in some cases made his argument stronger. The overkill hypothesis is strengthened by the apparent correspondence of New World extinctions with the arrival of humans, yet numerous Pleistocene megafauna survived in Africa, where humans originated. In some cases extinctions actually preceded the arrival of humans with advanced hunting technologies and involved more than merely big game species.[112] Direct overkill seems increasingly unlikely to have everywhere been the sole cause of these extinctions; rather, a combination of climatic and environmental changes, along with various indirect effects of human intervention, seem more likely causes of megafauna extinctions.[113]

Anthropological interpretations of hunting cultures suggest that overkill to the point of exterminating major prey species is theoretically very unlikely.[114] In the first place, hunters rarely relied exclusively on a single prey species, and often the bulk of their diet was based on plant foods. Furthermore, hunting systems stressed predictability and energy efficiency. As particular prey species become scarce it becomes inefficient to hunt them. Any subsistence system based on deliberately hunting key prey species to extinction would have been extremely unreliable, wasteful of time and energy, and disastrous in the long run. This is, of course, not to say that tribal hunters never wasted game animals because, even though there was often a strong ethic against wasteful over-hunting, certainly in many cases full utilization of game killed was impossible or impractical.

Impressive evidence of the long-term resilience of hunting cultures is found in the archaeological record left by mid– and late–Stone Age peoples in southern Africa, covering a time span from the recent past to over 130,000 years ago. Richard Klein[115] made a careful study of the age and sex distribution of the game animals taken by Stone Age hunters, based on an analysis of the bones left in their camps. He discovered that the pattern of human predation on large, dangerous game animals such as buffalo closely resembled that of natural predators such as lions. Human hunters took only the very young or very old individuals. He concluded that "the age distribution of buffalo in the archaeological kill samples is what one might expect if the Stone Age hunters were to enjoy a lasting, stable relationship with prey populations of buffalo."[116] Furthermore, he found no evidence of a decline in the buffalo population, even though they were hunted for tens of thousands of years. Klein found that even species of docile or small antelope, such as the eland and steenbok, which were easily driven or trapped, showed no evidence of any significant decline in numbers, even though they were utilized relatively intensively. Extinctions of game animals did occur during the period of human occupation, however, and Klein raised the possibility that improved hunting technology may have been a factor in some of these cases.

It is important to keep the issue of Pleistocene extinctions in perspective. Even if it can be demonstrated that tribal hunters did play a significant role in these extinctions, the losses are quite trivial compared to the scale of extinctions under way today. The speed, scale, and scope of the present extinction rate would appear to equal or exceed any mass extinctions in the recent geologic past, perhaps with the exception of a catastrophic meteorite collision with earth. The causes of the current extinctions are primarily landscape degradation, direct commercial exploitation, and pollution. The present extinction episode was initiated by the uncontrolled European invasion of the Western Hemisphere, which caused a massive die-off of native species severe enough to be called "biological imperialism."[117] The natural, background rate of extinction for all plant and animal species in geologic history is estimated to be from one to ten species a year, but the current rate of extinction may be as high as one thousand species per year.[118] Any estimates of extinction rates are of course problematic, but they provide a useful perspective on the present situation.

Tribal and Small-Scale Domestic Economies

Given the critical role that economics must play in any culture, some of the most important contrasts between tribal and small-scale indigenous societies and larger scale politically centralized and commercial societies should be expected to be seen in the organization and distribution of production and consumption, and related beliefs and practices. Small-scale societies include autonomous tribes existing historically in a world without governments, as well as relatively self-sufficient rural communities where householders may pay taxes or tribute and are often involved in varying degrees with the market economy. Such communities may also exist at widely different population densities, in different environments, and with different subsistence technologies. They may also differ in the extent to which resources are controlled by households or communally and in degrees of wealth inequality between households. What they have in common is their emphasis on local self-sufficiency and community sustainability, domestic-level management, and absence of community-level class divisions. These systems can all be disrupted by the intervention of governments or external commercial forces.

Unfortunately, attempts by earlier anthropologists to describe tribal economic systems as if they merely represented simplified capitalist market economies resulted in misunderstanding of the economic patterns of these domestic-scale societies. In the older anthropological literature it is not uncommon to find tribal economies described as if they were imperfectly developed market economies, with shell necklaces labeled money. At least one early economic anthropology textbook[119] attempted to follow classical economic analysis throughout, assuming that tribal systems displayed capitalist economic institutions, even if in a blurred and generalized fashion. This viewpoint has been called the formalist approach, in contrast to the substantivist anthropologists, who emphasized the unique features of tribal economies. Shed of some of the language of capitalist economics, the formalist view stresses that people everywhere are driven by self-interest and ever-expanding wants and always seek to maximize ends and minimize means.[120] Unfortunately, such interpretations have obscured both the significant accomplishments and the unique qualities of tribal economic systems.

Classical economic theory is an inadequate basis for understanding human behavior in any cultural world, because it assumes that as decision makers, people are either rational consumers seeking to maximize utility, or they are capitalist entrepreneurs, always seeking to maximize profits. From this theoretical perspective human decision makers are fully and consistently rational beings with clear goals. In the 1950s, Nobel Prize–winning cognitive psychologist and management specialist, Herbert A. Simon (1916–2001), found such models "inappropriate" when applied to the behavior of real individuals in social groups. As he explained:

> *The capacity of the human mind for formulating and solving complex problems is very small compared with the size of the problems whose solution is required for objectively rational behavior in the real world—or even for a reasonable approximation to such objective rationality.* (Simon 1957, italics original)[121]

According to Simon, human decision making and problem solving is very seriously constrained, or "bounded," by what we know, as well as our individual cognitive abilities, and the effects of decision making in groups. Making the most rational choice in the market place of classical economic theory requires perfect knowledge, which people are unlikely to possess, especially in a world where commercial advertising forcefully spins seductive illusions to sell products. Because people are not omniscient, they are forced to construct simplified mental models of reality to aid their decision making. People do the best they can, with the limited information available, and with their limited cognitive abilities. Everyone's rationality is bounded, and therefore, classical economic models are unrealistic. All peoples probably try to economize with their time and energy, as exemplified by the wide applicability of George Kingsley Zipf's "principle of least effort"[122] and as further demonstrated by optimal foraging theory,[123] but the specific goals of economic activity may vary widely in societies organized at different scales.

In capitalist economies, people produce not primarily for their own use but rather for sale or exchange, and land, labor, and money are all for sale. Of course, goods are both used and exchanged in both tribal and capitalist economies. However, in a tribal, or use value, economy, producers are directly involved in production decision making and are immediately concerned with both the environmental and the social consequences of production. These distinctions draw attention to the dual impact on the domestic, or household, economy of surplus extraction by the state, as well as the tendency of capitalist systems to alienate rural peoples from their subsistence bases and convert them into a wage-dependent labor force. Certainly the most significant contrast between tribal societies and both politically centralized and commercial societies hinges on the relative importance of markets and kinship-based social formations.

Substantivist anthropologists such as Robert Redfield[124] have emphasized the relative technological simplicity of tribal economies, the fact that there is a minimal division of labor or that everyone has equal access to the means of production, and that such small societies are basically economically self-sufficient. Paul Radin argued that tribal economies are distinguished most remarkably by their emphasis on the concept of an "irreducible minimum." According to Radin,[125] "primitive" economies operate on the principle that "every human being has the inalienable right to an irreducible minimum, consisting of adequate food, shelter and clothing." In other words, tribal economies are designed to satisfy basic human needs, in sharp contrast to imperial societies in which tribute supports an elite class, or the commercial system in which profit furthers capital accumulation.

Whereas tribal economies are often correctly described as cashless, subsistence based, and simple in technology, these obvious contrasts alone do not explain their achievements. Equally important are the built-in limits to economic growth that characterize tribal societies and the fact that tribal peoples explicitly recognize their dependence on the natural environment. In this respect, one of the key concepts in tribal economics is that of limited good, described by George Foster[126] as the assumption that "all desired things in life . . . exist in finite and unexpandable quantities." Tribals make this principle central to their economic system, while market economies operate on the diametrically opposed principle of unlimited good, assuming that "with each passing generation people on average will have more of the good things of life." Within a tribal economy several specific attributes, such as wealth-leveling devices, absolute property ceilings, fixed wants,[127] and the complementarity of production and needs, all center on the principle of limited good and contribute directly to the maintenance of a basically stable, no-growth economy.

In a tribal society, wants are not considered open to infinite expansion, and the economy is designed to fill existing wants by producing exactly what is culturally recognized as a need. Conspicuous wealth inequalities may be considered direct threats to the stability of a tribal community, and individual over-acquisitiveness may be countered with public censure, expulsion, or charges of witchcraft. At the same time, individuals may obtain prestige through generosity, and the redistribution or destruction of excess goods is accomplished through kinship and ceremonial obligations, feasting, and gambling. In contrast, the global market economy operates on the assumption that wants must be continually expanded. Specific institutions, such as advertising agencies, are employed to increase wants, and with individual acquisitiveness, conspicuous consumption brings greater prestige, as sociologist Thorstein Veblen[128] noted long ago.

Formalist anthropologists sometimes minimized the significance of growth-curbing mechanisms in tribal economies and instead incorrectly represented as cultural universals the unlimited acquisitiveness characteristic of our economic system and the parallel inability to satisfy all of our society's wants.

Cultural devices to curb wants in tribal societies are also sometimes attributed to unavoidable circumstances, such as the fact that any accumulation of unessential goods would merely be an undesirable and impossible burden for nomadic peoples, but this is not the case for sedentary villagers, for whom limits on property accumulation are also important. To explain their culturally imposed limits on economic growth, villagers often simply state that property must not be allowed to threaten their basically egalitarian social systems. This is a significant point, because tribally organized economic systems, with their careful limits on material wealth, do in fact occur within relatively egalitarian social systems. In contrast, market systems occur in significantly less egalitarian systems.

Some ethnocentric economic development writers have suggested that the only reason tribal societies curb their wants is because their technologies cannot fill them, the implication being that more productive techniques would free people's innate capacity for unlimited wants. Indeed, at various times anthropologists have dramatically overemphasized the supposed technological deficiencies of tribal economies.[129] Tribal systems have been described as barely able to meet subsistence needs, and it has been assumed that tribal peoples faced a daily threat of starvation that forced them to devote virtually all their waking moments to the food quest. This view remained almost unchallenged until careful studies of productivity and time-energy expenditure in tribal societies revealed that even the most technologically simple peoples were routinely able to satisfy all their subsistence requirements with relatively little effort. Much of the data was reviewed by Sahlins in his *Stone Age Economics*.[130] It has been shown, in fact, that many of these societies could have produced far more food if they had been so inclined; instead, people preferred to spend their time at other activities, such as socializing and leisure. It was discovered that hunters such as the Kalahari San (Bushmen) and certain Australian Aborigines, who were thought to be among those groups closest to the starvation level, put in on average no more than a twenty-hour workweek getting food.[131] Other researchers[132] have shown that shifting cultivation systems offer a reliable subsistence base that is actually more energy efficient than the "factory farm" techniques replacing them. On the basis of this kind of evidence, it can be assumed that tribals did not deliberately curb their wants and operate stable economies merely because they were incapable of either producing or desiring more or because circumstances automatically prevented the accumulation of goods. Rather, it would appear that such systems survived and proliferated because of their long-run adaptive value.

Wealth in Tribal and Commercial Worlds

In the 1980s the World Bank considered indigenous, or tribal, peoples to be the "the poorest of the poor,"[133] in part because they were completely outside of the world monetary economy. However, from a broader perspective, people in the tribal world may be considered very wealthy. Wealth can be compared cross-culturally by carefully distinguishing wealth from income, and by expanding the meaning of wealth to include things that are normally excluded from national monetary accounts, such as the value of human beings, the value of society and culture, and the value of nature. The narrow focus of the commercial culture on financial property, as well as moveable tangible property, land, and structures, leaves uncounted the primary determinants of human well-being.

For example, the household wealth of the tribal Matsigenka people of the Peruvian Amazon can be estimated for comparative purposes by assigning a monetary value to the hours they allocate to basic productive activities.[134] In the 1970s Matsigenka men and women spent about 10.5 hours a day in productive activities, about 5.5 at leisure, and about 8 hours sleeping. They spent about 70 percent of their productive time in food production and preparation, childcare, eating and hygiene, and various routine chores to maintain and reproduce their households. Only about 15 percent of their productive effort was devoted to manufacturing and maintaining their domestic goods. The remaining 15 percent of their productive time was devoted to household and community activities, including visiting and conversation that served to produce, maintain, and transmit their social networks and cultural information. Assigning an arbitrary dollar value of $9.08 per hour (the lowest average wage of service workers in the retail sector of the American economy in 1999), to the 7,811 hours the Matsigenka devoted to all of these productive activities yields an imputed income of $70,924 for a year. This is a measure of the Social Product of Matsigenka society, and assuming an average household size of five persons, could be considered broadly comparable to a Gross Domestic Product of $14,185 per capita in standard national accounts. This figure is roughly equivalent to the World Bank's 2004 ranking of Portugal, as a High Income OECD country with a per capita Gross National Income of $14,350 in U.S. market exchange dollars, or \$19,250 in PPP (Purchasing Power Parity) dollars.[135] PPP dollars reflect the prices of local consumer goods in each country, whereas exchange rate dollars represent the value of finance capital in global financial markets. Evaluating tribal Social Product at these levels may seem too high, considering their modest material culture, but in the tribal world the entire social product is consumed directly by households, and there is virtually no overhead paid for political institutions, or elite classes, in the form of tribute or taxes. People are able to maximize individual freedom and autonomy, which are important human values, and they live in absolute material comfort. They are well-fed, comfortably housed, and clothed according to the standards of their culture.

Tribal Social Product values can be converted to equivalent wealth values by considering the Social Product to be an annual investment in the production and maintenance of human beings, society, and culture, as well as assuming that it represents a modest 5 percent return on capital. This calculation, allowing for capital depreciation, produces an average wealth figure of \$1,032,873 for the Matsigenka household, suggesting that they are millionaires. Of course these wealth values are not negotiable in the present global market economy. In a real sense, Matsigenka society and culture are priceless, but this valuation suggests an underlying ranking that contrasts with market values in the commercial world. Family and household are the highest tribal values. This is the humanization process discussed in chapter 1. Most of the Matsigenka's effort (88 percent) is invested in producing and maintaining the members of their households. Society and non-material culture ranks next in value at 8 percent, and only 4 percent can be attributed to their material culture.

In the commercial world, balance sheets and wealth surveys show considerable variation in the composition of wealth in households in different countries. Human beings and nature are conspicuously absent from these accounts. In the financially rich United States in 2000, 42 percent of household wealth was in financial assets, and housing assets accounted for 55 percent of non-financial assets. In India, a financially poor country, only 5 percent of household wealth was in financial assets, and housing assets accounted for only 30 percent of non-financial assets. For the commercial world as a whole, household net worth was \$33,893 (exchange rate U.S. dollars) per adult, or \$43,628 in PPP dollars as a global adult average in 2000. These figures are based on a remarkable study sponsored by the United Nations World Institute for Development Economics Research that for the first time estimated household wealth for the entire world.[136] This assumes 3.6 billion adults and global household net worth of \$125 trillion (exchange rate), or $161 trillion in PPP dollars. Global wealth of $161 trillion PPP dollars for 6 billion people is $26,886 per capita, and would be $134,429 for a global average household of 5 persons, but of course global household wealth is not equitably distributed. These figures are not strictly comparable with the Matsigenka wealth figures, because they reflect differences in what culturally constitutes wealth in the commercial world, as well as how it is calculated.

Given that tribal peoples draw much of their material income directly from nature, it is also necessary to treat nature as part of their wealth. Environmental scientists have estimated that tropical forests worldwide produce ecosystem services worth $2,007 per hectare by recycling nutrients, microorganisms forming soil, plants converting carbon dioxide into food energy, provisioning fresh water, and maintaining biodiversity, etc.[137] This represents what it would cost if people took on these natural tasks themselves, for example, by building and maintaining factories and water purification plants, sequestering carbon, turning petroleum into plastics and petrochemicals, and adding synthetically manufactured fertilizer to the soil. We can do all of these things with the aid of machines, human labor, and fuels, but it is very costly. Nature's value as capital can be calculated at an absolute minimum by the biomass value in hectares of the biological product that households appropriate directly. For example, the Asháninka neighbors of the Matsigenka use the equivalent of all the biological product of 3 hectares of rain forest per household annually (table 2.1). At $2,007 per hectare for nature's ecosystem services, this would be $5,941, which if capitalized at 5 percent would be $118,814. This is just under the global average household wealth figure of $134,429 cited above. However, this is too low because it does not allow for the self-maintenance of the ecosystem. It is more meaningful to include the value of the 500 forest hectares per household needed to keep the Asháninka supplied with game,[138] or the 1,238 hectares per household that would conserve the entire forest ecosystem. This assumes an Asháninka population density of 0.4 persons/km² and best reflects the ecosystem area that is needed to sustainably provide their

Table 2.1. The Wealth of Nature in the Tribal World: Asháninka Household Natural Capital

	Hectares/ Household	Nature's Services $2007/Hectare	Capitalized 5% Value
Appropriated Biomass	3	$5941	$118,814
Game Conservation Area	500	$1,003,500	$20,070,000
Forest Conservation Area	1238	$2,484,857	$49,697,143

Note: Example of calculations: Value of appropriated biomass: 3 hectares x $5941 / .05 = $118,814.

material needs, allowing a wide margin that would accommodate future population growth without degrading the services that the tropical forest provides. The conservation area calculations, capitalized at 5 percent, yield figures of from $20 million to nearly $50 million for the value of natural capital per household. This would make these tribal peoples deca-millionaires, rather than simply millionaires.

Socio-Cultural Scale and the Environment

Anthropologists have widely discussed whether or not tribal peoples are more in balance with nature than people operating in the commercial world, or whether this is even a legitimate distinction to draw. Some cultural anthropologists reject the possibility that tribals could be in balance with nature, arguing that the terms "nature" and "balance" are simply culturally specific metaphors that exist only as narratives, or that balance cannot be meaningfully measured.[139] Some evolutionary anthropologists also argue that tribal peoples are not "true" conservationists.[140] These are false issues, because what matters is our ability to meet everyone's human needs over at least the next millennium, and that depends on the maintenance of many very real natural balances.

Some observers have maintained, in spite of overwhelming evidence to the contrary, that tribal cultures have no special advantages in their relationships to the environment in comparison to the global-scale commercial culture. For example, writing in the 1980s before global warming and deforestation were widespread concerns, anthropologist Terry Rambo[141] observed that forest clearing by the tribal Semang, shifting cultivators of Malaysia, modified the local climate and introduced particulate matter and carbon dioxide into the atmosphere. He described the Semang as "primitive polluters" who demonstrated "the essential functional similarity of the environmental interactions of primitive and civilized societies."[142] Exhaled carbon dioxide and wood smoke from a handful of small fires produced by a few hundred thinly scattered residents of a rain forest can be called pollution, but there is a crucial order-of-magnitude difference between this kind of pollution and the global climate-altering pollution produced by commercial societies. Equating these very different cultural phenomena obscures the environmental significance of scale and power.

The narrow range of environments that individual tribal societies exploit is a distinctive feature of tribal adaptations in contrast with global commercial societies. In 1976 distinguished ecologist and conservationist Raymond Dasmann[143] highlighted this contrast when he drew a distinction between

"Ecosystem" and "Biosphere" peoples. Dasmann's definition stressed the fact that Ecosystem peoples, or people living in tribal societies, depend on the resources supplied by local ecosystems and know immediately if their exploitation patterns are damaging. This distinction corresponds, respectively, to the categories *tribal world* and *commercial world*, as used in this book. Biosphere peoples extract resources from throughout the globe and may not even be aware of, or immediately affected by, the local destruction of ecosystems that they might cause. If too wide a range is exploited, a society might escape the ecological constraints of a given local environment and ignore its own detrimental impact on that environment. Commercial nations and global corporations are dependent on resources from throughout the world and can bring overwhelming forces to bear on particular local environments; in the short run, however, they remain immune to whatever damage they may cause. For example, at the present time the Amazon rainforest ecosystem is being systematically destroyed by remote decision makers in the commercial capitals of the world. The tribal peoples occupying the Amazon remain dependent on their local environments and can respond immediately to detrimental changes within them.[144] Anthropologist Roy Rappaport[145] made the same point using a New Guinea example. Recognizing this critical contrast does not mean that self-sufficient tribals or contemporary indigenous peoples are "ecologically noble" or intentional conservationists.[146]

Tribal hunters seldom display intentional conservation practices, which evolutionary ecologists narrowly define as trading off immediate benefits from unlimited hunting in exchange for the long-term benefits of a sustainable harvest. This definition would require tribal hunters to take into account future discount rates and marginal returns, just like any good market economist. Given the universality of bounded rationality, hunters may have many things in mind, including their beliefs in a supernatural world of spirits and beings that protect the game and punish human misbehavior. "True" conservation practices would also by definition need to have specific long-term selective advantages. This would exclude hunting practices that might have multiple, or unconscious, intentions, as well as sustainable outcomes that might be due to multiple causes. In such cases, "conservation" would be considered an "epiphenomenon," but such tribal harvesting practices might nevertheless be sustainable. When foragers move to a different area to harvest resources because their rate of return has fallen off, they may be merely trying to maximize their daily returns relative to effort expended, but the effect conserves game. Even a food preference for wild game, rather than domestic animals, is a cultural choice that presupposes low population density and a small society. The crucial underlying variable is the scale of tribal society, cultural intentions, and the limited demands they place on nature.

Nature, balance, and conservation are all measurable concepts grounded in the realities of the physical universe, and they all relate to the sustainability of societies and ecosystems. Nature is existence without people, even though people can be considered to be part of nature when they are viewed as biological organisms. Nature and culture are fundamental categories universally recognized by tribal peoples as complementary oppositions, which suggests the utility of such beliefs. It is often helpful to personify nature in thinking about how people relate to non-human reality. Humans of course are part of the physical world, but it is still useful to imagine the world as it exists apart from people. The specific metaphors that people use when they refer to the physical world may be less important than how their understandings shape their actions.

These problems of cross-cultural comparison can be clarified by taking into account the natural laws of the physical world as we now understand them. Pioneer French chemist Antoine Lavoisier discovered in 1789 that matter was conserved in chemical reactions, demonstrating that "balances" really do exist in nature. Furthermore, the laws of thermodynamics, which were barely understood until the late nineteenth century, tell us that both matter (mass) and energy are "conserved" as work is performed, and as matter and energy flow and change form. Neither can be created nor destroyed, but each can be transformed into the other, as demonstrated by the first intentional nuclear explosions in 1945. The commercial world has clearly caused some critical imbalances in nature, although often their direct effects are observable only in the laboratory. For example, the chemical element phosphorus (P) is a crucial component of living organisms and the soil, where it exists in measurable quantities, flows, and balances.[147] Human bone, blood, tissue, and DNA contain nearly a kilogram of phosphorus, and it is recycled at a rate of more than a kilogram per hour in energy transfers that power biochemical reactions that build proteins and contract muscles within the body. Industrial farmers create imbalance in soil phosphorus when they apply more than they withdraw in farm products.[148] Excess soil phosphorus runs off, causing eutrophication that kills aquatic animals and makes water undrinkable. Currently, the most dangerous worldwide imbalances are disruption of the natural carbon cycle causing global warming, and the sudden dominance of humans in global energy flows that reduces biodiversity and diminishes nature's ability to meet human needs.

Our cultural understanding of the physical world has grown in support of our increased demands for energy and materials. Societies that make light demands on nature do not require special institutions and specialists to produce and archive costly scientific knowledge of physics, chemistry, and biology. Tribal peoples metaphorically sorted reality into multiple sets of very basic opposing principles such as male and female, life and death, or nature and culture. They named plants and animals, and other natural phenomena, but did not need to know about atoms and molecules, or the laws of thermodynamics. Their epistemological framework worked for them very efficiently, because most of their needs came from nature's services with minimal human intervention. In the imperial world, ancient philosophers and medieval alchemists believed that matter consisted of just four elements—earth, air, fire, and water—and grouped them into four qualities—hot, cold, wet, and dry, much like tribal cosmologies. They were aware of seven metals—gold, silver, iron, mercury, tin, copper, and lead, and associated each with a planet. When European colonial expansion began by about 1500, only 15 elements were known to exist. By 1800, at the beginning of the industrial age, 32 of the 115 elements now known had been discovered.

Ecological Footprints

The change in the relationship of humans to the physical world caused by changes in the scale of societies and cultures is perhaps most strikingly seen in the increase in the energy and material requirements of people, both on a per capita basis and in absolute quantities, and in relation to the biological production of the non-human world. Human consumption of natural resources can be expressed as an ecological footprint.[149] The ecological footprint is measured using a standard global hectare of average biological productivity (the energy value of NPP, net primary plant biomass, per square meter per year) to calculate and compare the biological equivalent area that would be needed to produce the food, fiber, energy and materials that people consume and to recycle the waste generated. The ecological footprint is a useful measure of the human demand on nature, because it compares consumption to the potential biological production naturally available in a particular region, or the entire world. It accounts for the biological value of fossil fuel energy by estimating its biomass equivalent. The biological value of a standard global hectare in the present is here estimated at 56.7 million kcal per year, calculated by summing the caloric value in the 1970s of all net biomass produced in eleven different ecozones

Table 2.2.   Global Ecological Footprint, 2001

	Hectares/Capita		Percent	Percent
Energy	1.18		54	
Fossil Fuel		1.03		47
Nuclear		0.09		4
Fuelwood		0.06		3
Food & Materials	0.94		43	
Cropland		0.49		22
Forest		0.18		8
Grazing		0.14		6
Fishing		0.13		6
Built-up Land	0.07	0.07	3	3
Totals	2.19	2.19	100	100

Living Planet Report, 2004

throughout the world—exclusive of oceans, extreme deserts, polar, and alpine zones—and dividing by total hectares. By this measure a tropical rain forest (NPP 2,200 gms/m²/yr) is nearly 70 percent more productive than average cultivated land (NPP 650 gms/m²/yr).

Tribal societies have much smaller ecological footprints than the average of most nations in the contemporary world. They use a smaller proportion of the biological capacity of their territories, and their household footprints are much more equitably distributed. According to international footprint estimates in the *WWF Living Planet Report* for 2004,[150] the average ecological footprint for 148 countries ranged from 0.3 to 9.9 standard hectares per person, averaging 2.2 hectares for the world, based on data for 2001. The global footprint was about evenly divided between food and fiber production (agriculture), and energy, with 87 percent of the energy portion in fossil fuels. Significantly, the national footprints of 87 countries with some five billion people exceeded their national bioproductive capacities. These countries needed to import to make up their deficits, and/or they relied on fossil fuels (table 2.2). These realities highlight the enormous importance of global fossil fuel dependency.

Sample tribal footprints, according to my calculations, range from 0.08 to 1.1, based on my estimates for Australian foragers, African herders, and tropical forest gardener-foragers, but because their populations are so small relative to the natural resources available, their impact is typically miniscule. For example, the Asháninka, tropical forest village gardeners and hunters in the Peruvian Amazon, take less than 0.25 percent of the annual biological product of their territory. These calculations take into account not just a

Table 2.3.   Asháninka Ecological Footprint

	Kcal/Capita/Year	Percent	Global Hectares
Wild Plants	30,417	0.05	0.00
Insects	506,944	0.78	0.01
Game	21,900,000	33.61	0.39
Fish	4,562,500	7.00	0.08
Gardens*	32,657,813	50.12	0.58
House Site	5,500,000	8.44	0.10
Totals	65,157,674	100.00	1.15

* Note: Includes firewood & materials from forest, Global hectares = Kcal/capita/year / 56,742,424 global average kcal

per person daily average of 2,500 calories of food, but they also include an estimate of the primary biomass at the bottom of the food chain that ultimately produced the game animals, and the biomass of the gardens, and of the forest that was removed when gardens and house sites were cleared, including an allowance for forest fallow and garden production not consumed. The final figures suggest that half of the Asháninka ecological footprint is in the garden, and a third in game animals (table 2.3). There of course is no figure for fossil fuels. The most important point of comparison between tribal footprints, represented by the Asháninka example, and nation-state footprints in the commercial world, is that given their very low population density, the Asháninka, with a per capita footprint of only 1.1 global equivalent hectares, were using only 0.24 percent of the biocapacity of their territory. This very low demand guaranteed that their tropical rainforest environment could persist into the distant future, and could continue to supply the Asháninka with their basic needs. In comparison, Americans in 2001 were taking the equivalent of nearly 200 percent of the biological product of their territory, because their per capita ecological footprint was nearly an order of magnitude greater than the Asháninka's, and at 20 Americans per square kilometer (km^2) versus 0.2 Asháninka/km^2, the American population density was two orders of magnitude greater. Global trade and the extensive use of fossil fuels made this American hyper-consumption possible, at least in the short run.

Table 2.4 illustrates the ecological effects of changes in culture scale over the past 10,000 years at a global level, combining *Living Planet Report* estimates for global biocapacity in 2001 with my estimates for earlier periods. This shows that prior to AD 1500 the global ecological footprint was well under 10 percent of global biocapacity, and that it suddenly accelerated much faster than population growth after 1500 with the shift in global

Table 2.4.   Global Population and Ecological Footprint, 10,000 B.P.–A.D. 2001

	Footprint, Hectares (Millions)	Population, (Millions)	Percent of Capacity
Tribal World 10,000 BP	94	85	1
Imperial World AD 1	254	231	2
Early Commercial World AD 1500	658	438	6
Commercial World AD 2001	13,526	6,148	122

culture from the imperial to the commercial world. *Living Planet* estimates show the world exceeding 100 percent of global biocapacity in 1987, and reaching 122 percent by 2001. Figure 2.2 shows that after 1500 the global ecological footprint grew much faster than global population, suggesting that consumption and its distribution are more important than population growth alone.

Environmental modifications occurring as a result of the intervention of small-scale societies in general appear to be much more gradual and more akin to "natural" environmental processes than the modifications caused by the commercially driven global culture, which are often extremely rapid and qualitatively unusual. Commercial manufacturing processes often introduce completely new environmental pollutants that have the potential to disrupt natural biochemical processes. At the same time, ecosystems modified by the demands of commercial societies tend to become much simpler, less efficient, and more unstable than those affected by small-scale societies. Such differences sometimes result directly from contrasting subsistence systems. For example, the ecological advantages of traditional root-crop shifting cultivation over intensive monocrop systems in tropical areas have frequently been noted.[151] In their crop diversity and organization, the small garden plots of shifting cultivators structurally resemble the rainforest ecosystem and thereby utilize solar energy with great efficiency and minimize the hazards of pests and disease. Labor-intensive smallholder production systems, even when they are highly intensive and combine market and subsistence production, are likely to be more productive per unit of land, more energy efficient, more sustainable, and more conserving of nonrenewable resources than large-scale, capital-intensive, fully commercial agricultural systems.[152] These points are discussed more fully in chapter 4.

The massive, government-financed development programs of the twentieth century largely ignored the human advantages of small-scale production systems. Development planners arrogantly dismissed domestically organized systems as "primitive" and "pretechnological," assuming that peo-

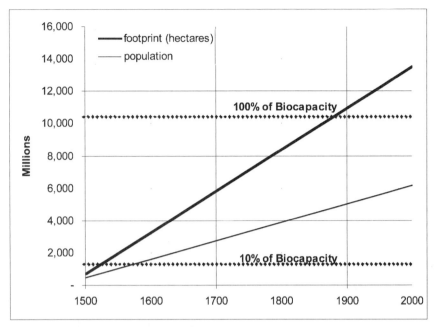

Figure 2.2.   Global Population and Ecological Footprint AD 1500–2001.

ple had little knowledge of their environment and no "control" over it. Yet the data provided by cultural ecological researchers indicate that small, indigenous societies actually possess deep and highly practical knowledge of their environments based on intimate experience accumulated over countless generations.

I have stressed that peoples living in self-sufficient small-scale societies, before they were engulfed by commercial-scale cultures, tended to maintain a dynamic and resilient relationship with the natural environment. They were not living in some passive "state of nature" surrounded by an undisturbed wilderness. Abundant evidence shows that tribal peoples actively managed local ecosystems, often on a large scale, to increase "natural" biological productivity for human benefit.[153] Intentional periodic burning of shrubs and grasslands was often a common management practice. Such burning increases both the quantity and the nutritional quality of the forage available to game animals. This elevates the game-carrying capacity three- to sevenfold and means that there will be more animals that are healthier and that reproduce faster. Hunting of game is also facilitated due to ease of moving through the forest and seeing game. Furthermore, frequent burning reduces the accumulation of combustible material and makes natural fires less destructive.

Many anthropologists have emphasized the fundamental contrasts in values, religion, and worldview between tribal and commercial cultures in relation to the natural environment.[154] The most remarkable general difference is that tribal ideological systems often express humanity's dependence on nature and tend to place nature in a revered, sacred category. The notion of a constant struggle to conquer nature, so characteristic of the commercially organized culture in which it may be supported by biblical injunction, is notably absent in tribal cultures.[155] Indeed, tribals generally consider themselves part of nature in the sense that they may name themselves after animals, impute souls to plants and animals, acknowledge ritual kinship with certain species, conduct rituals designed to help propagate particularly valued species, and offer ritual apologies when animals must be killed. Animals also abound in tribal origin myths, and at death, one's soul is often believed to be transformed into an animal.

Careful research has shown that many of these beliefs may contribute to the regulation of both population size and levels of resource consumption. Population growth, for example, is curbed by beliefs calling for sexual abstinence, abortion, infanticide, and ritual warfare, and various taboos control the exploitation of specific food resources. In Amazonia special taboos restricting the consumption of specific game animals by certain categories of people are most often applied to the animals that would be most vulnerable to over-hunting.[156] It has been argued that ceremonial cycles in highland New Guinea help maintain a balance between the human population, pig herds, and the natural environment.[157] Sacred groves in many parts of the world have maintained forest remnants and reduced soil erosion, while under Christian influence the forests have been chopped down, with unfortunate results.[158] It is significant that tribal belief systems often disintegrate under the impact of commercial culture and are replaced by beliefs that accelerate environmental disequilibrium.

Notes

1. Sahlins, Marshall, and Elman R. Service, eds. 1960. *Evolution and Culture.* Ann Arbor: University of Michigan Press, 26–27.

2. Boyd, Robert, and Peter J. Richerson. 1985. *Culture and the Evolutionary Process.* Chicago and London: University of Chicago Press, 9.

3. Cavalli-Sforza, L. L., and M. W. Feldman. 1981. *Cultural Transmission and Evolution: A Quantitative Approach.* Princeton, NJ: Princeton University Press;

Hewlett, Barry S., and L. L. Cavalli-Sforza. 1986. "Cultural Transmission Among Aka Pygmies." *American Anthropologist* 88: 922–34.

4. Levi-Strauss, Claude. 1966. *The Savage Mind.* Chicago: University of Chicago Press.

5. Durham, William H. 1991. *Coevolution: Genes, Culture, and Human Diversity.* Stanford, CA: Stanford University Press, 211.

6. Bodley, John H. 2005b. *Cultural Anthropology: Tribes, States, and the Global System.* New York: McGraw-Hill, 218–19.

7. Durham, *Coevolution*, 211.

8. Kardong, Kenneth V. 1998. *Vertebrates: Comparative Anatomy, Function, Evolution.* 2nd ed. Boston: WCB McGraw-Hill, 129–30.

9. Gould, Stephen Jay. 1996. *Full House: The Spread of Excellence from Plato to Darwin.* New York: Harmony Books.

10. Kardong, *Vertebrates*, 22–53; McMahon, T. A., and. T. Bonner. 1983. *On Size and Life.* New York: Scientific American Library.

11. Mayhew, Bruce H. 1973. "System Size and Ruling Elites." *American Sociological Review* 38: 468–75; Mayhew, Bruce H., and Paul T. Schollaert. 1980a. "Social Morphology of Pareto's Economic Elite." *Social Forces* 59(l): 25–43.

12. Fletcher, Roland. 1995. *The Limits of Settlement Growth: A Theoretical Outline.* Cambridge: Cambridge University Press, 71–81.

13. Fletcher, *The Limits of Settlement Growth*, 82–90.

14. Rappaport, Roy A. 1977. "Maladaptation in Social Systems." In *The Evolution of Social Systems*, edited by J. Friedman and M. J. Rowlands, 49–71. London: Duckworth.

15. White, Leslie A. 1959. *The Evolution of Culture.* New York: McGraw-Hill, 82–90.

16. Sahlins, Marshall, and Elman R. Service, eds. 1960. *Evolution and Culture.* Ann Arbor: University of Michigan Press.

17. Cohen, Yehudi, ed. 1974. *Man in Adaptation.* 2nd ed. Chicago: Aldine, 45–68

18. Turner II, B. L., William C. Clark, Robert W. Kates, John F. Richards, Jessica T. Mathews, and William B. Meyer. 1990. *The Earth as Transformed by Human Action: Global and Regional Changes in the Biosphere over the Past 300 years.* Cambridge, MA: Cambridge University Press.

19. Rummel, R. J. 1997. *Death by Government.* New Brunswick, NJ: Transaction.

20. United Nations. 2005. *The Millennium Development Goals Report.* New York: United Nations Department of Public Information, 8.

21. Cohen, *Man in Adaptation*, 45–68.

22. Asimov, Isaac. 1971. "The End." *Penthouse*, January.

23. Rojstaczer, Stuart, Shannon M. Sterline, and Nathan J. Moore. 2001. "Human Appropriation of Photosynthesis Products." *Science* 294(5551): 2549–52.

24. Smil, Vaclav. 2002. *The Earth's Biosphere: Evolution, Dynamics, and Change.* Cambridge, MA: The MIT Press, 183–97.

25. Vitousek, Peter M., Paul R. Ehrlich, Anne H. Ehrlich, and Pamela A. Matson. 1986. "Human Appropriation of the Products of Photosynthesis." *BioScience* 36(6): 368–73. This work was replicated by David Hamilton Wright producing an estimate of 20 to 30 percent human appropriation of potential prehuman global net biological production, which he estimated at 2800 Ej (2800*1018 joules). Wright, David Hamilton. 1990. "Human Impacts on Energy Flow Through Natural Ecosystems, and Implications for Species Endangerment." *Ambio* 19(4): 189–94.

26. Imhoff, Marc L., Lahouari Bounoua, Taylor Ricketts, Colby Loucks, Robert Harriss, and William T. Lawrence. 2004. "Global Patterns in Human Consumption of Net Primary Production." *Nature* 429: 870–73; Wackernagel, Mathis, Niels B. Schulz, Diana Deumling, Alejandro Callejas Linares, Martin Jenkins, Valerie Chad Monfreda, Jonathan Loh, Norman Myers, Richard Norgaard, and Jørgen Randers. 2002. "Tracking the Ecological Overshoot of the Human Economy." *Proceedings of the National Academy of Science* 99(14): 9266–71.

27. Richards, Paul W. 1973. "The Tropical Rain Forest." *Scientific American* 229(6): 58–67.

28. Wilson, Edward O. 2002. *The Future of Life.* New York: Alfred A. Knopf, 20.

29. Myers, Norman. 1992. *The Primary Source: Tropical Forests and Our Future.* New York: W. W. Norton.

30. Olson, Jerry S. 1985. "Cenozoic Fluctuations in Biotic Parts of the Global Carbon Cycle." In *The Carbon Cycle and Atmospheric CO2: Natural Variations Archean to Present,* edited by E. T. Sundquist and W. S. Broecker, 377–96. Geophysical Monograph 32. Washington, D.C.: American Geophysical Union.

31. Williams, Michael. 1990. *Americans and Their Forests: A Historical Geography.* New York: Cambridge University Press.

32. United Nations, Food and Agriculture Organization. 2006. *Global Forest Resources Assessment 2005: Progress Towards Sustainable Forest Management.* FAO Forestry Paper 147. www.fao.org/forestry/site/32039/en

33. Mather, Alexander. 2000. "South-North Challenges in Global Forestry." In *World Forests from Deforestation to Transition?* edited by Matti Palo and Heidi Vanhanen, 25–40. Dordrecht: Kluwer Academic.

34. Somer, Adrian. 1976. "Attempt at an Assessment of the World's Tropical Moist Forests." *Unasylva* 28: 5–23.

35. Myers, Norman. 1980. *Conversion of Tropical Moist Forests: A Report Prepared by Norman Myers for the Committee on Research Priorities in Tropical Biology of the National Research Council.* Washington, D.C.: National Academy of Sciences.

36. Fearnside, Philip M. 2005. "Deforestation in Brazilian Amazonia: History, Rates, and Consequences." *Conservation Biology* 19(3): 680–88.

37. Instiuto Nacional de Pesquisas Espacias (INPE). 2002. "Monitoring of the Brazilian Amazonian Forest by Satellite 2000–2001." www/inpe.br

38. Morton, Douglas C., et al. 2006. "Cropland expansion changes deforestation dynamics in the southern Brazilian Amazon." *Proceedings of the National Academy of Science* 103(39): 14637–41.

39. Kintisch, Eli. 2006. "Climate Change: Along the Road From Kyoto Global Greenhouse Gas Emissions Keep Rising." *Science* 311(5758): 1702–3; Fearnside, Philip M. 2006. "Tropical Deforestation and Global Warming." *Science* 312(5777): 1137.

40. Wright, "Human Impacts on Energy Flow," 189–94.

41. Williams, *Americans and Their Forests.*

42. Brown, Lester R., Michael Renner, Christopher Flavin, et al. 1998. *Vital Signs 1998: The Environmental Trends That Are Shaping Our Future.* Washington, D.C.: Worldwatch Institute.

43. American Forests. 1998. *Regional Ecosystem Analysis, Puget Sound Metropolitan Area.* www.amfor.org

44. Lathrap, Don W. 1970. *The Upper Amazon.* New York: Praeger; Meggers, Betty J. 1971. *Amazonia: Man and Culture in a Counterfeit Paradise.* Chicago: Aldine; Moran, Emilio. 1993. *Through Amazonian Eyes: The Human Ecology of Amazonian Populations.* Iowa City: University of Iowa Press.

45. Myers, *The Primary Source.*

46. Fearnside, "Deforestation in Brazilian Amazonia," 685.

47. Wallace, Scott. 2007. "Last of the Amazon." *National Geographic* 211(1): 40–71.

48. Feshbach, Murray, and Alfred Friendly Jr. 1992. *Ecocide in the USSR: Health and Nature under Siege.* New York: Basic Books.

49. Feshbach and Friendly, *Ecocide.*

50. Levintanus, Arkady. 1993. "On the Fall of the Aral Sea." *Environments* 22(l): 89–94.

51. Jones, Nicola. 2003. "South Aral Gone in 15 Years." *New Scientist* 179(2404): 9.

52. Greenberg, Ilan. 2006. "As a Sea Rises, So Do Hopes for Fish, Jobs and Riches." *New York Times* (April 6, 2006).

53. United Nations, *The Millennium Development Goals Report;* World Development Report 2006. *Equity and Development.* New York: Oxford University Press, 296, table 2.

54. Edwards, Mike. 1994. "Chernobyl: Living with the Monster." *National Geographic* 183(2): 100–15.

55. Clark, J. G. D. 1952. *Prehistoric Europe: The Economic Base.* New York: Philosophical Library; Frenzel, Burkhard, ed. 1992. *Evaluation of land surfaces cleared from forests by prehistoric man in Early Neolithic times and the time of migrating Germanic Tribes.* Stuttgart: G. Fischer.

56. Chew, Sing C. 2001. *World Ecological Degradation: Accumulation, Urbanization, and Deforestation 3000 B.C.–A.D. 2000.* New York: Altamira Press; Diamond, Jared. 2005. *Collapse: How Societies Choose to Fail or Succeed.* New York: Viking.

57. Tainter, Joseph A. 2006. "Archaeology of Overshoot and Collapse." *Annual Review of Anthropology* 35(1): 59–74.

58. Jacobsen, Thorkild, and Robert M. Adams. 1958. "Salt and Silt in Ancient Mesopotamian Agriculture." *Science* 128(3334): 1251–58.

59. Willey, Gordon R., and Demitric B. Shimkin. 1971. "The Collapse of Classic Maya Civilization in the Southern Lowlands: A Symposium Summary Statement." *Southwestern Journal of Anthropology* 27(10): 1–18; Culbert, T. Patrick. 1974. *The Lost Civilization: The Story of the Classic Maya*. New York: Harper & Row.

60. Demarest. Arthur A. 1993. "The Violent Saga of a Maya Kingdom." *National Geographic* 183(2): 94–111. Schele, Linda, and David Freidel. 1990. *A Forest of Kings: The Untold Story of the Ancient Maya*. New York: William Morrow & Co.

61. Meadows, Donella H., Dennis L. Meadows, Jorgen Randers, and William W. Behrens III. 1972. *The Limits to Growth*. New York: Universe, 126.

62. Meadows, et al., *The Limits to Growth*, 142.

63. Brown, Harrison. 1954. *The Challenge of Man's Future*. New York: Viking.

64. Heilbroner, Robert L. 1963. *The Great Ascent: The Struggle for Economic Development in Our Time*. New York: Harper & Row Torchbooks.

65. Meadows, et al., *The Limits to Growth*.

66. Simmons, Matthew R. 2000. *Revisiting the Limits to Growth: Could the Club of Rome Have Been Correct, After All? An Energy White Paper*. Simmons & Company International. www.simmonsco-intl.com/research

67. See especially Cole, H. S. D., ed. 1973. *Models of Doom*. New York: Universe.

68. Walter, Edward. 1981. *The Immorality of Limiting Growth*. Albany: State University of New York Press.

69. Simon, Julian. 1981. *The Ultimate Resource*. Princeton, NJ: Princeton University Press.

70. Meadows, Donella H., Dennis L. Meadows, and Jorgen Randers. 1992. *Beyond the Limits: Confronting Global Collapse, Envisioning a Sustainable Future*. Post Mills, VT: Chelsea Green Publishing Co.

71. Meadows, Donella, Jorgen Randers, and Dennis Meadows. 2004. *Limits to Growth: The 30-Year Update*. White River Junction, VT: Chelsea Green Publishing.

72. Simmons, *Revisiting the Limits to Growth*, 30.

73. Barney, Gerald O., ed. 1977–1980. *The Global 2000 Report to the President of the United States*. 3 vols. New York: Pergamon, vol. 1: xvi.

74. WCED (World Commission on Environment and Development). 1987. *Our Common Future*. Oxford: Oxford University Press.

75. WCED, *Our Common Future*, 43.

76. Millennium Ecosystem Assessment. 2005. *Ecosystems and Human Well-being: Synthesis*. Washington, D.C.: Island Press.

77. Millennium Ecosystem Assessment. 2005. *Living Beyond Our Means: Natural Assets and Human Well-Being. Statement from the Board*. Technical Volume. Washington, D.C.: Island Press, 5. www.maweb.org/en/Products.BoardStatement.aspx

78. Loh, Jonathan, and Mathis Wackernagel. 2004. *Living Planet Report*. Gland, Switzerland: WWF–World Wide Fund for Nature.

79. Warren-Rhodes, Kimberley, and Albert Koeing. 2001. "Ecosystem Appropriation by Hong Kong and Its Implication for Sustainable Development." *Ecological Economics* 39(3): 347–59.

80. BFF (Best Food Forward). 2002. *City Limits: A Resource Flow and Ecological Footprint Analysis of Greater London.* www.citylimitslondon.com

81. Commoner, Barry. 1971. *The Closing Circle.* New York: Knopf.

82. White, Lynn, Jr. 1967. "The Historical Roots of Our Ecological Crisis." *Science* 155(3767): 1203–7.

83. Sale, Kirkpatrick. 1985. *Dwellers in the Land: The Bioregional Vision.* San Francisco: Sierra Club Books.

84. Bookchin, Murray. 1991. *The Ecology of Freedom: The Emergence and Dissolution of Hierarchy.* Montreal and New York: Black Rose Books.

85. Headland, Thomas N. 1997. "Revisionism in Ecological Anthropology." *Current Anthropology* 38(4): 605–30; Krech, Shepard, III. 1999. *The Ecological Indian: Myth and History.* New York: W. W. Norton and Co.

86. Sahlins, Marshall. 1996. "The Sadness of Sweetness: The Native Anthropology of Western Cosmology." *Current Anthropology* 37(3): 395–428.

87. Weaver, Richard M. [1948] 1984. *Ideas Have Consequences.* Chicago and London: University of Chicago Press.

88. Weber, Max. 1930. *The Protestant Ethic and the Spirit of Capitalism.* London: George Allen & Unwin, 53

89. Weber, *Spirit of Capitalism*, 181.

90. Hardin, Garrett. 1968. "The Tragedy of the Commons." *Science* 162(3859): 1243–48.

91. Smith, Adam. [1759] 1976. *The Theory of Moral Sentiments.* Indianapolis, IN: Liberty Classics, 304.

92. Christensen, Kaare, Anne Maria Herskind, James W. Vaupel. 2006. "Why Danes are Smug: Comparative Study of Life Satisfaction in the European Union." *BMJ (British Medical Journal)* 333 (23–30 December): 1289–91.

93. UNCE. (United Nations Economic Commission for Europe). The Statistical Yearbook of the Economic Commission for Europe 2005. www.unece.org/stats/trends2005/Sources/110_Average%20annual%20population%20growth%20rate.pdf

94. Hardin, Garrett. 1991. "The Tragedy of the Unmanaged Commons: Population and the Disguises of Providence." In *Commons Without Tragedy*, edited by Robert V. Andelson, 162–85. London: Shepheard-Walwyn.

95. Netting, Robert McC. 1993. *Smallholders, Householders: Farm Families and the Ecology of Intensive, Sustainable Agriculture.* Stanford, CA: Stanford University Press.

96. McCay, Bonnie J., and James M. Acheson, ed. 1987. *The Question of the Commons: The Culture and Ecology of Communal Resources.* Tucson: University of Arizona Press; McCabe, J. Terrence. 1990. "Turkana Pastoralism: A Case Against the Tragedy of the Commons." *Human Ecology* 18: 81–103; McCabe, J. Terrence. 2004. *Cattle Bring Us to Our Enemies: Turkana Ecology, Politics, and Raiding in a Disequilibrium System.* Ann Arbor: University of Michigan Press.

97. Spooner, Brian. 1973. *The Cultural Ecology of Pastoral Nomads.* Module in Anthropology No. 45. Reading, MA: Addison-Wesley.

98. Ostrom, E. 1990. *Governing the Commons: The Evolution of Institutions for Collective Action.* Cambridge: Cambridge University Press.

99. Casimir, Michael J., R. P. Winter, and Bernt Glatzer. 1980. "Nomadism and Remote Sensing: Animal Husbandry and the Sagebrush Community in a Nomad Winter Area in Western Afghanistan." *Journal of Arid Environments* 3: 231–54.

100. Ruttan, Lore M., and Monique Borgerhoff Mulder. 1999. "Are East African Pastoralists Truly Conservationists?" *Current Anthropology* 40(5): 621–52.

101. Walker, B. H., et al. 1981. "Stability of Semi-Arid Savanna Grazing Systems." *Journal of Ecology* 69: 473–98.

102. Coughenour, M. B., J. E. Ellis, D. M. Swift, D. L. Coppock, K. Galvin, J. T. McCabe, and T. C. Hart. 1985. "Energy Extraction and Use in a Nomadic Pastoral Ecosystem." *Science* 230(4726): 619–25; Western, David, and Virginia Finch. 1986. "Cattle and Pastoralism: Survival and Production in Arid Lands." *Human Ecology* 14(l): 77–94.

103. Leeuw, Sander E. van der. 1997. *ARCHAEOMEDES: A DG-XII Research Programme to Understand the Natural and Anthropogenic Causes of Land Degradation and Desertification in the Mediterranean Basin.* Paris: University of Paris; Leeuw, Sander E. van der, and J. McGlade, eds. 1997. *Archaeology: Time and Structured Transformation.* London: Routledge.

104. McGlade, James. n.d. *ARCHAEOMEDES II. Proyecto Emporda: Human Ecodynamics and Land Use Conflict: Monitoring Degradation-Sensitive Environments in the Emporda North-East Spain.* www.ucl.ac.uk/archaeology/research/profiles/mcglade/archgld.htm.

105. IUCN (International Union for the Conservation of Nature). 2006. Red List of Threatened Species. www.iucnredlist.org/

106. Loh and Wackernagel, *Living Planet Report.*

107. Krech, *The Ecological Indian.*

108. Martin, Paul S. 1967. "Prehistoric Overkill." In *Pleistocene Extinctions: The Search for a Cause,* edited by P. S. Martin and H. E. Wright Jr., 75–120, Proceedings of the 7th Congress of the International Association for Quaternary Research. New Haven: Yale University Press. 1984; "Prehistoric Overkill: The Global Model." In *Quaternary Extinctions: A Prehistoric Revolution,* edited by Paul S. Martin and Richard G. Klein, 553–73. Tucson: University of Arizona Press.

109. Martin, "Prehistoric Overkill," 115.

110. Grayson, Donald K., and David J. Meltzer. 2002. "Clovis Hunting and Large Mammal Extinction: A Critical Review of the Evidence." *Journal of World Prehistory* 16(4): 313–59.

111. Grayson, Donald K., and David J. Meltzer. 2003. "A Requiem for North American Overkill." *Journal of Archaeological Science* 30: 585–93, 589.

112. Webster, David. 1981. "Late Pleistocene Extinction and Human Predation: A Critical Overview." In *Omnivorous Primates: Gathering and Hunting in Hu-*

man Evolution, edited by Robert S. Harding and Geza Teleki, 556–95. New York: Columbia University Press.

113. Grayson, Donald K. 1984. "Explaining Pleistocene Extinctions: Thoughts on the Structure of a Debate." In *Quaternary Extinctions*, edited by P. S. Martin and R. G. Klein, 807–23. Tucson: University of Arizona Press; Grayson, Donald K. 1991. "Late Pleistocene Mammalian Extinctions in North America: Taxonomy, Chronology, and Explanations." *Journal of World Prehistory* 5: 193–231; Politis, Gustavo G., Jose L. Prado, and Roelf P. Beukens. 1995. "The Human Impact in Pleistocene-Holocene Extinctions in South America: The Pampean Case." In *Ancient People and Landscapes*, edited by E. Johnson, 187–205. Lubbock: Museum of Texas Tech University; Barnosky, Anthony D., Paul L. Koch, Robert S. Feranec, Scott L. Wing, and Alan B. Shabel. 2004. "Assessing the Causes of Late Pleistocene Extinctions on the Continents." *Science* 306 (1 October): 70–75.

114. Lee, Richard B., and Irven De Vore. 1968. *Man the Hunter*. Chicago: Aldine; Hayden, Brian. 1981. "Subsistence and Ecological Adaptations of Modern Hunter/Gatherers." In *Omnivorous Primates: Gathering and Hunting in Human Evolution*, edited by Robert S. Harding and Geza Teleki, 344–421. New York: Columbia University Press; Webster, "Late Pleistocene Extinction;" Winterhalder, B., W. Baillargeon, F. Cappelletto, I. Daniel, and C. Prescott. 1988. "The Population Ecology of Hunter-Gatherers and Their Prey." *Journal of Anthropological Archaeology* 7: 289–328.

115. Klein, Richard G. 1979. "Stone Age Exploitation of Animals in Southern Africa." *American Scientist* 67(2): 151-60; Klein, Richard G. 1981. "Stone Age Predation on Small African Bovids." *South African Archaeological Bulletin* 36(1981): 55–65; Klein, Richard G. 1984. "Mammalian Extinctions and Stone Age People in Africa." In *Quaternary Extinctions: A Prehistoric Revolution*, edited by Paul S. Martin and Richard G. Klein, 354–403. Tucson: University of Arizona Press.

116. Klein, "Stone Age Exploitation," 158.

117. Crosby, Alfred W. 1972. *The Columbian Exchange: Biological and Cultural Consequences of 1492*. Westport, CT: Greenwood Publishing Co.; Crosby, Alfred W. 1986. *Biological Imperialism: The Biological Expansion of Europe, 900–1900*. Cambridge: Cambridge University Press.

118. Raup, David M. 1991. "A Kill Curve for Phanerozoic Marine Species." *Paleobiology* 17(1): 37; Pimm, Stuart L., et al. 1995. "The Future of Biodiversity." *Science* 269(5222): 347–50; Stork, Nigel. 1997. "Measuring Global Biodiversity and Its Decline." In *Biodiversity II: Understanding and Protecting Our Biological Resources*, edited by Marjorie L. Reaka-Kudla, Don E. Wilson, and Edward O. Wilson. Washington, D.C.: Joseph Henry Press; Tuxill, John. 1999. "Appreciating the Benefits of Plant Biodiversity." In *State of the World 1999: A Worldwatch Institute Report on Progress Toward a Sustainable Society*, edited by Lester R. Brown, Christopher Flavin, Hilary French, and Linda Starke, 96–114. New York and London: W. W. Norton and Co.

119. Herskovits, Melville J. 1952. *Economic Anthropology*. New York: Knopf.

120. For example, see discussion in Dowling, John H. 1979. "The Goodfellows vs. the Dalton Gang: The Assumptions of *Economic Anthropology*." *Journal of Anthropological Research* 35(3): 292–308.

121. Simon, Herbert A. 1957. *Models of Man: Social and Rational*. New York: John Wiley.

122. Zipf, George Kingsley. 1949. Reprint 1965. *Human Behavior and the Principle of Least Effort: An Introduction to Human Ecology*. Cambridge, MA: Addison-Wesley, New York and London: Hafner Publishing Co.

123. Winterhalder, B., and F. A. Smith, eds. 1981. *Hunter-Gatherer Foraging Strategies: Ethnographic and Archaeological Analyses*. Chicago: University of Chicago Press.

124. Redfield, Robert. 1947. "The Folk Society." *American Journal of Sociology* 52(4): 293–308.

125. Radin, Paul. 1971. *The World of Primitive Man*. New York: Dutton, 106.

126. Foster, George. 1969. *Applied Anthropology*. Boston: Little, Brown, 83.

127. Henry, Jules. 1963. *Culture Against Man*. New York: Random House.

128. Veblen, Thorstein. 1912. *The Theory of the Leisure Class: An Economic Study of Institutions*. New York: Macmillan Company.

129. For example, Herskovits, *Economic Anthropology*, 16; Levin, M. G., and L. P. Potapov. 1964. *The Peoples of Siberia*. Chicago: University of Chicago Press, 488–99; Nash, Manning. 1966. *Primitive and Peasant Economic Systems*. San Francisco: Chandler, 22; Dalton, George. 1971. *Economic Anthropology: Essays on Tribal and Peasant Economies*. New York: Basic Books, 27.

130. Sahlins, *Stone Age Economics*.

131. Lee, Richard B. 1968. "What Hunters Do for a Living, or How to Make Out on Scarce Resources." In *Man the Hunter*, edited by Richard B. Lee and Irven De Vore, 30–48. Chicago: Aldine; McCarthy, F. D., and Margaret McArthur. 1960. "The Food Quest and Time Factor in Aboriginal Economic Life." In *Records of the American-Australian Scientific Expedition to Arnhem Land*, edited by C. P. Mountford. Vol. 2, *Anthropology and Nutrition*, 145–94. Melbourne: Melbourne University Press.

132. Carneiro, Robert L. 1960. "Slash-and-Burn Agriculture: A Closer Look at Its Implications for Settlement Patterns." In *Men and Cultures*, edited by A. F. C. Wallace, 229–34. Philadelphia: University of Pennsylvania Press; Rappaport, Roy A. 1971. "The Flow of Energy in an Agricultural Society." *Scientific American* 224(3): 117–32.

133. Goodland, Robert. 1982. *Tribal Peoples and Economic Development: Human Ecological Considerations*. Washington, D.C.: World Bank.

134. Johnson, Allen. 2003. *Families of the Forest: The Matsigenka Indians of the Peruvian Amazon*. Berkeley: University of California Press. The present analysis was by Bodley in 2005(a) in a presentation entitled, "The Rich Tribal World: Scale and Power Perspectives on Cultural Valuation," at Society for Applied Anthropology, Annual Meeting, Santa Fe, New Mexico.

135. World Bank, *World Development Indicators, 2006*. devdata.worldbank.org/data-query/.

136. Davies, James B., Susanna Sandstrom, Anthony Shorrocks, and Edward N. Wolff. 2006. *The World Distribution of Household Wealth*. World Institute for Development Economics Research.

137. Costanza, Robert, et al. 1997. "The Value of the World's Ecosystem Services and Natural Capital." *Nature* 387 (15 May): 253–60.

138. Bodley, *Cultural Anthropology*, 75.

139. Weeratunge, Nireka. 2000. "Nature, Harmony, and the *Kaliyugaya*: Global/Local Discourses on the Human-Environment Relationship." *Current Anthropology* 41(2): 249–68.

140. Alvard, Michael S. 1998. "Evolutionary Ecology and Resource Conservation." *Evolutionary Anthropology* 7(2): 62–74.

141. Rambo, A. Terry. 1985. *Primitive Polluters: Semang Impact on the Malaysian Tropical Rain Forest Ecosystem*. Anthropological Papers No. 76. Ann Arbor: Museum of Anthropology, University of Michigan.

142. Rambo, *Primitive Polluters*, 78.

143. Dasmann, Raymond. 1976. "Future Primitive: Ecosystem People Versus Biosphere People." *Convolution Quarterly* 1 (Fall): 26–31.

144. Meggers, *Amazonia*.

145. Rappaport, "Flow of Energy," 117–32.

146. Redford, K. 1991. "The Ecologically Noble Savage." *Orion* 9: 24–29; Alvard, Michael S. 1993. "Testing the 'Ecologically Noble Savage' Hypothesis: Interspecific Prey Choice by Piro Hunters of Amazonian Peru." *Human Ecology* 21(4): 355–87.

147. Emsley, John. 2001. *Nature's Building Blocks: An A-Z Guide to the Elements*. Oxford: Oxford University Press, 310–17.

148. Sharpley, A. N., T. Daniel, T. Sims, J. Lemunyon, R. Stevens, and R. Parry. 1999. *Agricultural Phosphorus and Eutrophication*. United States Department of Agriculture, Agricultural Research Service. ARS-149.

149. Rees, William E., and Mathis Wackernagel. 1994. "Ecological Footprints and Appropriated Carrying Capacity: Measuring the Natural Capital Requirements of the Human Economy." In *Investing in Natural Capital: The Ecological Economics Approach to Sustainability*, edited by AnnMari Jansson, Monica Hammer, Carl Folke, and Robert Costanza, 362–90. Washington, D.C.: Island Press; Wackernagel, M., and W. E. Rees. 1996. *Our Ecological Footprint: Reducing Human Impact on the Earth*. Gabriola Island, British Columbia: New Society Publishers; Wackernagel, Mathis, and Judith Silverstein. 2000. "Big Things First: Focusing on the Scale Imperative with the Ecological Footprint." *Ecological Economics* 32: 391–94.

150. Loh and Wackernagel, *Living Planet Report*, Table 2.

151. Geertz, Clifford. 1963. *Agricultural Involution: The Process of Ecological Change in Indonesia*. Berkeley: University of California Press; Rappaport, "Flow of Energy," 117–32.

152. Netting, *Smallholders, Householders*.

153. Mellars, Paul. 1976. "Fire Ecology, Animal Populations and Man: A Study of Some Ecological Relationships in Prehistory." *Proceedings of the Prehistoric Society* 42: 15–45; Lewis, Henry T. 1982. *A Time for Burning*. Edmonton, Alberta: Boreal Institute for Northern Studies, Occasional Publications 17; Gould, Richard A. 1971. "Uses and Effects of Fire Among the Western Desert Aborigines of Australia." *Mankind* 8(1): 14–24; Hallam, S. 1975. *Fire and Hearth*. Canberra: Australian Institute of Aboriginal Studies.

154. Gutkind, E. A. 1956. "Our World from the Air: Conflict and Adaptation." In *Man's Role in Changing the Face of the Earth*, edited by William L. Thomas Jr., 1–44. Chicago: University of Chicago Press.; Spoehr, Alexander. 1956. "Cultural Differences in the Interpretation of Natural Resources." In *Man's Role in Changing the Face of the Earth*, edited by William L. Thomas Jr., 93–102. Chicago: University of Chicago Press.

155. White, "Historical Roots," 1203–7.

156. McDonald, David. 1977. "Food Taboos: A Primitive Environmental Protection Agency (South America)." *Anthropos* 72: 734–48.

157. Rappaport, Roy A. 1968. *Pigs for the Ancestors: Ritual in the Ecology of a New Guinea People*. New Haven, CT: Yale University Press.

158. Bartlett, H. H. 1956. "Fire, Primitive Agriculture, and Grazing in the Tropics." In *Man's Role in Changing the Face of the Earth*, edited by William L. Thomas Jr., 692–720. Chicago: University of Chicago Press.

Natural Resources and the Culture of Consumption

3

The biosphere with industrial man suddenly added is like a balanced aquarium into which large animals are introduced. Consumption temporarily exceeds production, the balance is upset, the products of respiration accumulate, and the fuels for consumption become scarcer and scarcer until production is sufficiently accelerated and respiration is balanced. In some experimental systems balance is achieved only after the large consumers which originally started the imbalance are dead. Will this happen to man?

—HOWARD T. ODUM, *ENVIRONMENT, POWER, AND SOCIETY*[1]

IN THE PREVIOUS CHAPTER, two specific aspects of the environmental crisis—resource depletion and pollution—were related to over-consumption. This chapter further explores the problem of over-consumption because it appears to be the critical defining feature of the global culture in contrast with the tribal world and because it is the feature that contributes most to the present instability of the contemporary world. Here we will be concerned specifically with how globally organized commercially driven systems extract and utilize energy and other natural resources in comparison with patterns typical of small-scale, tribal societies and how these commercial patterns relate to the environmental crisis.

Energy and Culture: Basic Considerations

It becomes the primary function of culture, therefore, to harness and control energy so that it may be put to work in man's service. . . . The functioning of culture as a whole therefore rests upon and is determined by the amount of energy harnessed and by the way in which it is put to work. (Leslie White 1949)[2]

Culture evolves as the amount of energy harnessed per capita per year is increased, or as the efficiency of the instrumental means of putting the energy to work is increased. (Leslie White 1949)[3]

Anthropologist Leslie A. White elaborated a simplistic but important theory of the evolution of culture based largely on energy utilization. In White's view, the earliest tribal societies necessarily remained at a very low level of evolutionary complexity as long as they relied on their own human energy and minimal use of wind, water, and fire. The additional control of solar energy through domesticated plants and animals released vast amounts of energy and made possible higher levels of social complexity, greater productivity per unit of area, and greater population density. These developments culminated with the appearance of state organization.

Since White first published this evolutionary scheme in 1949, other researchers have shown that his theory was misleading. In fact, prior to the use of fossil fuel energy sources, per capita energy use did not increase significantly—humans remained the basic source of mechanical energy. The real difference was that domestication of plants and animals supported higher population densities and larger total populations,[4] and thus elites could direct larger total energy to promote growth and build cultural complexity. The fact that increased complexity can arise without domestication, or with only minimal use of domesticates, is demonstrated by the emergence of complex chiefdoms along the desert coast of Peru 4,000 years ago based on the exploitation of rich marine resources rather than cultivated food crops.[5]

White felt that the full potential for cultural evolutionary advance on the basis of agriculture alone was realized before the Christian era and that further advance into industrial civilization was only made possible by the *fuel revolution*, his term for the utilization of fossil fuels. With the discovery of nuclear energy, White felt, culture was poised on the verge of a major new energy revolution that could lead to even higher levels of evolutionary progress. Brazilian anthropologist Darcy Ribeiro[6] infelicitously applied the term *thermonuclear revolution* to this new era, but neither White nor Ribeiro considered the full cost of nuclear energy.

It is certainly reasonable and useful to describe general evolutionary progress in terms of energy utilization, but if we are concerned with the environmental crisis and with achieving a successful and sustainable cultural adaptation it is more useful to compare cultures according to the rate at which nonrenewable resources are being depleted. The global energy resources that are most significant for human use can be divided into three categories: (1) solar radiation, (2) fossil fuels, and (3) nuclear energy. Solar radiation can be considered a steady "income" energy source that is renewed daily or annually and is converted by green plants, or through the movement of water and wind, into other usable forms of energy. Solar energy may also be concentrated and converted directly to heat for human use. Only a very small, relatively constant quantity of energy can ever be provided by this source, and because of the Second Law of Thermodynamics the amount of energy available for use is constantly reduced at each conversion.

Fossil fuels supply solar energy that has been trapped by green plants and stored in the earth through incomplete oxidation over the past 600 million years. The process of fossil fuel formation is still under way but at a rate too slow in relation to human needs for this energy source to be considered anything other than nonrenewable. Any use of this stored energy is a withdrawal from a steadily dwindling stock.

Nuclear energy can be released from its storage within the atomic structure, but the most easily utilized radioactive fuels are in limited supply and all controlled releases of nuclear energy require enormous additional inputs from other energy sources in order to be safely maintained, to deal with the waste heat, and to warehouse the dangerous radioactive by-products for millennia. Nuclear energy also has serious limitations because it is primarily a source of heat that must be converted into electrical energy before it can be widely used, and thus it seems an unlikely replacement for all present uses of fossil fuels.

Societies can be divided into "high-energy societies" and "low-energy societies" in regard to energy use. These categories have immediate implications for both evolutionary "progress" and adaptive success. The quantitative differences between high- and low-energy societies can be seen easily by reference to per capita levels of energy consumption. It has been estimated that prior to the fuel revolution no state-organized societies utilized more than 26,000 kilocalories per capita daily, whereas small, domestically organized tribal societies, whether foragers or farmers, utilized between 5,000 and 12,000 kilocalories per capita daily (see figure 3.1). These societies could all be considered low-energy societies, especially because these

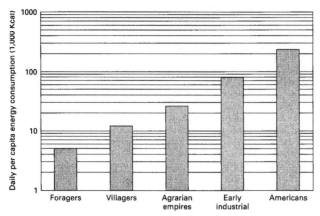

Figure 3.1.   Energy Consumption by Culture Scale.
Earl Cook. 1971. "The Flow of Energy in an Industrial Society." *Scientific American* 224(3):134–44.

rates include only the energy cost of domestic cooking and an average of 2,500 kilocalories of food energy needed for daily per capita human nutrition. In contrast, early industrial commercial societies utilizing fossil fuels consumed approximately 70,000 kilocalories per capita daily, and by 1970 American consumers had elevated that rate to 230,000.[7] Between 1970 and 2005, average daily American per capita energy consumption has averaged 235,000 kilocalories. It increased by 50 percent during the decades of 1953 to 1973, when the OPEC oil crisis caused a sudden dip.[8] Significantly, after 1958 Americans imported more energy than they exported, until by 2005 more than 34 percent of the energy Americans consumed was being imported. At the global level, per capita energy consumption increased only gradually from an average of 43,000 kilocalories in the 1970s to 46,000 kilocalories between 2000 and 2004, but because of continued increases in global population the aggregate human demand on the world's energy resources more than doubled between 1970 and 2004. However, the actual distribution of consumption is extremely unequal. For example, ranking countries by their per capita energy consumption in 2003 and adding up global population shows that 10 percent of the world's people consume 44 percent of global energy. The median per capita consumption is only 24,000 kilocalories per day. This means that half the world, approximately 3 billion people, get by on 24,000 kilocalories of commercial energy or less. This is about the same as the 26,000 hectares estimated for preindustrial England in 1400, if 2,000 kilocalories are added for food energy. In 2003, 2 billion people were consuming less

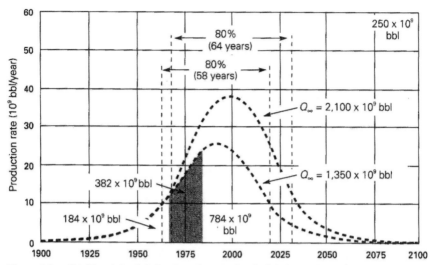

Figure 3.2.   "Hubbert's Peak," the Complete Cycle of Global Petroleum Production.
Petroleum is perhaps global culture's most vital nonrenewable resource, yet its total availability is strictly limited, as this chart of complete cycles of world crude-oil production demonstrates. Hubbert, M. King. 1996. "Energy Resources," in *Resources and Man*, edited by National Academy of Sciences. San Francisco: W. H. Freeman, 196.

than 12,000 kilocalories daily, not counting food energy and any firewood that they might have collected.

Given the apparently immutable laws of thermodynamics and the physical limitations of the global energy budget, any culture that relies on renewable solar energy sources must necessarily remain a low-energy culture relative to cultures drawing on stored, depletable sources. Theoretically, low-energy cultures could exist another 5 billion years until the sun burns out, whereas high-energy cultures must be transformed to low-energy cultures when their depleted energy stores are burned up. Or their growth may be halted by the adverse impacts of the waste heat or global warming produced through energy conversion. High-energy cultures thus have limited life spans that can easily be predicted as compared to the 5-billion-year life expectancy of low-energy cultures.

Estimates of the depletion rates of fossil fuels vary considerably, depending on accepted rates of utilization and estimates of total reserves, but the general magnitude of the problem is clear. Global production of petroleum seems to be following the total life cycle projected by geologist M. King Hubbert in 1969 (figure 3.2), although there are many adjustments to the model. Hubbert assumed a total global supply of from 1.3 to 2.1 trillion barrels and projected that 25–37 billion barrels a year would be the peak of global production and would be reached by approximately 1990–2000, followed by a decline. This would mean that 80 percent of the world's oil would be consumed over a span of about sixty years. Hubbert's Peak, or Peak Oil, would be the point at which half of all the oil that could ever be produced would have been consumed, and that after that point production would necessarily decline because of the increasing difficulty of oil discovery and extraction. In fact, Hubbert's 25 billion barrels figure was actually reached in 2000,[9] and by 2005 it had reached 30 billion barrels. How much higher production figures can rise remains to be seen. Some analysts argue that the total global supply might actually be 3.5 trillion barrels, rather than Hubbert's 1.3 to 2.1, and that rather than a peak, global production will be an extended plateau.[10] At 30 billion barrels a year, 3.5 trillion barrels would be totally consumed within eighty years, so this does not extend the prospect for a petroleum-based world system very far. The magnitude of the petroleum depletion problem, not precise depletion dates, is what matters. Even if oil production continues to rise, oil prices and the environmental costs of petroleum production and consumption will also rise. These facts and the need to reduce total energy consumption and shift to alternative energy resources were certainly known to the leaders of the oil industry by the end of the twentieth century, as evidenced by a prophetic 1999 statement by Mike Bowlin, chief executive officer of ARCO: "We've embarked on the beginning of the Last Days of the Age of Oil."[11]

The depletion problem affects all fossil fuels and makes any fossil fuel–based culture ultimately maladaptive. Petroleum is especially important because it has so many uses, but its use as a high-energy liquid fuel will be difficult to replace. Coal is relatively abundant, but using it will only accelerate global warming. The overall magnitude of the fossil fuel problem suggests that consumption patterns that characterized the second half of the twentieth century will not continue indefinitely. The most likely outcome will be dramatic decreases in per capita energy use early in the twenty-first century and a widespread shift to renewable energy sources.

The commercial world is clearly approaching a critical energy threshold. Even if fossil fuel reserves were to prove virtually inexhaustible, continued use of these fuels at present rates is not sustainable. Atmospheric carbon dioxide averaged 383 ppm in 2007.[12] This is 27 percent above preindustrial levels of 280 ppm that lasted until 1750, after 10,000 years of stability. As is now well known, increased human releases of carbon dioxide and other greenhouse gases trap heat and are the primary cause of global warming. The UN-sponsored Intergovernmental Panel on Climate Change (IPCC) estimated in its third report in 2001 that the greenhouse effect could cause global mean temperature to rise from 1990 levels by between 1.4 to 5.8° C (2.5 to 10.4° F), and sea level by 0.09 to 0.88 meters (4 to 35 inches) by 2100.[13] Global warming is melting the polar ice caps and will flood many of the world's urban centers; it is causing enormous adverse changes in world vegetation, disrupting human society. Even without the greenhouse effect, within 200 years a mere 5 percent annual increase in world energy production would produce waste heat equal to that received from the sun, and all life on earth would cease.[14]

Thus, a continually expanding high-energy culture will be self-terminating, and its maximum life expectancy can be no more than a few hundred years. It is doubtful that relatively high levels of energy utilization can be stabilized at safely sustainable levels even with nuclear technology, because of its known and unknown risks and because of the uncertainty that unstable high-energy societies will evolve the social mechanisms needed to achieve a safe transition to full use of nuclear energy. All of these projections about fossil fuels are based on differing assumptions concerning future economic conditions, population growth, and the way "known reserves" are calculated. However, in spite of all the unknowns, the overall magnitude of the fossil fuel problem suggests that energy consumption patterns that characterized the second half of the twentieth century will not continue indefinitely. We can anticipate dramatic decreases in per capita energy use in the first half of the twenty-first century and a widespread shift to renewable energy sources. Any culture defined by perpetual growth in either consumption or population is certain to be self-limiting. Although it is not possible to precisely estimate the life expectancy of a global commercial culture as presently organized, it can confidently be stated that it will not exceed the 50,000-year record of Australian aboriginal culture, or the 3,500-year span of political-scale ancient Mesopotamian civilization. A drastic restructuring of contemporary culture seems virtually certain.

Capitalism and the Culture of Consumption

The first edition of this book (1976) defined the global culture as an unsustainable "culture of consumption." This characterization derived from my earlier conclusion that since 1800, autonomous tribal peoples throughout the world had been deprived of their resources, territories, and independence because of a seemingly insatiable demand for resources emanating from industrial nations.[15] At that time I hesitated to label the culture of consumption "capitalism" because commercially driven unsustainable consumption may take many forms, but by the end of the twentieth century, with capitalism triumphant worldwide and resource consumption accelerating, there was no doubt that capitalism was the dominant culture of consumption. A focus on resource consumption raises many troubling questions about the nature of commercial societies, capitalism, and sustainability. The consensus among economists is that economic growth is the very essence of capitalism. Historically, capitalist growth has invariably meant increased consumption, but it is possible to imagine capitalism without growth, development without growth, and development without capitalism as we know it. The fundamental anthropological questions to ask are, why and how did expanding resource consumption become so important, and how long can it be maintained?

Social scientists at first focused on European science, exploration, and technology to explain the origins of the modern capitalist world. Initially, they considered the Industrial Revolution, conceptualized as science-based social and technological changes in production, to be the principal architect of material progress. Consumption, rather than production, became a subject of widespread scholarly research only in the 1980s, when the global economy entered a dramatic new expansion phase widely attributed to the liberalization of trade under "free market" capitalism and new computer-based information technologies. At this time many anthropologists, historians, and cultural studies researchers began to view commodities as cultural objects.[16] They examined the symbolic cultural meanings of commodities for individual consumers and their use in the construction of self-identity. Some anthropologists argued that markets, commodities, consumption patterns, and their cultural meanings are mutually constructed by marketers and consumers.[17] While no doubt correct in a general sense, this interpretation makes capitalism and the culture of consumption seem both natural and inevitable, avoiding the crucial issues of class, social power, and sustainability raised by capitalism.

Even when human problems are the focus of a cultural approach to understanding capitalism, an emphasis on the mutual construction of cultural meanings can obscure the dominant directing role of specific human agents and make everyone appear equally responsible for the problems created by elevated consumption. For example, anthropologist Richard H. Robbins described the cultural construction of capitalism as follows: "The culture of capitalism is devoted to encouraging the production and sale of commodities. For capitalists, the culture encourages the accumulation of profit; for laborers, it encourages the accumulation of wages; for consumers, it encourages the accumulation of goods. In other words, capitalism defines sets of people who, behaving according to a set of learned rules, act as they must act."[18]

This interpretation is technically accurate, but it makes a disembodied capitalism the active agent and relegates capitalists, laborers, and consumers to the role of passive entities. This led Robbins to state that the culture of capitalism itself "has reshaped our values . . . *it* has largely dictated the direction that every institution in our society would take. . . . *It* has produced wave after wave of consumer goods" (italics added).[19] Robbins concluded that "the culture" takes advantage of the natural inclination of people to consume. He further explains that "the desire, indeed the necessity of people to consume more and more is the force that drives the society of perpetual growth." In reality, the primary human agents who created capitalism were elites with vested interests in increasing the scale of consumption in order to disproportionately enhance their own power. This is not to deny that many other people also benefited from improved material conditions, but the point is that a few people produced a cultural system that worked for them but may not have been the best, or most sustainable, human alternative. Capitalism is not just a culture, it is also a society that takes the shape of overlapping networks of individuals with varying degrees of ability to influence material outcomes.

The most important task is to understand how the culture of consumption originated, how material benefits were distributed, and what increased consumption means for human problems and sustainability. Increased consumption also cannot be explained by human greed or selfishness because these traits are presumably universal, albeit differentially distributed in degree among individuals. Furthermore, from a scale and power perspective the problem is neither the specific technology of production nor the detailed symbolism or individual psychology of consumption. The critical issues are the scale and organization of the commercial exchanges that support increased consumption and the manner in which the system of exchanges concentrates social power and reduces sustainability. This view of consumption is one of political economy and political ecology.[20] Nor was the consumption culture just a product of the market economy or the use of money; organized markets and money have existed for millennia, economically linking villages, towns, and cities in all of the major civilizations. When markets are controlled by many buyers and many sellers, they can be minimally hierarchical, can respond to supply and demand as shaped by domestic needs, and are more likely to remain stable and sustainable. This is how the "invisible hand" of the "free market" can benefit society, as Adam Smith originally envisioned in his famous 1776 book, *Wealth of Nations*.

However, when a few aggrandizing people gain monopoly or oligopoly access to global-scale transactions and can gain disproportionate benefits from directing these transactions, elites have an immediate incentive to expand the scale and scope of the "market" and to push resource consumption beyond sustainable limits. This growth-oriented monopolistic commerce is far removed from the local and regional markets that support communities.

The History of Capitalism

The new global culture of consumption was the historical product of a hierarchical, capitalist world economic system based on long-distance commerce that began in about 1400 and was developed by merchants and investors centered successively in Venice, Antwerp, Genoa, Amsterdam, London, and New York.[21] The elites in these urban centers enjoyed the highest living standards and consumption levels in the world, while the lower classes everywhere lived as wage workers, serfs, or slaves. Genocide, ethnocide, and ecocide were the external costs that initially subsidized the consumption culture. This outcome was not simply the result of the operation of comparative advantage in a free market. French historian Fernand Braudel argued in 1977 that a few elite commercial families succeeded because they were able to merge political and economic power within very hierarchical, but not totally closed, European societies and transmit and accumulate their power and control over generations.

The European Origins of Capitalism

The culture of consumption was created by European elites during the three centuries between 1500 and 1800, well before the Industrial Revolution gained momentum. The resources that boosted increased consumption came from a variety of elite-funded enterprises, including long-distance trade, conquest, colonization, looting, and piracy. In England between 1575 and 1630 the initiators and prime beneficiaries of these power-concentrating projects were centered in London. At any one time no more than 2,500 individual investors owned the thirty-three joint-stock companies that conducted these activities.[22] Most investors were wealthy but socially inferior large merchants who picked the only route open to them for material advancement. The remaining fourth of investors were drawn from the landed hereditary aristocracy, the top 2 percent of England's social hierarchy. Aristocrats invested in development because their privileged status was threatened by the unsettled conditions accompanying the end of feudalism. During this time Europeans experienced a prolonged episode of famine, disease, war, inflation, political upheaval, and bad weather that paradoxically created opportunities for the elite.[23] This handful of venture capitalists represented a mere 0.25 percent of the households in the kingdom of 5 million people. Perhaps only 100 men in any given year headed the corporations that actually organized and directed much of England's overseas expansion, which ultimately transformed the world.

The largest English investments during this period were in privateering—the looting of Spanish galleons of gold and silver previously looted from the Aztecs and Incas or extracted from the Potosí mines of Bolivia by means of slave labor. The quantity of gold and silver "imported" to Europe between 1500 and 1680 represented more than a tenfold increase in the existing stock and certainly boosted European development. The British East India Company, founded in 1600, was the largest English development enterprise of the era, after privateering, and it was fabulously profitable. For example, seven East India Company trading expeditions carried out from 1601 to 1612 produced a return of 155 percent on an investment of £517,784 for 550 investors at a time when 98 percent of households lived on less than £120 a year.[24] Between 1600 and 1688 the wealth of England more than tripled, fueling a frenzy of luxury building and consumption by the elite. By 1688 some 2,000 large merchant traders were earning £400 a year, putting them economically at the same level as the gentry class and almost equal with knights and esquires.[25] The very high rate of return realized on these investments was a result not only of the unique opportunity afforded by low-wage workers, slavery, and privateering but also of the ability of aristocrats at the highest level of government to systematically enrich themselves with royal favors, bribes, and the abuse of public office.[26]

The 1500–1800 period in the expansion of capitalism is remarkably similar to the period of "free market" globalization that began in 1980. In both periods increased resource consumption by a few households conferred a decisive advantage in a cultural environment of intense competition for social power. Massive inequality does indeed appear to be a dominant feature of the historic development of capitalist economic growth. However, rapid growth in wealth and income may not be an obvious advantage in a society that distributes resources equitably. This suggests that the emergence of capitalism as we know it was not inevitable. It cannot be attributed to universal human greed or selfishness or to an innate desire for accumulation, because domestic-scale societies successfully curbed this desire.

Capitalism resulted from a unique, dynamic, and multi-determined process that operated in a highly stratified cultural world shaped by commercial competition and status-seeking in which individual households followed their natural desire to ensure the well-being and success of their children, unhindered by the effects of their success on the larger society. In this peculiar cultural environment, the scale of consumption and accumulation increased because people felt compelled to intensify their productive labor, to innovate, to take risks, and to take advantage of new economic opportunities to expand trade, markets, money, and overseas exploration and conquest. In important respects this development was both an elite-directed and a historically determined process that people of all social strata participated in, but this particular path toward a particular kind of mass culture of consumption was not the only possible path or outcome. There were many different ways in which the development might have unfolded, and it is quite possible that other configurations of mass consumption would be sustainable.

A persistent central belief in capitalist cultures is that everyone benefits from elevated consumption, but this belief needs to be carefully qualified. Some historians speak of a "consumer revolution" or a "democratization of consumption" occurring in England and America as early as the eighteenth century.[27] In reality, living standards were extremely inequitably distributed in politically centralized pre-capitalist societies, and the benefits of higher consumption levels produced by the early commercial world spread very slowly. In many countries it was well into the twentieth century before more than half the population realized significant improvement in work loads, nutrition, life expectancy, and overall household well-being. The notion of a "spirit of equality" or a democratization of consumption really refers to the *possibility* of everyone's being able to experience material benefits; in reality, vast income differences always prevent full democratization in class-stratified societies. At the same time, any discussion of consumption must acknowledge the cultural relativity of concepts such as material luxury and deprivation, human needs, human desires, and consumer demand. Consumer demand for commercial products is not a human universal but rather is determined by the balance between the actual market availability of goods and the willingness and ability of households to produce for themselves, household income, and perceived needs. However, elevated consumption of commodities is a necessary feature of a political economy in which elite households control commercial transactions in order to disproportionately concentrate their own social power. There is an absolute minimum level below which deprivation measurably reduces the life chances of households and individuals, but the cultural definitions of *poverty* and *luxury* are variable. Although people may disagree as to the precise meaning of insufficiency or superfluity of goods,[28] consumption patterns are crucial to any understanding of contemporary human problems.

The emergence of fashion, defined as rapid style changes in commodities, is sometimes cited as an example of consumption democratization. In 1982 historian Neil McKendrick[29] attributed the virtual absence of fashion in most precapitalist cultures to the "consumer vacuum" caused by material poverty and sumptuary laws, which made it impossible for most people to follow the whims of fashion. For example, in Tudor England consumption defined social rank, and sumptuary laws specified the color, styles, and material of clothing, and even the number of dishes that could be served at meals, according to income and rank.[30] When these laws were suddenly repealed in 1604 in order to stimulate trade, a flurry of competitive emulation began, but much of this new consumption involved luxury goods and was necessarily restricted to a tiny minority in the upper ranks of society. At this time the English categorized consumer goods as (1) *necessities* such as food and domestic durables; (2) *decencies* such as house, groceries, bedding, and tableware; and (3) costly *luxuries* of the leisured lifestyle. These categories corresponded respectively to the social distinctions of the relatively powerless poor in the vast lower class; the shopkeepers, merchants, and professionals in the small middle class, who could maintain themselves in "decent" comfort; and the handful of households in the upper gentry and aristocracy.

In our English example, new trade goods generally were first consumed as luxuries by the highest social ranks and then very gradually diffused downward, driven by the pressures of competitive emulation and shrewd marketing. In 1559 the primary grocery imports consumed by the English were pepper and dried fruit. Mass consumption of tobacco began by 1650, sugar by 1690, and tea by 1730.[31] By the 1680s English merchants were importing grades of cloth specifically to reflect social ranks, with different colors and qualities designed for each rank. Merchants made gifts of the finest materials to the nobility to stimulate top-down emulation. These new consumer markets did not just happen but were to a great extent propelled by intense competition between rival investor-driven international trade monopolies.[32]

The Culture of Over-Consumption

In a fully developed consumption culture as it had evolved by the mid-twentieth century, the elite shape the major economic, social, and ideological subsystems to promote ever-higher per capita levels of resource consumption that were patently unsustainable. This is *over-consumption,* not only in terms of reduced cultural viability but also in a strictly biological sense, as ecologist Howard Odum explains it:

> In the industrial system with man living off a fuel, he manages all his affairs with industrial machinery, all parts of which are metabolically consumers. . . . The system of man has consumption in excess of production. The products of respiration—carbon dioxide, metabolic water, and mineralized inorganic wastes—are discharged in rates in excess of their incorporation into organic matter by photosynthesis. If the industrialized urban system were enclosed in a chamber with only the air above it at the time, it would quickly exhaust its oxygen, be stifled with waste, and destroy itself since it does not have the recycling pattern of the agrarian system."[33]

Odum estimated that on a global scale "human industries add about a 5 percent excess of consumption over production." Over-consumption also produces a phenomenal quantity of garbage that can be a gold mine for archaeologists, both today and in the future,[34] but clogged landfills also suggest waste and system imbalance.

Growth through increased consumption is so much a part of our present economy that most economists find it difficult to imagine any other state, even though perpetual growth is possible only in an infinite environment. Some writers characterized the present growth economy as a "frontier" or "cowboy" economy,[35] meaning that it is the type of economic system that might be appropriate to a particular period of expansion into a new environment, but that it becomes inappropriate when that historical period has passed and further expansion threatens to become destructive. The important point is that such a system is defined by a continual increase in "throughput," that is, production and consumption measured variously as gross domestic income or product (GDI, GDP). The by-products of the process, such as waste, depletion, pollution, and various indirect social costs or "externalities," do not immediately detract from growth measured as GDP and may actually increase it. For example, accidents and diseases caused by the production and consumption process contribute to economic growth because further goods and services are required to deal with them. Business consultant Ralph Estes[36] estimated in 1996 that corporate business produced costs to American society at large of $2.6 trillion (1994 dollars) for injuries, price-fixing, dangerous products, pollution, environmental damage, and illegal activity—more than one-third of American GDP in 1994. This pattern of "externalized" costs resembles the piracy and injustice that accompanied the original creation of the culture of consumption and is clearly counter-productive in a human sense, if not illegal. Many of these practices are a form of elite deviance, or "higher immorality," that characterizes corporate business and government.[37] Corporate crime and immorality occur in large-scale corporations because power is relatively anonymous, the personal rewards are extremely high, and punishment is either very light or unlikely. Adverse side effects of growth will be certain to make growth self-limiting in the long run, but because of the investment process a consumption economy is focused only on the immediate future and typically disregards impacts even only twenty-five to fifty years into the future.

Perpetual economic growth is firmly entrenched in the culture of consumption and has become the way to both produce and sustain a grossly stratified, non-egalitarian social system. Disruptive dissatisfaction among the lowest classes due to poverty and unemployment can be prevented without the wealthy sacrificing their positions if the total volume of wealth can be steadily increased or if people believe that they have the possibility of improving their material condition. In this way the poor gradually become "wealthy," or nurture hope of doing so, while their relative position remains constant or declines. The same principle operates between countries at the global level. "Poor" nations might be prevented from warring against rich nations if the possibility of certain minimal levels of economic growth can be maintained.

Sociologist Leslie Sklair[38] calls the culture-ideology of consumerism "the fuel that powers the motor of global capitalism." In his view the global system is driven by a powerful, elite-generated ideology that convinces people that perpetual economic growth will benefit everyone. Social science theorist Immanuel Wallerstein[39] called this the "myth of the rising standard of living" because it masks the realities of poverty and the unequal economic relationships between rich and poor countries, as well as the physical impossibility of a perpetual expansion of consumption. As discussed in chapter 1, Leslie Sklair[40] identified "consumerism," as it is promoted by the transnational mass media and advertising, as the dominant element in the ideology of the global system. This "consumption project" works best where people's prospects for self-sufficiency in basic needs such as food and shelter are reduced at the same time that they are exposed to mass-media advertising. He states: "The cultural-ideological project of global capitalism is to persuade people to consume above their own perceived needs in order to perpetuate the accumulation of capital for private profit, in other words, to ensure that the global capitalist system goes on forever."[41]

Media studies expert Stuart Ewen argues in his book *Captains of Consciousness*, which tells the social history of advertising in the United States during the 1920s,[42] that in the same way that clocks shaped people for factory work, advertising was needed to make people predictable consumers of factory-made commercial products. Creating an American consumer culture also helped deflect the social movements that at that time were seeking greater social equality and more government regulation of commerce. In Sklair's view, the advertising "project" seeks to make consumption of commercial products the center of people's lives. As he observes: "The culture-ideology of consumerism proclaims, literally, that the meaning of life is to be found in the things that we possess. To consume, therefore, is to be fully alive, and to remain fully alive we must continuously consume."[43]

Media specialist Sut Jhally[44] suggests that advertising works by promoting fantasies that persuade people that their real desires "for love, family, for friendship, for adventure, and sex" can be obtained by purchasing commodities. These cultural messages emphasize individual, rather than social, interests and make people less responsive to the social and political issues that really matter.

The importance of advertising in promoting consumption is illustrated by the example of the United States where $271 billion was expended on advertising in 2005.[45] This was 85 percent of the $315 billion spent by all degree-granting institutions (colleges and universities) in the country in the 2003–2004 academic year.[46] Radio and television are virtually entirely dependent on advertising revenues. American advertising expenditures were highly concentrated in a relatively few corporations. The one hundred largest corporate advertising expenditures accounted for 37 percent of all advertising expenditures in 2005. The top nine corporations—Procter & Gamble, General Motors, Time Warner, Verizon, AT&T, Ford, Walt Disney, Johnson & Johnson, and GlaxoSmithKline—accounted for 10 percent of all advertising expenditures. This shows that a handful of business executives have enormous influence over the culture.

The transnational corporations and the transnational elite that own and manage them will certainly prosper as formerly self-sufficient peoples become wage earners and consumers of commercial products, but the outcome for those marginalized in the process is less promising. Higher "standards of living" or improved "quality of life" may be illusory when they are measured by ever-increasing per capita consumption of energy, rising GNP, or national income averages. This illusory quality of the consumer culture is shown by other cross-national measures such as the Physical Quality of Life Index (PQLI) developed by David M. Morris in 1979. This index averaged national-level data on infant mortality rates, life expectancy at age one, and literacy rates into a single index value. The PQLI is a simple, comprehensive, and relatively non-ethnocentric measure of overall quality of life, at least for literate national societies. The PQLI demonstrates that there is no absolute relationship between quality of life and GNP. In the 1970s there were nations with low GNP that had high life-quality indices, such as Sri Lanka, Cuba, and Western Samoa, and nations with high GNP and low life quality, such as Libya and Saudi Arabia. Cross-national surveys suggest that only up to a certain point do increases in energy use correspond with rises in commonly accepted measures of quality of life in industrial countries, such as health care, education, and "cultural" activities.[47] Very high energy levels may be part of evolutionary progress as Leslie White defined it, but they make little contribution to improving the quality of life. There are even indications that very high energy consumption rates are related to negative qualities such as high suicide and divorce rates, but the causal relationships have not been fully explored.

A new measure of the effects of economic growth and consumption, the *Genuine Progress Indicator*, GPI, was developed in 1995 by researchers at Redefining Progress, a socio-economic policy institute.[48] The GPI offers a separate accounting of consumption that directly supports human well-being, including things that benefit households, communities, society, and the natural environment, listing these things apart from other things that benefit only the "economy." Genuine Progress Indicators also include things that enhance human well-being but are ignored by GDP, such as unpaid domestic labor, volunteer work, services provided by domestic consumer goods, and community infrastructure. These measures were included in our previous discussion of noncommercial income and wealth in the tribal world in chapter 2. Genuine Progress Indicators are adjusted downward for the costs of crime, pollution, and environmental degradation, and for the benefit-concentrating effects of inequality that shift costs to the majority. In the United States personal consumption has historically been the primary component of GDP, but beyond a certain point increased domestic consumption and overall economic growth as traditionally measured by GDP may actually erode quality of life. For example, in 2002 personal income in the United States was $6.5 trillion dollars in 2000 dollars ($22,835 per capita), and constituted two-thirds of GDP. To measure Genuine Progress, some $3.1 trillion in well-being would be added to account for non-market household services and public goods, but $6.2 trillion is subtracted in social and environmental costs attributable to economic growth. A final

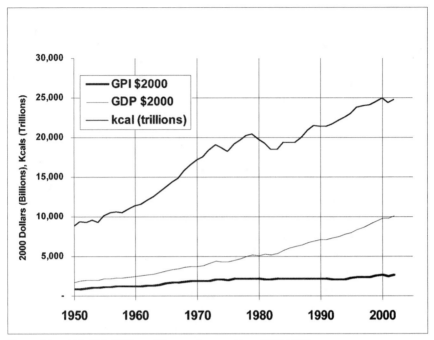

Figure 3.3.   U.S. GPI, GDP, and Energy Consumption, 1950–2002.

adjustment for capital investment and foreign lending and borrowing yields a Genuine Progress Indicator of $2.7 trillion ($10,033 per capita), only some 40 percent of the apparent personal consumption value as it appears in the standard GDP calculation for 2002. When U.S. GPI, GDP, and energy consumption are plotted together over time from 1950 to 2002, it can be seen that GPI has remained relatively flat, whereas GDP and total energy consumed have increased steeply (figure 3.3). This suggests that the benefits of economic growth have been very costly, and to a considerable degree are accounting illusions.

It is widely believed that the historically ever-increasing output of household appliances meant a steady reduction in housework and an increase in leisure time. Consumer appliances thus became principle indicators of a high standard of living. Anthropological research among foragers and shifting cultivators, however, has shown that tribal people work far less at household tasks, and indeed at all subsistence pursuits, than any modern populations.[49] Aboriginal Australian women, for example, were found to spend an average of approximately twenty hours per week collecting and preparing food,[50] whereas women in rural America in the 1920s, without the benefit of labor-saving appliances, devoted approximately fifty-two hours a week to their housework.[51] Some fifty years later, contrary to all expectations, urban women who were not employed outside of the home were putting in fifty-five hours a week at their housework, in spite of all their new "labor-saving" dishwashers, washing machines, vacuum cleaners, and electric mixers. This increase in work time shows how illusory the idea of an increased standard of living may be when judged according to the consumption culture's traditionally accepted measures. Some of this increased workload may be due to the need to spend more time on consumption-related tasks such as shopping and caring for an increased volume of clothing. Furthermore, the thirty hours a week of television that Americans were watching in 2002[52] could be considered a loss of leisure time, because television viewing is consumption of a commercial product and because, through advertising, it promotes further consumption.

The relationship between a culture of consumption and the natural environment can be seen more clearly through the examination of specific examples. The examples that follow deal primarily with the United States in order to illustrate specific principles that may be valid for all consumption cultures and that show how environmental crises may be precipitated by over-consumption.

Resource Consumption in America

The United States is without question the leading example of a culture of consumption. Shortly after World War II, it had become the world's major consumer of nonrenewable resources on both an absolute and a per capita basis. In 2004 the United States, with less than 5 percent of the world's population, consumed 100 quadrillion BTUs, which represented 22 percent of the world's total consumption. In 1970 Americans accounted for 35 percent of the world's energy consumption.[53] Worldwide economic development meant that the rest of the world was catching up with America in energy consumption; nevertheless, in 1996 total American consumption was still more than all the energy consumed by China, Japan, and India combined. China, with 21 percent of the world's population, still consumed less than 12 percent of the world's commercial energy, about half the American total. The historic pattern of American consumption illustrates important trends that may be generally characteristic of consumption cultures. If China continues to follow America's energy consumption example, pressures on the global environment will accelerate dramatically above their already unsustainable levels.

High and rapidly increasing rates of American energy consumption were made possible by a switch from primary dependence on theoretically renewable "income" sources, such as fuel wood, to nonrenewable "capital stock" resources, such as coal. In 1850 approximately 90 percent of America's energy was derived from fuel wood, but by 1890 over 50 percent was supplied by coal. By 1960 nearly 70 percent came from oil and natural gas, and optimists hoped that in the near future nuclear energy would replace depleted fossil fuels.[54] In a mere 100 years Americans tripled their per capita use of energy and increased their total use thirty times. They have already made two major shifts in their basic energy sources and face shortages and further adjustments in the foreseeable future. Much of this increased use has carried an enormous environmental cost due to air pollution from burning the fuels and to disturbances caused by drilling and mining operations and accidents such as oil spills. As more easily exploited energy resources have become depleted, higher extraction costs have forced the United States to rely heavily on imported energy. By 2005 nearly 30 percent of American energy was imported. Oil and natural gas were still predominant, accounting for 63 percent of consumption, with coal approximately 22 percent and nuclear 8 percent.[55]

Certainly, a critical question to ask is how a society based on ever-expanding consumption such as the United States responds to the impact of its own consumption on what must be an ever-dwindling resource base. Tribal societies, as noted earlier, tend to respond quickly to adverse impacts on their resource base because they are immediately dependent on local resources. However, commercially organized societies may lack this instant responsiveness because of their complexity and specialization. They are especially vulnerable to overgrowth and collapse because of their rapid expansion. More importantly, they lack substitute response mechanisms, and the market system seems to thrive on resource depletion. Governments have occasionally stockpiled certain critical resources as strategic military reserves, but in general present political institutions prefer to let market forces detect potential shortfalls. Some of the special commissions that have historically examined the problem are discussed in the following.

Taking Stock

Our nation, looking toward a future of continuing economic progress, is well-advised to take stock of its natural resources. Industry can expand only so far as raw materials are available. (Dewhurst)[56]

After World War II, in 1949, the United Nations brought together in New York over 700 scientists from over fifty nations to exchange information on world problems of conservation and resource utilization. In assessing the world mineral situation, H. L. Keenleyside, Canada's deputy minister of mines and resources, noted that between 1900 and 1949 more world mineral resources had been consumed than during all of humanity's previous existence. He felt that there were as yet no critical mineral shortages developing, but he recognized future limitations: "Thus it is quite clear that the combination of an increasing population and rising standards of living will place a strain on our metal resources which will almost certainly in the end prove beyond the capacity of man and nature to supply" (Keenleyside).[57]

To postpone the inevitable, Keenleyside recommended increased exploration for minerals, improved extraction and processing technology, conservation, and substitution. Given increasing demands, his warning was clear: "[Unless] there is a fundamental change in the economic fabric of human society we will ultimately be faced with the exhaustion of many of our mineral resources."[58]

In the United States no comprehensive inventory of natural resources was undertaken until 1908. There were early moves toward conservation but little concern that serious problems might arise. A major study published in 1947, titled *America's Needs and Resources*,[59] attempted to project national requirements for resources for 1960. It reported that no real resource exhaustion was likely within twenty years, although high-grade zinc, lead, and bauxite ores might be exhausted by that time and soil shortages might occur somewhat later. The report recognized that domestic mineral resources would ultimately be depleted, but it was felt that, given free access to foreign resources, an "expanding American economy" could be supported for "many decades" to come. Supporting an ever-expanding American culture of consumption has major implications for global resources. This, of course, is one of the reasons why global "free trade" is such an important part of the political ideology of the American elite.

Eight years later, the study *America's Needs and Resources* was updated with the publication of a new edition[60] that displayed a greater appreciation for the incredible consumption rates that Americans were developing. But this awareness was more than overshadowed by an even greater confidence in the country's ability to solve any problem. The study noted that by 1950 Americans were consuming some eighteen tons of raw materials per capita and as much of many important minerals as the rest of the world combined. In spite of these staggering facts, the authors of the report were certain that there would be no insurmountable problems that would limit further growth. "Despite man's seemingly devastating exploitation, he has merely scratched a small segment of this gigantic ball of resources on which he lives. Our power to use the materials in nature is growing rather than diminishing, through favorable technology and economic organization."[61]

While in 1955 we may have been only scratching the surface of the globe's resources, the suddenly increased extent of this scratching was put in perspective in President Truman's study *Resources for Freedom*.[62] This study pointed out that American consumption of most minerals and fuels since 1914 exceeded total world consumption from the dawn of human existence up to 1914. Furthermore, other projections showed how quickly this minor scratching could have a serious impact on a finite earth. In 1956 geochemist Harrison Brown calculated that a world population of 30 billion (which will be reached by 2136 if the 1999 world population of 6 billion continues to grow at 1.2 percent per year), with nuclear breeder technology and the ability to extract all needed mineral resources directly from ordinary rock and seawater, would literally eat up the continents. The crust of the earth would be skimmed off at the rate of 3.3 millimeters a year, or over 3 meters every 1,000 years. Of course this scenario ignores conservation and recycling. Furthermore, the world population growth rate can be expected to continue to drop. It has now become apparent that the use of and availability of energy to move and transform materials is the most critical limiting factor.

In 1963 a third major assessment of American resources was published by *Resources for the Future* (RFF). The 1,000-page report, titled *Resources in America's Future*,[63] attempted to project supply and demand for natural resources up to the year 2000. The authors of the study recognized the general difficulty of such projections but felt they were essential for decision making. They recommended that such studies be conducted or updated by a government agency every five years, perhaps through computer simulation techniques. This study, like earlier assessments, could foresee no immediate critical general shortages. Although the authors felt that some specific problems might arise, they correctly assumed that any problems would be solvable. New technology, world trade, and careful utilization would maintain continued high consumption rates. On the basis of careful projections, which considered the interrelatedness of population, technology, and "demand" levels, and assumed continued imports and no major wars or economic depressions, the RFF report concluded that by the year 2000 the United States would triple its annual consumption of energy, metals, and timber. According to the RFF report summary: "Neither a long view of the past, nor current trends, nor our most careful estimates of future possibilities suggest any general running out of resources in this country during the remainder of this century. The possibilities of using lower grades of raw material, of substituting plentiful materials for scarce ones, of getting more use out of given amounts, of importing things from other countries, and of making multiple use of land and water resources seem to be sufficient guarantee against across-the-board shortage."[64]

This optimistic view was quite in agreement with earlier America's Needs and Resources studies on this point: "On the whole, it seems clear that we shall not be hampered in meeting future needs by a shortage of raw materials."[65]

America's Forests as Resources

The RFF projections accurately predicted the continued technological advances, greater efficiency, and continued substitution of synthetics for natural materials that occurred in subsequent decades. Without constant technological "advance," it is clear that the culture of consumption would rapidly be faced with what the RFF report called "inconvenient and perhaps critical material limitations." For example, it was estimated that 64 percent of the fibers consumed by the year 2000 would be synthetics drawn largely from fossil fuel stocks. The report noted that by 1952 western softwood forests were already being cut at over their replacement rate and warned that unless we wished to be extremely optimistic we could expect a continued depletion of western forests. This prediction also seems to have been accurate.

Softwood (primarily fir and pine) lumber and plywood, primarily from the Pacific Northwest, was a crucial building material for America's suburban expansion that was well under way by the 1950s, and was heavily dependent on the rapid spread of private cars and the availability of cheap and abundant petroleum. RFF projected that Americans would be consuming a maximum of 28 billion board feet of softwood lumber by the year 2000.[66] This figure proved to be about half of the total U.S. consumption of 53 billion board feet reached by 2001, according to lumber industry sources.[67]

By 1992 an inventory by the Forest Service showed that large-diameter softwoods had steadily decreased in the west since 1952, such that "for the first time in history, the United States does not have a large reserve of high quality softwood saw timber available for harvest."[68] The 1992 Forest Service study suggested that eastern hardwood forests and imports would make up for the decline in western forests. By the 1990s the value of American forest product imports had roughly tripled 1960 levels, and American forestry planners acknowledged that American consumption patterns were having a global impact.[69] As the discussion on tropical deforestation in chapter 2 showed, the world's forests will probably not sustain the perpetual increase in harvests that commercial uses demand. Eastern hardwoods will replace western softwoods, and tropical hardwoods may in turn replace the eastern hardwoods. Plastics will replace tropical trees, until petroleum depletion makes plastics too expensive.

The RFF researchers viewed western forests simply as sources of lumber, or inventory, and growing stock. They did not see forests as ecosystems, and they did not consider the cascading effects of intensified cutting. From their perspective, old growth western forests were a mature, unproductive standing crop. Old forests were not growing and therefore needed to be cut to increase growth. They correctly anticipated that in order to meet growing demand western forests would be cut at greater than their growth rates through the twentieth century, but they called this "inventory reduction" rather than deforestation. However, they did warn that over-cutting "would very soon raise the most serious issues of conservation over a broad field far exceeding forestry matters."[70] The RFF researchers also correctly projected that removing these forests would still not meet the growing demand, so they called for more intensive forestry management to improve growth rates and reduce mortality from insects and fire. They also advocated fertilizer, genetic improvement, and the introduction of tree farming. Even taking their most optimistic outlook, there would still be a huge gap between production and demand that could only be met by imports from Canada. After that, tropical hardwoods would substitute for softwoods. The world's tropical rainforest would need to be cut to satisfy American demands. Finally we would need to find synthetic substitutes for wood. They considered everything but actually reducing growth in "demand." Perhaps even more seriously they also failed to anticipate the effects of forest clearing on global warming, and global warming on the forests.

The curious part of the Pacific Northwest's participation in the global lumber market is that at the national level in 2001 the United States imported 394 million board feet (bd ft) of softwood logs and 18.5 billion bd ft in lumber, mostly from Canada, and exported 1.4 billion in logs back to Canada and to Japan, and exported nearly a billion bd ft of softwood lumber.[71] So, logs and lumber were moving in both directions, as if the flow of material mattered more than consumption. This is a good example of the difference between what is good for the economy, measured as GDP, and what is good for human well-being.

It is difficult to escape the conclusion that the consumption culture is fighting a losing battle to support a rising level of consumption that must ultimately be insupportable. At any given moment some important material subsystem of the culture appears about to exhaust a particular resource and is forced to intensify its technology or move on to another resource to keep the system functioning a little longer through any means short of reduced consumption.

Shortly after publication of the RFF study, the National Academy of Sciences conducted its own two-year study, which took a much broader approach to the question of resources and consumption. This work, *Resources and Man*, published in 1969, was concerned with the entire globe and looked beyond the year 2000. The outlook was far more sober and raised serious questions about the long-term viability of an ever-expanding industrial culture. It recognized that supplies of nonrenewable resources such as oil and coal were finite, and in the near future might need to be replaced by nuclear technology. Some authors even felt that there were serious possibilities that certain critical mineral shortages might arise before 2000. The report was clear on one point—even given technological breakthroughs, continued expansion in consumption rates cannot be supported indefinitely. The report held out the hope that, if population and consumption could be stabilized at reasonable levels, industrial society could last for centuries or millennia.

The National Academy of Sciences' 1975 report *Mineral Resources and the Environment*[72] carried the most pessimistic warning of all: "Man faces the prospect of a series of shocks of varying severity as shortages occur in one material after another, with the first real shortages perhaps only a matter of a few years away." Echoing Hubbert's oil depletion projections, this report suggested that world oil supplies might effectively be gone within fifty years and, for the first time ever, called for a massive conservation program and an actual reduction in consumption: "Because of the limits to natural resources as well as to means of alleviating these limits, it is recommended that the federal government proclaim and deliberately pursue a national policy of conservation of material, energy and environmental resources, informing the public and the private sectors fully about the needs and techniques for reducing energy consumption, the development of substitute materials, increasing the durability and maintainability of products, and reclamation and recycling."

According to these findings, the United States, the world's leading culture of consumption, went from just scratching the surface of its own resources to the "bottom of the barrel" in a mere twenty years and was forced into increasing dependency on foreign resources.

The Economics of Resource Depletion

> Sooner or later, the market price will get high enough to choke off the demand entirely. At that moment production falls to zero . . . the last ton produced will also be the last ton in the ground. The resource will be exhausted at the instant it has priced itself out of the market. The Age of Oil or Zinc or Whatever It Is will have come to an end. (Solow, "Economics of Resources")[73]

The culture of consumption has clearly developed within the framework of an economic system that advances systematically from one resource to another, supported by theoretical economic assumptions that deny that "real" scarcity or limits to further growth can exist. We already have seen how industrialized centers in the global culture moved rapidly through several alternative energy sources as they became depleted or inadequate. This process occurs with different grades of ore and virtually every other depletable resource from whales to timber, and represents the predictable operation of market principles in combination with continuing technological advances.

To orthodox economists, the simple solution to the obvious incompatibility of an ever-expanding economy and a finite world is to "redefine" resources. The whaling industry in the 1940s provides an example.[74] Blue whales were being exterminated, then fin whales were declared a replacement resource, then Sei whales, and then sperm whales. When the whales were exhausted the whaling industry could convert itself into a krill-catching industry. Krill are an Antarctic shrimp eaten by whales. Indeed, by 1984 krill were labeled an "untapped bounty" and their commercial exploitation was already under way.[75]

A theoretical charter for such a process of self-perpetuating depletion and never-ending technical progress was clearly spelled out by economists Harold Barnett and Chandler Morse in their influential study *Scarcity and Growth: The Economics of Natural Resource Availability*, published in 1963 for the Resources for the Future Corporation.[76] The primary objective of this study was to disprove the notion of classical economists such as Thomas R. Malthus (1766–1834), David Ricardo (1772–1823), and John Stuart Mill

(1806–1873) that resource scarcity would ultimately halt economic growth, leading to a stationary economy. Such an outcome, according to Barnett and Morse, would be possible only in a world without technological progress and is therefore quite unrealistic. What Barnett and Morse were saying, of course, was that progress will end when progress ends, but they could not conceive of such a contingency. They declared: "The notion of an absolute limit to natural resource availability is untenable when the definition of resources changes drastically and unpredictably over time."[77]

In other words, today trees and whales will be depleted, tomorrow plastic and granite. According to these enthusiastic consumption economists, depletion of resources will make way for economic alternatives of equal or even superior quality and at reduced cost. Using language that contemporary ecofeminists would eagerly deconstruct, Barnett and Morse argued that industrial technology was virtually "turning the tables on nature, making her subservient to man." In their view, whatever resource scarcity may exist is always relative, never absolute, and substitution always solves it. Resource limits cannot be defined in economic terms, so their argument went, and therefore they must not exist. Attempting to conserve resources in the present might actually reduce the "heritage" of future generations because it could preclude future technological advances. Economist Julian Simon, writing in 1981, continued this anti-conservation argument, urging that the market price of resources should be the sole measure of their status. He maintained that trends in prices suggested that "future generations will be faced by no greater economic scarcity than we are, but instead will have just as large or larger supplies of resources to tap, despite our present use of them."[78]

Sustainable Development for the Common Good

Barnett, Morse, and Simon represent the super-optimistic economic view that sustains the culture of consumption. The process of relative scarcity and substitution they describe typifies the operation of the consumption economy thus far, but there is no solid evidence that it will be able to continue to grow in this way indefinitely into the future, or that it would even be desirable for it to do so. Less-orthodox economic theorists Herman E. Daly and John B. Cobb argued in 1989 that a weakness of perpetual growth economic models is that they externalize, and thus disregard, the physical/biological realities that real human communities depend on. They noted that money is an abstract symbol and suggested that it is "money fetishism" to believe that "if money balances can grow forever at compound interest, then so can real GNP, and so can pigs and cars."[79] The assumptions of Barnett and Morse were based largely on trends in the mining industry between 1870 and 1957 and ignored clear cases of increased costs and diminishing returns, especially as can now be seen in the energy sector. By 1987, as discussed in chapter 2, the mounting evidence of poverty, environmental deterioration, and resource depletion had become so undeniable at the global level that the UN-sponsored Brundtland Commission called for redirecting global economic goals toward sustainability. Unfortunately, some policymakers still seemed to deny the reality of limits to growth. For example, the 1993 study *World Without End*,[80] commissioned by the World Bank, argued that simply correcting "economic distortions" would make growth sustainable. It must be stressed that while development may indeed become sustainable, growth, by definition, cannot be sustained indefinitely.

The real problem in replacing the consumption culture is how best to conceptualize genuinely sustainable development, because sustainability will require a major change in the global economic order. Daly and Cobb point the way in their book *For the Common Good: Redirecting the Economy toward Community, the Environment, and a Sustainable Future*. Development for Daly and Cobb refers to an increase in Hicksonian Income (HI), as defined by Nobel Prize–winning British economist Sir John R. Hicks (1904–1989). Hicksonian Income is the amount that can be consumed over a given period without impoverishment and is calculated as GNP minus Production Costs minus Depletion of Natural Capital. HI is "a practical guide to avoid impoverishment by overconsumption."[81] An increase in HI would be sustainable by definition and does not require the continuous quantitative economic expansion implied in the usual meaning of economic growth. For example, development can be achieved by simply reducing the costs of pollution control or by improving conservation of resources. This HI concept of development recognizes that GNP by itself is a poor measure of the economic welfare of households and communities. In addition, this concept forces planners to take into account ecological carrying capacity. The HI approach also highlights the problem of global trading systems' permitting one region of the world to draw down the natural capital of another region, thereby extending what would otherwise be unsustainable consumption at someone else's expense.

Embracing sustainable development also means rejecting orthodox economic models that assume an insatiable individual human desire for commodities as the primary human motivation. Daly and Cobb note that aggressive advertising would be unnecessary if human acquisitiveness were truly insatiable and always satisfied within the marketplace. They point out that relative well-being within a society may be more important than absolute levels of economic wealth. Arguing in favor of local self-reliance, they cite resource economist Thomas M. Power, who suggests that the real economic base of a community includes, in addition to commodities, "all those things that make it an attractive place to live, work, or to do business. This means the economic base includes the quality of the natural environment, the richness of the local culture, the security and stability of the community, the quality of the public services and the public works infrastructure, and the quality of the workforce. None of these things are produced by the commercial economy or produced for export."[82]

Shifting the focus of economic activity away from perpetually acquisitive individuals to the long-term needs of communities and households for meaningful employment, security of access to resources, and the noncommercial things that make life worthwhile certainly does not mean that market systems must be abandoned. They simply need to be reshaped. The case study that follows is an example of the cost of a business-as-usual culture of consumption.

The Consumption Culture's Environmental Cost: Western Coal

Any culture that continues to accelerate consumption in a fixed environment will eventually be forced into making trade-offs between environmental quality and a continuation of its consumption pattern. By 2005 it was obvious that the fossil fuel base of America's consumption culture was seriously threatened—71 percent of its petroleum resources were being imported, up from 60 percent in 1998.[83] In the early 1970s, when petroleum imports stood at approximately 25 percent and it was recognized that nuclear energy would be more costly and hazardous than supposed, the government readied a plan to strip the coal reserves of the western states. The objective was to meet the projected needs of the country for ever-expanding energy consumption. In reality, energy consumption did not rise as rapidly as projected, but it did continue to increase. Under the new federal coal-leasing program, vast areas of the West, which had remained in almost pristine condition despite supporting Native American cultures for perhaps 20,000 years, were slated to be strip-mined on a massive scale to perpetuate the culture of consumption for a few more decades.

The 1974 *Draft Environmental Impact Statement*[84] dealing with the coal-leasing program and written by the Bureau of Land Management made clear the rationale for the stripping and concisely summarized the costs. The entire procedure is a remarkable example of the extremes to which over-consumption can drive a society. The fundamental assumption underlying the proposed stripping program was simply that economic growth could not be sustained without it: "We assume the first principal demand pressure for coal development will be from the physical and economic inability of the United States to obtain sufficient oil supplies to meet the demand generated by normal growth rates of the national economy."[85]

"Normal growth rates" meant that by the year 2000 the population was expected to have increased by less than 50 percent, but total energy consumption would have doubled. If we were having difficulties meeting our energy requirements in 1974, it should be no surprise that if total consumption more than doubled by the year 2000 it would be at an enormous cost. In fact, total American energy consumption did double between 1975 and 2000.[86]

Strip-mining coal involves removing all the overlying surface material, placing it to one side, and extracting the coal. Federal regulations require "rehabilitation" of the site, but this term must be broadly interpreted. The impact statement carefully summarized the immediate effects of surface mines in a way that implied that rehabilitation would be possible: "The operation completely eliminates existing vegetation, disrupts soil structure, alters current land uses, and to some extent changes the general topography of the area."[87]

The details buried in the report made it clear that rehabilitation would be very limited. Vegetation might re-grow, but surface drainage patterns may be disrupted, water sources might be eliminated, streams may be silted in and contaminated with toxic materials, big game wintering grounds and migration routes and wildlife habitat in general would be destroyed, archaeological sites would be destroyed, geological features and scenic resources would be destroyed or "disrupted," and miles of impassable "high walls" might be left. Where underground mining takes place, surface collapses might occur. Contamination by radioactive fly ash would occur in the vicinity of the coal-fired electric plants. Local communities would be disrupted by a temporary influx of outsiders. A variety of other detrimental impacts could be predicted. In summary, the "grand scale of the operation impacts significantly on the environment."

In 1978 President Carter confirmed in a speech to Congress that a major expansion in American coal production would indeed be pursued as a way of coping with the "energy crisis" and the country's increasing dependence on foreign oil. He asked for an increase in coal production by more than two-thirds by 1985. The bulk of the targeted coal reserves in the West were on Native American lands, and as the new energy development programs were implemented, there was widespread protest by impacted Native American communities angered over the potential destruction of their grazing land, the pollution, and the loss of critical irrigation water."[88]

"Restoration" of stripped areas was expected to require from twenty to thirty years, but the impact statement was concerned only with the period before 1985. "More lengthy projections" were considered "impractical." The statement glibly notes, however, that "man cannot immediately restore natural biotic communities." Experience with strip-mining in Appalachia indicates that the worst erosion and pollution problems may occur up to twenty-five years after mining; in some cases, spoil piles were still eroding sixty-five years after the coal had been extracted. Some researchers estimate that 800 to 3,000 years may be needed before toxic wastes will leach away.[89] We know for certain that the leased areas will never be the same again, but the total cost is incalculable. The major cost will be increased global warming, because burning coal is a major source of atmospheric carbon dioxide. Any technological cleanup operation to reduce carbon emissions from coal-fired plants will add costs to electric power. The best solution to the energy crisis is to reduce total demand.

Elite Decision Makers and the Consumption Culture

Perhaps the most critical anthropological question is this: Who are the human decision makers that ultimately drive the present consumption patterns of the consumption culture? We can say that over-consumption is not an innate human trait; it is culturally determined. It is also clear that high rates of consumption, or a lack of cultural limits on consumption, relate to social stratification and inequality within a culture, but there were many highly stratified, large-scale ancient civilizations that set limits to consumption. In those cases wealth was concentrated primarily in support of the political system. Perpetual wealth accumulation and increasing consumption are intrinsic to the commercial world that concentrates the greatest power in business corporations. First and foremost, this system disproportionately serves the personal interests of the global elite who control the great multinational corporations and financial institutions. This is not a mysterious, decentralized, amorphous system. Control functions and the distribution of costs and benefits can be identified. This chapter has shown how since 1400 a relatively few business managers and investors have made the crucial decisions that have created and maintained the culture of consumption. This means that other socio-cultural developments might produce more humane and more sustainable systems.

Because food is such a key human need, the following two chapters will further explore the problem of over-consumption, the distribution of costs and benefits, and control functions in the global system by comparing food systems in the tribal and commercial worlds.

Notes

1. Odum, Howard T. 1971. *Environment, Power, and Society.* New York: Wiley, Inter-Science.

2. White, Leslie A. 1949. *The Science of Culture.* New York: Grove, 367–68.

3. White, *Science of Culture*, 368–69.

4. Sahlins, Marshall. 1972. *Stone Age Economics.* Chicago: Aldine, 5–6.

5. Moseley, Michael Edward. 1975. *The Maritime Foundations of Andean Civilization.* Menlo Park, CA: Cummings; Quilter, Jeffrey, and Terry Stocker. 1983. "Subsistence Economies and the Origins of Andean Complex Societies." *American Anthropologist* 85(3): 545–62.

6. Ribeiro, Darcy. 1968. *The Civilizational Process.* Washington, D.C.: Smithsonian Institution Press.

7. Cook, Earl. 1971. "The Flow of Energy in an Industrial Society." *Scientific American* 224(3): 134–44.

8. United States Department of Energy. 2006. Annual Energy Review 2005. Energy Information Administration. Report No. DOE/EIA-0384(2005), Table 1.5, page 13. www.eia.doe.gov/emeu/aer/pdf/aer.pdf

9. United States Department of Energy. International Energy Annual, 2004. Energy Information Administration. Table F.2.

10. Cambridge Energy Research Associates (CERA), Press Release Nov. 14, 2006, "Correct Model for Post-2030 Oil Supply is Undulating Plateau." www.cera.com

11. Mike R. Bowlin. 1999. "Clean Energy: Preparing Today for Tomorrow's Challenges," Cambridge Energy Research Associates 18th Annual Executive Conference: Globality & Energy: Strategies for the New Millennium, Houston, TX. Cited in Brown, Lester R. 2000. "Challenges of the New Century." In *State of the World 2000: A Worldwatch Institute Report on Progress Toward a Sustainable Society*, edited by Lester R. Brown, Christopher Flavin, Hilary French, and Linda Starke, 1–21. New York and London: W. W. Norton and Co.

12. National Oceanic & Atmospheric Administration (NOAA), Earth System Research Laboratory, Global Monitoring Division. www.cmdl.noaa.gov/ccgg/trends/. Recent Monthly Mean CO2 at Mauna Loa.

13. IPCC (Intergovernmental Panel on Climate Change). 2001. *Climate Change 2001: Synthesis Report. Contribution of Work Groups I, II, and III to the Third Assessment.* Report of the Intergovernmental Panel on Climate Change. Edited by R. T. Watson. Cambridge and New York: Cambridge University Press.

14. Luten, Daniel B. 1974. "United States Requirements." In *Energy, the Environment, and Human Health,* edited by A. Finkel, 17–33. Acton, MA: Publishing Sciences Group, Inc.

15. Bodley, John H. 1975. *Victims of Progress.* Menlo Park, CA: Cummings, 4–5.

16. Fox, Richard Wightman, and T. J. Jackson Lears, eds. 1983. *The Culture of Consumption: Critical Essays in American History, 1880–1980.* New York: Pantheon Books; McCracken, Grant. 1988. *Culture and Consumption: New Approaches to the Symbolic Character of Consumer Goods and Activities.* Bloomington and Indianapolis: Indiana University Press; Miller, Daniel. 1987. *Material Culture and Mass Consumption.* Oxford and New York: Basil Blackwell, Inc.; Mills, C. Wright. 1963. "A Diagnosis of Our Moral Uneasiness." In *Power, Politics, and People,* edited by I. H. Horowitz. New York: Ballantine.

17. Applbaum, Kalman. 1998. "The Sweetness of Salvation: Consumer Marketing and the Liberal-Bourgeois Theory of Needs." *Current Anthropology* 19(3): 323–49.

18. Robbins, Richard H. 1999. *Global Problems and the Culture of Capitalism.* Boston: Allyn and Bacon, 12.

19. Robbins, *Global Problems,* 9.

20. Carrier, James G., and Josiah McC. Heyman. 1997. "Consumption and Political Economy." *Journal of the Royal Anthropological Institute* (N.S.) 3: 355–73.

21. Braudel, Fernand. 1977. *Afterthoughts on Material Civilization and Capitalism.* Baltimore and London: Johns Hopkins University Press; Braudel, Fernand. 1992. *Civilisation materielle, economic et capitalisme* (Civilization and Capitalism, 15th–18th Century). Berkeley: University of California Press; Wallerstein, Immanuel. 1974. *The Modern World-System: Capitalist Agriculture and the Origins of the European World-Economy in the Sixteenth Century.* New York: Academic Press; Wolf, Eric R. 1982. *Europe and the People Without History.* Berkeley: University of California Press.

22. Rabb, Theodore K. 1967. *Enterprise and Empire: Merchant and Gentry Investment in the Expansion of England, 1515–1630.* Cambridge, MA: Harvard University Press.

23. Stone, Lawrence. 1965. *The Crisis of the Aristocracy 1558–1641.* London: Oxford University Press; Fischer, David Hackett. 1996. *The Great Wave: Price Revolutions and the Rhythm of History.* New York and Oxford: Oxford University Press.

24. Chaudhuri, K. N. 1965. *The English East India Company: The Study of an Early Joint-Stock Company 1600–1640.* London: Frank Cass & Co.

25. King, Gregory. 1936. *Two Tracts: (a) Natural and Political Observations and Conclusions upon the State and Condition of England and (b) Of the Naval Trade of England Ao. 1688 and the National Profit Then Arising Thereby*, edited by George E. Barnett. Baltimore: Johns Hopkins University Press. Originally published in 1696.

26. Stone, Lawrence. 1965. *The Crisis of the Aristocracy 1558–1641*. London: Oxford University Press, 3–15.

27. McKendrick, Neil. 1982b. "The Consumer Revolution of Eighteenth-Century England." In *The Birth of a Consumer Society: The Commercialization of Eighteenth-Century England*, edited by Neil McKendrick, John Brewer, and J. H. Plumb, 9–33. Bloomington: Indiana University Press.

28. Berry, Christopher J. 1994. *The Idea of Luxury: A Conceptual and Historical Investigation*. Cambridge: Cambridge University Press.

29. McKendrick, Neil. 1982a. "The Commercialization of Fashion." In *The Birth of a Consumer Society: The Commercialization of Eighteenth-Century England*, edited by Neil McKendrick, John Brewer, and J. H. Plumb, 34–99. Bloomington: Indiana University Press.

30. Hooper, Wilfrid. 1915. "The Tudor Sumptuary Laws." *English Historical Review* 30(119): 433–49.

31. Shammas, Carole. 1990. *The Pre-industrial Consumer in England and America*. Oxford: Oxford University Press; Shammas, Carole. 1993. "Changes in English and Anglo-American Consumption from 1550 to 1800." In *Consumption and the World of Goods*, edited by John Brewer and Roy Porter, 177–205. London and New York: Routledge.

32. Wills, John E., Jr. 1993. "European Consumption and Asian Production in the Seventeenth and Eighteenth Centuries." In *Consumption and the World of Goods*, edited by John Brewer and Roy Porter, 133–47. London and New York: Routledge.

33. Odum, Howard T. 1971. *Environment, Power, and Society*. New York: Wiley, Inter-Science, 17.

34. Rathje, William L., and Cullen Murphy. 1992. *Rubbish: The Archaeology of Garbage*. New York: HarperCollins Publishers.

35. Boulding, Kenneth. 1966. "The Economics of the Coming Spaceship Earth." In *Environmental Quality in a Growing Economy: Essays from the Sixth Resources for the Future Forum*, edited by Henry Jarrett, 3–14. Baltimore: Johns Hopkins University Press.

36. Estes, Ralph. 1996. *Tyranny of the Bottom Line: Why Corporations Make Good People Do Bad Things*. San Francisco: Berrett-Kohler Publishers, 177–78.

37. Mills. "A Diagnosis of Our Moral Uneasiness," 33; Simon, David R. 1999. *Elite Deviance*. 6th ed. Boston: Allyn and Bacon.

38. Sklair, Leslie. 1991. *Sociology of the Global System*. Baltimore, MD: Johns Hopkins University Press, 42.

39. Wallerstein, Immanuel. 1990. "Culture as the Ideological Battleground of the Modern World-System." *Theory, Culture, and Society* 7: 31–55.

40. Sklair, *Global System*, 54.

41. Sklair, *Global System*, 41.

42. Ewen, Stuart. 1976. *Captains of Consciousness: Advertising and the Social Roots of the Consumer Culture*. New York: McGraw-Hill.

43. Sklair, *Global System*, 41

44. Jhally, Sut. 1997. *Advertising and the End of the World*. Transcript. Northampton, MA: Media Education Foundation, 10. www.mediaed.org/handouts/pdfs/AEW.pdf

45. *Advertising Age*. 2006. "Special Report: 100 Leading National Advertisers." Supplement (June 26), 5.

46. U.S. Department of Education, National Center for Education Statistics. 2005. *Revenues and Expenditures for Public Elementary and Secondary Education: School Year 2002-2003* (NCES 2005-353), nces.ed.gov/ccd/pubs/npefs03/findings.asp#3

47. Mazur, Allan, and Eugene Rosa. 1974. "Energy and Life Style." *Science* 186(4164): 607–10.

48. Venetoulis, Jason, and Cliff Cobb. 2004. *The Genuine Progress Indicator 1950–2002 (2004 Update)*. Oakland, CA: Redefining Progress. www.rprogress.org/projects/gpi/

49. Johnson, Allen. 1975. "Time Allocation in a Machiguenga Community." *Ethnology* 14(3): 301–10; Johnson, Allen. 1985. "In Search of the Affluent Society." In *Anthropology: Contemporary Perspectives*, edited by David E. K. Hunter and Phillip Whitten, 201–6. Boston: Little, Brown. First published in *Human Nature*, September 1978; McCarthy, F. D., and Margaret McArthur. 1960. "The Food Quest and Time Factor in Aboriginal Economic Life." In *Records of the American-Australian Scientific Expedition to Arnhem Land*, edited by C. P. Mountford, vol. 2, *Anthropology and Nutrition*, 145–94. Melbourne: Melbourne University Press.

50. McCarthy and McArthur, "Food Quest," 145–94.

51. Vanek, Joann. 1974. "Time Spent in Housework." *Scientific American* 23(15): 116–20.

52. *World Almanac and Book of Facts*. 2004. New York: World Almanac Books, 268.

53. Cook, "Flow of Energy," 134–44.

54. Landsberg, Hans H. 1964. *Natural Resources in America's Future: A Look Ahead to the Year 2000*. Baltimore, MD: Johns Hopkins University Press; Landsberg, Hans H., Leonard L. Fischman, and Joseph L. Fisher. 1963. *Resources in America's Future: Patterns of Requirements and Availabilities 1960–2000*. Baltimore, MD: Johns Hopkins University Press.

55. U.S. Department of Energy, Energy Information Administration. 2007. *Monthly Energy Review*. (January), Table 1.2 Energy Consumption by Source.

56. Dewhurst, J. Frederic, and Associates. 1955. *America's Needs and Resources: A New Survey*. New York: Twentieth Century Fund, 754.

57. Keenleyside, H. L. 1950. "Critical Mineral Shortages." In *Proceedings of the United Nations Scientific Conference on the Conservation and Utilization of Resources*, August 17–September 6, 1949, 38–46. Lake Success, NY: United Nations, 38.

58. Keenleyside, "Mineral Shortages," 38.

59. Dewhurst, J. Frederic, and Associates. 1947. *America's Needs and Resources: A Twentieth Century Fund Survey Which Includes Estimates for 1950 and 1960*. New York: Twentieth Century Fund.

60. Dewhurst, J. Frederic, and Associates. 1955. *America's Needs and Resources: A New Survey*. New York: Twentieth Century Fund.

61. Dewhurst, *America's Needs: New Survey*, 754–55.

62. U.S. President's Materials Policy Commission. 1952. *Resources for Freedom*. Paley Commission Report. Washington, D.C.: U.S. Government Printing Office.

63. Landsberg, Hans H., Leonard L. Fischman, and Joseph L. Fisher. 1963. *Resources in America's Future: Patterns of Requirements and Availabilities 1960–2000*. Baltimore, MD: Johns Hopkins University Press.

64. Landsberg, *Natural Resources*, 13.

65. Dewhurst, *America's Needs: New Survey*, 939.

66. Landsberg, Fischman, and Fisher, *Resources in America's Future*, 256.

67. Western Wood Products Association. 2002. *Lumber Track*. (Oct. 2002). www.wwpa.org/econpubs.htm

68. Powell, Douglas S., Joanne L. Faulkner, David R. Darr, Zhiliang Zhu, and Douglas W. MacCleery. 1993. *Forest Resources of the United States, 1992*. Rocky Mountain Forest and Range Experiment Station, General Technical Report RM-234. Fort Collins, CO: USDA, Forest Service, 20.

69. Brooks, David J. 1993. *U.S. Forests in a Global Context*. USDA Technical Report RM-228. Fort Collins, CO: U.S. Department of Agriculture, Forest Service, Rocky Mountain Forest and Range Experiment Station.

70. Landsberg, Fischman, and Fisher, *Resources in America's Future*, 365.

71. Western Wood Products Association, *Lumber Track*.

72. National Research Council, Committee on Mineral Resources and the Environment. 1975. *Mineral Resources and the Environment*. Washington, D.C.: National Academy of Sciences.

73. Solow, Robert M. 1974. "The Economics of Resources or the Resources of Economics." *American Economic Review* 64(2): 1–14.

74. Payne, Roger. 1968. "Among Wild Whales." *New York Zoological Society Newsletter*, November, 1–6.

75. Nicklin, Flip. 1984. "Krill: Untapped Bounty from the Sea?" *National Geographic* 165: 626–43.

76. Barnett, Harold, and Chandler Morse. 1963. *Scarcity and Growth: The Economics of Natural Resource Availability*. Baltimore, MD: Johns Hopkins University Press.

77. Barnett and Morse, *Scarcity and Growth*, 7.

78. Simon, Julian. 1981. *The Ultimate Resource*. Princeton, NJ: Princeton University Press, 149.

79. Daly, Herman E., and John B. Cobb. 1989. *For the Common Good: Redirecting the Economy Toward Community, the Environment, and a Sustainable Future*. Boston: Beacon Press, 37.

80. Pearce, David W., and Jeremy J. Warford. 1993. *World Without End: Economics, Environment, and Sustainable Development*. New York: Published for the World Bank by Oxford University Press.

81. Daly and Cobb, *For the Common Good*, 84.

82. Power, Thomas Michael. 1988. *The Economic Pursuit of Quality*. Armonk, NY: M. E. Sharpe, 127.

83. U.S. Department of Energy. 2006. *Annual Energy Review 2005*. Energy Information Administration. Report No. DOE/EIA-0384(2005), Table 1.1.

84. U.S. Department of the Interior, Bureau of Land Management. 1974. *Draft Environmental Impact Statement: Proposed Federal Coal Leasing Program*. 2 vols. Washington, D.C.: U.S. Government Printing Office.

85. U.S. Department of the Interior, Bureau of Land Management, *Coal Leasing Program*, part 1, 8.

86. U.S. Department of Energy, Energy Information Administration. 2006. *Annual Energy Review 2005*. Report No. DOE/EIA-0384(2005), Table 1.1.

87. U.S. Department of the Interior, Bureau of Land Management, *Coal Leasing Program*, part 3, 33.

88. Anthropology Resource Center. 1978. *Native Americans and Energy Development*. Cambridge, MA: ARC.

89. Spaulding, Willard M., Jr., and Ronald D. Ogden. 1968. *Effects of Surface Mining on the Fish and Wildlife Resources of the United States*. Bureau of Sport Fisheries and Wildlife Resources Publication 68. Washington, D.C.: U.S. Government Printing Office.

Malnutrition and the Evolution of Food Systems

4

[The] power of obtaining an additional quantity of food from the earth by proper management and in a certain time has the most remote relation imaginable to the power of keeping pace with an unrestricted increase of population.

—THOMAS R. MALTHUS,
AN ESSAY ON THE PRINCIPLE OF POPULATION[1]

As long as food is something bought and sold in a society with great income differences, the degree of hunger tells us nothing about the density of the population.

—FRANCES MOORE LAPPÉ AND JOSEPH COLLINS,
FOOD FIRST: BEYOND THE MYTH OF SCARCITY[2]

FOOD SYSTEMS ARE CULTURAL MECHANISMS for meeting basic human nutritional needs. Every food system must confront two general problems if it is to continue to perform satisfactorily: (1) It must avoid long-term depletion of the natural resource base; and (2) It must equitably distribute essential nutrients to people. The existence of widespread malnutrition in the modern world indicates that many food systems are not performing adequately, but in many cases the immediate problem is distribution, not production. Ultimately, there are physical limits to food production, but culturally defined dietary patterns, production technologies, and distribution systems have a great effect on per capita energy costs of food production.

Since the Paleolithic, production techniques have steadily intensified as human populations have increased. Yet it also seems clear, as British economist Thomas R. Malthus observed, that population always has the potential of increasing more rapidly than production. It also seems likely that chronic malnutrition is rooted in the structural aspects of society, particularly inequalities of wealth and power, in cultures that make food a commercial commodity and thereby limit its distribution to people.

The Malthusian Dilemma

The power of the earth to produce subsistence is certainly not unlimited, but it is strictly speaking indefinite; that is, its limits are not defined, and the time will probably never arrive when we shall be able to say that no further labour or ingenuity of man could make further additions to it. But the power of obtaining an additional quantity of food from the earth by proper management and in a certain time has the most remote relation imaginable to the power of keeping pace with an unrestricted increase of population. (Malthus)[3]

Malthus was certainly the most influential early writer to raise the fundamental question of the relationship between population growth and food production. Along with prominent fellow, now "classical," economists of his day—including Adam Smith and David Ricardo—Malthus had concluded that economic growth would ultimately be limited by the productivity of land and nature. In effect, they all believed that economic growth could not continue indefinitely, and they anticipated a stationary economy in the future. Modern economist E. A. Wrigley[4] argues that these classical economists did not appreciate the growth potential of the technological transformations that were under way at the time. In 1798 Malthus was viewing the middle period of the early Industrial Revolution of 1760–1830. The newly developing use of fossil fuels was indeed a "technological paradigm shift," as Wrigley observes, that at least temporarily raised the growth threshold beyond what Malthus had imagined, but even Wrigley acknowledges that it is now "questionable whether indefinite growth is compatible with a safe and stable environment."[5]

Writing in 1798, Malthus argued that, if unchecked, human population has the natural capacity to expand at a geometric, or exponential, rate, while over the long run food production could only be expected to increase at an arithmetic, or linear, rate. The capacity for population growth is largely an empirical question, and Malthus had data to support the view that a doubling every twenty-five years was possible. Reliable data on food production through time were unfortunately not available, but Malthus merely assumed that there were in fact ultimate limits and that, whatever those limits were, food production could not long be expected to keep pace with a doubling population. He felt that as population began to press on the subsistence base, "misery," in the form of poverty, would tend to reduce population growth, while greater efforts would be made to increase production through opening new land and improving agricultural methods until eventually a balance would be restored. Malthus was convinced that these principles were self-evident laws of nature. Unfortunately, Malthus succeeded in making poverty appear to be *natural* rather than *cultural* and provided a seemingly scientific justification for either refusing aid to the poor or sending them surpluses, and promoting capital-intensive factory farming rather than advocating political and economic democracy.[6]

In many respects cultural evolution has been based on efforts to avoid hunger by maintaining a secure subsistence base while minimizing the pain of regulating population. Diminishing returns are experienced in the intensification of food production systems. This is the Malthusian dilemma, and in a general sense Malthus was quite right. The evolution of food systems in the tribal world can often be reasonably viewed in these terms, but in a world dominated by commercial interests and characterized by great inequality it would be a mistake to assume that natural limits such as overpopulation and inadequate production are the primary causes of hunger. It now seems obvious that hunger is also caused by powerlessness, landlessness, and poverty and can be reduced by changes in social and economic policies designed to provide people with the resources to feed themselves. Hunger was not a characteristic of the tribal world because tribal peoples made the equitable satisfaction of the most basic human needs a primary social objective.

To illustrate the operation of his "laws," Malthus projected population and food production trends for Britain and the world and correctly showed how quickly an exponentially growing population would surpass a linearly expanding food production system. Many of his critics misunderstood him on this point. He did not make specific predictions for future demographic patterns but merely tried to show how unchecked population growth would compare with what he felt were optimistic projections for increases in food production, assuming the operation of diminishing returns. There is remarkable evidence of an apparent Malthusian food shortage in central Europe that was occurring when Malthus first published *An Essay on the Principle of Population* in 1798, but social inequality and the maldistribution of capital remained the most crucial problems. Europeans were experiencing another wave of declining wages, escalating rents and food prices, and increasing returns on capital. The elite were flourishing, while the poor were declining into misery.[7] Using government records, John Komlos[8] documented a prolonged decline in the average height of military recruits in the Hapsburg monarchy from 1740 to 1800, which he attributed to a decline in food intake. In this case, just as Malthus predicted for a land-constrained system, population growth produced by an earlier episode of favorable weather and good crops was followed by a decline in production and wages, reduced consumption of meat and grain, and stunted growth for children. Most elites probably avoided the food shortages, but not everyone ignored the plight of the poor. The Hapsburg rulers responded to the emergency by redistributing income to the peasantry and encouraging increased industrial production.

The Malthusian theoretical model of world population growth with a doubling time of twenty-five years was three times higher than what actually occurred between 1800 and 2000, but by 1800 world population was growing exponentially. Viewed from the perspective of the actual history of population growth from 1500 to 2000, Malthus's projection of an unprecedented expansion of population was correct. Remarkably, his estimate for a linear increase in food production yields figures that would support a global population of 9 billion in the year 2000, even more optimistic than the actual population of 6 billion. Judged by history up to the year 2000, his theory was wrong; food production stayed ahead of population growth far longer than he expected. By the year 2000, however, it was clear that many regional food-producing systems were experiencing seriously diminishing returns and were approaching or exceeding crucial thresholds.

Thanks to dramatic technological advances, great expenditures of fossil fuel energy, and expansion into marginal agricultural lands, it appears that from 1950 to 1984 global food production stayed ahead of the unprecedented expansion of population. Since then food production seems to be faltering as both absolute and per capita yields level off or even decline.[9] This does not mean that absolute global food production limits are being reached, because there is still enormous elasticity in subsistence choices and food allocation systems. Nevertheless, as we will explore shortly, hunger has become a serious global problem, making it appear that in some areas human "misery" could act as a "natural" check on population growth just as Malthus predicted. In a general sense the statistics on hunger suggest that the world is now experiencing a "Malthusian crisis," but it must be emphasized that it is largely a cultural, not a natural, problem, because many cultural choices remain that would not violate the physical limits on the expansion of subsistence. Social inequality within and between nations and the specific ways in which the global food system is commercially organized can significantly accelerate the appearance of Malthusian symptoms.

The Evolution of Food Systems

In a sense, the Malthusian dilemma—the need to balance the power of population with the power of food production—is the most basic adaptive problem that any society must successfully solve if it is to survive for any length of time. Anthropologists have devoted a large share of their research efforts to examining subsistence systems in various cultures, and archaeologists have focused much of their research on the evolution of food-producing systems. The major findings in both fields have contributed to a better understanding of today's food systems.

Much of the early theoretical literature on the evolution of food systems was cluttered by a consistent tendency to view each change in subsistence as a hard-won major improvement that was achieved only through some brilliant invention. Furthermore, "advances" in food production have traditionally been considered prerequisites for increases in population and other forms of evolutionary progress. These views apparently reflect the popular tendency to view all problems as simple technological issues and to underrate the intelligence of peoples in domestic-scale cultures. More recent approaches to food systems have been more balanced. At least three different interpretations of the causal factors underlying changes in subsistence technologies in the tribal world have been proposed.

The first approach, the Population Pressure Model, argues that increases in population mean that more food must be produced per unit of space.[10] This model reverses the earlier view that new inventions allowed population to increase. A second approach, the Optimization Model, assumes that people are striving for the most energy-efficient production techniques that will satisfy basic nutritional needs.[11] This interpretation meshes well with the Population Pressure Model and allows one to predict what new techniques might be adopted if efficiency declines as population increases. However, efficiency analyses are usually based on average production rates and might not adequately consider long-term fluctuation in resource availability or environmental variables. Finally, the Risk-Minimizing, Subsistence Security Model argues that people are always most concerned with the long-run security of subsistence.[12] This argument is not a revival of the earlier view that tribal peoples are always on the brink of starvation; instead it calls attention to the diverse measures these peoples have applied to maintain long-term subsistence reliability, or resilience. Certainly all these factors—population stress, energy efficiency, and overall security—in varying degrees shaped the food systems in the tribal world for tens of thousands of years. Politically centralized imperial societies, with their built-in incentives to increase food production to support political elites and non-food producing specialists, along with the commercially driven economic structures of the global system, have distorted and displaced these adaptive processes such that today famine and malnutrition are commonplace and food systems are very complex and fragile.

Foraging and Subsistence Security

Anthropologist Brian Hayden[13] presented an overview of subsistence strategies from the first appearance of hominids to the beginnings of farming following the Subsistence Security approach. Throughout, it appears that people have consistently sought to maintain maximum subsistence security and stability at the lowest possible cost in subsistence effort or population regulation. This involves difficult decisions, and people probably leaned toward security in spite of the cost. A successfully balanced food system can be disturbed by either natural decline in the resource base (caused perhaps by climatic changes) or a relative increase in the human population. Regulating population involves personal and psychological as well as social costs, as we will discuss later, but it certainly contributes to subsistence security. Increased subsistence effort and regional exchange backup networks also mean greater security.

According to Hayden, during the Lower Paleolithic early hominids were probably able to scavenge and opportunistically capture only a few species of small animals. As both organizational and physical abilities increased during the Middle Paleolithic, archaic Homo sapiens and Neanderthal subsistence diversified to include larger herbivores. Because a wider range of food sources became available, subsistence presumably became more reliable. During the Upper Paleolithic, beginning perhaps 50,000 years ago, physically modern humans developed highly effective hunting techniques and tools, including spear-throwers and finely made stone projectile points. During this period, virtually all game animals, including carnivores, were possible prey. This wide inventory of food resources would have helped minimize the stress caused by the large-scale climatic and environmental fluctuations that occurred throughout the Pleistocene.

Further increases in subsistence reliability during the Mesolithic, beginning about 14,000 years ago, involved significant use of small, rapidly reproducing, short-lived species (which biologists have called "r-species"), such as insects, fish, shellfish, and grasses. These species were available in relative abundance but required special techniques to harvest and process efficiently. Thus, during this time grinding tools, nets, hooks, baskets, the bow and arrow, and hunting dogs all came into common use in many parts of the world. These new production and processing methods certainly expanded the available range of food and would have provided a greater cushion against resource shortages, but they also involved greater effort and reduced energetic efficiency. Wild grass seeds, for example, may be very abundant seasonally, but they are not easy to harvest in quantity and must be threshed, winnowed, milled, and cooked before they can be consumed. It seems unlikely that people would have included grass seeds in their diets unless they significantly increased subsistence security.

Even the most reliable local system of food production might still be vulnerable to unpredictable environmental factors such as periodic drought, so tribal peoples evolved mechanisms for maintaining permanent home territories while encouraging use of their resources by outsiders. Kinship ties and ritual practices provided opportunities for widespread sharing of resources, thereby providing an extra margin of security.

It appears that during the Mesolithic people began to culturally manipulate their food resources by methods such as selective burning, as discussed earlier, and also by replanting roots, scattering seeds, and diverting water to increase wild plant productivity.[14] The productivity of game would be further increased by selectively killing certain age or sex categories, removing competing predators, and holding and breeding captives.[15] The result of these practices may ultimately have been "domestication" as it is usually conceived.

Ironically, although the drive to maintain subsistence security may have ultimately resulted in domestication, it is not totally clear that settled farm life was an obvious improvement over nomadic or semi-nomadic foraging. Foragers generally have a convenient cushion against food shortages because their subsistence depends on collecting food from a diverse range of species drawn from complex and stable natural or only partially modified ecosystems. Hunters can easily switch and choose among a variety of wild foods in the event that specific food sources fail, and if local conditions become very bad they may temporarily join their kin in more favorable areas. Farmers, however, must rely on a few domestic species grown in artificial, highly simplified, and relatively unstable ecosystems vulnerable to many kinds of disruptions. When crop failures occur, famine is almost certain to follow if people do not have access to alternative resources or if elites remove storable surpluses. Even regular seasonal scarcity, such as that preceding harvest, may be more exaggerated among farmers. For example, Richard Lee found no significant weight loss for the !Kung Bushmen during the severest season of the year, whereas West African farmers showed losses of 6 percent of body weight before harvest season.[16]

Clear testimony to the greater overall security of foraging adaptations is also afforded by the cases on record of farming peoples joining neighboring foragers in order to weather droughts,[17] and by the common tendency of foragers to reject farming until it is absolutely forced on them. There are also cases of farmers who became foragers when the right conditions presented themselves. This is, of course, not to argue that occasional hungry times never occurred before farming. We know that people have sometimes starved in the harsh and often unpredictable conditions of the Arctic, yet it seems that hunger is less frequent and less devastating for foragers.

The Shift to Farms and Gardens

Not only is farming less secure than food collecting, but it often involves longer, more monotonous work and a loss of independence and mobility. In some cases it has even meant a switch to nutritionally inferior foods. Some anthropologists also point to demographic evidence of a decline in life expectancy for some populations after domestication, as well as a significant increase in women's domestic work loads.[18] Given so many disadvantages, it seems remarkable that people ever bothered with domestication. Indeed, the explanation for domestication has been one of the longest-running theoretical debates in anthropology.

It has become increasingly apparent that domestication was not a sudden or unique technological discovery. At best, it was a long process of transformation that occurred independently in perhaps five or more major areas of the world. Theories that stress the "invention" aspect of the process are quite misleading because there is no reason to believe that peoples with the accumulated knowledge of many thousands of years of plant collecting would not realize that plants grew from seeds and cuttings. There are also many examples of food collectors who lived next to, or maintained trade contacts with, food producers for centuries and were well acquainted with the basics of farm life but apparently had no desire to emulate it. Australian Aborigines, for example, maintained contacts with New Guinean village people who raised pigs and planted gardens, but they did not themselves take up farming.

The Domestic Mode of Food Production

In addition to the obvious technological differences, food production in the tribal world, whether by foraging, gardening, farming, or herding, differs in other very important respects from production in the food systems found in politically centralized, or commercial, cultures. Many of these critical differences were outlined in 1972 in an important book by Marshall Sahlins, *Stone Age Economics*.[19] According to Sahlins, when food production is primarily for local, household, or village domestic consumption, as in all tribal cultures, actual production tends to be far below the maximum that might be sustained given the potential limitations of technology, labor force, and natural resources. The result of this "underproduction" is that the danger of a tribal society ever exceeding the carrying capacity of its environment at a given technological level is greatly reduced, as is the likelihood of environmental deterioration and famine. On the other hand, as political development occurs and social scale and complexity increases, food production must accelerate, as does the possibility of overshooting carrying capacities and the attendant famine and environmental deterioration.

The concept of carrying capacity is a crude device for discussing the relationships among population, technology, and resource base. In theory, all these are in relative balance in tribal societies over the long run because even slight imbalances over 1,000 years would almost certainly force a system change. However, any balance is always relative and can be disrupted frequently and easily. Balance is also difficult to demonstrate empirically because it might be impossible to realistically calculate the food production potential of any particular environment for a given tribal group, especially when cyclical fluctuations in resource availability are involved.[20] Because of such complexity, resilience and ecological footprints are more useful measures of successful human interaction with natural systems.[21]

Another approach to underproduction, which avoids the problem of carrying capacity, is simply to assess the labor potential of a given culture and evaluate how hard the population is working at food production.[22] There is actually very wide cross-cultural variation in the length of average working life span, the division of labor by gender, and seasonal labor. The outputs of individual households also vary within a given society. For example, young adults may often be only marginally involved in food production, and tribal societies often retire adults far sooner than may be the case in the imperial and cultural worlds. In tribal societies generally labor tends to be irregular and intermittent. Particular tasks are easily and frequently postponed for what might seem to be trivial reasons—because of the weather, for a nap, for visiting, for feasting, or for no reason at all.

Among farming peoples, and in some cases even among hunters, there can be seasonal slack periods with virtually no hunting or farming. There are also wide tolerances of individual variation in work load; some persons do far more than their "share" while others consistently loaf. The concept of "work" as opposed to "play" or "leisure" may not even be an important distinction in all cultures. There seems little doubt that most tribal peoples could easily produce a "surplus" of food above their own immediate subsistence needs if they merely worked a little harder, put in a few more hours a week, or slightly reshuffled their labor force. The limitation on production, then, is not inadequate technology or a scarcity of natural resources. It is the presence of a built-in cultural limit; phrased negatively, there is a cultural lack of incentive to raise production in tribal societies in which production is essentially for domestic use.

Sahlins argues that what makes "Stone Age" or tribal economies unique in comparison with "more advanced" economies is that in tribal economies the basic production unit, and therefore the dominant institution, is the household. This creates a qualitatively very remarkable kind of economy whose operation can be understood only on its own terms. Most important, within this domestic mode of production lies a major key to the adaptive success of tribal societies.

The domestic mode of production is created by marriage, a minimal division of labor by gender, and a materially simple technology that is available to all and in which each household can perform all the technological functions itself. The critical point is that the primary objective of production is domestic use—the satisfaction of the most basic human needs such as nutrition. Food production goals are thus set by the individual food-consuming household. When the specific need is met—daily in the case of foragers, annually in the case of garden planting—labor ceases. The system is not normally designed to produce an exchangeable surplus above domestic needs. In a commercial market economy, production is for exchange, for cash, or for profit. There is no culturally recognized limit to production because the need for financial wealth is infinitely expandable. The distinctive features of food production in the commercial world will be discussed in detail in chapter 5, but here it may be noted that the contrasts between the mode of production in a tribal society and the capitalist mode of production are so great that much of the economic behavior of tribal peoples in contact with market-oriented outsiders has been considered quite irrational. What has been interpreted as laziness or ignorance on the part of tribals is actually the operation of a unique and very adaptive system of food production.

The general egalitarianism of tribal cultures is an obvious element in the success of tribal subsistence systems. All households typically enjoy free access to the natural resources needed for their subsistence. Various redistributive mechanisms may be initiated when serious local imbalances result because of random fluctuations in demography or subsistence success. A further stabilizing factor is reciprocal pooling of food and redistribution along kinship networks, which assure a relatively uniform distribution of nutrients. As a result, everyone is likely to enjoy the same nutritional standard.

Technological Advances in Food Production

If population densities are to rise, food production must be intensified either by increased labor or by technological improvements, or both. How this might occur in a tribal culture is an interesting theoretical problem because, as we have seen, food production is relatively frozen by the shutoff factors inherent in the domestic mode of production in the absence of either political or market incentives, and population growth is normally minimized by the operation of the equilibrium mechanisms outlined in chapter 6. In effect, there is normally no Malthusian dilemma in tribal culture because the forces of population and food production are continuously kept in check. Thus, we must reconsider the question of whether technological advances in food production cause population growth or whether population growth itself causes advances in food production. The most basic determining factors would appear to lie in the actual arrangement of the social system. Tribal social systems, as we have seen, are structured to restrain both population and food production. They are, by definition, no-growth systems. Growth of either population or food production—or both—may, however, be deliberately promoted and even institutionalized within more complex social systems.

Within societies organized around the domestic mode of production there is a constant struggle to balance the demands of the society at large, which extracts food from individual households by means of kinship obligations based on the immediate self-interest of each individual household. If growth of either population or food production is to occur, a social system must develop that will tap "underdeveloped" resources and transform the domestic mode of production into something else. Political authority must overcome the natural tendency of individual households to set their own production goals and to maintain their economic autonomy over and against the interests of the larger society or against the self-interest of aspiring rulers. The political order must establish a public economy. "Big-man" leadership systems, segmentary lineage and clan systems, and hierar-chical chiefdoms all represent different sociopolitical strategies for mobilizing productivity above the cutoff point normally operating in the domestic mode of production while still remaining within the limitations of a kin-based, non-state social system. Historically, the initial step was the construction of political economies, and what archaeologist Timothy Earle calls "Bronze Age Economics."[23]

Population growth, subsistence intensification, and increasing social complexity are so interrelated that it is not easy to decide which process most influences the structure of a food system, although population growth has often been regarded as a primary factor. Many theorists assume that technological improvements that demand greater intensification of la-bor will come about only in the presence of population pressure. Con-versely, they may be facilitated by the prior existence of certain levels of sociopolitical organization. A complex irrigation system, for example, would probably not be initiated by a society that lacked effective supralo-cal forms of political control, although a full-time central authority might not be required. For their part, more complex forms of social organization may often become necessary as disputes over access to resources begin to arise under increasing population pressure.

Danish economist Ester Boserup[24] (1910–1999) argued that all techno-logical changes in "primitive" agriculture can be viewed as responses to population pressure. Her approach is very similar to that used by anthro-pologists to explain the transition from hunting to farming. She assumes that the earliest, simplest farming techniques, such as shifting cultivation, were more productive per hour of labor than the more advanced systems but less productive per unit of land. People would automatically prefer such extensive methods; that is, these methods simply required less work to produce food than more intensive methods. There is indeed a clear rela-tionship between the frequency of cropping in a given unit of land and the density of population. Denser populations require more intensive land use. Fallow periods may well be shortened as a direct response to increased pop-ulation in local areas, and this shortening of fallow periods or more intense land use will initiate ecological changes that force the use of new technol-ogy. Under a typical swidden or "forest fallow" system, a simple digging stick is all that is required for planting in newly cleared, virtually weed-free forest. However, when the fallow cycle is shortened because of the need to increase food production in a limited area, the increasing appearance of weeds makes hoes necessary. Continued shortening of fallow periods will lead to grasses that can only be cultivated effectively with plows.

From this viewpoint, advances in food production can be seen not as brilliant inventions that in turn cause population growth, but rather as being forced on people by prior population growth. It would make no sense at all for shifting cultivators with adequate forest resources to invent a plow, because it simply would not fit their mode of land use and would not be an advantage. It must not be forgotten, however, that intensification in food production will, of course, reinforce the need for further intensification by supporting and amplifying the prior deviation from population equilibrium. Archaeologist Kent Flannery called this process of population growth and subsistence intensification "deviation amplification,"[25] describing it as a self-intensifying spiral.

Politically Directed Food Systems

The coercive food systems directed by politically centralized societies such as chiefdoms and agrarian civilizations contrast sharply with the relative autonomy and abundance enjoyed by households in the tribal world. Political elites used military force and ideological compulsion to extract food surpluses from local villages and households in the form of taxes or tribute far above the levels that people would require for their own needs. Ancient civilizations required permanent administrative bureaucracies, but they also had to support large labor forces on massive construction projects. Most of the grain that fed these non-food-producing specialists was extracted from the peasantry or produced on state-run farms by peasant labor. For example, in Ch'ing dynasty China under the Manchu rulers (1644–1911) some 40,000 people were part of the formal administrative bureaucracy, in addition to the 700 people who belonged to the emperor's clan. Another 1.5 million scholar-bureaucrats were a privileged elite with significant degrees of local control.[26] All of these elites and their non-food-producing specialists were provisioned by the labor of peasant-farmer households that constituted more than 90 percent of the total population. In ancient China, in addition to the permanent bureaucracy and specialists, a vast conscripted labor army was mobilized for construction projects such as the 1,400-mile (2,250-kilometer) Great Wall and the 1,000-mile (1,600-kilometer) Grand Canal. Furthermore, virtually all ancient city-states, kingdoms, and empires were on a permanent war footing and needed vast stores of surplus food in order to provision armies engaged in military campaigns.

In politically directed food systems elites allocate access to productive resources such as land and water according to social class and status, and as shown previously, significant segments of the population have no direct involvement in food production decision making. This arrangement makes it quite likely that nutrients will no longer be equally distributed—some classes may indeed be relatively hungry while other classes are "over-nourished." For example, even as commercial elites began to take political power in Europe from 1760 to 1800, there were dramatic differences in height and growth rate for boys by social class.[27] At age fifteen poor boys in London averaged 8.3 inches (21 cm) shorter than their gentry counterparts. A combination of differential access to subsistence resources and inequitable distribution of nutrients by social class is, as we have seen, one of the basic correlates of hunger in the modern world. However, because ancient rulers derived their power from human labor it would have been counterproductive for them to allow large segments of the population to be malnourished. The rulers of the commercial empires of today's multinational corporations are subject to no such constraints.

Thus, there are three aspects of the food problem that might be considered adverse side effects of evolutionary "progress." First, the adoption of agriculture creates an ecologically less resilient food system that is inherently more prone to famine-causing fluctuation. Second, as a deviation amplification, technological advances in food production tend to reinforce an accelerating spiral of population and further subsistence intensification that must inevitably place greater strains on the ecosystem and increase the likelihood of further environmental deterioration, which results in an approach close to—if not beyond—the ultimate carrying capacity of the resource base. Finally, social stratification can create an imbalance in the availability of food to the population, especially when food becomes a commercial commodity.

It would appear from this analysis that many of the food problems the world is now experiencing are predictable cultural evolutionary processes and intrinsic features of imperial and commercial societies. While some of these difficulties have been with us since the first appearance of agriculture some 10,000 years ago, they were clearly intensified and enlarged by the elite-directed construction of states and urban civilization some 5,000 years ago. The fact that these problems are still unsolved suggests that they may well be overcome only through a drastic transformation process. The food problem clearly has dramatically intensified over the past 200 years with the emergence of the culture of consumption and its unique food system.

The Commercialization of Grain: England 1500–1700

The cultural shift from the imperial to the commercial world can be observed in the transformation of the English grain distribution system between 1500 and 1700.[28] This change removed an ancient agrarian food system in which a hereditary land-owning aristocracy extracted surplus grain from a largely self-provisioning rural peasantry and replaced it with a highly centralized mercantile capitalist market system that allowed a few grain dealers to accumulate profits from global-scale transactions. In this transformation process the market value of grain ultimately became more important than its nutritional value, and a decentralized, locally controlled market system that had focused on the subsistence needs of local consumers in villages, manors, and small towns was replaced by a concentrated market system largely serving a few economic elites with financial interests in metropolitan and foreign markets.[29]

In medieval England during the centuries following the withdrawal of the Romans in AD 410 up to approximately 1500, a local and regional grain distribution system evolved in which the great lords shifted grain between their manors to meet local shortages and the peasants sold their surpluses in small, local, municipally regulated markets. The lords themselves sometimes moved from manor to manor to consume the surpluses. The Domesday Survey shows that in 1086 the top 2 percent of the population of 2 million controlled virtually all the land, either as members of the hereditary aristocracy or as religious leaders. All food was produced by the 90 percent of the population who were village farmers, most of whom were dependent on the manors, the country estates of the elite who coordinated the extraction of surplus production and labor from the peasantry according to an elaborate code of feudal rights and duties. The degree to which power was concentrated even among the elite was astounding. Over 45 percent of the manors were controlled by the king and the ten most powerful lords. However, manorial control over grain distribution eventually declined in response to new economic opportunities for the elite, as well as to direct pressure from the peasants. The aristocracy eventually found it advantageous to allow farmers to pay their land rents with cash obtained from selling their surplus grain in local markets.

Small towns gradually grew up around hundreds of local marketplaces. Before 1500, fifteen regional markets emerged in which grain from adjacent local markets was sold at the same price because of similar conditions.[30] Even though the domestic market was unrestricted and people could sell in any of

Britain's eight hundred market towns, these regional markets remained relatively isolated. Few specialist merchants transported grain to higher-priced markets. Many local municipal regulations were applied to grain handling and marketing, all apparently designed to protect the consumer from price manipulation, poor quality, or dishonest measures. Ordinances specified the hour and place at which grain could be traded, sometimes specified maximum prices, and in some cases even restricted the role of brokers in order to ensure that consumers could buy directly from producers. Middleman grain traders, or wholesalers, were tolerated but were generally regarded with suspicion and considered to be disreputable.

The phenomenal growth of the city of London from 1500 to 1700, stimulated by the expanding global economy, produced a greater than tenfold increase in population. This order-of-magnitude change could not be sustained by the existing food system, and the increased demand for grain soon overwhelmed Britain's medieval system of local and regional grain distribution. London in 1250, like all English towns, drew on a local grain market within a radius of twenty-five miles, but by 1500 the city had grown to some 50,000 people, and the local market proved totally inadequate. A much larger distribution system, with the metropolitan center drawing on a vast market area, was required. Grain was soon being shipped to London from all over England. Between 1580 and 1680 the volume of coastal grain shipments increased tenfold. Grain prices in London now affected the entire country, and distinct regional markets began to disappear. Previously, overseas grain had been imported by foreign merchants only under emergency conditions, but after 1500 imported grain became increasingly important. From 1514 to 1678 London's municipal authorities bought and sold grain, established public granaries, and urged the guilds to buy and store grain when prices were low and hold it for resale to consumers at reasonable prices during shortages. By a royal decree in 1587 county officials watched fields and households throughout the kingdom to ensure that all surplus was marketed. When these measures failed, the grain trade was turned over to private, profit-seeking merchants who were even encouraged to engage in overseas import and export. By the late seventeenth century London merchants were sending grain to Scandinavia, central Europe, Holland, Spain, the Caribbean, New England, Virginia, and Canada. A global food market was in place, but an elite few were reaping the largest benefits. For example, during three trading seasons between 1676 and 1683, a mere four merchants handled half of London's wheat export business.[31] At this time there were perhaps only 2,000 large merchants engaged in all of England's overseas trade.

By 1700, when the scale transformation of the grain market was virtually complete, the majority of the English population was no longer in control of their food distribution system, and most households had lost control over food production as well. Grains, along with most other foods, had become commodities that people had to purchase with cash, but market value now responded to international conditions and the previously "free" markets were now in the hands of just a few merchants. London's population had reached 700,000; it soon became the largest city in Europe, housing a vast number of impoverished people.

Famine in the Modern World

[Despite] the enormous sums invested, the impressive technical progress we have made, and the extraordinary efforts by governments, by international bodies, and by scientific and technical communities—mankind has by and large failed in its supreme effort to feed adequately those billions of people now living on earth. Of these, at least one billion are undernourished, and the diets of an additional eight hundred million are deficient in one or several key nutrients. (Borgstrom 1967: xi)[32]

Famine is not new. It has been, and continues to be, a chronic hazard of civilization. Famines of varying degrees and intensity were recorded in China at the rate of 1,828 over the 2,019 years up to 1911. Four million people may have died in China in 1920–1921. Three million died in the Indian famine of 1769–1770, and 2 to 4 million in West Bengal in 1943. Russian famines from 1918 to 1934 may have claimed 5–10 million lives. Famines have ravaged Europe many times, and even England counted more than 200 famines between AD 10 and AD 1846.[33] Since Malthus outlined the dangers in 1798, Europe has moved to the brink of famine, and sometimes beyond, several times. By the middle of the nineteenth century a general food crisis was developing in Europe, but it was alleviated by emigration and food imports from the United States. The most notable problem during this period was the Irish "potato famine" of 1845–1846. The introduction of the potato to Ireland permitted rapid population growth up to some 8 million people by 1841, but a blight struck the monocrop and more than 1 million people died and another million emigrated. The Irish population has since stabilized at half its preblight level. A second European food crisis developed early in the twentieth century, but famine was averted when vast acreages in Australia, Argentina, and Canada were taken from aboriginal hunting peoples and put into production for the world market.

In 1905 Harvard geologist Nathaniel S. Shaler warned that the world was very near the limits of food production; he doubted that a threefold population expansion could be supported. World population then stood at well under 2 billion. Forty years later the United Nations declared that much of the world suffered from malnutrition and launched a major "freedom from hunger" campaign. In 1965, food scientist George Borgstrom declared that the world had already failed in its effort to feed itself.

Recognizing the dangers, American president Lyndon B. Johnson declared that the world food problem was "one of the foremost challenges of mankind today," and in 1966 he directed his Science Advisory Committee to investigate the problem and look for solutions.[34] The committee brought together 115 experts on all aspects of the problem from universities, industry, and government agencies. They worked for a year, with subpanels devoted to topics such as food supply, population, nutritional needs, plant and animal productivity, soils and climate, marketing, processing, and distribution. Finally, in 1967 the committee issued a three-volume, 1,200-page report confirming all the dire predictions that had been made before. Their major conclusion was that "the scale, severity, and duration of the world food problem are so great that a massive, long-range, innovative effort unprecedented in human history will be required to master it."[35]

The report dealt with the basic problem of the food crisis in the immediate future, the twenty years from 1965 to 1985, on the mistaken assumption—or at least the hope—that effective family-planning programs would be initiated immediately and would stabilize global population by 1985. The panelists felt that if the food problem was solved by 1985 it would be manageable well into the future. At the first United Nations World Food Conference, held in Rome in 1974 and sponsored by the United Nations in an effort to deal with hunger as a global problem, experts reported that 460 million people were threatened with immediate famine. By 1984 it was clear that the food problem was not going away; hunger was occurring throughout the world, although it was perhaps less dramatic than had been predicted.

Global Malnutrition

Since the United Nations system was established in 1945 there has been a continuous international effort to statistically assess the effectiveness of food systems throughout the world, as measured by the availability of food supplies and the total number of malnourished people. Over the years the definition of malnutrition and the specific methods of measurement have varied. The most dramatic assessments of the global food system suggested that by the year 2000 three billion people, half the world's population, were malnourished, either from calorie and protein deficiency or vitamin and mineral deficiency or from over-consumption.[36] A later World Health Organization estimate put the figure at 30 percent of humanity, or nearly two billion malnourished people, so these figures are very rough estimates.[37] It is astounding that the number of malnourished people in the year 2000 could have been as high as the entire population of the world in 1960.

Four decades of economic progress in the commercially organized global system may have actually magnified malnutrition. The UN Food and Agriculture Organization's narrower definition of malnutrition, focused solely on "food security" in the developing world and countries in "transition" to capitalism in the former Soviet Union and Eastern Europe, listed 845 million "undernourished" people in 2001–2003. This was a decline of only 1.3 million undernourished in the same areas since 1990–1992, implying abysmal progress in a decade.[38] Although much international attention has focused on the problem of food production and food stocks, it has become apparent that access to the means of food production and adequate household income are the most important factors in reducing hunger. The primary causes of malnutrition and food insecurity in a commercially organized world are social, political, and economic. As long as food is a commodity in a world market dominated by highly concentrated commercial power, malnutrition may remain an intractable problem.

The Persistence of Food Insecurity

For many years the UN and governmental development agencies viewed hunger as a problem of technological backwardness and poverty to be treated with relief operations, new technology, and increased economic growth. A vast institutional structure was developed to implement these solutions. Policies were fine-tuned and targets set by the UN's "Development Decades" initiated early in the 1960s. In order to monitor the food crisis and help individual nations design specific programs to increase their food productivity, the UN established four separate bureaucracies, all headquartered in Rome: the Food and Agriculture Organization (FAO, 1945), the World Food Program (WFP, 1961), the World Food Council (WFC, 1974), and the International Fund for Agricultural Development (IFAD, 1977). After 1960 steady improvement was seen in the availability of grain per capita at the global level, with production peaking in 1985 (figure 4.1). However, global food productivity figures are less significant than social and economic

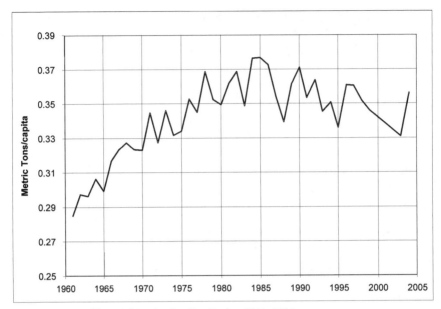

Figure 4.1.   World Cereal Production Per Capita, 1961–2004.
Source: FAO, Food and Agriculture Organization of the United Nations. 2007. FAOSTAT. FAO
Statistics Division.

conditions in individual regions and countries. For example, per capita cereal production in sub-Saharan Africa remained far below the world average and displayed a downward trend from 1960 to 1999. Some war-torn
African countries such as Mozambique were far below the African average.

At the 1996 World Food Summit development leaders pledged to reduce
the number of hungry people in the world by half by the year 2015. Within
three years the UN Food and Agriculture Organization published a new assessment of the food problem, *The State of Food Insecurity in the World 1999*.
The FAO report concluded that 790 million people in the developing world
were undernourished—40 million fewer than in 1992 and 100 million fewer
than in 1970.[39] However, at that rate of improvement there would still be
more than 600 million hungry people by 2015. Surprisingly, this net reduction in the number of hungry people was almost offset by an increase of 34
million undernourished people in developed countries. Incredibly, there
were more hungry people in 1997 than the entire population of the world
(720 million) in 1750. As noted earlier, the *Food Insecurity* report in 2006
listed 845 million undernourished in the developing and "transition" countries in 2001–2003. The FAO defines food insecurity as a low level of food
intake that could be either temporary or chronic. Hunger is now defined as

"undernourishment," or chronic food insecurity based on estimates of the caloric needs of a country's population in relation to the availability and distribution of food supplies. The UN World Health Organization (WHO) offered a higher figure for the world's hungry in 1998 based on physical condition as an indication of undernutrition. WHO relied on anthropometric measures of children, distinguishing among wasting (low weight-for-height), stunting (low height-for-age), and underweight (low weight-for-age) as indicators of malnutrition. WHO estimated that overall there were 1.2 billion malnourished people due to caloric and protein deficiencies.[40]

FAO figures show that in 1997 almost two-thirds of the world's hungry were in Asia, but in more than a dozen sub-Saharan African countries more than 35 percent of the population was considered hungry. Overall, six countries had hunger rates above 60 percent: Haiti, Afghanistan, Mozambique, Burundi, Eritrea, and Somalia. An estimated fifty-nine hungry countries actually experienced increases in the number of hungry people or remained even between 1980 and 1996, whereas forty countries in which the benefits of economic growth were being widely shared were reducing their hunger problem. Estimates comparing 1990–1992 with 2001–2003 show 46 million fewer undernourished people in Asia and the Pacific, but 50 million more in Africa and the Middle East. There were many "setbacks" in sub-Saharan Africa.[41]

A close look at individual countries revealed many critical localities within these countries where specific factors put large numbers of people at risk of severe food insecurity. Obviously vulnerable groups included the elderly and disabled, victims of conflict, migrant workers, the urban poor, minorities, and numerous low-income groups in "vulnerable livelihood systems" such as landless peasants, agricultural workers, pastoralists, subsistence farmers, fishers, forest dwellers, and small-scale market gardeners. Most of these vulnerable livelihood groups either were being displaced by economically more competitive capital-intensive enterprises or occupied marginal, sometimes degraded environments. However, capital-intensive agricultural systems were also proving to be extremely vulnerable to political instability, as illustrated by the sudden collapse of the Democratic People's Republic of Korea's food production system in the 1990s when it lost access to crucial chemical inputs and machinery from China and the former USSR. The chaotic transition from state socialism to new forms of capitalism in fifteen Eastern European countries had produced 26 million undernourished people by 1997. The financial crisis that struck many Asian banking systems in 1997 caused an immediate decline in food consumption and doubled the proportion of undernourished people from 6 percent in 1997 to 12 percent in 1999.

Food Over-Consumption

Over-consumption of food, or an excess of calories, is another dimension of the culture of consumption, and it is a form of malnutrition often accompanied by a deficiency of vitamins and minerals. At the end of the twentieth century an estimated 1.2 billion people were considered malnourished from over-consumption.[42] Fifty-five percent of American adults were overweight as measured by body mass indexes of 25 or above (weight in kilograms divided by the square of height in meters). The proportion of American children who were overweight doubled to 20 percent in twenty years. Over-consumption malnutrition was becoming a global health problem attributed to the "nutrition transition"—the pervasive change from diets rich in complex carbohydrates, whole grains, and vegetables to diets based on fats and simple carbohydrates, or sugars.[43] The nutrition transition, which seems to be an intrinsic feature of the global market economy, is a circular process in which the development of capitalist commercial enterprises causes social changes that over-stimulate the natural human appetite for fat and sweets and provide the commodities and the incomes to meet the almost unrestrained demand. The universal shift to urban life with both parents working outside the home, combined with massive commercial advertising, has dramatically increased the worldwide appeal of and market for highly processed and packaged convenience foods, as well as "fast foods" that are high in fat and sugar and low in nutrients. At the same time over-consumption has become more likely because urban life is physically less strenuous than rural life.

The Political Economy of Hunger: Bangladesh

Except for cases of blatant genocide and war-related famine, the political economy of hunger is usually ignored by international agencies such as the United Nations, even though these agencies can readily identify poverty and "vulnerable livelihood systems" as important causes of hunger and food insecurity. Political economy refers to the interconnections between government and the distribution of economic power. Governments are organized for the legitimate use of force, backed by military power and by legislative and judicial systems to maintain order and protect private property. When the power of government is used to impose or perpetuate the economic interests of an elite over the interests of the majority, poverty can be created and millions of people can be denied access to adequate subsistence. The history of the political economy of South Asia from the beginnings of British colonial rule in 1757 up to the present demonstrates that politics can be a more important cause of hunger than population growth and limited resources.

Bangladesh, the former East Pakistan, is often presented as one of the most extreme cases of hopeless population pressure and Malthusian famine and malnutrition. The human problem is certainly conspicuous, with a population of 147 million and a density of 1,023 people per square kilometer in 2006.[44] It might not seem surprising that millions died here in the great famine of 1943, 100,000 people died of starvation in 1974, and 131,000 died in the cyclone and floods of 1991. A nutrition survey conducted in 1975–1976 found that over half of the families in the country were eating fewer calories than they needed and suffered from protein deficiencies. Not surprisingly, life expectancy stood at just forty-seven years.[45] Near the end of the twentieth century conditions had improved somewhat but still remained grim. The FAO reported that 30 percent of Bangladesh's population, some 43 million people, were undernourished in 2001–2003.[46] It also estimated that 56 percent of children were underweight, 55 percent were stunted, and 18 percent were wasted in 1995.[47] According to the World Bank's figures,[48] in 1998 Bangladesh was a low-income country, with a per capita GNP of $350, but in 1997–1998 its economy was growing at 5 percent a year. Life expectancy at birth had risen to fifty-eight years for both men and women, and infant mortality was 75 per 1,000. In comparison, at that time the U.S. per capita GNP was $29,340 and was growing at 3.7 percent a year, life expectancy was seventy-three for men and seventy-nine for women, and infant mortality was 7 per 1,000. Five years later, Bangladesh's economy was still growing at nearly 4 percent annually, and life expectancy had increased to 62 and 63 years for men and women respectively, infant mortality had declined to 69, but there were almost 4 million more undernourished people than in 1990.

With one of the largest and densest populations in the world, Bangladesh would certainly seem to be a prime example of a Malthusian "basket-case" country. However, reexamined from a perspective emphasizing cultural rather than biological constraints in the food system, the picture changes considerably. Such a perspective emerged dramatically in 1977 with the publication of two important books: *Food First: Beyond the Myth of Scarcity*, by Frances Moore Lappé and Joseph Collins for the Institute for Food and Development Policy, and *How the Other Half Dies: The Real Reasons for World Hunger*, by Susan George. These two books convincingly argued that the world potential for food production was not yet being strained by overpopulation. On the contrary, grain production was still so

Table 4.1.   Bangladesh and the United States, GDP, Household Wealth, and Well-Being, 2000–2005.

	Bangladesh	USA	World
Population	129,277,579	284,776,554	6,097,999,006
GDP (exchange rate)	$144,859,319,888.00	$10,143,456,061,973.00	$37,838,083,832,230
Net Worth (exchange rate)	$161,596,973,659	$40,935,775,247,493	$125,319,977,574,000
GDP/Capita	$347	$35,619	$6,205
Net Worth/Capita	$1,250	$143,747	$20,551
Life Expectancy, Male	62	75	65
Life Expectancy, Female	63	80	69
Infant Mortality	69	8	84
Percent of World Population	2.12	4.67	100
Percent of World Income	0.14	31.49	100
Percent of World Net Worth	0.13	32.65	100

abundant that wealthy countries could turn vast quantities into animal feed. People were hungry because they had been removed from the land by large landowners and multinational agribusiness interests and because they could not earn enough to purchase the food they could no longer grow. Poor people's demand for food could not even be expressed in the marketplace because their purchasing power was too weak.

The relationship between global distribution of wealth and income and material conditions in Bangladesh in 2000 is illustrated in table 4.1 comparing Bangladesh with the United States. Bangladesh has 2 percent of global population but only 0.1 percent of global GDP and household wealth. The United States has less than 5 percent of global population, but 32 percent of global GDP and household wealth. The contrast stands out sharply when Bangladesh's per capita GDP of $347 and net worth of $1,250 is compared with the United States' per capita GDP of $35,619 and $143,747 respectively. Both countries have similar population magnitude, but their total economies are two orders of magnitude apart, $45 billion versus $10 trillion. The vastly greater economic wealth in the United States, and its unequal wealth distribution, meant that the six wealthiest American individuals had combined net worths of $172 billion, which exceeded all household net worth in Bangladesh.[49]

Paradoxically, Bangladesh is a very rich agricultural land with excellent climate, abundant water, and fine alluvial soils. Before the British arrived in 1757, the region (then called Bengal) supported a prosperous local cotton industry. The peasantry was quite capable of feeding itself because land was not privately owned and was not part of the market economy. The British East India Company forcibly introduced cash cropping for export, first of indigo and then of jute, and made land a commodity to be individually owned. Through a variety of legal and extralegal means the peasantry was steadily deprived of the land. A study published in 1977 showed that nearly two-thirds of the rural households held less than 10 percent of the land, whereas one-third were totally landless.[50] Since then land ownership has become even more concentrated. In 1999 the FAO reported that more than 60 percent of the rural population was "functionally landless" and identified many subareas of Bangladesh as "severely famine-prone."[51] Not having access to land can mean being unable to eat adequately. In the 1970s landless peasants were consuming 22 percent less grain than small landholders, whereas they burned 40 percent more calories because of their increased workloads.[52] Many of the landless worked as sharecroppers, providing labor, and often seeds and fertilizer, while the owner claimed at least half of the crop. Those who worked as wage laborers earned twenty to thirty cents per day. The local elites used their power to manipulate wages and prices to ensure that the peasantry was invariably underpaid, relative to official prices, for the crops they produced while being overcharged for the commodities they had to purchase. International development aid and even emergency food aid were invariably monopolized by the landed elite. Researchers Hartmann and Boyce, after two years in the country from 1974 to 1976, including nine months in a representative village, clearly place the blame for hunger on the cultural system: "Hunger in Bangladesh is neither natural nor inevitable. Its causes are deeply rooted, but they are man-made. The surplus siphoned from the peasants is squandered; land, labor and water are underutilized; and, at the national level, financial resources and skilled manpower are allocated for the benefit of a few rather than for the well-being of the majority."[53]

Nobel Prize–winning economist Amartya Sen[54] analyzed the Bangladesh famines of 1943 and 1974 and demonstrated that people died because they lacked adequate entitlements to food, not because food was scarce. Entitlement is a person's or a household's ability to secure food, either as a *direct entitlement* from primary production, such as from a subsistence crop, or by *exchange entitlement* when food must be purchased or obtained by trade in the market. The 1974 famine was related to a severe flood, but production levels were at a decade peak. Prices nevertheless soared and wages dropped, such that many could not afford to buy enough to eat. Those who died were primarily landless laborers or farmers with tiny plots. At the same time, the government's stocks of grain for public distribution were low and the United States chose that moment to hold up its deliveries of relief aid until Bangladesh agreed to stop exporting jute to Cuba. Thus, in a market economy, people with weak entitlements to food may be extremely vulnerable to famine if the government is unwilling or unable to supplement their entitlements. Markets will not be particularly responsive to the demands of the poor for food because when the poor lack exchange entitlements, that is, if they have no money, they cannot be part of the market. In contrast, in the tribal world each household has virtually the same entitlement to food.

Even though maldistribution of social power is the most important cause of malnutrition, the physical limits to food production in particular areas remain an important factor. Many production systems are being pressed beyond sustainable limits by capital-intensive production methods. For example, in Bangladesh cereal production between 1961 and 1999 did not keep pace with population, in spite of enormous capital investments in agricultural technology. However, FAO figures since 2000 show per capita levels returning to the peaks levels of the 1960s.[55]

Notes

1. Malthus, Thomas R. 1895. *An Essay on the Principle of Population*. Parallel chapters from the 1st and 2nd editions. New York: Macmillan. Originally published in 1798, 2nd edition originally published in 1807.

2. Lappé, Frances Moore, and Joseph Collins. 1977. *Food First: Beyond the Myth of Scarcity*. Boston: Houghton Mifflin.

3. Malthus, *Essay on Population*, 110.

4. Wrigley, E. A. 1994. "The Classical Economists, the Stationary State, and the Industrial Revolution." In *Was the Industrial Revolution Necessary?*, edited by Graeme Snooks, 27–42. London and New York: Routledge.

5. Wrigley, "Classical Economists," 30.

6. Ross, Eric. 1998. *The Malthus Factor: Poverty, Politics and Population in Capitalist Development*. New York: Zed Books.

7. Fischer, David Hackett. 1996. *The Great Wave: Price Revolutions and the Rhythm of History*. New York and Oxford: Oxford University Press.

8. Komlos, John. 1989. *Nutrition and Economic Development in the Eighteenth-Century Habsburg Monarchy: An Anthropometric History*. Princeton, NJ: Princeton University Press.

9. Brown, Lester R. 1994. "Facing Food Insecurity." In *State of the World, 1994*, edited by Lester R. Brown et al., 177–97. New York and London: W. W. Norton and Co.

10. Boserup, Ester. 1965. *The Conditions of Economic Growth*. Chicago: Aldine.

11. Winterhalder, B., and F. A. Smith, eds. 1981. *Hunter-Gatherer Foraging Strategies: Ethnographic and Archaeological Analyses*. Chicago: University of Chicago Press; Johnson, Allen, and Clifford A. Behrens. 1982. "Nutritional Criteria in Machiguenga Food Production Decisions: A Linear-Programming Analysis." *Human Ecology* 10(2): 167–89.

12. Gould, Richard A. 1981. "Comparative Ecology of Food-Sharing in Australia and Northwest California." In *Omnivorous Primates: Gathering and Hunting in*

Human Evolution, edited by Robert S. O. Harding and Geza Teleki, 422–54. New York: Columbia University Press; Hayden, Brian. 1981a. "Research and Development in the Stone Age: Technological Transitions Among Hunter-Gatherers." *Current Anthropology* 22(5): 519–48.

13. Hayden, "Research and Development," 519–48.

14. Harris, David R. 1989. "An Evolutionary Continuum of People-Plant Interaction." In *Foraging and Farming: The Evolution of Plant Exploitation*, edited by D. R. Harris and G. C. Hillman, 11–26; Campbell, Alastair. 1965. "Elementary Food Production by the Australian Aborigines." *Mankind* 6: 206–11, discusses some of these practices by Australian aboriginal foragers.

15. Hecker, Howard M. 1982. "Domestication Revisited: Its Implications for Faunal Analysis." *Journal of Field Archaeology* 9: 217–36.

16. Lee, Richard. 1979. *The !Kung San: Men, Women and Work in a Foraging Society*. Cambridge and New York: Cambridge University Press, 294–302.

17. Woodburn, James. 1968a. "An Introduction to Hadza Ecology." In *Man the Hunter*, edited by Richard B. Lee and Irven DeVore, 49–55. Chicago: Aldine; Colson, Elizabeth. 1979. "In Good Years and in Bad: Food Strategies of Self-Reliant Societies." *Journal of Anthropological Research* 35(1): 18–29.

18. Harris, Marvin, and Eric B. Ross. 1987. *Death, Sex, and Fertility: Population Regulation in Preindustrial and Developing Societies*. New York: Columbia University Press, 41–43, 49–50.

19. Sahlins, Marshall. 1972. *Stone Age Economics*. Chicago: Aldine, especially chapters 2 and 3.

20. Hayden, Brian. 1975. "The Carrying Capacity Dilemma: An Alternate Approach." *American Antiquity* 40(2): 11–19, Memoir 30.

21. Gunderson, Lance H., and C. S. Hilling, eds. 2002. *Panarchy: Understanding Transformations in Human and Natural Systems*. Washington, D.C.: Island Press.

22. Sahlins, *Stone Age Economics*.

23. Earle, Timothy. 2002. *Bronze Age Economics: The Beginnings of Political Economies*. Boulder, CO: Westview Press.

24. Earle, *Bronze Age Economics*.

25. Flannery, Kent V. 1969. "Origins and Ecological Effects of Early Domestication in Iran and the Near East." In *The Domestication and Exploitation of Plants and Animals*, edited by Peter J. Ucko and G. W. Dimbleby, 73–100. London: Duckworth.

26. Stover, Leon N., and Takeko Kawai Stover. 1976. *China: An Anthropological Perspective*. Pacific Palisades, CA: Goodyear Publishing Co.

27. Komlos, *Nutrition and Economic Development in the Eighteenth-Century Habsburg Monarchy*. 94–95.

28. Gras, Norman S. B. 1915. *The Evolution of the English Corn Market: From the Twelfth to the Eighteenth Century*. Cambridge: Harvard University Press.

29. This transformation process is detailed in Bodley, John H. 2003. *The Power of Scale: A Global History Approach*. Armonk, NY, and London: M. E. Sharpe, chapter 5.

30. Gras, *English Corn Market.*

31. Gras, *English Corn Market,* 197.

32. Borgstrom, Georg. 1967. *The Hungry Planet.* New York: Macmillan, xi.

33. Ehrlich, Paul, and Anne Ehrlich. 1972. *Population, Resources, Environment.* San Francisco: W. H. Freeman.

34. U.S. President's Science Advisory Committee. 1967. *The World Food Problem: A Report of the Panel on the World Food Supply.* 3 vols. Washington, D.C.: U.S. Government Printing Office.

35. U.S. President's Science Advisory Committee, *The World Food Problem,* vol. 1, 11.

36. Gardner, Gary, and Brian Halweil. 2000. "Nourishing the Underfed and Overfed." In *State of the World 2000: A Worldwatch Institute Report on Progress Toward a Sustainable Society,* edited by Lester R. Brown, Christopher Flavin, Hilary French, and Linda Starke, 59–78. New York and London: W. W. Norton and Co.

37. WHO, World Health Organization. 2003. *Diet, Nutrition and the Prevention of Chronic Diseases.* Report of a Joint WHO/FAO Expert Consultation. WHO Technical Report Series 916. Geneva: WHO, 8.

38. FAO, United Nations, Food and Agriculture Organization. 2006. *The State of Food Insecurity in the World 2006: Eradicating world hunger—taking stock ten years after the World Food Summit.* Rome: UNFAO. www.fao.org/docrep/009/a0750e/a0750e00.htm

39. FAO, Food and Agriculture Organization of the United Nations. 1999. *The State of Food Insecurity in the World 1999.* Rome.

40. Gardner and Halweil, "Underfed and Overfed," 59–78.

41. FAO, *Food Insecurity in the World 2006.*

42. Gardner and Halweil, "Underfed and Overfed."

43. Drewnowski, Adam, and Barry M. Popkin. 1997. "The Nutrition Transition: New Trends in the Global Diet." *Nutrition Review* 55(2): 31–43; Popkin, Barry M. 1998. "The Nutrition Transition and Its Health Implications in Lower-Income Countries." *Public Health Nutrition* 1(1): 5–21.

44. U.S. Central Intelligence Agency (CIA). *The World Factbook 2007.* www.cia.gov/cia/publications/factbook/index.html

45. Hartmann, Betsy, and James Boyce. 1982. *Needless Hunger: Voices from a Bangladesh Village.* San Francisco: Institute for Food and Development Policy, 9.

46. FAO, *Food Insecurity in the World 2006,* Table 1.

47. FAO, *The State of Food Insecurity in the World 1999.*

48. World Bank. 1999. *Entering the 21st Century: World Development Report 1999/2000.* New York: Oxford University Press.

49. Davies, James B., Susanna Sandstrom, Anthony Shorrocks, and Edward N. Wolff. 2006. *The World Distribution of Household Wealth.* World Institute for Development Economics Research; World Bank. 2006. *World Development Report 2006: Equity and Development.* New York: Oxford University Press; *Forbes Magazine.* "Forbes 400 2001. " (Sept. 27, 2001) www.forbes.com/2001/09/27/400.html

50. Jannuzi, F. Tomasson, and James T. Peach. 1977. *Report on the Hierarchy of Interests in Land in Bangladesh.* Washington, D.C.: Agency for International Development, September 1977, xxi, 30.

51. FAO, *The State of Food Insecurity in the World 1999.*

52. Jannuzi and Peach, *Land in Bangladesh.*

53. Hartmann and Boyce, *Needless Hunger,* 35.

54. Sen, Amartya. 1981. *Poverty and Famines: An Essay on Entitlement and Deprivation.* Oxford: Clarendon Press.

55. FAO, *FAOSTAT.* 2007. FAO Statistics Division. faostat.fao.org/default.aspx

Commercial Factory Food Systems   **5**

If we insist on a high-energy food system, we should consider starting with coal, oil, garbage—or any other source of hydrocarbons—and producing in factories bacteria, fungi, and yeasts. These products could then be flavored and colored appropriately for cultural tastes.

—JOHN S. STEINHART AND CAROL E. STEINHART,
ENERGY USE IN THE U.S. FOOD SYSTEM[1]

GLOBAL-SCALE COMMERCIAL FOOD SYSTEMS represent an enormous advance in evolutionary progress and a proportionate loss in long-run adaptive success. Primary technical features of these factory systems are their costly fossil fuel energy subsidies and their reliance on sophisticated biological engineering, which permit very high crop yields for very low inputs of human labor. Other critical cultural aspects are the extreme complexity of the production-consumption market chain and the tendency to increase the per capita energy and resource cost of food consumption through expanded dependence on synthetic and highly processed foods and inefficiently produced animal protein. Because the primary objective of a commercial food system is to produce a financial return for investors, the system's ability to satisfy human nutritional needs on a sustained basis is a secondary, virtually irrelevant consideration for those who direct the system. Commercially driven food systems are not only far more costly in per capita demand for energy and resources, but ultimately less sustainable than small-scale, noncommercial systems and much less responsive to basic human needs. Global-scale commercial food systems involve substantial social and cultural, as well as environmental, costs. As noted in the previous chapter, people who lack sufficient financial resources may be excluded from commercial food markets while at the same time small-scale productive systems are displaced by politically and economically more powerful commercial systems.

Commercial factory food systems involve an enormous concentration of political and economic power that produces vast profits for global elites, but they are inherently insensitive to the needs of local human communities and ecosystems. These global-scale commercial systems place great demands on natural resources and consequently have great potential for producing environmental deterioration. Most critically, perhaps, they cannot be sustained indefinitely at present rates of growth, or even at present levels, without drastic restructuring to make them more responsive to basic human needs and the requirements of natural systems. These are critical issues because the present global strategy for promoting economic development and reducing world hunger continues to promote large commercial systems at the expense of locally controlled food systems.

Factory Food Production

By the 1940s and 1950s tractors and farm chemicals were turning farms throughout the world into factories. The demand for farm labor began a drastic decline, and development planners everywhere hailed the efficiency of the new technology. If we ignore the nonhuman energy expended in the production, processing, distribution, storage, and preparation of food in America, the system may indeed appear to be very efficient. Before the full costs of the fossil fuel subsidy were widely acknowledged, anthropologist Marvin Harris[2] gave the American food system highest ratings in "techno-environmental advantage" in comparison with the energy efficiency of foragers, shifting cultivators, hoe farmers, and wet-rice growers. His figures were based on a simple estimate of the hours expended per farm worker, multiplied by a fixed rate of 150 calories expended per hour and divided into the quantity of food calories produced in a given period of time. These calculations may be a reasonable approximation of energy input-output ratios for small-scale foragers and farmers, but they are completely inadequate for the American system unless they include fossil fuel energy inputs.

Harris corrected his figures in 1975 as shown in table 5.1, which gives the basic techno-environmental efficiency ratings of the five cultures originally evaluated by Harris, with an adjustment made to the efficiency of

Table 5.1.   Energy Input-output Efficiency in Five Food Systems.

Culture	Technology	Calories Produced/Calorie Expended
!Kung San	Foraging	9.6
Tsembaga	Shifting cultivation	18
	Pig raising	2.1
	Total	9.8
Genieri	Hoe farming	11.2
China	Irrigated rice	53.5
United States	Factory farming	
	Human labor	210.0
	Nonhuman energy	0.13

Sources: Harris, *Culture, Man and Nature,* 203–17; Steinhart and Steinhart, "Energy Use in the U.S. Food System," 307–16.

the American system by counting separately the nonhuman energy inputs from production to consumption. The surprising fact is that whereas American farm laborers were expending only 1 calorie of human energy for every 210 food calories they produced, approximately 8 calories of nonhuman energy, primarily in the form of fossil fuels, were also required for each calorie produced. It is apparent that the industrial food system is actually operating at an energy efficiency deficit.

Ecologist Howard T. Odum[3] brilliantly outlined the energy flow systems underlying subsistence patterns at different scales of cultural development, using carefully designed circuit board–like diagrams. Odum used a variety of symbols to represent the pathway of energy through an ecosystem, from the sun through green plants and herbivores to the human consumers. The resulting diagram resembles an electrical schematic with switches, gates, heat sinks, and so on, all showing how energy is transformed, stored, and regulated. One need not understand all the complexities of this method of analysis to appreciate how it illustrates the general design of different subsistence systems and their relationship to the ecosystem. These diagrams dramatically show how commercial food systems use fossil fuels to replace energetic functions performed more efficiently and at lower cost by tribal societies and small-scale producers that rely directly on natural solar-powered production.

As foragers, humans were dependent for their subsistence on highly complex and stable ecosystems that were largely self-regulating, relatively closed information systems. Foragers let the diverse natural species of the ecosystem do all the work of concentrating energy and nutrients and regulating their flow, with no intentional human intervention needed. Nutrients are largely stored in the living plants and animals and are quickly and efficiently recycled after their deaths. Tribal shifting cultivators adjusted to their forest ecosystem by making use of the artificial energy pulse generated each time a forest plot was cut and burned. This pulse temporarily eliminated competitor species and concentrated nutrients to briefly channel the energy flow into food crops. Except for this minor intervention, the system continued to be basically self-regulating and immediately began to return to its starting point; that is, natural forest succession began at once. Thus, nature did most of the work, and as long as their power base remained restricted to local inputs of solar energy, tribal societies generally did not harness enough power to seriously disrupt their supporting ecosystems.

When modern commercially driven nations began to channel fossil-fuel energy into their food systems the picture was suddenly and radically changed. Odum describes the new fossil-fuel food systems very concisely: "One of the results of industrialization based on the new concentrated energy sources was abundant food rolling out from huge fields which were sowed with machinery, tilled with tractors, and weeded and poisoned with chemicals. Epidemic diseases were kept in check by great teams of scientists in distant experiment stations developing new and changing varieties to stay ahead of the evolution of disease adaptation. Soon a few people were supporting many, and most of the rural population left the little farms to fill the new industrial cities."[4]

The greater crop yields that followed industrialization must not be considered simply the result of brilliant inventions, education, determination, and great technological know-how. An enormous energy subsidy was essential. Factory farms do not achieve more efficient rates of photosynthesis and energy conversion. Actually, even some of the most productive factory farms, such as industrialized rice farms, convert only about 0.25 percent of incoming solar radiation into useful food energy, whereas a tropical rain forest operates at 3.5 percent efficiency.[5] Larger per-acre yields are possible on factory farms because fossil fuels replace the energy loop the natural ecosystem reserved for its own mechanisms of self-regulation. This system is simply a means of converting oil into food. In effect, as Odum phrased it, in a factory agricultural system "fossil fuel supported works of man have eliminated the natural species and substituted industrial services for the services of those natural species, releasing the same basic production to yield."[6]

A factory farm is actually an extremely costly and inefficient attempt to replace nature with a very simplified, humanly maintained and subsidized machine. Chemical fertilizers manufactured and transported with fossil fuels replace the tightly calibrated nutrient cycles of the natural ecosystem. More chemicals and machinery control the weeds that in a swidden system are merely part of the restart mechanism and are shaded out as the successional pattern they initiate proceeds. Plant geneticists working in laboratories replace the natural process of biological evolution based on natural selection and species diversity. The delicate natural balances that prevent consumer species from overgrazing are eliminated by heavy application of chemical poisons. Pollution and environmental deterioration are unintended by-products of industrial farming because the exotic nutrients and pesticides do not fit into natural ecosystem cycles but instead merely pile up in unexpected places to block these cycles. The massive use of chemical pesticides also has serious direct implications for public health and has stirred widespread public concern and controversy on many occasions, as demonstrated in the Soviet example in chapter 2.

Much of the energy and work force needed to support an industrial food system is disguised by statistics that focus on farm labor and yields per acre. An industrial food system necessarily engages many more sectors of the economy than those directly involved in primary agricultural production. In 1992–1993 there were more than 11 million full-time workers in the food system as a whole, including primary producers, food processors, and distributors, not counting farm owners and operators. This includes 2 million farm laborers and support workers in the manufacturing of farm machinery and chemicals and in the federal Department of Agriculture, but there were more than 9 million people involved in food processing and distribution, not counting the transportation sector. Thus, food processing and distribution engaged far more labor than primary production. The farm labor force has continued to decline; for example, in 2002 there were 3 million farm operators, and they hired only 966,000 workers in July of 2002.[7] These figures help explain why American food distribution is much more costly than food production.

Anthropologists have pointed out that factory farming's capital-intensive dependence on machinery and expensive fossil fuel energy and the continuing maintenance requirements for specialized technical skills and manufactured imports make such production methods a poor choice for the world's domestic-scale farmers.[8] Massive federally subsidized water development projects have supported factory farming in the arid regions of the American West, but these giant projects have led to soil salinization[9] and they involve enormous social costs, as we will see in a later section.

Factory Potatoes versus
Swidden Sweet Potatoes

Profit is the only reason for growing potatoes. (Knudson 1972: 76)

The extent to which fossil fuel–subsidized factory farming systems have artificially replaced the functions of the natural ecosystem and the incredible energy and environmental costs of this change stand out with remarkable clarity when we compare the commercial production of Irish potatoes by large-scale American agribusiness in the 1960s and 1970s with the methods of raising sweet potatoes for local consumption by tribal gardeners in New Guinea during the same time.[10] Potatoes (Irish or sweet) occupy roughly the same position in each culture, in that they are quantitatively the most important single vegetable consumed and are unquestionably basic staples in the diet. In many American households meat and potatoes were traditionally thought to make a meal complete.

Sweet potatoes directly contributed 21 percent of the diet by weight for the local group of 204 Tsembaga people who were actively cultivating about 1,000 acres in highland Papua New Guinea in 1962.[11] Much of their sweet potato crop was fed to domestic pigs and thus indirectly contributed animal protein to their diet in the form of pork. They carried out their basic cultivation system entirely by hand. They cleared and burned the forest, built fences to keep out the pigs, and planted crops with a sharpened stick. They harvested their crops by hand and carried them in handcrafted net bags to their houses for consumption. There was no elaborate processing; potatoes were simply roasted whole in the fire or steamed in earth ovens. There was also no significant storage, except in the ground until harvest.

Energy-wise, the Tsembaga system was quite efficient, with approximately 16 kilocalories of sweet potatoes produced for each kilocalorie of human labor. Only about 10 percent of the easily arable land was under active cultivation at a time, and there appeared to be no immediate danger of resource depletion, although in some areas of highland New Guinea there has been a long-term trend toward more intensive cultivation and replacement of forest with savanna. The basic objective of Tsembaga gardening was to meet human nutritional needs, and they did this very well. They grew no crops for the market, although other New Guinea peoples raised cash crops for local markets and produced coffee for the world market while still maintaining subsistence production for household use.

On a factory farm in the United States, potatoes can be grown as a successful monocrop only with the help of vast energy inputs to maintain correct soil conditions, moisture, and nutrients and to control weeds, epidemic diseases, and insect infestations. On the swidden sweet potato farm all of these functions are carried out by the natural ecosystem and by the diversity of the garden plantings, which imitates the natural system. No irrigation or fertilizer is required on swidden plots, while factory potato farmers must apply chemical fertilizer constantly and in many areas must irrigate to maintain high yields. In areas where overhead sprinklers are used, special chemicals may be applied to the soil to prevent compaction and lost filtration caused by the perpetual mechanical rain.[12] Weeds, insects, and diseases may be variously controlled before planting by chemical treatment of the tubers, by application of chemical herbicides and insecticides to the soil, and sometimes even by soil fumigation that kills virtually all soil organisms. Specialized pre-emergence weed killers and a wide variety of other herbicides and insecticides may be applied while the crop is growing. In some cases special chemicals are sprayed on the crop to inhibit sprouting after harvest or to intensify the red skin color of certain potatoes to increase their market value. Note that part of this energy-expensive chemical program is a cosmetic treatment to prevent unsightly blemishes that may lower consumer acceptance, with little effect on increasing actual yields. Where potatoes are contracted to go into chips, the vines must be chemically killed weeks before harvesting to prevent starch buildup in the tubers, which causes an undesirable darkening in the finished potato chips.

The Commercialization of the American Food System, 1850–1890

In 1790 America was 95 percent rural. Most farm families at that time were self-provisioning and produced small marketable surpluses. By 2000 America was 79 percent urban,[13] and agriculture was large scale, capital intensive, and fully commercialized. This cultural transformation was a result of policy decision making by America's political and commercial elite that promoted a form of economic growth that disadvantaged small-scale agricultural producers.[14] The commercial revolution that totally transformed the way food was produced, processed, and distributed in America was an elite-directed process that occurred within the space of four decades, between 1850 and 1890. It involved a rapid succession of changes in transportation, communication, production, distribution, and the organization of business enterprise itself that collectively expanded the speed and scale of commercial transactions.[15] These changes were financed and directed by a relative handful of commercial elites. At the very top were an even smaller number of millionaire investors, centered in Boston, New York, and Philadelphia, whose numbers expanded from an estimated 40 in 1860 to 2,500 in 1870 and to 3,800 in 1897.[16] This was a time when more than half of the adult male population remained landless in spite of the Homestead Act of 1862 and the westward expansion movement. By 1900 perhaps 1,500 industrial corporations, directed by some 18,500 corporate board members and major stockholders, had capital assets of $1 million or more.[17] Collectively these 22,000 financiers and corporate directors formed an economic elite that represented less than 0.15 percent of American households. By their joint decisions to expand the scale and scope of commerce and their success at enlisting political support, these few transformed the nation and the world before the end of the nineteenth century.

America's great national expansion and the commercial transformation that propelled it were initiated in the 1850s by a tiny group of some 200 Boston families. These aggrandizing families, each worth at least $100,000 in 1848, owned 37 percent of the personal property in the city and were the major shareholders in Boston's fifty largest banks and insurance companies.[18] Boston in 1850 was a city of 137,000 people and was the banking center for the entire country. Its financial elite directed a massive, self-serving culture-change project in the same way that London's elite, in a city of 123,000, had initiated British expansionism 270 years earlier. The Boston elite amassed financial capital by investing prudently, marrying carefully, and forming dynastic trusts that allowed them to accumulate vast, transgenerational family fortunes.[19] These wealthy New Englanders not only financed the first great American business corporations but they also used their philanthropy to create the private foundations and elite private colleges, such as Harvard and Yale, that trained the professionals who went on to build the institutional and ideological infrastructure for a commercially focused, elite-directed American nation.[20]

The decline and near disappearance of small farms in America was neither a natural nor an inevitable process. It was the result of a hard-fought political struggle in which a few centrally located, politically and economically powerful commercial leaders were pitted against a great mass of small farmers scattered across rural America. Thomas Jefferson's vision of America as an agrarian democracy was shared by millions of independent farmers who enthusiastically joined the Granges and the Populist Party between 1870 and 1900 and tried to gain control of state and federal governments.[21] The agrarian populists envisioned a rural America that was the exact opposite of the factory-farm, corporate agribusiness system that came to dominate the twentieth century. In 1920 there were 6.5 million farms. In

2002 there were 2.1 million farms, but a mere 143,547 farms representing fewer than 6.7 percent of the total number of farms accounted for 75 percent of total farm product sales.[22] The real function of factory farming is concentrating economic power, not producing food.

By the 1930s the land grant colleges, the Department of Agriculture, and the Extension Service came to serve the interests of the largest commercial farmers, in the process causing small farmers to be steadily marginalized. Agribusiness leaders formed a single, very powerful lobby—the American Farm Bureau Federation—that constructed a successful partnership between large landholder farmers and government bureaucrats, politicians, and expert advisers.[23] These institutional structures, in combination with the railroads, financier investors, farm machinery manufacturers, the emerging petroleum and chemical industries, and mass merchandisers, made the large-scale factory farm dominant over the small family farm in America.

Social Costs of the Food Production System

> The growth of corporate agriculture is neither inevitable nor simply a product of efficiency, but it is rather a result of the emergence of national policies favorable to large-scale enterprises. Some of these policies were promulgated by corporate interests. Others, ostensibly at least, were formulated in the desire to protect the family farmer but have had the opposite effect. (Goldschmidt, *As You Sow*, 1978)[24]

The growth of factory farming has dramatically transformed rural society throughout the world, generally reducing the number of people supported directly from the land, increasing inequality, and often lowering the quality of life for those at the bottom of the economic hierarchy. This process can easily be documented in the United States, where there has been a steady decline in rural population and a decrease in the number of farms as farming has become a business rather than a way of life. Between 1930 and 1990 in the United States as a whole two-thirds of the farms disappeared while those that remained increased in size more than threefold. This transformation occurred within less than a single lifetime.

Contrary to popular wisdom, this dual process of economic concentration and impoverishment is not solely driven by economies of scale resulting purely from improvements in technology. We have seen that less fossil fuel–intensive food production systems are energetically both more efficient and more sustainable. Furthermore, a wide-ranging comparative study published by the U.S. Department of Agriculture demonstrated that fully mechanized farms operated by one person were economically more efficient than much larger operations.[25] Anthropologist Walter Goldschmidt, who studied California agribusiness, emphasized that smaller farms maximized income for the maximum number of people more effectively than larger farms. Smaller farms also supported more prosperous farm towns. Goldschmidt[26] attributed the concentration of American farm ownership to public policies that for decades systematically favored large owners over small. Giant corporate farms did not emerge because of the efficiencies of nature. Goldschmidt observed that under federal subsidy programs larger owners received larger support payments. The progressive income tax encouraged high-income people to acquire farms as tax shelters so they could write off losses, while reductions in capital gains taxes made farms attractive investments for wealthy financiers and giant corporations. Farm labor has also been a special bonus for large farm operators because seasonal farm workers have few legal protections, especially when, as is often the case, they are not citizens. Goldschmidt also noted that agricultural research sponsored by the federal government through the Department of Agriculture and the land grant universities has often been directed toward the needs of agribusiness rather than those of the family farm.

In 1940 Goldschmidt was commissioned by the federal Bureau of Agricultural Economics to study the effects of limiting the size of farms that used federally subsidized irrigation water. This was a special issue in central California, where a few very large estates, a heritage of Spanish land grants, and nineteenth-century railroad grants were monopolizing the Bureau of Reclamation's water projects. Subsidizing large farms seemed to contradict the bureau's mission, which since 1902 had been to promote water development to support family farms on arid western land. In order to assess the social impact of farm size, Goldschmidt selected two communities in the Central Valley of California, Dinuba and Arvin. Both had approximately 4,000 people, the same environment, and the same overall level of agricultural productivity. Dinuba and Arvin differed only in farm size. Goldschmidt found that Dinuba, surrounded by small farms, had twice as many local businesses as Arvin and two-thirds more local retail trade. Dinuba's farms averaged only 57 acres but supported a richer community life with more people and a higher living standard per dollar of agricultural production than Arvin. Dinuba had better community infrastructure, including streets, sidewalks, sewage disposal, and recreational facilities; better schools; more civic organizations; more churches; and more democratic local government. The farms around Arvin averaged 497 acres and individually generated more dollars, but income was skewed toward the upper end of the social hierarchy and wealth was more externally directed. In Dinuba more than half the work force was business professionals and farm operators, while in Arvin 80 percent were low-paid farm laborers.

The policy implications of Goldschmidt's research were obvious, and the local elite attempted unsuccessfully to use their political influence in Washington, D.C., to stop the project. They then tried to publicly discredit Goldschmidt and suppress his findings, and they succeeded in closing down the Bureau of Agricultural Economics and blocking a follow-up study. However, a repeat study thirty and forty years later found that social conditions in portions of the Central Valley Water Project had deteriorated even further than in the 1940s.[27] Researchers Dean MacCannell and Jerry White investigated the federally supported Westland Water District developed in Fresno County in the 1960s. They found sharp class divisions, with a small prosperous elite and an impoverished majority. Many of the wealthy farm owners lived in Los Angeles or in lavish houses on their 2,000-acre estates, while community infrastructure in the district's towns declined. In 1970 farm-worker housing was often overcrowded and grossly inadequate, and in some communities more than half the population lived below the official poverty level. Not surprisingly, MacCannell and White advocated land reform and adherence to the acreage limitations as a solution. Other researchers have examined the social consequences of large-scale, factory-style pig production, following Goldschmidt's methods of analysis.[28]

In the United States overall, where the economic interests of agribusiness and corporate food processors and distributors have prevailed, the food system has become remarkably centralized, in ways that give food production decision-making power to a very few people who have little economic incentive to concern themselves with the long-term social consequences of their actions. For example, in 1990 California produced well over half the nation's vegetables, including some 90 percent of its tomatoes and more than 75 percent of its lettuce. In 1982 Fresno County, discussed earlier, produced nearly $1.5 billion in crops, the highest in the state. Land ownership in Fresno County was extremely concentrated, with 7.6 percent of the farms—a mere 568—controlling more than 80 percent of the land.[29] In 1990 just 513 corporations, less than 0.5 percent of the nation's 126,423 agricultural corporations, held one-third of the nation's corporate agricultural assets. Food processors are also highly concentrated. From 1995 to 2004 the four largest cattle-packing houses accounted for 80 percent of the market, whereas in 1980 they controlled only 36 percent. Similarly, the top four hog packers controlled 64 percent in 2004, twice their market power in 1980, and the top four poultry packers controlled 54 percent in 2004.[30] In 1992 the 59 largest of some 1.4 million American food manufacturing companies accounted for some 75 percent of sales. At a global level the marketing and intercontinental movement of grain was controlled by five privately held corporations.[31]

Energy Costs of the Distribution System

In a tribal culture, as we have seen, food is largely produced by the households that consume it. Only small quantities are normally distributed beyond individual households, and this distribution occurs within a framework of reciprocal sharing between close kin. In small chiefdoms, the simplest politically centralized societies, production and consumption still remain largely at the household level, although some foodstuffs may be concentrated by chiefs as tribute to be redistributed at feasts or in times of crisis and to support craft specialists for the production of sumptuary goods. With the evolution of the state and the establishment of politically centralized governments, large quantities of food had to be transferred from the rural subsistence farmers or peasants to the cities to maintain permanent food storehouses for state use. This transfer has been variously carried out through the payment of taxes, the operations of special trader classes, or well-developed market exchanges. Reliance only on solar energy–powered agriculture apparently placed severe limitations on the extent to which the population of a given society could be concentrated in cities, especially because of the energy costs of transportation relative to the cost of food production. With the tapping of fossil fuels and the rise of industrialized urban centers, where up to 95 percent of the population in particular countries became concentrated, the energy costs of the food distribution system quickly came to totally overshadow the costs of primary production.

It is possible to make only a very rough estimate of the total energy costs of the American food system. In a now classic study, John S. Steinhart and Carol E. Steinhart[32] calculated that in 1970 between 8 and 12 calories were expended in the production, distribution, and consumption of a single calorie of food. These findings show that industrial commercial societies reverse the energy input-output relationship of the food system typical of the tribal world, in which 10 or more kilocalories are produced for each kilocalorie expended. The Steinhart figures include energy costs such as the manufacturing and operation of farm machinery, fertilizer, irrigation, food processing, packaging, transportation, manufacturing of trucks, and both industrial and domestic cooking and refrigeration. Higher estimates would include the energy cost of shipping food by rail, ship, and air; disposal of food-related wastes; maintenance of buildings and equipment; a percentage of highway construction costs; agricultural research; and domestic use of private automobiles to move food from supermarket to home. Other estimates of the energy costs of the American food system calculated by different researchers for 1994 show a similar expenditure of approximately 7 kilocalories for each kcal of food available.[33] According to these figures more energy is expended at the household level in trips to the grocery store, and in storage and cooking, than in primary agricultural production.

According to Steinhart and Steinhart's conservative estimate, less than 25 percent of the total energy expended in the American food system actually went to support primary production on the farm; the other 75 percent plus went to processing, marketing, and domestic uses. Significantly, much more of the work force was engaged in the food processing and distribution network than on the farm, even disregarding labor costs in the transportation system. Clearly the distribution component of the industrial food system is responsible for much of the enormous energy cost of the total system, and for this reason it deserves special investigation. The 1994 estimates show 47 percent of the energy in the food system consumed in commercial processing and marketing, 32 percent by households, and only 21 percent in primary agricultural production (table 5.2). It would be difficult to argue that energy-expensive commercialization has improved the nutritional quality of the American diet.

Many of the increased energy costs of the American food system appear to be related solely to the marketing process. Despite the biological limits to per capita food consumption, between 1950 and 1990, under the commercial urging of the food industry, the apparent per capita consumption of

Table 5.2.   Daily per capita energy consumption in the U.S. food system, 1994 (based on Heller and Keoleian. 2000, figure 5).

	Kcal/capita/day	Percent
Household	8,530	32
Production	5,774	21
Processing	4,409	16
Transportation	3,648	14
Packaging	1,779	7
Food Service	1,772	7
Retail	989	4
Totals	26,901	100

calories by Americans increased by almost 20 percent, with protein consumption up 13 percent.[34] Between 1970 and 1990 American soft drink consumption increased more than 80 percent, exceeding 50 gallons per person annually by 1999.[35] Much of this can be explained as a marketing effort to dispose of vast quantities of corn produced in the Midwest on petroleum-fueled factory farms by converting it to corn syrup sweeteners and animal protein from grain-fed livestock and poultry.[36] These changes in diet dramatically elevate total American energy consumption but produce few nutritional benefits, and have detrimental effects. Even by 1990 nearly one-third of the American population was 20 percent or more above desired weight standards set by life insurance companies. Between 1990 and 2004 Americans added another 400 kilocalories to their daily consumption, raising the figure from 3,500 to 3,900.[37]

A national-scale food distribution system is costly to grow and maintain. Between 1940 and 1970 the per capita energy costs of American food doubled. During this period the energy costs of food packaging increased by 119 percent, while the overall per capita costs of processing, packaging, and transportation from factory to marketplace increased by 95 percent.[38] Increases in food-related energy use and changes in the cost of petroleum and natural gas are also reflected in the dollar cost of food. Between 1970 and 2004 per capita marketing costs in the food system increased by 47 percent in constant dollars,[39] reducing the effects of technological efficiencies gained in primary agricultural production. Larger-scale markets have produced little benefit for most farmers, because they have driven down the returns to the farmer in relation to the total costs of food to the consumer, such that in 2004 the farmer was receiving only 20 cents out of the consumer's food dollar. In 1950 the farmer's share of the food dollar was 41 cents.[40]

After 1950 there was a dramatic switch to the consumption of more energy-intensive processed food. By 1970 America's food was transported farther and more expensively processed and packaged than ever before. For example, it has been estimated that fresh produce travels an average of 1500 miles from producer to consumer, because most produce comes from California.[41] These cultural changes were seen in many areas. The introduction of frozen foods raised energy requirements because their distribution required additional preparation and packaging, along with special transportation and storage facilities. Certain new food products, such as potato chips, were far more costly to transport and store because of their increased bulk and fragility compared to their less processed counterparts. Since 1950 energy costs rose due to trends in packaging such as the general increase in the use of packaging solely to enhance the consumer appeal of foodstuffs and the switch to more energy-expensive materials. Wood, paper, and reusable glass bottles were steadily replaced by plastic, non-returnable bottles, and aluminum cans. The latter require approximately twice the energy to manufacture than the steel cans they replaced.

Cultural changes in patterns of food consumption account for part of the increase in energy use. The per capita retail consumption of beef increased steadily from a low of 37 pounds per capita per year in 1932 during the Depression, to a peak of 94 pounds in 1976, but by 2004 it had declined to 66 pounds. Cattle are relatively inefficient converters of vegetable protein, requiring approximately 20 pounds of protein to produce 1 pound for human consumption. This ratio would not be critical if cattle were grazed on rangeland that would not produce other food crops, but a high proportion of America's beef cattle are fed high-quality grains in feedlots before being slaughtered. In 1991 approximately two-thirds of the American grain crop was used as animal feed (U.S. Department of Agriculture, 1992). Pork and chicken are more efficient protein producers, and it is significant that since 1992 Americans have begun eating more chicken than beef, and per capita chicken consumption had increased more than fivefold since 1909 (figure 5.1).[42]

Food Marketing

The National Commission on Food Marketing's findings in a study of the marketing practices in the American food system conducted at the request of President Lyndon B. Johnson in the 1960s continue to be relevant for understanding America's commercial food system.[43] This study was based on the work of nineteen academicians and seven private researchers and considered the cost structure of food from farmer to consumer, product innovation and competition, and consumer "needs." This helped to pinpoint factors in the processing and distribution components of the food system that promote increased energy costs.

It is striking that productivity in the food-marketing industry is measured not by how efficiently human need–satisfying nutrients can be distributed to the population but by dollar output per hour of labor or return on investment. In this accounting staple foods such as meat, flour, and sugar, which require little processing, are considered less productive because they have a relatively low "value added" in comparison to snack foods, cold breakfast cereals, or other highly processed food "products." If the population is growing very slowly and is already satisfying its basic food needs, then logically the only way for food companies to increase their domestic profits

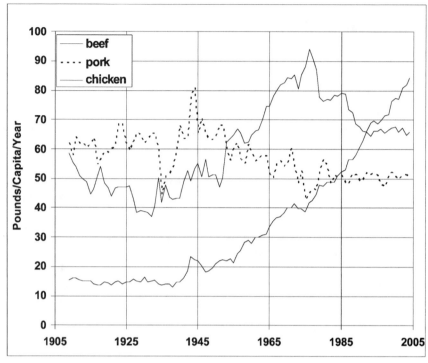

Figure 5.1.   U.S. Retail Beef, Pork, and Chicken Consumption, 1909–2004.

is through increased competition between companies or through the production of increasingly more expensive new food products. Food markets may also be increased through exports in a world market system. Limited increases have also been achieved by raising the nutritional standard for domestic pets. New food products are one of the most important tools used by giant food corporations competing for larger shares of the relatively fixed market. The importance of new food products was underscored by the comments of a president of Campbell Soup Company, cited in the National Commission study, to the effect that a company without new products would see a 50 percent drop in profits within a year and would be losing money within five years.

Thus, the introduction of new food items and a corresponding continual upgrading of the energy intensity of subsistence seem to be a logical outgrowth of an expanding economy in a culture of consumption. However, the food habits of any society, including societies based on a culture of consumption, undoubtedly will be relatively conservative and can be changed only with difficulty, regardless of the need of manufacturers to continually create and market new food products. The findings of the National Commission clearly bear out this generalization: Manipulating American tastes in food—introducing totally new foods or even permutations of existing products—has not been easily accomplished. It is instructive that ideas for new products do not normally originate with the consumer. Only 3 percent of the suggestions for 127 new products in a sample examined by the National Commission actually came from future consumers. Consumers were not clamoring for new products. New product development is in fact a very expensive, very lengthy, and uncertain process of trial and error in which most ideas prove unmarketable. In the mid-1960s a typical new cold breakfast cereal product required 4.5 years of development activity and nearly $4 million invested in physical design, market research, and advertising before full distribution could be achieved. Only some 5 percent of new product ideas reached full distribution, and only about 10 percent of these became well established. Of those products that made it all the way to the test-market stage, 22 percent were withdrawn short of full development. Beyond that point, another 17 percent were quickly withdrawn. Manufacturers assumed that every new product had a "life cycle" beginning with a very slow rise in sales or consumer acceptance and leading to a saturation point. A gradual decline would then set in as customers dropped the product entirely or shifted to rival brands. There may be a saturation point beyond which perpetually new products lose their appeal. The introduction of new American food products peaked in 1995 at more than 22,500, and had declined to some 16,200 by 1992.[44] There were 128 new breakfast cereals in 1995, but only 88 in 2000. Approximately one-fourth of new food products in 2000 claimed nutritional benefits such as reduced calories, fat, or cholesterol.

The amount of money spent on advertising and promotion of new products totally dwarfed expenditures for research and development. Only the largest food corporations could afford to develop new products, but the heavy advertising expenses were made less burdensome because they were tax deductible, thereby shifting costs to consumers. Enormous advertising expenditures are an accepted part of the process, as the National Commission study explained, because of the "inertia" of consumers, "arising primarily from reluctance to change established behavior patterns which delays customer acceptance of the new product."[45] The entire process bears a disturbing resemblance to the work of cultural change experts attempting to convince reluctant self-sufficient villagers that they should adopt expensive factory farm techniques. Food manufacturers happily concluded that those products that survive the risky promotion process do so because they satisfy a "real" consumer "need."

The non-random pattern of advertising expenditures clearly demonstrates that the reluctance to change established food habits is strongest when such habits already adequately satisfy basic nutritional needs. Products that appear to have little nutritional value or that at least do not offer a clear nutritional gain over the foods they would replace often require the most intensive advertising campaigns. The study found this to be true for cold cereals but considered it merely the reflection of "higher-than-average uncertainty as to consumer acceptance."[46] This generalization continues to be valid. For example, in 1992 the Kellogg Company, with some thirty-one brands of breakfast cereal on the market, spent $630 million on advertising.[47] Kellogg spent $715 million on national advertising in 2005.[48]

In general, staple foods such as fresh fruit, vegetables, meat, and milk, which could form the basis of a nutritionally sound diet yet require minimal processing and have little "added value," are promoted very little. "Impulse" items such as soft drinks, candy, and other snack foods, and new products generally, are heavily dependent on continual promotion. Companies spent $7 billion advertising processed food in the United States in 1999; $2 billion of this was to sell candy, snacks, and soft drinks and bottled water, but only $165 million on fruits, vegetables, and grains.[49] For example, the two largest candy manufacturers, Hershey's and Mars, spent $170 million advertising their products. Coca-Cola, one of the world's most profitable companies, spent $703 million on its American advertising in 2005 and sold $6.6 billion in soft drinks in North America, and $23 billion worldwide.[50] Coke executives calculated in the early 1990s that Americans were drinking an average of thirty-seven gallons of Coke products per capita per year, which is remarkable for a food product whose only nutritional ingredient, sugar, is often replaced with a non-nutrient substitute.[51] People must be persuaded to accept food products that are not necessarily good for them, just as peasant farmers must be urged to accept energy-intensive farming practices that in the long run may prove highly detrimental.

The "need" for new food products is sometimes explained by the argument that food habits are not necessarily "rational" from a nutritional viewpoint anyway and that food may often serve critical cultural functions other than nutrition.[52] This generalization is of course true, but it seems to be only in commercial societies that nutritional needs become secondary to other cultural functions, such as maintaining food industry profits. This seems to be a very crucial difference between major cultural systems. As noted in the discussion of potato production on the factory farm, profit was the only reason for growing potatoes; in food marketing the only reason for new food products may also be profit. As the National Commission study explained, "[The] risky and expensive venture of new product development and introduction is undertaken in hopes of finding a new product which yields a higher gross contribution to overhead and profit on invested assets."[53] This is the fundamental logic of the market economy as it is presently organized.

It is also sometimes argued that people have a basic "need" for new products as an escape from food monotony. Variety is, of course, also a nutritional advantage, and people may have a basic need for a varied diet to the extent that it is nutritionally adequate. However, local farm produce can be highly varied and nutritious, and new manufactured food products may offer no special advantage in that regard. Furthermore, people may eat food they know to be harmful, but this does not absolve the food industry from criticism for actively promoting nutritionally inferior but profitable foods. Perhaps more crucial is the reality that in the late 1990s some $10 billion was being spent on advertising directed at children and adolescents in the United States, including special packaging and toys designed to appeal to children, the use of cartoon characters in television ads, in-school marketing, kids' clubs, and special websites. This advertising was predominately for branded processed food, and not for fruits or vegetables. American children now receive more than half of their calories from fat and sugar, and this has been implicated in their soaring weight problems.[54]

Food Quality and Market Scale

People who routinely obtain their daily subsistence from supermarkets that are supplied by giant farms, processors, and warehouses from throughout the world may not realize how much food quality is lost when food must move great distances through such a vast marketplace. A large-scale market is good for investors because it means a larger volume of sales for a smaller number of merchants, but this scale change also makes it physically impossible to market many natural foods, such as delicate fruits at their sweetest, juiciest, most aromatic best. Genetic engineering may produce larger, firmer, and redder strawberries that store and ship well and look fabulous on the supermarket shelf, but they will never taste as good as fragile vine-ripened berries. Many fruits are genetically engineered as patented brand-name products that thrive on brand-name pesticides, herbicides, and fertilizers. These fruits are also designed to mature at the right time for ease of mechanical harvesting. Because urban consumers often select fruit by color rather than aroma, they can be deceived into choosing inferior fruit by artificially colored, waxed, gassed, or genetically altered crops. Food expert Jeffrey Steingarten[55] reminds us that most fruits taste best when ripe, but ripening is a complex biochemical process involving maturation to full size and shape, followed by enzymatic changes that produce softening, color changes, and the conversion of starches into sugars. All of this may take place very quickly or relatively slowly and may involve many combinations of variables, all of which can be affected by marketing practices. Some ripe fruits survive only a single day. Many fruits—such as blackberries, cherries, grapes, grapefruit, lemons, limes, litchis, mandarins, oranges, pineapples, raspberries, strawberries, and watermelons—will never ripen after they are picked. These fruits need to be ripened on the plant, harvested ripe, and consumed immediately. In contrast, apples and pears must be harvested at maturity, but they store well and will ripen and sweeten long after harvest and thus are ideal food products for global marketers.

Factory-Processed Potato Chips versus Manioc Cakes

Food processing and varied, nutritious diets were not invented by industrial civilization; they have been with us since the beginning of culture and humans' first use of fire. There is a clear difference, however, between food processing in tribal societies, where it is unquestionably "consumer oriented," and industrial food processing for a profit. Some of these differences have already been demonstrated, but a brief comparison between manioc cakes and potato chips will heighten the contrasts.

One of the finest examples of food processing in tribal cultures can be seen in the South American manioc complex. Bitter manioc is the staple food crop for many Amazonian Indians.[56] Before the starchy tuber can be eaten it must be peeled and grated and the pulp must be squeezed to separate the poisonous juice from the flour. This process is accomplished by means of a variety of specialized graters and squeezing devices (figure 5.2). The end products may then be further processed into a wide range of foods. The Waiwai of Guyana developed at least fourteen different kinds of bread and thirteen beverages based on bitter manioc and its by-products.[57] The flour may be sifted in various ways, baked in bread, eaten toasted, or used in soups and stews. The juice is used in soups, and the tapioca extracted from it finds a variety of food uses, sometimes in combination with the flour. All of these processes, of course, take place in the household. They involve no external energy inputs and no extended shipping or storage. Tribal diets should not be considered dull and monotonous simply because

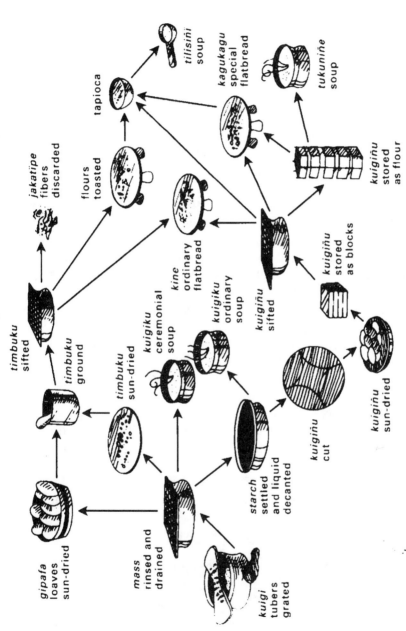

Figure 5.2. Steps in the Preparation of Manioc among the Kuikuru.
Dole, "Use of Manioc among the Kuikuru."

they do not benefit from supermarkets. There is also no possibility of eating potentially harmful food to assure someone else's profit.

In the United States in 2001 only about 30 percent of the marketed potato crop was shipped to consumers as raw tubers to be processed in the household.[58] Even these "unprocessed" potatoes had to be washed mechanically, chemically treated to inhibit sprouting, in some cases colored or waxed, and transported and stored under temperature-controlled conditions. The potato industry was transformed by the development of frozen French fries for the fast food industry in the 1950s. By 1993 Americans were consuming more fried frozen potatoes than fresh, with the added oil more than tripling their caloric intake from potatoes.[59] Potatoes destined for chips—and in 2001 these made up about 13 percent of the crop—would go through washing, sprout inhibition, and temperature control and in addition might sit in storage for six to eight months. Further chemical treatments might include gases or chemical solutions to prevent discoloration of peeled potatoes before cooking and again to avoid after-cooking darkening that occurs as a natural enzymatic process and has no effect on taste or nutritive qualities but is thought to reduce consumer appeal.[60] Oils, salt, preservatives, and sometimes special artificial flavoring are added in the final processing, and the end product is packed and shipped in special containers. Then, of course, millions of advertising dollars must be spent to convince people to eat the product. After critics attacked chips for their high fat and salt content, an experimental, vitamin-enriched chip made a brief appearance in 1974. In 1998 Frito Lay began marketing potato chips made from *olestra*, an indigestible synthetic fat-like molecule that sometimes caused diarrhea. Of course, the success of the potato chip as a food product is attributable not to its nutritional qualities but rather to the fact that at the retail level it is many times more expensive per pound than the ordinary raw potato.

An important dimension of factory food systems that should not be overlooked is that marketing requirements—food that looks attractive, ships well, and can be stored for extended periods in warehouses and on supermarket shelves—mean that many new chemical ingredients are added for strictly economic, non-nutritional reasons. A bewildering array of food additives, by 1972 estimated at some 2,500, is being added to food products as coloring agents, synthetic flavors, and preservatives; to prevent caking or separation; to provide body; and for a wide range of other specialized functions.[61] Only a few of these additives are used to replace some of the nutrients destroyed in processing. As with pesticide residues, much controversy has arisen over the possible dangers of these additives, but few people question the basic marketing system that makes them nec-essary. Since 1972 many new additives have, of course, appeared; others were discovered to be harmful and were subsequently banned. Health au-thorities and the food industry are engaged in an ongoing struggle over how to control non-nutritional additives.[62]

Fishing, Global Trade, and "Ghost Acres"

Some modern nations have so far managed to keep ahead of their food problems by supplementing their own limited food production capabilities through heavy reliance on fishing and international trade. Fish may be eaten directly or used as a substitute for feed crops for the production of meat, milk, eggs, and poultry. This seems to be a logical step to stay ahead of the Malthusian controls on overpopulation. When the intensification of agriculture has reached the point at which further increases can be achieved only if truly prohibitive energy deficits are incurred, fishing fleets may be expanded and favorable trade agreements reached with nations producing food surpluses.

In 1965, food scientist Georg Borgstrom introduced the concept of ghost acres, referring to the fact that trade and fishing were ways of gain-ing extraterritorial acres. Ghost acres were calculated as the amount of land a given country would need to put into production to gain an amount of animal protein equivalent to its net food imports and fishery production. Ghost acres have also been called "phantom carrying capacity."[63] Accord-ing to this reckoning many nations had already far exceeded the carrying capacity of their farmlands—at least given their culturally prescribed food patterns—and had become precariously dependent on uncertain interna-tional markets and frail marine resources. At that time Borgstrom calculated that Japan's ghost acres exceeded its agricultural acreage by more than six times and the United Kingdom's effective acres were nearly tripled by ghost acres. Japan's fishing industry was the third largest in the world in 1990, with its fleet spread throughout the Pacific and Atlantic. Fish products then accounted for 28 percent of the daily protein supply in Japan, the highest in the world.[64] Furthermore, in 1992 Japan imported more grain than any other nation, more than double its domestic production.[65]

The problem with subsisting on ghost acres is that global fisheries are now heavily over-exploited and in danger of collapse. By 2003, seven of the top-ten species, constituting 30 percent of global wild fisheries, were considered to be fully exploited or already overexploited.[66] The global trend in loss of marine species since 1950 led a team of marine biologists and ecologists in 2006 to project the collapse of all species currently fished by 2048.[67] The ecological footprint concept and the closely related ecological fishprint also help put ghost acres in perspective.[68] For example, the world was taking 157 percent of global marine biocapacity in 2003. At that time Japan was using more than 6 times its ecological footprint biocapacity, and its ecological fishprint was nearly 8 times its fisheries biocapacity. The fishprint takes into account the trophic level of fish harvested and reductions in capacity as overfishing occurs. Trophic level matters because for example it takes over 1.7 million tons of primary biological productivity to produce 1 ton of Bluefin tuna at the top of the marine food chain, but only 79 tons to produce 1 ton of anchovies near the bottom of the food chain.

The global trade component of ghost acreage is not presently operating as a means of allocating food to countries on the basis of critical nutritional requirements; rather, as with other facets of the global market economy, it supports and reflects the interests of the world's financial elite. Scarce protein resources in the form of meat, fish and fish products, nuts, and oilseed cakes move with bananas, cocoa, coffee, and tea from protein-poor, hungry nations to rich, well-fed nations, propelled by the exigencies of the world's financial markets. Under the General Agreement on Tariffs and Trade (GATT), finance capital moves freely between countries seeking the highest returns on investment. Peruvian traders, for example, instead of satisfying the obvious needs of Peru's protein-deficient people, find it more profitable to ship Peru's rich fish meal resource to the United States, where it is fed to chickens to subsidize energy-intensive egg industries. Likewise, Indian oilseed cakes are fed to European cattle while millions of Indians are starved for protein and Indian cattle scavenge for refuse.

Borgstrom pointed out that the world's refrigerator ships were almost exclusively engaged in moving bananas and frozen meat from Central and South America, Australia, and New Zealand to Western Europe and North America, where they will bring the highest prices. The curious feature of this trade is that in many cases it fills a nutritional need in the rich countries that could be satisfied by simply replacing the imported supplies with domestic equivalents. Brazilian meat and Peruvian fish meal in the United States might be considered an anomaly, but actually they are the logical outgrowth of a system of world market exchanges between nations that have institutionalized inequality.

In many cases this system quite literally plucks food from the hands of starving people while also indirectly depriving them of the ability to produce their own badly needed food. Millions of acres in Africa, Latin America, and Asia presently devoted to the satisfaction of the culturally prescribed "need" of the developed nations for chocolate, coffee, and tea might instead be converted to the production of food to satisfy local needs.

Trading patterns are directly related to malnutrition in Brazil.[69] By the 1970s vast areas of the Brazilian northeast were converted from subsistence farms feeding peasants to large-scale sisal plantations on which the peasants became poorly paid laborers. The sisal plantations supplied twine to the United States, where it was used to tie bales of hay, which in turn were fed to American cattle. Unfortunately, the former subsistence farmers whose lands were converted from food crops to an export crop found themselves unable to buy enough food with their meager wages to satisfy the minimal nutritional needs of their families. Systematic malnutrition resulted as the peasants were forced to rely on cheap, high-calorie foods that were low in protein. Different permutations of the same situation have occurred throughout the world where the growing of cash crops for export, either to world or to national markets, has replaced food crops grown to satisfy the nutritional requirements of local peoples.

Such disparity between the nutritional needs of people and the distribution of food has no parallel in tribal culture. In fact, while food may circulate between local households according to need, it is very unusual for cultures not to be totally self-sufficient in their subsistence requirements. In a remarkably few cases cultures are unable to satisfy their needs either because of periodic misfortunes or because of peculiarly limiting environmental factors. Food can then indeed be distributed through an "international" trade system that characteristically does not operate by normal market principles that determine prices and profits.[70] The critical aspect of these systems is that exchange rates are socially prescribed, not set by market competition. The obvious conclusion is that applying the market rationale is not always the best means of satisfying human nutritional needs.

The present world food distribution system reflects the economic ranking of nations and of rich and poor within nations. In 1965 Borgstrom computed agricultural self-sufficiency ratings for various nations on the basis of their reliance on ghost acres and showed that poor Asian nations such as China and India were more than 90 percent self-sufficient, whereas the wealthy Western European nations such as England, the Netherlands, Belgium, and West Germany were only 37–60 percent self-sufficient. Clearly these "developed" nations were being supported by a costly food system that could not long be sustained if world fisheries declined from overfishing or if the world trade system were to break down. In effect there is an international series of trophic levels in which the nations at the bottom are supported by high-calorie, low-protein diets while supplying their high-protein resources to the nations at the upper levels. The upper-level nations are able to consume the highest-quality animal protein and a wide array of very costly sumptuary foods imported from nations where these foods are economically inaccessible to the bulk of the population.

The continued expansion of world trade and the proliferation of new food products in rich nations add enormously to the energy costs of food, not only because of additional processing, but also because of the further requirements of storage and transportation. There are also diminishing energy returns due to increasing waste and losses. Normally at least 10 percent of the food supply of a given nation is lost annually to spoilage and pests before it even reaches consumers. This loss may be serious enough in a market system that moves food from one end of the country to the other through complex networks of intermediary wholesalers and retailers. It becomes critical in a system in which food may be shipped halfway around the world.

The Limits of Food Production

Increased resource use and improvements in technology and efficiency have increased global food production more rapidly than population in recent decades, but 800 million people remain food insecure. . . . Meanwhile, growth in global agricultural productivity appears to be slowing, and land degradation has been blamed as a contributing factor. (Wiebe, "Global Resources and Productivity")[71]

More intensive subsistence technology has been one of the principal components of international proposals for dealing with the food problem for decades. The famous "Point Four" program of technical assistance launched by the United States in 1949 made this a prime objective. Since then the United States has been heavily committed to speeding the diffusion of agricultural technology through official agencies such as the Agency for International Development (USAID), the Consultative Group on International Agricultural Research (CGIAR), and the Board for International Food and Agricultural Development (BIFAD) working through the U.S. land grant universities. Private foundations such as the Ford Foundation, Rockefeller Foundation, and Kellogg Foundation have devoted millions of dollars since the 1950s to programs of agricultural extension and research designed to raise food production in poor countries. The United Nations Food and Agriculture Organization (FAO) has been dedicated to increasing food production throughout the world since its inception. Agricultural development was a key element in UN proposals for the Second Development Decade (1970–1980) and continued to be a central focus in the Fourth and Fifth Development Decades, and is part of the strategy for meeting the UN Millennium Goals. In 1969 the FAO unveiled its Indicative World Plan for agricultural development as the basis for UN food strategy. The plan called simply for "increasing productivity through more intensive use of physical resources and modern agricultural technology."[72] Cereal production, because of its crucial dietary role, was singled out for special attention. The plan assumed continued economic growth to support the further development of technology and to help poor nations purchase the food imports they would still require even if agricultural development succeeded.

The strategy of intensifying production was pioneered by the Rockefeller Foundation and by Nobel Prize–winning plant scientist Norman Borlaug. It involves simply exporting the fossil fuel–subsidized capital intensive factory farm systems of the highly industrialized nations to the rest of the world. More specifically, it means applying biological engineering to the design of specialized plants that will respond to the application of large doses of chemical fertilizer, pesticides, and water with high yields. In this case the domestication process itself has become a commercial enterprise. For example, in 1999 the Monsanto corporation, with annual sales of $9.1 billion, was marketing Roundup, which it described as "the world's leading nonselective agricultural and industrial herbicide," as well as Roundup Ready canola, cotton, and soybeans, YardGard insect-protected corn, and NewLeaf insect-protected potatoes.

This Green Revolution was quickly hailed as an enormous success when per-acre yields in many countries soared with the application of these new techniques in the late 1960s, and there were many optimistic statements about rapid doublings in food production and a final conquest over all of nature's limitations. Malthus, it seemed, had been refuted.

Many agricultural success stories have been cited as justification for renewed faith in the unlimited power of technology. Mexico, for example, was able to triple its wheat production and double its corn output within roughly twenty years after agricultural scientists financed by the Rockefeller Foundation began applying modern technology to the development of miracle plants in 1944.[73] World grain production more than doubled between 1962 and 1992, actually staying ahead of population growth. Furthermore, large surpluses in some farm products continued to pile up in the United States, and even India has had sporadic surpluses since the late 1970s.[74]

Despite the outstanding successes, however, in some countries many problems have arisen that have made implementation of the new technology difficult. Many agricultural extension workers have been frustrated by stubborn peasants who refuse to believe that the new crops would really be an advantage for them because of their obvious vulnerability and the increased dependence on outsiders that these crops imply. There have also been serious problems in financing the new technology at both national and local levels. Small farmers cannot afford the investment in expensive seeds and chemicals, nor can poor nations. As noted earlier, this system ultimately depends on a vast fossil-fuel subsidy that has seldom been readily available to poor countries. Escalating petroleum prices on the world market since the early 1970s and general increases in the cost of agricultural intensification contributed to the enormous debt burdens that poor nations faced in the 1980s and 1990s.

Even if financing and the energy base were not limiting factors, water availability and unfavorable weather conditions such as global warming could be. Even unlimited energy would not solve all the problems involved in getting enough water to enough acres to support an unlimited Green Revolution. Some of the new technology may require so little labor that unemployment might result and more rural people may be forced to move to the cities. In some countries the new crops have been monopolized by large agribusinesses and wealthy landowners, driving small farmers off their lands. In some cases, transportation and storage facilities have been inadequate to handle either the increased crops or the needed fertilizer. High production may reduce prices below the profit margin, but the prices may still be higher than the poor can pay. Indeed, the social and economic barriers to further intensification of food production may be so critical that the ultimate physical limits may never be reached.

Some experts fear that the successes achieved to date in the Green Revolution might be only temporary and that serious reversals may occur if potential biological liabilities of the high-yield varieties emerge. It must be assumed that these plants will turn out to be highly susceptible to many new pests and blights or to minor fluctuations in weather. A further unknown is the extent of the ecological impact of factory farming on a global scale. Further eutrophication will almost certainly clog inland waters as fertilizer use increases, and pesticides will further threaten already overstressed marine food resources. With the full application of fossil fuel–powered factory farm food production humanity may be taking an irreversible step with implications fully as grave as when tribal foragers first turned to simple farming. This time, however, the price could be much higher. Optimists have argued that with the proper application of technology we could intensify production to feed 10 billion people by 2050.[75] The removal of farm subsidies and trade barriers would allow food prices to rise to levels that would no doubt spur production. However, unless these changes also allow the world's poor to participate in the market, billions will be shut out.

Notes

1. Steinhart, John S., and Carol E. Steinhart. 1974. "Energy Use in the U.S. Food System." *Science* 184(4134): 307–16.

2. Harris, Marvin. 1971. *Culture, Man and Nature*. New York: Crowell.

3. Odum, Howard T. 1971. *Environment, Power, and Society*. New York: Wiley, Inter-Science.

4. Odum, *Environment, Power, and Society*, 115.

5. Odum, *Environment, Power, and Society*.

6. Odum, *Environment, Power, and Society*, 117.

7. NASS (National Agricultural Statistics Service) Farm Labor, August 16, 2002. usda.mannlib.cornell.edu/MannUsda/homepage.do; U.S. Census Bureau, 2007. *Statistical Abstract of the United States: 2007*. Washington, D.C.: U.S. Government Printing Office, Table 803.

8. Barlett, Peggy F. 1987. "Industrial Agriculture in Evolutionary Perspective." *Cultural Anthropology* 2: 137–54; Barlett, Peggy F. 1989. "Industrial Agriculture." In *Economic Anthropology*, edited by Stuart Planner, 253–91. Stanford, CA: Stanford University Press; Netting, Robert McC. 1993. *Smallholders, Householders: Farm Families and the Ecology of Intensive, Sustainable Agriculture*. Stanford, CA: Stanford University Press.

9. Reisner, Marc. 1986. *Cadillac Desert: The American West and Its Disappearing Water*. New York: Viking Penguin.

10. Talburt, William E., and Ora Smith. 1967. *Potato Processing*. Westport, CT: Avi; Various *Proceedings of the Annual Washington Potato Conference and Trade Fair*, Washington Potato Commission; Rappaport, Roy A. 1971. "The Flow of Energy in an Agricultural Society." *Scientific American* 224(3): 117–32.

11. Rappaport, Roy A. 1968. *Pigs for the Ancestors: Ritual in the Ecology of a New Guinea People*. New Haven, CT: Yale University Press; Rappaport, Ray. "The Flow of Energy."

12. Hagood, Mel A. 1972. "Which Irrigation System?" *Proceedings of the 11th Annual Washington Potato Conference and Trade Fair*, 83–86. Washington Potato Conference, Moses Lake, Washington.

13. U.S. Census Bureau. 2007. *Statistical Abstract of the United States: 2007*, Table 33.

14. Berry, Wendell. 1977. *The Unsettling of America: Culture and Agriculture*. San Francisco: Sierra Club Books.

15. Chandler, Alfred D., Jr. 1977. *The Visible Hand: The Managerial Revolution in American Business*. Cambridge, MA, and London: Belknap Press of Harvard University Press.

16. Soltow, Lee. 1975. *Men and Wealth in the United States, 1850–1870*. New Haven, CT, and London: Yale University Press, 112–13; Beard, Charles A., and Mary R. Beard. 1934. *The Rise of American Civilization*. New York: Macmillan, 383–84.

17. Roy, William G. 1983. "Interlocking Directorates and the Corporate Revolution." *Social Science History* 7(2): 143–64.

18. Pessen, Edward. 1973. *Riches, Class, and Power Before the Civil War*. Lexington, MA: Heath and Company.

19. Friedman, Lawrence M. 1964. "The Dynastic Trust." *Yale Law Journal* 73: 547–92; Marcus, George E., with Peter Dobkin Hall. 1992. *Lives in Trust: The Fortunes of Dynastic Families in Late Twentieth-Century America*. Boulder, CO: Westview Press, 60–70; Farrell, Betty G. 1993. *Elite Families: Class and Power in Nineteenth-Century Boston*. Albany: State University of New York.

20. Hall, Peter Dobkin. 1982. *The Organization of American Culture, 1700–1900: Private Institutions, Elites, and the Origins of American Nationality*. New York: New York University Press.

21. Clanton, Gene. 1991. *Populism: The Humane Preference in America, 1890–1900*. Boston: Twayne Publishers.

22. U.S. Census Bureau. 2007. *Statistical Abstract of the United States: 2007*, Table 802; U.S. Department of Agriculture (USDA). 2002. *Census of Agriculture*, vol. 1, chapter 1: U.S. National Level Data. Table 41. www.nass.usda.gov/census/census02/volume1/us/index1.htm

23. McConnell, Grant. 1953. *The Decline of Agrarian Democracy*. Berkeley and Los Angeles: University of California Press; Domhoff, G. William. 1996. *State Autonomy or Class Dominance?: Case Studies on Policy Making in America*. New York: Aldine de Gruyter.

24. Goldschmidt, Walter. 1978. *As You Sow: Three Studies in the Social Consequences of Agribusiness*. Montclair, NJ: Allanheld, Osmum & Co, xlviii.

25. Madden, J. Patrick. 1967. *Economics of Size in Farming: Theory, Analytic Procedures, and a Review of Selected Studies*. Economic Research Service, USDA. Agricultural Economic Report 107, cited in Goldschmidt, *As You Sow*, xxx–xxxi.

26. Goldschmidt, *As You Sow*, xxxii–xxxix.

27. MacCannell, Dean, and Jerry White. 1984. "The Social Costs of Large-Scale Agriculture: The Prospects of Land Reform in California." In *Land Reform, American Style*, edited by Charles C. Geisler and Frank J. Popper, 35–54. Totawa, NJ: Rowman & Allanheld.

28. Thu, Kendall M., and E. Paul Durrenberger, eds. 1998. *Pigs, Profits, and Rural Communities*. Albany: State University of New York Press. See also Stull, Donald D., and Michael J. Broadway. 2004. *Slaughterhouse Blues: The Meat and Poultry Industry in North America*. Belmont, CA: Wadsworth/Thomson Learning.

29. U.S. Department of Commerce. 1984. *1982 Census of Agriculture.* vol. 1, pt. 5, *Geographic Area Series.* California. Washington, D.C.: U.S. Government Printing Office.

30. U.S. Department of Agriculture (USDA), Grain Inspection, Packers and Stockyards Administration. 2006. *Assessment of the Cattle, Hog, and Poultry Industries. 2005 Report.* archive.gipsa.usda.gov/pubs/05assessment.pdf

31. Morgan, Dan. 1979. *Merchants of Grain.* New York: Viking Press; Sewell, Tom. 1992. *The World Grain Trade.* New York: Woodhead-Faulkner.

32. Steinhart and Steinhart, "Energy Use," 307–16.

33. Heller, Martin C., and Gregory A. Keoleian. 2000. *Life Cycle-based Sustainability Indicators for Assessment of the U.S. Food System.* Report No CSS00-04 Center for Sustainable Systems. Ann Arbor: University of Michigan, 41, Figure 5.

34. U.S. Department of Commerce, *Statistical Abstract of the United States, 1994,* 146.

35. Capps, Oral, Jr., Annette Clauson, Joanne Guthrie, Grant Pittman, and Matthew Stockton. 2005. *Contributions of Nonalcoholic Beverages to the U.S. Diet.* USDA, Economic Research Service, Economic Research Report Number 1. www.ers.usda.gov/publications/err1/err1.pdf

36. George, Susan. 1977. *How the Other Half Dies: The Real Reasons for World Hunger.* Montclair, NJ: Allanheld, Osmum & Co; Manning, Richard. 2004. "The Oil We Eat: Following the Food Chain Back to Iraq." *Harper's Magazine.* (February); Manning, R. 2004. *Against the Grain: How Agriculture Has Hijacked Civilization.* New York: North Point Press; Pollan, Michael. 2006. *The Omnivore's Dilemma: A Natural History of Four Meals.* New York: Penguin Press.

37. U.S. Department of Agriculture (USDA), Economic Research Service. 2006. "U.S. Food Supply: Nutrients and Other Food Components, 1909 to 2004." *Nutrient Availability Spreadsheet* (March 3).

38. Steinhart and Steinhart, "Energy Use," 307–16.

39. U.S. Department of Agriculture (USDA), Economic Research Service. 2007. *Food Price Spreads.* Table 1—Marketing bill and farm value components of consumer expenditures for domestically produced farm foods. www.ers.usda.gov/Briefing/FoodPriceSpreads/bill/table1.htm

40. USDA, Economic Research Service. 2007. *Food Price Spreads,* Table 1; U.S. Department of Agriculture (USDA). 2000. "Annual Spotlight on the U.S. Food System, 2000." *FoodReview* 23(3).

41. Heller and Keoleian, *Life Cycle-based Sustainability Indicators,* 40; Barton, J. 1980. *Transportation and Fuel Requirements in the Food and Fiber System.* USDA, Agricultural Economic Report No. 444. Economic, Statistics, and Cooperative Service.

42. USDA, Economic Research Service. 2006. *U.S. Food Supply: Nutrients and Other Food Components, 1909 to 2004.* Nutrient Availability Spreadsheet, food consumption (per capita) data system, food availability (March 3).

43. Marple, Gary A., and Harry B. Wissman, eds. 1968. *Grocery Manufacturing in the United States.* New York: Praeger.

44. U.S. Department of Agriculture (USDA), Economic Research Service. 2002. *The U.S. Food Marketing System, 2002.* Agricultural Economic Report No. 811. Appendix Table 33.

45. Marple and Wissman, *Grocery Manufacturing*, 40.

46. Marple and Wissman, *Grocery Manufacturing*, 185.

47. *Advertising Age.* 1993 (Sept 29).

48. *Advertising Age.* 2006. *100 Leading National Advertisers.* Supplement (June 26).

49. USDA, Economic Research Service. 2002. *The U.S. Food Marketing System, 2002.* Agricultural Economic Report No. 811. Appendix Table 30.

50. *Advertising Age.* 2006. *100 Leading National Advertisers.* Supplement (June 26).

51. Huey, John. 1993. "The World's Best Brand." *Fortune* (May 31): 44–54.

52. Sofer, Cyril. 1965. "Buying and Selling: A Study in the Sociology of Distribution." *Sociological Review* (July): 183–209.

53. Marple and Wissman, *Grocery Manufacturing*, 7.

54. Story, Mary, and Simone French. 2004. "Food Advertising and Marketing Directed at Children and Adolescents in the U.S." *International Journal of Behavioral Nutrition and Physical Activity* 1(3).

55. Steingarten, Jeffrey. 1997. *The Man Who Ate Everything and Other Gastronomic Feats, Disputes, and Pleasurable Pursuits.* New York: Random House, Vintage Books, 74–88.

56. Dole, Gertrude. 1978. "The Use of Manioc Among the Kuikuru: Some Implications." *Anthropological Papers* (Ann Arbor: University of Michigan Museum of Anthropology) 67: 217–47; Lancaster, P. A., et al. 1982. "Traditional Cassava-Based Foods: Survey of Processing Techniques." *Economic Botany* 36(l): 12–45.

57. Yde, Jens. 1965. "Material Culture of the Waiwai. Narionalmuseets Skrifter." *Etnografisk Roekke* 10. Copenhagen: National Museum, 28–51.

58. U.S. Department of Agriculture (USDA), Economic Research Service. 2007. *Potato Statistics* (91011), Table 52—Utilization of U.S. potatoes, 1959–2001.

59. Buzby, Jean C., and Hodan A. Farah. 2006. "Findings: Americans Switch From Fresh to Frozen Potatoes." *Amber Waves* 4(3): 5.

60. Talburt and Smith, *Potato Processing.*

61. Kermode, G. O. 1972. "Food Additives." *Scientific American* 226(3): 15–21.

62. Freydberg, Nicholas, and Willis A. Gortner. 1982. *The Food Additives Book.* Toronto: Bantam; Hunter, Beatrice Tram. 1982. *Food Additives and Federal Policy: The Mirage of Safety.* Brattleboro, VT: Greene.

63. Catton, William. 1980. *Overshoot: The Ecological Basis of Revolutionary Change.* Chicago: University of Illinois Press.

64. FAO, Food and Agriculture Organization of the United Nations. 1992. *The State of Food and Agriculture.* Rome.

65. World Bank. 1994. *World Development Report 1994: Infrastructure for Development.* New York: Oxford.

66. FAO Fisheries Department 2004: 32. FAO, Food and Agriculture Organization of the United Nations. 2004. *The State of the World Fisheries and Aquaculture*

2004. Rome: Food and Agriculture Organization of the United Nations. ftp://ftp.fao.org/docrep/fao/007/y5600e/y5600e00.pdf

67. Worm, Boris, et al. 2006. "Impacts of Biodiversity Loss on Ocean Ecosystem Services." *Science* 314 (Nov. 3): 787–90.

68. WWF International. 2006. *Living Planet Report 2006.* World Wildlife Fund. www.panda.org/news_facts/publications/living_planet_report/index.cfm; Talberth, John, Karen Wolowicz, Jason Venetoulis, Michel Gelobter, Paul Boyle, and Bill Mott. 2006. *The Ecological Fishprint of Nations: Measuring Humanity's Impact on Marine Ecosystems.* Oakland, CA: Redefining Progress. http://www.rprogress.org/newprograms/sustIndi/fishprint/index.shtml

69. Gross, Daniel R., and Barbara A. Underwood. "Technological Change and Caloric Costs: Sisal Agriculture 1971." *American Anthropologist* 73(2): 725–40.

70. Sahlins, Marshall. 1972. *Stone Age Economics.* Chicago: Aldine, chapter 6.

71. Wiebe, Keith. 2006. "Global Resources and Productivity." In *Agricultural Resources and Environmental Indicators,* edited by Keith Wiebe and Noel Gollehon, 81–88; Economic Information Bulletin 16. USDA Economic Research Service, 81.

72. Boehma, Addeke H. 1970. "A World Agricultural Plan." *Scientific American* 223(2): 54–69.

73. Fabun, Don. 1970. *Food: An Energy Exchange System.* Beverly Hills, CA: Glencoe.

74. Hazell, Peter B. R. 1994. "Rice in India." *National Geographic Research & Exploration* 10(2): 172–83.

75. Bongaarts, John. 1994. "Can the Growing Human Population Feed Itself?" *Scientific American* 270(3): 36–42.

The Population Problem 6

The explosive growth of the human population is the most significant terrestrial event of the past million millennia. . . . No geological event in a billion years—not the emergence of mighty mountain ranges, nor the submergence of entire subcontinents, nor the occurrence of periodic glacial ages—has posed a threat to terrestrial life comparable to that of human overpopulation.

—PAUL AND ANNE EHRLICH,
POPULATION, RESOURCES, ENVIRONMENT 1972[1]

IT HAS BEEN RELATIVELY EASY for Americans and citizens of the other comfortably wealthy industrial nations to see overpopulation as the "root" of all the world's environmental problems and of many of its other difficulties as well. In this simplistic view resource depletion, food shortages, and environmental deterioration, along with war and poverty, must all be caused by the presence of too many people in the world. Birth control and family planning programs are the obvious solutions. In 1968 biologist Paul Ehrlich presented this viewpoint dramatically in his book *The Population Bomb*, which popularized the expression "population explosion" and focused wide attention on population growth as *the* cause of global problems. Ehrlich emphatically linked "too many people" with "too little food" and named it as the cause of hunger in poor countries and environmental troubles worldwide. On the latter issue he declared: "The causal chain of the deterioration is easily followed to its source. Too many cars, too many factories, too much detergent, too much pesticide, multiplying contrails, inadequate sewage treatment plants, too little water, too much carbon dioxide—all can be traced easily to too many people."[2]

In 1972 Paul and Anne Ehrlich declared in "The Crisis," the first chapter of their human ecology textbook, that the population explosion was "the most significant event of the past million millennia" and dramatically warned that it was suddenly bringing all life on earth to the edge of extinction. In their later popular writings the Ehrlichs offer a more nuanced view of the role of population.[3] The *Population Bomb* was of course much too simple. Discussions between biologists Paul Ehrlich, Barry Commoner, and environmental scientist John Holdren quickly led to the formulation of the IPAT equation to explore the complexity of the problem. In this equation, I = PAT, where I = impact on the environment, P = population, A = affluence, or per capita level of consumption, and T = technology.[4] The IPAT equation reformulates Leslie White's anthropological model of cultural evolution, highlighting the negative effects of progress.

Paul Ehrlich's 1991 address delivered in London for the Worldwide Fund for Nature's annual World Conservation Lecture emphasized the scale dimensions of human problems. He expressed his shock that world population was reaching 5.5 billion—an increase of 2 billion people in the twenty-four years since the publication of *The Population Bomb*. He argued emphatically that "the strategic problem for humanity is that the *scale* of our activities is too large."[5] He maintained that sustaining the present population required eating into the world's capital resources and that it was pure folly to suggest that further growth was supportable.

Many other writers reject the notion of a population crisis. They argue that if we simply achieve full economic development the earth can comfortably support many billions more people. British economist Colin Clark (1905–1989) even suggested that population growth itself will be the means of bringing further progress to poor peoples:

> It [population growth] brings economic hardship to communities living by traditional methods of agriculture; but it is the only force powerful enough to make such communities change their methods, and in the long run transforms them into much more advanced and productive societies. The world has immense physical resources for agricultural and mineral production still unused. In communities, the beneficial economic effects of large and expanding markets are abundantly clear.[6]

There can be little doubt that rapid population growth and the absolute level of population are important aspects of the environmental crisis as Ehrlich suggests, but as the IPAT equation shows, the level of consumption is in many respects more critical than population size alone. At the same time, Clark is correct that population growth has promoted techno-logical growth and economic development, but when development means growth in per capita consumption the human impact on the earth increases disproportionately, such that greater numbers have a more negative impact in the long run. Ehrlich[7] calculated in 1992 that since his birth in 1932 world population had nearly tripled, but because of economic develop-ment the effective human impact on the planet had increased perhaps six-fold. He estimated that on a per capita basis Americans had a fifty times greater impact on the earth's life support system than people in the poor-est countries. As we will see, quality of life, or standard of living, "A" in the IPAT equation, must be considered in any attempt to assess carrying capacities for given environments. Population pressure is always relative to particular cultural conditions.

Instead of treating population as the sole problem, this chapter exam-ines population in broad cross-cultural and evolutionary perspectives. The elevated population growth rates that presently characterize world demog-raphy will be seen as one problematic symptom of a world dominated by commercially organized societies. Given present consumption patterns it would be misleading to deny the reality of the environmental crisis that ac-celerates with each increase in either population or consumption. Global economic growth may well be a false hope, both because it may be unat-tainable and because, if attained, it would only elevate consumption and cancel any environmental gains that might be achieved, even if world pop-ulation can be stabilized. Rather than focusing on economic growth, the world needs to focus on socio-cultural development and the politics of wealth distribution to meet existing human needs. As Ehrlich argued in 1968, rather than planning technological advances to meet the future needs of another 5 or 10 billion people, "it would be more prudent to take proper care of 3.5 billion people [the 1968 population] before boasting about how easy it was to do the same for much greater numbers."[8]

There is no disagreement on the basic fact that world population has grown enormously since the beginning of the industrial era and that un-sustainable growth continues in much of the world. With few apparent ex-ceptions,[9] most writers also agree that present growth patterns cannot continue indefinitely. It is easy to demonstrate the impossibility of perpet-ual growth. For example, in 1968 Paul Ehrlich calculated that, given a dou-bling time of 37 years (the estimated world rate at that time), there would be 60 million billion people, or 100 persons per square yard over the entire surface of the earth, within just nine hundred years. Biochemist and science fiction author Isaac Asimov (1920–1992) calculated in 1971 that at growth rates prevailing at that time the human population would equal the mass of the globe within a mere 1,560 years, and within 4,856 years it would equal the mass of the universe. The real question is obviously not whether growth will continue but rather how and when it will stop, and whose decision making shapes the social and cultural conditions driving both population and consumption. Technological optimists feel confident that the world can support more than 10 billion people,[10] while some super-optimists feel that we might in theory accommodate well over 100 billion under special circumstances. Optimum global population will certainly be far lower than any theoretical maximum.

Maximum Global Population Estimates

There have been many modern attempts to estimate how many people the world could support, but they have varied widely because of differing assumptions about the natural capacity of the world and the cultural demands that people might make.[11] Based on population densities by land type in 1890, British geographer E. G. Ravenstein calculated a maximum global population of 5.9 billion, which he projected could be reached by 2072.[12] In 1925 German human geographer Albrecht Penck treated food as the limiting factor. Calculating human nutritional requirements and agricultural potential for eleven climatic zones, Penck estimated a probable maximum global population of 8 billion, and an absolute maximum of about 16 billion.[13] Based on the photosynthetic potential of the earth by latitude, and human nutritional requirements of 1 million kilocalories per capita per year, Dutch biochemist C. T. De Wit calculated in 1967 that the earth could theoretically feed an incredible 1 trillion people, but allowing for their needs for urban and recreational space, he set the upper limit at 79 to 146 billion.[14] These estimates would of course leave nothing for nature. De Wit assumed that water and minerals would not be limiting factors, and recognized that the amount of meat people wanted would reduce maximum population.

Following similar methods, Stanford geneticist H. R. Hulett calculated an American-defined optimum global population in 1970.[15] Based on American apparent daily consumption of 3,200 kcal per person, with one-third in animal products, Hulett estimated that because of the energy requirements of animal food production, the actual per capita caloric consumption of Americans was equivalent to 7 million kilocalories annually. Comparing this figure with the global potential suggests that the world could support only 1.2 billion people on the American diet. Global forest resources at the 1965 harvest level would likewise support just over one billion people at the American rate of consumption. Based on photosynthetic potential, or net primary biological productivity (NPP), Hulett estimated that at the American rate of consumption the 1965 population of 3.5 billion people would consume 10 to 40 percent of the world's total biological product for food and fiber. Burning the entire global NPP as a renewable fuel, rather than burning fossil fuel, would support at most 1 to 4 billion people at the American per capita energy consumption rate, leaving nothing for food and fiber. Hulett also considered American consumption of steel, aluminum, and fertilizer and likewise concluded that a global population of about one billion would be the maximum supportable. These results did not anticipate the dramatic increases in agricultural productivity that occurred after 1965, or the extent to which diets could change. For example, even though American caloric consumption increased from 3,200 in 1970 to 3,900 by 2000, the use of animal products declined from 1,130 to 810 kcal, or from 35 percent to 21 percent of total calories.[16]

Colin Clark calculated a maximum global population of 28 billion in 1958, assuming 77 million square kilometers of good temperate agricultural land cultivated at an intensive Dutch agricultural level of productivity. This would theoretically support 365 persons per square kilometer with food and fiber at a Dutch dietary standard.[17] In 1977 Clark calculated that an American diet would require 2,000 square meters of agricultural land per capita per year. Another 250 square meters would be needed for wood fiber. He then estimated a value of 10.7 billion hectares of global equivalent agricultural land to support a global population of 47 billion people. Clark estimated that only 680 square meters of agricultural land per capita would support 157 billion people at an Asian standard of subsistence living with reduced caloric and wood fiber requirements, and consumption of only a "small quantity" of animal products.[18] The wide range of Clark's figures show how sensitive his model is to small changes in his assumptions. His assumption that wood would be replaced by other fuels and his failure to consider loss of food before consumption were important shortcomings in his analysis.

These earlier estimates can more realistically be recalculated based on the *Living Planet 2006* figures of 11.2 billion global hectares of equivalent biocapacity in 2003, and average per capita demand for cropland, grazing, forest products, fishing, CO_2 emissions, nuclear power, and built-up land.[19] The world would sustain only 1.1 billion people at the average American footprint of 9.6 global hectares, but it would support 2 billion Danes,

French, Germans, British, and Japanese, 7 billion Chinese, or 14 billion Indians at their respective footprints. Culture does matter. The most important unmet assumption behind all such maximum sustainable population
estimates based on food requirements and global productive capacity is that
food, labor, and resources would be equitably distributed. The global "population problem" is most fundamentally a distribution, not a production,
problem.

Predictions of global population based on conditions in the late 1960s
warned that there could be 8 billion people in the world by the year 2000.
However, after peaking at over 2 percent a year in about 1970, the actual
rate of increase declined, and the world population officially reached only
6 billion on October 12, 1999, doubling in forty years (figure 6.1). Projections by the United Nations Population Division in 2004 predict continuing declines in rate of population growth and show a global population
in the range of 8 to 12 billion by 2050, depending on varying assumptions
about fertility patterns.[20]

A major assumption concerning the origin of the population problem,
which provides the basis for much current policy making, is that the rapid
growth now experienced in the poor countries of the world is simply the
result of the combination of traditionally high fertility rates and the sudden lowering of traditionally high mortality rates that has accompanied in-

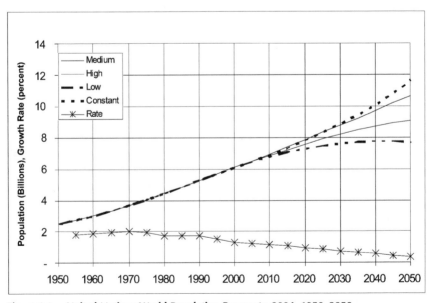

Figure 6.1.   United Nations World Population Prospects, 2004, 1950–2050.

complete economic development. Most of those holding this view feel that values relating to family size have somehow not caught up with the drop in mortality and that further economic growth and education will correct the situation such that people everywhere will experience the "demographic transition" to low fertility and low mortality enjoyed by rich nations. This interpretation may place too much emphasis on continued economic growth, and it does not acknowledge the demographic advantages of small-scale societies with relative social equality demonstrated by the tribal world. Many demographers are appropriately shifting their attention to the role of women in family planning decisions, emphasizing that when women have greater personal autonomy and economic power total family size is likely to be smaller and populations more stationary. Before examining these issues in more detail, we will first look at population history from a broad global perspective.

Great Waves of Population Growth

Global population has increased in five great waves of expansion, with each wave representing an order-of-magnitude scale increase. Figure 6.2 depicts these waves on a log graph to emphasize the scale differences. "Waves" are major transformations, or development episodes, that produce particular socio-cultural systems presumably defined by scale limits, or thresholds. "Cycles" are repetitive sequences of system growth and decline that may be somewhat regular. The Early Human Wave encompassed the biocultural evolution of human hominid ancestors from 4 million years ago to the emergence of physically modern, but culturally archaic, Homo sapiens by perhaps 100,000 years ago. At that time global population may have been less than 1 million, and people were not yet capable of occupying the entire globe. The Forager Wave, from 100,000 to 12,000 BP, saw the evolution and global diffusion of hunting and gathering societies and the formation of small seasonal villages based on fully human symbolic culture and speech. This growth and development wave produced a forager world of perhaps 10 million people distributed across all the continents except Antarctica. The next development, the Neolithic Wave, from 12,000 to 8,000 BP, saw the emergence of settled village life based on domesticated plants and animals and produced a tribal world of some 85 million people. The fourth wave, the Agrarian Civilization Wave, from 8,000 to 600 BP, saw the cyclical rise and collapse of numerous sequences of politically organized chiefdoms, city-states, kingdoms, and agrarian empires throughout the world. This wave may have peaked in AD 1200 when global population

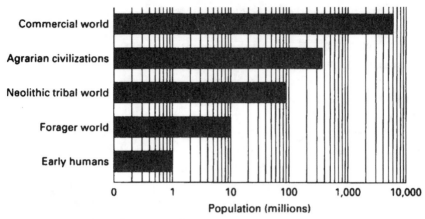

Figure 6.2.   Global Population Growth Waves.

reached 360 million people, a figure that may represent the maximum potential population for a world dominated by politically organized societies dependent on renewable solar energy. The most recent growth and development episode, the Commercial Wave, began in about 1400 and produced a global population of 1 billion by 1825 and 6 billion by 2000. Only with the development of commercially organized culture did the global population become organized as a single, globally integrated system.

Figure 6.3 depicts the last 10,000 years of global population history from the Neolithic to the present. On a linear scale global population appears virtually flat until the last 500 years when global population suddenly expands by two orders of magnitude, reaching 1 billion by 1820.

The geographic size and the cyclical rise and collapse of all historically documented agrarian civilizations have been graphically plotted by historian Rein Taagepera. He discovered that most empires did not last more than 130 years, and very few survived longer than 300 years.[21] David Fischer distinguished other economically defined waves, or price revolutions, for the millennium from AD 1000 to 2000 that also correspond to demographic trends. Other detailed refinements in world population history can be discerned.[22] Demographic historians Colin McEvedy and Richard Jones[23] have described a Primary Cycle in which global population peaked at 200 million people by AD 200, followed by demographic collapse in both Europe and Asia. They then distinguished a Medieval Cycle (from AD 500 to 1400) during which global population reached 360 million in AD 1200 only to decline due to plagues and invasions. They attributed the end of each growth cycle to either Malthusian limits or unfavorable climatic shifts,

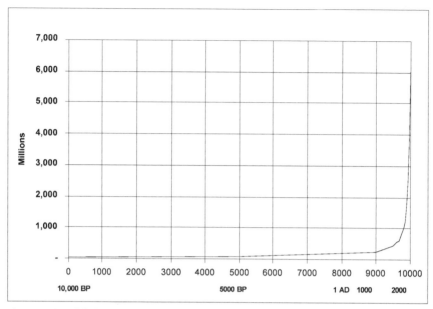

Figure 6.3.   Global Population, 10,000 BP–AD 2000.

but the inherent instability of politically organized cultural systems, compounded by the persistent rise and fall of grain prices, was probably the principal limiting factor.[24] McEvedy and Jones have suggested that global population might peak at 8 billion by 2100, which is below the UN's medium projections in 2004.

Population Pressure, Carrying Capacity, and Optimum Population

> [P]reindustrial population rates reflect some form of optimization effort engaged in by individuals and groups, rather than a culturally unregulated surrender to sex, hunger, and death. Among preindustrial populations both age-specific fertility and age-specific mortality could readily be raised or lowered in conformity with optimizing rationalities which maintained or enhanced the well-being of individuals and groups—although seldom with equal or even beneficial results for all. (Harris and Ross, *Death, Sex, and Fertility*, i)[25]

It makes little sense to speak of overpopulation and the need to halt growth without further discussing carrying capacity, optimum population size, and what constitutes population pressure. Surprisingly these topics are often completely ignored in population programs, even though they may be at least implicit in any attempt to regulate population or set demographic goals. The failure to adequately deal with these aspects of the population problem is perhaps understandable when we realize that they are culturally and environmentally relative concepts and directly involve the most basic characteristics of any culture.

An optimum population would exist at what archaeologist Fekri Hassan[26] called the optimum carrying capacity for its technology and environment—that is, the level of population that could safely maintain itself over several generations without drastic crashes as the resource base fluctuates. This is precisely where a culture concerned with minimizing subsistence risk would find itself.[27] Small-scale tribal societies have in effect been designed by the collective decisions of people organized in independent bands and villages seeking to satisfy their basic human needs on a long-term basis, such that they have always attempted to maintain themselves at optimum population levels. The important thing is that maximum decision-making authority for production, reproduction, and consumption is at the individual and household levels. Thus, people are free to make the decisions that best meet their needs. This is the freedom that is too often missing in the commercial world where decision-making power is so concentrated.

Population pressure is a widely discussed component of the population problem and is frequently assumed to be some readily apparent, absolute quality. However, like carrying capacity, on closer analysis it proves to be neither easily recognized nor absolute. Population pressure cannot be profitably treated in isolation from other cultural, demographic, and environmental factors.[28] The problem with the concept of population pressure is that it places undue emphasis on population, while the real issue is how to maintain a balance between the total human demand for resources in a given area and the sustainable supply, given a certain technology. Such balances may be attained most easily in relatively egalitarian societies, where competition over natural resources is likely to be reduced. In fact, population pressure is culturally defined and is meaningful only in relation to particular technological systems, environments, and per capita consumption levels.

In New Guinean tribal societies population pressure occurred only rarely in an absolute sense but was frequently manifested as a local imbalance between people and land experienced by particular clans.[29] Local imbalances may occur even when the total population is stable simply because random demographic processes, including variation in sex ratio, birthrates,

and mortality, may under different cultural circumstances have widely varying impacts on local groups of different size. As a result, certain clans may
outgrow their land base while neighboring clans dwindle to extinction.
This is a distribution problem. Tribal peoples employ many cultural devices
to relieve this pressure of population on land resources, including transfers
of land and people between clans through gifts, adoption, and warfare.
Where population pressure is not compensated for by normal redistributive
measures it may be felt as a steady reduction in the culturally defined standard of living, with people forced to work longer hours to increase food
production. Eventually there may be a switch to less desirable food
sources[30] or a move to marginal ecological zones.[31] Thus, "absolute" population pressure might be relieved by a simple redefinition of what the
members of a culture consider an acceptable standard of living, by technological innovation, or by a reduction in population.

Population redistribution has sometimes been developed to a high degree, particularly in island cultures in which adoption is widely used, but
it can be only a temporary solution. Resource redistribution may help raise
regional carrying capacity by evening out local surpluses or seasonal fluctuations, but elaborate redistribution systems are usually dependent on formal political offices and thus can occur only in political-scale cultures.
Migration to relieve population pressure is probably a normal response that
people resort to automatically whenever ecologically similar territory is
readily available for occupation.[32]

A final option, population control, has been practiced by virtually all
tribal societies to some degree. Tribal foragers have followed this course almost exclusively and achieved remarkably stable populations that must have
maintained a long-term dynamic equilibrium with shifts in their environments. Cultivators may sometimes have established equilibrium systems as
well balanced as those of foragers but have far more often slipped into subsistence intensification and predatory expansion against their neighbors as
their populations have gradually increased.

Population Control among Foragers

Although many demographers believe that the human population has
grown at a slow and steady rate from its very beginnings to the origins of
agriculture, anthropological research suggests that the thousands of years
before domestication were characterized by relative population equilibrium, punctuated by only occasional and unusual growth phases as people
settled new territories. By the eve of the transition to settled farm life the

human population had grown to an estimated 8–9 million over a span of a million years.[33] Much of this increase represented expansion into empty lands. Only very slight local increases in density occurred prior to the introduction of agriculture. As a general principle it can be assumed that tribal societies quickly established a culturally regulated equilibrium as soon as their populations had grown to a culturally defined carrying capacity within specific environments.

Cultural factors, not food shortages or high mortality rates, seem to have been the primary factors in setting limits to population growth in tribal societies. This is a particularly significant point, because it is still widely assumed that tribal peoples were characterized by uniformly high fertility and mortality rates and a precarious food supply, but such was decidedly not the case. Tribal societies were generally stabilized at levels considerably below the maximum population densities that their technologies and environments might potentially have sustained if increasing absolute population had been a cultural objective. Even Paleolithic hunters, if their political structures had forced them to work harder and if they had adjusted their food preferences away from big game to a concentration on small mammals, might have increased their population densities many times over. This is of course precisely what happened during the Mesolithic period. It is also likely that real famines were rare during the Paleolithic period, although it has been established both archaeologically and ethnohistorically that hunting peoples did sometimes starve in the Arctic when relatively minor shifts in climate made critical food resources unavailable. In such unstable and marginal environments population equilibriums were very dynamic.[34] Dramatic shifts in the environment probably occurred throughout the last great Ice Age, such that population/resource balances were continuously interrupted. Nevertheless, while the availability of game certainly influenced population densities among hunting and foraging peoples, food shortages per se appear not to have been the primary factor limiting population growth; rather, as we will see, the limiting factor was the cultural organization of tribal societies themselves.

Overwhelming evidence suggests that mortality was also not a significant limiting factor for tribal hunters and foragers. Deaths due to epidemic disease were apparently far fewer before the establishment of permanent villages than at any time thereafter. Tribal hunting peoples were consistently well nourished, they led physically active lives, and they apparently avoided most infectious epidemic diseases by maintaining dispersed populations, preventing these diseases from becoming established and spreading. Foragers may also have developed high levels of natural immunity thanks to strong selective pressure enforced by relatively high infant mortality rates and constant exposure to endemic pathogens. Deaths due to warfare, feuding, and violence may have been more variable and sometimes much higher among certain tribal societies than previously believed,[35] but such deaths probably were not normally a significant means of population regulation. Demographic data based on age estimates of selected prehistoric skeletal populations and modern ethnographic data reveal that foragers at age fifteen could expect to live an average of twenty-six additional years. This is more than half the average for people in industrialized nations today but roughly the same as life expectancy at age fifteen in thirteenth-century England and higher than has been described for some Neolithic populations.[36]

Tribal societies held in reserve an enormous potential for rapid population growth that was activated only under special conditions. Even if mortality rates as high as 50 percent to age fifteen are assumed to have been typical for foraging peoples (half of the population dying before reaching reproductive age)[37]—and this is by no means easily demonstrated—it still would have been quite possible for the population to have doubled each generation if high fertility was culturally encouraged. Such rapid growth probably did occur at times but was common only when previously unoccupied territory was first entered or when a population was recovering from some natural disaster, such as an unfavorable shift in the ice in the Arctic.[38] In the New World, for example, people were well established in North America by 10,000 BC and were settled in the southern tip of South America by 9000 BC. Such a rapid spread could hardly have been achieved by cultures that were barely keeping ahead of extinction.

The full significance of this picture of the demography of early foraging peoples can perhaps best be appreciated when considered in contrast to the grim view presented by modern demographers in their assessment of the history of population growth and the origin of our present dilemma. Paul Ehrlich, for example, in *The Population Bomb*, stated that "our ancestors were fighting a continual battle to keep the birth rate ahead of the death rate."[39] The distinguished demographer Donald T. Bogue summarized this period in his major textbook, *Principles of Demography*, as follows:

> During the many thousands of years of man's existence on the earth before the beginning of civilization, the population problem facing most communities was that of survival—to offset successfully the terrible attrition of death on their numbers. . . . When population did manage to grow, there was always the threat of famine, war, and epidemics. Such a situation is the only conjecture that is consistent with the facts. . . . We are forced,

therefore, to conclude that the human race has been required by circumstances of high mortality to reproduce at near-biological capacity and that a whole system of fertility-promoting practices has evolved as an integral part of every culture.[40]

In fact, precisely the opposite situation now appears to have been the case, and chronic waves of famine, war, and epidemics seem to have been characteristic of civilizations, not of the tribal world. The question that remains to be answered is precisely what fertility-dampening practices helped to maintain tribal populations in dynamic equilibrium.

Among hunters, density limits seem to have been set by the availability of culturally recognized food sources and by the lack of formal political structures to deal with conflict. Small local bands of twenty-five to fifty people were apparently the most efficient hunting and gathering groups. Fewer people would have difficulty feeding themselves due to random accidents or runs of bad luck, whereas larger groups would experience diminishing returns as local resources were depleted too quickly. Expansion of subsistence through intensified collecting or domestication was apparently rejected as a solution far more often than not and seems to have been a course that was followed only reluctantly in the face of either political pressures or environmental changes. Migration certainly occurred among hunters as new bands on the fringes of occupied territories moved steadily into vacant lands, but this migration would not have been at the expense of other groups already firmly in possession of their territories.[41] There is little evidence of warfare or territorial conquest between bands. Perhaps most critical was the fact that there was no culturally encouraged reason for increasing population density beyond the minimum needed to reproduce healthy domestic units and local communities. Birth spacing by deliberate abortion and infanticide seems to have been the primary mechanism of fertility regulation, although indirect physiological factors must have played a role.

Infanticide has received much attention as the basic method of population control among foraging peoples, but this is a complex issue and many questions remain unanswered. Some writers have argued that baby girls were killed or neglected so that boys could be raised to become warriors or hunters.[42] However, computer simulations suggest that selective female infanticide could never have been very common because it would easily cause an irreversible decline in a small population.[43] It has also been argued that detailed census data provide no real evidence for selective female infanticide.[44] Furthermore, both the actual rates and individual motives for even general infanticide are not well known. J. B. Birdsell[45] suggests that 15–30 percent of births in aboriginal Australia ended in infanticide, but convincing supporting evidence has not been provided and is unlikely ever to be obtained. Some authors offer antagonism between the sexes as an important motivation for infanticide,[46] but it seems more likely that it occurs primarily as a birth-spacing mechanism when a woman realizes that attempting to raise a new baby might threaten the welfare of her older child.

It has been assumed that women in nomadic foraging societies were forced to space their children approximately four years apart because of the difficulty of carrying two dependent children on daily foraging expeditions and on the frequent moves to new camps.[47] This may have been a critical consideration motivating, or at least rationalizing, the family planning decisions of individual women, but if it were an absolute necessity it would be difficult to explain the rapid growth known to have occurred when virgin territories were occupied. Whatever the motivation for such spacing and regardless of the method employed, it would yield a stationary, no-growth population, assuming that an average woman attempts to raise four children and that half of them survive to reproduce.

Population Equilibrium in Aboriginal Australia

One of the most provocative and best-documented arguments that tribal foragers maintained culturally regulated optimum populations is presented in J. B. Birdsell's analysis of Australian Aborigines, based on twenty-five years of intensive research. According to Birdsell's estimates,[48] Australia supported a constant population of 300,000 Aborigines, the maximum that could be sustained by a hunting and gathering technology, for perhaps 30,000 years with only minor fluctuations related to overall changes in the environment. They were not constantly tottering on the edge of disaster, with their numbers held in check by high mortality rates, and they did not continually outstrip their meager resources only to crash precipitously and later rebound. In contrast, the commercial society now controlling Australia grew to 17 million within two hundred years of the first European settlement and continues to grow at more than 1 percent per year. By 2005 there were some 20 million people in Australia.

The forces that may have contributed to the relative stability in the aboriginal population involved not only environmental factors but also culturally defined territorial spacing mechanisms. According to Birdsell's analysis,

Australian cultures were organized into linguistically distinct tribal groups averaging five hundred people that were in turn divided into bands of twenty-five people composed of individual families of five persons. Tribal territories were large enough to provide a reliable subsistence base for the population roughly 98 percent of the time, while individual band territories might be somewhat less self-sufficient, with resources from neighboring bands needed in perhaps ten to fifteen out of every one hundred years. Band territories were carefully laid out to ensure that they allowed access to all critical food resources in sufficient quantity for long-range survival. In some coastal regions, where a tribal territory included several diverse ecological zones with different resource potentials, each band territory would include portions of each zone. Interband and intertribal ceremonies normally occurred in times of plenty. These ceremonies helped distribute seasonal or random concentrations of food and served to equalize resources, thus helping to bring population densities closer to the maximum carrying capacity for the technology. Bands in drought-stricken areas might be temporarily taken in by more comfortably situated neighbors. Individuals were so emotionally attached to the sacred sites within their traditional territories representing their totemic origin points that there was no danger that they would ever choose to remain permanently in their refuge. Boundaries were also clearly defined by the wanderings of spirit beings, which were recorded in myths and commemorated in intergroup ceremonies. The religious and ceremonial system played a vital role in supporting population balances through boundary maintenance and resource redistribution.

The upper limit for tribal population was set by the density of the communication network that could be supported by foragers restricted to foot travel. As tribes grew larger, it became more difficult for the bands within them to remain in contact. When more bands appeared, the frequency, intensity, and length of interactions such as joint ceremonies and intermarriage declined and linguistic diversity increased, making further communication more difficult. Tribes that lost bands until they dropped below 500 members would automatically interact more with bands in neighboring tribes and eventually be absorbed into them. Bands needed to include at least twenty-five people in order to maximize the availability of food, given random variations in hunting success; to provide task groups of optimum size; to ensure demographic viability, given gender variations at birth; to defend themselves; and to ensure a large enough pool of marriageable individuals to meet the cultural requirements of band exogamy, that is, marriage outside the band. Upper limits to band size were apparently set by the absence of strong political controls, which meant that increased conflicts that might arise with denser population could be adequately controlled only by fissioning, or splitting a large band into two or more smaller bands. The need to minimize the strain on local ecosystems also determined maximum band sizes. Random fluctuation in local band size was regulated through selective infanticide, adoption, and transfers of people in "violation" of normal residence and exogamic norms. Local boundaries were also adjusted by means of occasional duels and skirmishes.

Actual tribal densities varied from as low as perhaps 80 square miles per person in the interior deserts, where rainfall might drop to a mean of only 4 inches per year, to as high as 2 square miles per person in rich coastal or riverine environments. Optimum carrying capacities for tribal territories remained within 10–20 percent of the maximum density that could be supported in the best years, thanks to the cultural mechanisms that helped level out the long-range fluctuations in resources due to droughts and other unpredictable events.

It is uncertain what means of birth spacing were most common, but it is clear that infanticide was often practiced by Australians; abortion and contraception may also have been important spacing mechanisms. It is important to note in this context that the distinction between abortion and infanticide may not be culturally meaningful. Some tribes may induce labor in the third trimester of pregnancy and then kill the fetus if it survives. "Birth" itself, as well as "humanness," may be culturally defined at a quite different point than that normally recognized by state legal systems.[49]

It appears from the data Birdsell presents that a system of density equilibrium was indeed operating among Australian tribes and bands. The primary density determinant seems to have been environmental, as reflected by a statistically significant inverse relationship between rainfall and size of tribal territory. Deviation from this mathematical relationship can be accounted for by the presence of extra water and consequently greater biological productivity in riverine or coastal regions, where carrying capacity is higher than would be expected otherwise. Further evidence is provided in the reports that large tribes were in the process of splitting into small tribes of five hundred members when they were first contacted by Europeans. It has also been shown that tribes initially fragmented by the acquisition of new initiation ceremonies quickly returned to their original size after the diffusion wave had passed.

Some authorities argue that Aborigines did not quickly establish an equilibrium but rather steadily and gradually expanded both population and technology.[50] This viewpoint is supported by the appearance in Australia of some technological improvements, such as the spear-thrower and the dingo, within only the past 5,000 years. However, Aborigines were in contact with gardeners and pig raisers in New Guinea for thousands of years without borrowing their more intensive production techniques.

The Neolithic Population Explosion

The relatively rapid growth in population that accompanied and perhaps contributed to the adoption of farming is one of the most significant demographic events in human history. It marked the end of the long period of relative population equilibrium that foraging peoples established and initiated a period of almost continuous population growth and a rapid series of interrelated changes associated with political centralization, the emergence of large-scale urban societies, and finally the rise of global commercial cultures. It has been estimated that world population suddenly jumped from approximately 10 million in 12,000 BP to 85 million by 8000 BP.[51] The scale of the Neolithic expansion was even more dramatic in specific countries. France, for example, experienced a hundred-fold population increase by 3000 BC over densities during the Upper Paleolithic period and only a tenfold increase between 3000 BC and the twentieth century.

Since the earliest development of cultural evolutionary theory it has been assumed that the "Neolithic," conceptualized as settled village life with domesticated plants and animals, as well as ceramics, was a package of cultural traits that constituted a necessary and irreversible step on the pathway to the inevitable transformation of small-scale tribes into larger chiefdoms and states. However, many archaeological researchers no longer consider the Neolithic itself to be a package deal in which sedentism, pottery, agriculture, and social complexity necessarily occur together.[52] These patterns can occur independently, and in various combinations. They are not parts of a one-way street that inevitably involves growth in population and social inequality. Sedentism is not all or nothing. It can exist in degrees, and over the past 12,000 years peoples have moved back and forth from village to nomadic life, and it can be supported by different productive systems. In many parts of the world—including the Pacific Northwest Coast, Scandinavia, China, North Africa, the Levant, and coastal Peru—fishing, hunting, and gathering supported permanent villages. Likewise, even monumental constructions such as Stonehenge may not have involved sedentism. Sedentary foragers have become nomadic pastoralists, and village farmers have become nomadic bison hunters.

Explaining the breakdown of "Paleolithic" dynamic population equilibrium mechanisms and the shift to sedentary village life must surely be one of the most critical theoretical problems in anthropology. Numerous specific explanations have been proposed for the Neolithic transition that occurred independently in different parts of the world about 5,000 to 10,000 years ago. The common element is the enormous environmental changes that occurred in the post-Pleistocene world at the end of the last Ice Age. Climate became milder, especially in the temperate zones; vegetation zones shifted; many large animals became extinct; and sea levels rose, flooding many coastal plains and separating many formerly connected land areas. Many authors explain the Neolithic as a relatively gradual process of subsistence intensification designed to increase food production in the face of dwindling resources and great instability.[53] More intensive use of local resources may involve sedentism, with people maintaining a relatively fixed residence throughout the year. Sedentism could in itself encourage population expansion because it eliminates at least one incentive to birth spacing—the inconvenience of more than one dependent child needing to be carried every time camp was moved. However, Barry Hewlett[54] argues that foragers and simple horticulturalists do not differ significantly demographically. It is quite possible that foragers spaced births to protect the health of mother and child as well as to maintain mobility, and thus the practice might have been continued even after sedentarization. It is well known that many settled village peoples space births four years apart, or even longer, for precisely this reason. Late weaning can be very important to the health of an infant, particularly where protein is scarce. Furthermore, there is evidence that prolonged lactation may suppress ovulation and thus serve as a natural contraceptive.

Some writers attribute population growth to the increased food supply made available by domestication. This argument is the opposite of the Boserup subsistence intensification theory discussed in chapter 4 and in the preceding paragraph, which sees population pressure or resources/population imbalance as leading to more intensive resource use, including sedentism and domestication. Increases in food production in a given region are thus more likely to be results rather than causes of imbalance in the resources/population equation.

Randel A. Sengel[55] suggested a rather novel solution to this vexing problem. He argued that in the Near East an increased reliance on wild grains, ultimately caused by climatic changes that increased their prevalence, may have resulted in a significant augmentation of the protein intake of the population, which in turn lowered the age of menarche and increased the reproductive span of the women. Empirical evidence from Europe indicates that nutritional improvement has apparently had that effect in modern times, and it is by no means certain that the age of menarche is a constant in all human populations. Some writers, however, have suggested that the domestication process resulted in the displacement of wild plant foods that were richer in protein than domesticated varieties, so the argument is by no means settled.[56]

It is clear that even a slight increase in the reproductive span could result in a gradual population growth even if the original pattern of birth spacing were retained. It might be assumed that such increased growth would quickly be recognized and the birth-spacing mechanism adjusted to restore equilibrium. However, it is not likely that population control in tribal cultures was actually carried out with long-range social goals in mind; rather, individual women made "family planning" decisions for their immediate self-interest, and in the aggregate these decisions proved to be highly adaptive for the entire culture.

Although these demographic changes, whatever their causes, were in the long run revolutionary in their impact, they were so slow that, like the domestication process, they would have been imperceptible to the actors. In the Near East, for example, the population may have grown from 100,000 in 8000 BC to 12 million by 4000 BC, an annual growth rate of only 0.12 percent.[57] At such a gradual rate a tribe of five hundred people would add only about twelve people in a generation.

Population Control among Tribal Village Farmers

Population growth was a much more difficult force to contain for sedentary or semi-sedentary cultures based on domesticated, and thus inherently more elastic, food sources. Tribal farmers certainly have in many cases achieved remarkable population equilibrium, as we will show in the examples that follow. In general, however, domestication touched off a period of great cultural instability throughout the world. Suddenly expanding farming societies pushed hunters out of the most fertile lands only to be themselves incorporated into expanding conquest states and ultimately into an expanding global commercial society. Foragers, newly transformed into farmers, found their resource bases increasingly inadequate for the support of their growing populations and were forced into more difficult environments or into cultural transformations that they might not otherwise have chosen. In some cases growing populations may have expanded beyond the carrying capacities of their fluctuating environments and collapsed without the development of complex political systems or more "advanced" technology.

The American Southwest offers an example of this latter outcome. From approximately 7000 BC to AD 100 that area was occupied by hunters and seed collectors who made up what archaeologists have called the "desert tradition," which must have constituted an enduring, relatively stable adaptation. Toward the end of that period domesticated plants from Mesoamerica were gradually adopted, and by AD 400 farming villages were becoming established.

The archaeological record for one small valley in Arizona from 1,400 years from the beginning of domestication up to AD 1400 shows a steady increase in population and a continual expansion into marginal environments as the most favorable zones were filled.[58] The population peaked shortly after people began to irrigate their fields in approximately AD 1000 and then began to decline when changes in the rainfall pattern beginning in AD 1150 drastically lowered the carrying capacity of the valley. Population densities plunged rapidly between AD 1100 and 1200 to a small fraction of the peak, and by 1400 the valley had been abandoned completely. Thus, a society of village farmers expanded for perhaps 700 years and then collapsed, at least locally. This record stands in striking contrast to the 7,000 years of success that foragers previously enjoyed in the same general environment. Similar patterns occurred in other areas in the Southwest at the same time. For example, in northwest New Mexico farming peoples constructed an architecturally imposing society centered on Chaco Canyon that seemingly flourished for about a century, until it also collapsed around AD 1130. People were presumably forced to relocate.[59]

The archaeological and ethnographic record also contains many examples of village farmers who were able to support their population growth by pushing out their neighbors. The Neolithic population expansion carried speakers of Indo-European languages—with their farming village lifestyle based on sheep, cattle, and grain crops—throughout Europe over a 2,000-year period beginning about 6500 BC or earlier. The fate of the prior European foragers is uncertain. Although some may have adopted farming or been incorporated into the invading culture, it seems more reasonable to guess that many resisted the change and simply moved into marginal environments and gradually declined. Austronesian speakers carried taro, bananas, breadfruit, and pigs from Southeast Asia to the most remote parts of the Pacific from about 4000 BC to AD 600. Bantu-speaking peoples carried cattle and millet throughout Central and Southern Africa beginning about AD 200. In East and South Africa, Bantu farmers and herders were still expanding into territory occupied by foraging peoples in the seventeenth century. Their growth was not halted until the militaristic Zulu empire was finally overwhelmed by the British army in the late nineteenth century. Marshall Sahlins[60] has shown how growing African tribal cultures such as the Nuer and Tiv, in the absence of formal political leadership, have utilized their segmentary lineage systems as a means of mobilizing on their boundaries to expand their territory against weak neighbors.

Village farmers were probably well established in the central Amazon Basin by 3000 BC, utilizing manioc as their primary staple.[61] The evidence suggests that almost from that point on a continuous period of population growth, migration, displacement, and differentiation of cultures continued into modern times. However, many uncertainties remain. Some archaeologists attribute prehistoric population movements in Amazonia to the periodic effects of long-term climate fluctuations, thus emphasizing population equilibrium rather than continuous population expansion.[62] Smaller societies may have simply been pushed up the smaller tributaries of the Amazon, and finally into the interfluvial hinterlands, by successive migration waves from the expanding centers.[63] Among these expanding Amazonian village farmers the best known historically were Tupi-speaking peoples. They, like the Zulus in South Africa, were still spreading south and east up the Amazon and even down the Brazilian coast, pushing aside prior foragers and more stable village peoples, when the Spanish and Portuguese arrived in the sixteenth century. The difference between the migratory expansion waves of small-scale Amazonian and African tribes and politically organized chiefdoms and European colonialism is that the former were driven by demographic and political processes, whereas Europeans were motivated primarily by commercial economic forces as the global culture developed.

Chronic raiding and head-hunting for shifting cultivators in many other parts of the world, including New Zealand and Southeast Asia, may also be viewed as responses to a failure to maintain population equilibrium. The Ibans in Borneo were actively expanding against their neighbors, some of whom were foragers, in the late nineteenth century and well into the twentieth. Traditionally oriented hill tribes in northwestern Thailand were growing rapidly in the 1960s but maintained intact cultures without warfare by crowding out neighbors and through high rates of migration into lowland areas, where excess population was absorbed into other ethnic groups.[64]

In spite of these examples of population growth among village farmers, considering the time periods involved it is apparent that very few such cultures reproduced at maximum feasible fertility rates for more than a very brief time. Cultural regulation of population growth certainly continued to be a very significant factor even after domestication began. As with foragers, fertility control was probably the most important regulating mechanism for village farmers, although increased mortality through raiding was at times an additional means of control. Abortion, infanticide, contraception, and birth spacing remained the primary means of limiting fertility, although many specific cultural practices that limited the frequency of coitus or shortened the fertile period by delaying marriage also became important.

One of the most common birth-spacing practices is the long postpartum taboo on sexual intercourse that occurs widely among shifting cultivators in tropical climates.[65] The taboo often extends for more than a year after the birth of each child and has been shown to be related to reduced fertility rates in cultures that practice it. The taboo correlates with a number of other cultural practices, and elaborate causal explanations for its occurrence have been proposed.[66] It is quite possible that it is not an intentional means of birth spacing, but whatever its "cause" it serves as a critical check on fertility.

Island Population Problems

Perhaps the severest example of a test of a culture's ability to regulate population growth was the problem of maintaining equilibrium on the small islands and coral atolls of the Pacific. Certainly cultures with such restricted land bases would run up against physical limits to population expansion much more quickly than would cultures in continental areas.

Tim Bayliss-Smith[67] outlined the general process of adjustment to island environments in a theoretical model that recognized three phases of population growth and cultural response. Following the initial settling of an island, there may be rapid expansion and an extensive—that is, low labor input—subsistence system, which continues until the available land base is filled. Intensification of the food production system may follow, with greater labor inputs and new technology, or "lower" dietary standards may be introduced. Finally, emigration and direct cultural controls on population growth become necessary. Many of these islands have been settled for a very long time; much of Micronesia, for example, may have been occupied for 1,000 years, and the maximum practical limits of technological intensification of food production must have been reached very early, quickly exhausting this solution. Actually, many of the coral atolls required an extremely high degree of technological development before any kind of gardening could be established because of the absence of soil and the shortage of fresh water.

In practice, various cultural controls helped maintain population well below any theoretical maximum carrying capacity based on the ultimate limits of food production. In the Polynesian outlier atolls, the critical population ceiling seems to have been set by the environmental limits to taro production. Taro was a daily element in the diet and a prime measure of the overall adequacy of the food supply. If cultural preferences were not a factor, then presumably these cultures might simply have switched to crops that provided more calories per acre or per unit of labor, such as coconuts, and supported even denser populations. However, the ideal seems to have been for taro to supply approximately 50 percent of the caloric intake, and it was culturally intolerable for it to drop below 25 percent. Coconuts were not expected to constitute more than 25 percent of the diet. Population pressure was clearly present to the extent that the proportions of these critical foods deviated from the cultural ideals. Further forms of cultural control of carrying capacity were the planting of non-subsistence crops, such as ritually important turmeric, that displaced food crops, and the social and ceremonial stress placed on certain marine resources.

Various social and political adjustments helped maximize available resources while minimizing possible ecological stresses to the food systems from overuse. For example, political-scale cultures, with higher levels of social stratification in which political leaders were given authority to regulate the production and distribution of food, seem to have arisen in both Micronesia and Polynesia wherever resources were sufficient to support such developments. Shortages of food and "overpopulation" here, as in the New Guinea example, were in effect treated as problems of allocation, but in this case they were critical enough that political authority was needed to solve them. Other social mechanisms for allocating people to land, and vice versa, were also widely employed. For example, cognatic descent systems, which allow descent to be traced through either parent, were common in the Pacific and were easily manipulated to relieve local pressures. Adoption was also practiced; in some Micronesian islands as many as half of all children were adopted.[68]

At the inter-island level, various cultural practices helped relieve local problems and permitted larger densities than might otherwise have been possible, in much the same manner as intertribal relations in aboriginal Australia. For example, if typhoons temporarily destroyed the food resources of a particular atoll, the residents might be temporarily taken in by the residents of unaffected high islands or might be sent emergency food. Likewise, if a critical imbalance in the sex ratio developed, individuals might in effect be exported or imported as needed.

Virtually the entire range of fertility control mechanisms was practiced by Pacific island cultures. In Micronesia a woman was often restricted to no more than three children, and abortion, infanticide, coitus interruptus, and frequent periods of ritual celibacy all occurred. In Tikopia,[69] in addition to these controls, younger males could not marry if productive land was not available. These unmarried men often set out on overseas voyages and never returned, although if they remained, extramarital access to women was not denied them. When population pressures became intolerable on Tikopia, an entire clan or other social segment was simply driven away, although this was a very rare event. Raymond Firth's conclusion with regard to Tikopia is probably applicable to the Pacific as a whole before European intervention: "It can be safely said that until recent years the population of Tikopia was normally in a state of equilibrium with its food supply."[70]

Archaeological research revealed evidence of 3,000 years of continuous human occupation on Tikopia.[71] During that time the population of the three-square-mile island probably did not exceed its historically known population range of 1,000–1,700 people. However, maintaining this balance required converting virtually the entire island to human use. Shifting cultivation eventually gave way to permanent gardening, and selectively planted domesticated forest replaced the original forest cover. In the intensification process, erosion from the island's volcanic slopes filled in part of the lagoon and increased the land area. At least one wild bird species was locally exterminated, but supernatural sanctions mediated by the island chief apparently protected some of the marine life from overexploitation. Tikopia's extremely remote location and small size allowed its people to maintain their autonomy and self-sufficiency.

The Case of Rapa Nui (Easter Island) "Collapse"

Jared Diamond's[72] popularized account of Rapa Nui as an example of overpopulation caused "full-fledged collapse" in a chapter of his book *Collapse*, may be misleading. Citing existing accounts, Diamond assumed that people arrived on Rapa Nui by AD 400, after which population peaked in about 1600, followed by a collapse. For Diamond, Rapa Nui represented a clear case of human population growth leading to over-consumption followed by environmental destruction, social collapse, conflict, and population decline, but this was largely conjectural history. The island had been covered by Jubaea palm trees for some 35,000 years, but they had mostly disappeared by 1722. More recent archaeological research, new radiocarbon dates, and reinterpretation of older material shows that people did not reach Rapa Nui until about AD 1200, and that the deforestation was caused by the Polynesian rat that accompanied them.[73] The rats multiplied rapidly and ate the palm nuts, thereby inhibiting their reproduction. Rat damage drastically reduced the palm population well before clearing and burning by humans would have been significant. If 50 people colonized the island in AD 1200 and the population grew at 3.4 percent annually, a rate documented for other Pacific islands, the population would have reached a peak of about 3,000 people by AD 1323. The population apparently remained fairly stable at that level up to European contact in 1722. By the 1870s, after more than a century of European contact, European diseases, slave raiding, and cultural disturbance, the population had plummeted to 100 survivors. This means that major environmental damage was caused by rats rather than over-consumption by humans, and the population collapse was caused primarily by European intrusion.

State Intervention and Population Control Mechanisms

When autonomous tribal societies came under the influence of commercial societies, three things drastically modified the demographic picture. In the first place, traditional population control mechanisms invariably dropped out. The disappearance of these control measures may have been due to deliberate pressures aimed at eliminating them, as when missionaries halted abortion and infanticide, or the government forbade raiding and warfare. Many important regulating practices may simply have been abandoned as other practices that supported them were modified. For example, the traditional religious system provided essential support for the postpartum taboo and a variety of other ceremonial regulations. Even if no other modifications in the culture occurred, the elimination of traditional population controls would be certain to lead to rapid population growth.

The second factor affecting tribal societies under the influence of commercial systems was that the politicization process that created the state initially provided positive incentives for population expansion, through conquest and internal growth, because a growing population was the primary way in which political rulers extended their power. Furthermore, the extraction of taxes and tribute from formerly autonomous villages and households increased the demand for labor at the domestic level and made larger families a rational choice. For example, villagers in India and other poor countries were especially pleased to add sons to their families because they could help on the farm.[74] Extra children contributed more to the labor force than their maintenance cost, at least until the limits of labor intensification were exceeded. Anthropologist Clifford Geertz[75] provided a well-documented case study of such a situation in Java. It is not surprising that societies based on intensive agriculture, which is likely to be associated with state organization, show higher fertility rates and higher population growth than either foragers or simple horticulturalists.[76]

The third effect of the incorporation of autonomous groups into commercial systems was the reduction of traditionally high mortality rates. This process has received the most attention as the principal cause of the modern worldwide population explosion, but in regard to tribal societies this common interpretation needs to be qualified in important ways. As I argued earlier in this chapter, the mortality rates of independent tribal societies may not have been as high as commonly thought, and high mortality was clearly not the primary mechanism of population control. During the early phase of state intervention in tribal cultures, mortality rates were typically elevated because of frontier violence and the disruption of forced cultural change. In many cases whole tribes were simply exterminated at this point.[77] Extinction was sometimes actually accelerated by the retention of traditional fertility checks even in the face of severe depopulation. Examples of this process can be drawn from South America[78] and Micronesia.[79] On the Micronesian island of Yap the continuation of traditional abortion practices may not have been a major factor in depopulation as some have suggested, but other traditional controls could certainly have come into play.[80]

When it was advantageous to retain a native labor force, administrative authorities usually regulated the cultural change process to minimize undue increases in mortality. New health measures to reduce infant mortality and control endemic diseases such as malaria in the long run succeeded in lowering overall mortality rates. It is quite possible that, if the traditional culture remained intact and new incentives for population growth were introduced, a reduction in mortality rates might be easily countered with an adjustment in fertility control mechanisms, and no dramatic population explosion would need to occur. Unfortunately, a real test of this hypothesis might never be possible, because modern medical technology has invariably been accompanied by both a loss in traditional fertility controls and the appearance of new incentives for growth. The main point is clear, however—traditional cultures are not in themselves the primary cause of the present population explosion.

Policy Implications

Population policy has largely been based on the demographic transition model, which described the way population growth first soared and then declined in Europe and North America as economic growth occurred. Improvements in public health and the availability of antibiotics reduced mortality rates, making it more likely that each child would survive, while increasing numbers of urban wage workers found large families to be a disadvantage as their material condition improved. Therefore, family size declined rapidly, and population growth slowed. It was widely believed that the same demographic pattern would occur in the rest of the world as the global economy grew, and many planners argued that promoting economic growth everywhere was the best way to reduce population growth. However, the flaw in this theory is that the material benefits of economic growth have not been distributed widely enough in the "developing world" to make smaller families more attractive. As I will show in the following chapter, income and wealth inequalities are enormous and are increasing, and population in poor countries also continues to increase. Under poverty conditions, especially in rural, subsistence economies, large families often continue to be an economic asset, whereas in urban settings they may be a disadvantage. Since the 1970s urban fertility rates have dramatically declined even though living standards may actually have declined for most people in poor countries.[81] Worsening living standards in urban settings may make large families a liability, while at the same time the availability of new contraceptive technologies makes family planning more attractive. A more equitable distribution of economic resources would help slow population growth; however, it is crucial that improvements in the economic conditions of households be accompanied by policy changes that give women more control over fertility decision making. It seems likely that women exercised such control in autonomous tribal societies but tended to lose control when male-dominated politically centralized societies and great tradition civilizations such as Imperial China, Hindu India, and Islam developed. The increasing use of contraceptive technology by urban women in poor countries and the related reduction in family size has been called a "demographic revolution" that may significantly reduce population.[82] Balanced populations require an equitable distribution of social power.

Notes

1. Ehrlich, Paul, and Anne Ehrlich. 1972. *Population, Resources, Environment.* San Francisco: W. H. Freeman.

2. Ehrlich, Paul. 1968. *The Population Bomb*. New York: Ballantine, 67.

3. Ehrlich, Paul R., and Anne H. Ehrlich. 2004. *One with Ninevah: Politics, Consumption, and the Human Future*. Washington, D.C.: Island Press, Shearwater Books.

4. Chewtow, Marian R. 2001. "The IPAT Equation and Its Variants: Changing Views of Technology and Environmental Impact." *Journal of Industrial Ecology* 4(4): 13–29. Ehrlich, Paul R., and John P. Holdren. 1971. "Impact of Population Growth." *Science* 171(3977): 1212–17; York, Richard, Eugene A. Rosa, and Thomas Dietz. 2003. "STIRPAT, IPAT and ImPACT: Analytic Tools for Unpacking the Driving Forces of Environmental Impacts." *Ecological Economics* 46: 351–65.

5. Ehrlich, Paul. 1992. "Environmental Deterioration, Biodiversity and the Preservation of Civilization: The Ninth World Conservation Lecture." *The Environmentalist* 12(1): 9–14; Ehrlich, Paul, and Anne Ehrlich. 1990. *The Population Explosion*. New York: Simon and Schuster.

6. Clark, Colin. 1968. *Population Growth and Land Use*. London: Macmillan, preface.

7. Ehrlich, "Environmental Deterioration," 9–14.

8. Ehrlich, "Environmental Deterioration," 10.

9. Simon, Julian. 1981. *The Ultimate Resource*. Princeton, NJ: Princeton University Press.

10. Bongaarts, John. 1994. "Can the Growing Human Population Feed Itself?" *Scientific American* 270(3): 36–42.

11. Cohen, Joel E. 1995. *How Many People Can the Earth Support?* New York: W.W. Norton. Cohen reviews a wide range of estimates for how many people the earth can support.

12. Ravenstein, E. G. 1891. "Lands of the Globe Still Available for European Settlement." *Proceedings of the Royal Geographical Society* 13: 27–35.

13. Cohen, *How Many People*, 165–72.

14. De Wit, C. T. 1967. "Photosynthesis: Its Relationship to Overpopulation." In *Harvesting the Sun: Photosynthesis in Plant Life*, edited by Anthony San Pietro, Frances A. Greer, and Thomas J. Army, 315–20. New York: Academic Press.

15. Hulett, H. R. 1970. "Optimum World Population." *BioScience* 20(3): 160–61.

16. U.S. Department of Agriculture (USDA), Economic Research Service. 2006. "U.S. Food Supply: Nutrients and Other Food Components, 1909 to 2004." Nutrient Availability Spreadsheet (March 3).

17. Clark, Colin. 1958. "World Population." *Nature* 181 (May 3): 1235–36.

18. Clark, Colin. 1977. *Population Growth and Land Use*. 2nd edition. London: Macmillan.

19. WWF International. 2006. *Living Planet Report 2006*. World Wildlife Fund. www.panda.org/news_facts/publications/living_planet_report/index.cfm

20. United Nations Secretariat, Department of Economic and Social Affairs, Population Division. 2004. *World Population Prospects: The 2004 Revision and World Urbanization Prospects*. esa.un.org/unpp

21. Taagepera, Rein. 1978a. "Size and Duration of Empires: Systematics of Size." *Social Science Research* 7: 108–27; Taagepera, Rein. 1978b. "Size and Duration of Empires: Growth-Decline Curves, 3000 to 600 B.C." *Social Science Research* 7: 180–96; Taagepera, Rein. 1997. "Expansion and Contraction Patterns of Large Polities: Context for Russia." *International Studies Quarterly* 41: 475–504.

22. Fischer, David Hackett. 1996. *The Great Wave: Price Revolutions and the Rhythm of History*. New York and Oxford: Oxford University Press.

23. McEvedy, Colin, and Richard Jones. 1978. *Atlas of World Population History*. Middlesex, England, and New York: Penguin Books.

24. Fischer, *The Great Wave*.

25. Harris, Marvin, and Eric B. Ross. 1987. *Death, Sex, and Fertility: Population Regulation in Preindustrial and Developing Societies*. New York: Columbia University Press.

26. Hassan, Fekri A. 1981. *Demographic Archaeology*. New York: Academic Press, 167.

27. Gould, Richard A. 1981. "Comparative Ecology of Food-Sharing in Australia and Northwest California." In *Omnivorous Primates: Gathering and Hunting in Human Evolution*, edited by Robert S. O. Harding and Geza Teleki, 422–54. New York: Columbia University Press; Hayden, Brian. 1981a. "Research and Development in the Stone Age: Technological Transitions Among Hunter-Gatherers." *Current Anthropology* 22(5): 519–48.

28. Cowgill, George L. 1975. "Population Pressure as a Non-Explanation." *In American Antiquity* 40(2): 127–31, part 2, Memoir 30; Hassan, *Demographic Archaeology*.

29. Kelly, Raymond C. 1968. "Demographic Pressure and Descent Group Structure in the New Guinea Highlands." *Oceania* 38(1): 36–63.

30. Bayliss-Smith, Tim. 1974. "Constraints on Population Growth: The Case of the Polynesian Outlier Atolls in the Precontact Period." *Human Ecology* 2(4): 259–95.

31. Zubrow, Ezra B. 1975. *Prehistoric Carrying Capacity*. Menlo Park, CA: Cummings.

32. Dumond, Don E. 1972. "Population Growth and Political Centralization." In *Population Growth: Anthropological Implications*, edited by Brian Spooner, 286–310. Cambridge: MIT Press.

33. Hassan, *Demographic Archaeology*, 199; Deevy, Edward S. 1960. "The Human Population." *Scientific American* 203(3): 195–204; Coale, Ansley J. 1974. "The History of the Human Population." *Scientific American* 231(3): 40–51; Demeny, Paul. 1990. "Population." In *The Earth as Transformed by Human Action: Global and Regional Changes in the Biosphere Over the Past 300 Years*, edited by B. L. Turner et al., 41–54. Cambridge: Cambridge University Press.

34. Smith, E. A., and S. A. Smith. 1994. "Inuit Sex-Ratio Variation: Population Control, Ethnographic Error, or Parental Manipulation?" *Current Anthropology* 35: 595–614.

35. Keeley, Lawrence H. 1996. *War Before Civilization*. New York and Oxford: Oxford University Press.

36. Hassan, *Demographic Archaeology*, 118.

37. Weiss, K. M. 1973. "Demographic Models for Anthropology." *American Antiquity* 38(2), pt. 2, Memoir 27.

38. Smith and Smith, "Inuit Sex-Ratio Variation," 595–614.

39. Ehrlich, *The Population Bomb*, 29.

40. Bogue, Donald T. 1969. *Principles of Demography*. New York: Wiley, 53–54.

41. Krantz, Grover S. 1976. "On the Nonmigration of Hunting Peoples." *Northwest Anthropological Research Notes* 10(2): 209–16.

42. Riches, David. 1974. "The Netsilik Eskimo: A Special Case of Selective Female Infanticide." *Ethnology* 13(4): 351–61; Divale, W. I., and Marvin Harris. 1976. "Population, Warfare, and the Male Supremacist Complex." *American Anthropologist* 78(3): 521–38.

43. Schrire, C., and W. L. Steiger. 1974. "A Matter of Life and Death: An Investigation into the Practice of Female Infanticide in the Arctic." *Man* 9(2): 161–84.

44. Yengoyan, Aram A. 1981. "Infanticide and Birth Order: An Empirical Analysis of Preferential Female Infanticide Among Australian Aboriginal Populations." In *The Perception of Evolution: Essays Honoring Joseph B. Birdsell*, edited by Larry L. Mai, Eugenia Shanklin, and R. W. Sussman, *Anthropology UCLA* 7: 255–73. See also Smith and Smith, "Inuit Sex-Ratio Variation," 595–614.

45. Birdsell, J. B. 1979. "Ecological Influences on Australian Aboriginal Social Organization." In *Primate Ecology and Human Origins: Ecological Influences on Social Organization*, edited by Invin S. Bernstein and Euclid O. Smith, 117–51. New York: Garland STPM.

46. Freeman, M. M. R. 1971. "A Social and Ecological Analysis of Systematic Female Infanticide." *American Anthropologist* 73(5): 1011–18; Cowlishaw, Gillian. 1978. "Infanticide in Aboriginal Australia." *Oceania* 48(4): 262–83.

47. Sussman, Robert W. 1972. "Child Transport, Family Size, and Increase in Human Population During the Neolithic." *Current Anthropology* 13(2): 258–59.

48. Birdsell, J. B. 1953. "Some Environmental and Cultural Factors Influencing the Structure of Australian Aboriginal Populations." *American Naturalist* 87: 171–207; Birdsell, J. B. 1971. "Ecology, Spacing Mechanisms, and Adaptive Behavior in Aboriginal Land Tenure." In *Land Tenure in the Pacific*, edited by Ron Crocombe, 334–61. Melbourne: Oxford University Press; Birdsell, J. B. "Ecological Influences on Australian Aboriginal Social Organization," 117–51.

49. Neel, James V. 1968. "Some Aspects of Differential Fertility in Two American Indian Tribes." *Proceedings of the Eighth International Congress of Anthropological and Ethnological Sciences* 1: 356–61. Tokyo: ICAES.

50. Bowdler, S. 1977. "The Coastal Colonization of Australia." In *Sunda and Sahul: Prehistoric Studies in Southeast Asia, Melanesia and Australia*, edited by J. Allen, J. Golson, and R. Jones, 205–46. London: Academic Press; Lourandos, Harry. 1985. "Intensification and Australian Prehistory." In *Prehistoric Hunter-Gatherers: The*

Emergence of Cultural Complexity, edited by T. Douglas Price and James A. Brown, 385–423. New York: Academic Press; Lourandos, Harry. 1987. "Pleistocene Australia: Peopling a Continent." In *The Pleistocene Old World: Regional Perspectives*, edited by Olga Soffer, 147–65. New York: Plenum Press.

51. Deevy, "The Human Population," 195–204. Polgar, Steven. 1972. "Population History and Population Policies from an Anthropological Perspective." *Current Anthropology* (132): 203–11; Coale, "The History of the Human Population," 40–51; Hassan, *Demographic Archaeology*.

52. Marshall, Yvonne. 2006. "Introduction: Adopting a Sedentary Lifeway." *World Archaeology* 38(2): 153–63.

53. Cohen, Mark Nathan. 1977. *The Food Crisis in Prehistory: Overpopulation and the Origins of Agriculture*. New Haven, CT: Yale University Press. See also Hayden, "Research and Development in the Stone Age."

54. Hewlett, Barry. 1991. "Demography and Childcare in Preindustrial Societies." *Journal of Anthropological Research* 47(1): 1–37.

55. Sengel, Randal A. 1973. "Comments." *Current Anthropology* 14(5): 540–42.

56. Flannery, Kent V. 1969. "Origins and Ecological Effects of Early Domestication in Iran and the Near East." In *The Domestication and Exploitation of Plants and Animals*, edited by Peter J. Ucko and G. W. Dimbleby, 73–100. London: Duckworth.

57. Carneiro, Robert L., and D. F. Hilse. 1966. "On Determining the Probable Rate of Population Growth During the Neolithic." *American Anthropologist* 68(1): 177–81.

58. Zubrow, *Prehistoric Carrying Capacity*.

59. Noble, David Grant, ed. 2004. *In Search of Chaco: New Approaches to an Archaeological Enigma*. Santa Fe, NM: School of American Research Press; Stuart, David E. 2000. *Anasazi America: Seventeen Centuries on the Road from Center Place*. Albuquerque, NM: University of New Mexico Press.

60. Sahlins, Marshall. 1961. "The Segmentary Lineage: An Organization of Predatory Expansion." *American Anthropologist* 63(2), pt. 1, 322–45.

61. Lathrap, Don W. 1970. *The Upper Amazon*. New York: Praeger.

62. Meggers, Betty J. 1995. "Judging the Future by the Past: The Impact of Environmental Instability on Prehistoric Amazonian Populations." In *Indigenous Peoples and the Future of Amazonia: An Ecological Anthropology of an Endangered World*, edited by Leslie E. Sponsel, 15–43. Tucson and London: University of Arizona Press.

63. Lathrap, *Upper Amazon*.

64. Kunstadter, Peter. 1971. "Natality, Mortality and Migration in Upland and Lowland Populations in Northwestern Thailand." In *Culture and Population*, edited by Steven Polgar, 46–60. Cambridge, MA: Schenkman.

65. Whiting, John M. 1969. "Effects of Climate on Certain Cultural Practices." In *Environment and Cultural Behavior: Ecological Studies in Cultural Anthropology*, edited by A. P. Vayda, 416–55. New York: Natural History Press.

66. Saucier, Jean-Francois. 1972. "Correlates of the Long Postpartum Taboo: A Cross-Cultural Study." *Current Anthropology* 13(2): 38–49.

67. Bayliss-Smith, "Constraints on Population Growth," 259–95.

68. Knudson, Kenneth E. 1970. "Resource Fluctuation, Productivity, and Social Organization on Micronesian Coral Islands." Doctoral dissertation, University of Oregon.

69. Firth, Raymond. 1957. *We the Tikopia.* New York: Barnes and Noble.

70. Firth, *We the Tikopia,* 414.

71. Kirch, Patrick Vinton, and D. E. Yen. 1982. *Tikopia: The Prehistory and Ecology of a Polynesian Outlier.* Bernice P. Bishop Museum Bulletin 238. Honolulu: Bishop Museum Press.

72. Diamond, Jared. 2005. *Collapse: How Societies Choose to Fail or Succeed.* New York: Viking.

73. Hunt, Terry L. 2006. "Rethinking the Fall of Easter Island: New Evidence Points to an Alternative Explanation for a Civilization's Collapse." *American Scientist* 94(5): 412–19; Hunt, Terry L., and Carl P. Lipo. 2006. "Late Colonization of Easter Island." *Science* 311(5767): 1603–6.

74. Mamdani, Mahmood. 1973. *The Myth of Population Control: Family, Caste, and Class in an Indian Village.* New York: Monthly Review Press.

75. Geertz, Clifford. 1963. *Agricultural Involution: The Process of Ecological Change in Indonesia.* Berkeley: University of California Press.

76. Bentley, Gillian R., Tony Goldberg, and Grazyna Jasienska. 1993. "The Fertility of Agricultural and Non-Agricultural Traditional Societies." *Population Studies* 47: 269–81.

77. Bodley, John H. 1988. *Tribal Peoples and Development Issues: A Global Overview.* Mountain View, CA: Mayfield Publishing; John H. Bodley. 1999b. *Victims of Progress.* 4th ed. Mountain View, CA: Mayfield Publishing.

78. Wagley, Charles. 1951. "Cultural Influences on Population." *Revista do Museu Paulista* 5: 95–104.

79. Schneider, David. 1955. "Abortion and Depopulation on a Pacific Island: Yap." In *Health, Culture, and Community,* edited by B. D. Paul, 211–35. New York: Russell Sage Foundation.

80. Underwood, Jane H. 1973. "The Demography of a Myth: Abortion in Yap." *Human Biology in Oceania* 2: 115–27.

81. Robey, Bryant, Shea O. Rutstein, and Leo Morris. 1993. "The Fertility Decline in Developing Countries." *Scientific American* 269(6): 60–67.

82. Robey, Rutstein, and Morris, "Fertility Decline," 60–67.

Poverty and Conflict   7

*A large number of people on this planet, to whom the comfort
and stability of a middle-class life is utterly unknown, find war
and a barracks existence a step up rather than a step down.*

—ROBERT D. KAPLAN, *THE COMING ANARCHY*[1]

IN ADDITION TO ESTABLISHING A SUCCESSFUL ADAPTATION to the natural
environment, every human society must maintain a certain minimal
level of internal order and security to survive. Conflict and violence,
both internal and external, must be carefully regulated. Individuals, households, and other social units must have access to basic resources and sufficient involvement with decision-making processes to protect their
self-interests. During the thousands of years before the first large-scale, politically centralized societies appeared, domestic-scale tribal societies successfully minimized these universal problems by maintaining the household
as the primary institutional structure, with decision-making power widely
dispersed throughout society. This allowed these small societies to be
highly responsive to internal problems. Differential access to wealth and
power was unlikely to provide a systematic source of conflict, because individuals' social action occurred in small, face-to-face communities where
everyone could participate according to his or her individual abilities.
Poverty and powerlessness were not institutionalized. Feuding and raiding
were chronic problems but often took the form of interpersonal conflicts
and were part of the established social order. There were no professional
armies and no permanent war leaders.

With the arrival of political centralization and the resulting social stratification and economic specialization that accompanied the appearance of
the first states a mere 6,000 years ago, social order became a far more difficult and dangerous problem. Whole segments of a society were sometimes denied direct control over their basic subsistence requirements, and
real political power came to rest with an elite few. Monumental royal
tombs, palaces, and temples were constructed to reinforce the legitimacy of
the ruling elite and the social order. For the first time in human experience, political power and religious ideology were used to compel households to provide labor and to produce basic subsistence for an elite few
who controlled the political system and its supporting institutions. However, because human labor was the primary source of energy in ancient
civilizations it was crucial that the peasantry remain healthy. Thus, it would
have been counterproductive for ancient rulers in the imperial world to
have ignored the basic needs of the populace that ultimately sustained
them. Although they sought to meet the basic needs of their populations,
pre-capitalist states were precarious systems because they engendered internal political conflict and external wars and because they depended on
intensive agriculture operating close to the regional carrying capacity.
Throughout history states have been subject to frequent collapses of social
order through civil wars, peasant revolts, and popular uprisings that, in
combination with foreign invasions, have destroyed many individual states.
Indeed, seldom have any states survived more than a few centuries.

The social order problem changed again with the recent emergence of
a globally organized commercial society because the scale of elite power
became far greater than in any ancient civilization. The institutions that the
elite control have enormous power over the daily lives of people everywhere. Commercially controlled and highly concentrated communication
systems, including radio, television, cinema, and the print media, now
shape virtually everyone's thought and behavior, creating passive consumers
and wage laborers worldwide. At the same time, industrial technology reduces the requirement for human labor and makes the basic welfare of millions of people irrelevant to those in power. Relative and absolute poverty
and powerlessness are intrinsic aspects of the global system that continue to
threaten the internal security and domestic tranquility of people in virtually all states.

The potential collapse of democratic political systems and their replacement by overwhelmingly powerful and oppressive totalitarian forces
would represent the ultimate political crisis. Such an event would mean
the curtailment of many individual freedoms now enjoyed in most indus-

trial nations and might be followed by a period of intensifying civil strife. Such an outcome might occur independently of international conflict. Disastrous internal disorders could be precipitated by a major downturn or collapse of our precarious consumption-based economic system, by unresolved urban stresses, or by unresponsive political processes. Terrorist acts and civil disturbances on the part of dissident political groups, spontaneous urban riots and looting, labor strife, organized crime, corruption among high political officials, illegal use of power, rising rates of violent crime and juvenile delinquency, and drug abuse are all symptoms of serious underlying conflicts and contradictions in commercially organized cultures.

Anthropologists have traditionally been concerned with a variety of problems related to social order that are directly relevant to a better understanding of our present crisis. However, before considering the anthropological perspective in detail, we will present a brief historic review of the social order crisis in America to clarify both the nature of the crisis and current attempts at its solution. The United States provides an excellent starting point for any treatment of this topic because culturally it has long been a world leader—yet its violent crime and incarceration rates are far higher than those of any other modern nation. Perhaps even more important, in recent decades the American government commissioned several major studies of the problem of violence in an attempt to pinpoint its causes and to work toward the prevention, or at least the reduction, of violence and disorder.

Violence and Insecurity in America

Violent crime, political terrorism, assassination, rioting, and various other forms of social disorder have always been part of the American scene. It was not until the assassination of President John F. Kennedy in 1963 and the outbreak of widespread urban rioting in 1967—followed in 1968 by violent political demonstrations, campus disturbances, and the assassination of Martin Luther King Jr. and Senator Robert E. Kennedy—that the government began to ask serious questions about violence. Several national commissions were convened in the late 1960s to examine various aspects of the problem. Perhaps the most comprehensive of these commissions was the National Commission on the Causes and Prevention of Violence, established in June 1968 by President Lyndon Johnson. He directed it to "go as far as man's knowledge" could take it in the search for the causes and prevention of violence.

The final report of the commission[2] concluded that the 1960s saw virtually all types of violence increase dramatically over the levels of prior decades. Over the decade between 1958 and 1968 the rate of reported violent crimes (homicide, forcible rape, robbery, and aggravated assault) doubled, reaching nearly 300 cases per 100,000 people. After the commission report was published, the violent crime rate continued to escalate until by 1992 it had reached 646 per 100,000.[3] Since then the rate of violent crime has declined steadily, dropping in 2005 to the still historically high level of 402 per 100,000 (figure 7.1). Some of these fluctuations can be attributed to demographic shifts in the population. However, it is remarkable that the proportion of the population incarcerated or under "correctional supervision" (incarceration, probation, or parole) in the United States rose steadily from 1980 through 2005 even as the violent crime rate rose and fell, seemingly independently. The elevated incarceration rate was largely due to the large increase in drug-related arrests. Homicide rates also soared during this period, reaching 10 or more per 100,000 for twelve years between 1973 and 1993, whereas from 1949 to 1964 it did not exceed 5 per 100,000.[4] However, from 1997 to 2002 homicides also declined, but less dramatically

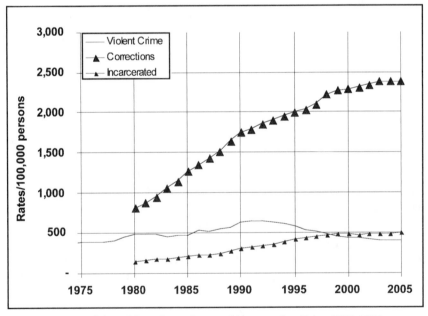

Figure 7.1.   U.S. Violent Crime, Corrections, and Incarceration Rates, 1975–2005.
Source: U.S. Department of Justice, Bureau of Justice Statistics. 2006. *Uniform Crime Reports,* www.ojp.usdoj.gov/bjs/glance/tables/4meastab.htm.

than overall violent crime rates, to 6 to 7. This was still a relatively high rate; by comparison, Norway recorded only 55 homicides in 1990, a rate of 1.1 per 100,000.[5]

In view of the overall increase in violence in America, the commissioners felt that the basic foundations of our society were clearly being threatened and urged immediate action to control the problem. The dangers of internal disorder were considered fully as serious as any external threats, requiring a reassessment of national priorities along with a scaling-down of military expenditures for national defense. As the commissioners stated, "We solemnly declare our conviction that this nation is entering a period in which our people need to be as concerned by the internal dangers to our free society as by any probable combination of external threats."[6] This was a remarkable conclusion, given that this was during the Cold War with the Soviet Union.

The commissioners called for a doubling of expenditures on the criminal justice process and greater coordination and efficiency in law enforcement activities in general. If drastic action was not taken quickly, they foresaw a bleak future for Americans. Our inner cities would be dotted with isolated "safe" areas occupied by upper-income families protected by armed guards and electronic surveillance equipment, while crime and terror would prevail for the poor at night, when there would be no possible security. Public facilities such as schools, libraries, and playgrounds would also require armed guards. Commuters from safe suburban compounds would travel carefully patrolled and "sanitized" corridors in armored cars, while guards would "ride shotgun" on public transportation. These defensive measures would in turn lead to further intensification of terror and violence as those at the bottom of the social order became increasingly desperate. This picture has proven to be remarkably prophetic. Since then we have seen an increasing tendency for upper-income households to move into gated communities, and safety and security issues have become widespread concerns, quite apart from the elevated concerns of terrorist attack since 2001.

The commissioners recognized that merely increasing the efficiency of law enforcement was not sufficient if the underlying causes of violence were not corrected. In their view, violence was a sickness, a social pathology. To discover the underlying causes of violence, the report attempted first to pinpoint where crimes were committed most often and who committed them. It confirmed that violent crimes were most prevalent in cities of over 50,000 people, where crime rates were eleven times greater than in rural areas. Crimes were most often committed by young, low-income males living in urban slum conditions. An earlier national commission[7] had declared that this association between crime and slum living conditions was "one of the most fully documented facts about crime." This commission, known as the Kerner Commission, readily identified issues of unemployment and poverty as primary underlying social causes. The solutions they advocated were jobs, education, housing, livable incomes, and enforcement of civil rights laws.[8] Some improvements in economic conditions during the 1970s also benefited the poorest Americans, but the economic transformations of the 1980s and 1990s actually increased both the absolute number and the percentage of the officially poor over the levels in 1970.

In-depth life history research and basic ethnography on street criminals by anthropologist Mark S. Fleisher in 1995 vividly demonstrated that when family life disintegrates under conditions of extreme urban poverty and children are damaged by persistent parental brutality, criminality can become a way of life. There is also a common pattern of non-criminal coping responses to material deprivation throughout the underdeveloped world and in urban slums in developed nations that is strikingly similar to the behavior patterns of the urban poor in early industrial England.[9] Nontraditional marriage arrangements; the matrifocal family; and various forms of petty marketing practices, such as children hawking gum on the streets are simply ways of making the best of a difficult situation. Poverty behavior indeed presents a consistent picture, but it does so because people are adapting to the same problems, not because they are locked in their own self-replicating culture of poverty.

Social Order in the Tribal World

Solving our social order problem is indeed a formidable task, particularly in view of the fact that the most humane societies known are institutionally far different from the highly stratified urban societies that we often mistakenly assume are based on the fundamentals of human nature. A very high level of social disorder is not just a problem of human nature, because we can treat human nature as a constant. It is a cultural and social organizational problem whose solution may require drastic cultural and social change. More relatively egalitarian modern nations, such as Norway, clearly show levels of violence that are dramatically lower than America's. Furthermore, it is instructive to note that most of the criminogenic factors identified in the Kerner Report are absent in tribal societies. This is not to suggest of course that tribals have no bad people. The key factors seem to be the small absolute size of tribal societies, as well as their relatively greater

level of basic equality and shared decision making in comparison with politically centralized states. With low population densities, little concentrated social power, no emphasis on material wealth as the primary source
of social status, and access by all households to basic subsistence resources,
tribal societies face very different internal social order problems and are
able to solve them very effectively. Also important is the tribal emphasis on
the distribution of wealth and income as a primary social objective, rather
than an emphasis on continually increasing production.

Anthropologists who have observed the most autonomous foraging societies have generally been impressed with their relatively low levels of internal violence. Some societies, such as the San Bushmen of southern Africa
and the Semai of Malaysia,[10] have been characterized as almost totally non-
violent, but it would be misleading to assume that all tribal peoples lead perpetually harmonious social lives. It is important to distinguish between the
relative harmony of day-to-day life within camps or settlements and the frequently less peaceful relations between local communities and ethnic groups
prior to government-imposed control: Externally directed conflict was a
fact of life in autonomous domestic-scale societies, and in some cases loss of
life was high.[11] Some tribal societies, such as the Yanomamo Indians of the
upper Orinoco rain forests, have been described as highly violent.[12]
Chronic feuding is characteristic of tribal societies, but it is usually externally directed. The very existence of the Yanomamo is threatened by violence related to the intrusion of commercially motivated peoples, and it is
possible that external factors may have increased the recently described levels of violence that anthropolist Napoleon Chagnon found in Yanomamo
life.[13] The basic survival of autonomous tribal societies was seldom threatened by internal conflict, although internal and external is not always readily defined in these very small societies. It could hardly have been otherwise,
considering the thousands of years that tribal societies endured. There was
no "war of all against all" that Thomas Hobbes (1588–1679) envisioned,[14]
nor was there total harmony. Strictly speaking, tribal societies were anarchic,
in that they lacked government.[15] They were also characterized by autonomy (self-rule, freedom) and economic autarky (self-sufficiency). However,
they maintained internal order without formal legal codes and specialized
law enforcement institutions, and even without formal political offices invested with coercive authority. Tribal societies are dramatic proof that the
expensive law-and-order machinery that we now require is not the only,
and perhaps not the best, route to social order.

The maintenance of social order by tribals is not a result of any moral
superiority of "noble savages." It is due to social and cultural conditions. In

tribal societies individual self-interest is unlikely to conflict with the long-range interests of society. Excessive conflict, theft, use of force, or hoarding of resources for exclusive use would all be self-defeating in a tribal society in which everyone's survival ultimately depended on mutual trust and cooperation. As noted in earlier chapters, this same correspondence of interests has also contributed to the ecological success of tribal societies and to the maintenance of population equilibrium.

In low-density tribal societies, conflict was unquestionably further minimized by extreme flexibility in group membership and by the small size of the local, face-to-face residential group. A typical hunting band averaged only twenty-five to fifty people, including children; thus, relatively few adults were ever forced into close interaction. Camps shifted location every few days or weeks, and such moves were often used as an excuse for changing band personnel. Careful studies of modern hunting bands such as the San Bushmen have revealed that individuals and families constantly shuffle between bands and that many of these shifts are simply a means of resolving interpersonal conflicts without violence.[16]

The Importance of Social Equality

The concept of equality is critical to an understanding of the differences between tribal societies and the imperial and commercial worlds. Equality is a fundamental feature of tribal societies, and it makes early human society strikingly different from the hierarchical societies of our closest non-human primate relatives, and the more recent hierarchical imperial and commercial societies.[17] No one of course is ever totally equal with anyone else in any society, but in tribal societies the differences that separated people were exclusively age, gender, and unique personal qualities. Positions of prestige and influence were open to all persons qualified to occupy them. For example, anyone with sufficient skill could become a respected hunter or a band leader. Anthropologist Morton Fried defined an egalitarian society very concisely, as follows:

> An egalitarian society is one in which there are as many positions of prestige in any given age-sex grade as there are persons capable of filling them. Let it be put even more strongly. An egalitarian society does not have any means of fixing or limiting the number of persons capable of exerting power. As many persons as can wield power—whether through personal strength, influence, authority, or whatever means—can do so, and there is no necessity to draw them together to establish an order of dominance and paramountcy.[18]

Some anthropologists point out that in tribal societies, where social classes and political hierarchy are by definition absent, some forms of social inequality may be produced by marriage exchanges and by a gendered division of labor.[19] In such cases, equality still prevails between households. Social equality may be said to exist when opposing categories are seen as morally equivalent, or complimentary oppositions, as in many tribal moiety systems. Even with this kind of equality, people may still be distinguished by different levels of "moral worthiness," producing a moral hierarchy, or prestige hierarchy, as demonstrated by tribal examples from New Guinea.[20] Witches and sorcerers may be stigmatized, and even killed, whereas shamans may be accorded special respect. However, regardless of differences in "virtue," the distribution of basic physical necessities of life is expected to be fundamentally egalitarian in the tribal world. No one in a tribal society is routinely denied access to basic subsistence, or the means to subsistence. Fried is emphatic on this point: "In no simple society known to ethnography is there any restriction on access to the raw materials necessary to make tools and weapons. This statement can be made flatly about resources in the habitation area of a given unit."[21]

Land, water, and game are always accessible by claims of kinship and marriage. This is the "irreducible minimum" referred to in chapter 2. Although boundaries may be recognized for tribal, band, and occasionally family territories, trespass regulations usually mean that permission to use an area must be requested but cannot reasonably be denied.[22] Group membership also fluctuates widely. The trespass rules themselves often serve the important function of helping people monitor who is using resources to better manage their availability. Among tribal horticulturalists, access to land may be regulated by descent groups, but these are not rigid organizations, and membership changes may commonly occur if land shortages arise. Individual ownership of property certainly does occur, but it is normally restricted to personal weapons and artifacts, herd animals, and crops—things in which personal labor has been invested. With use-access to basic resources in effect open to all, particularly when residential shifts are part of the subsistence round, there are no real advantages to be gained by asserting individual title to land. In regard to movable property, one can make practical use of only so many goods; given both the need for mobility and the cultural emphasis on generosity, there is no incentive either to hoard or to steal property. Furthermore, in a small society a thief would be unable to hide. All these factors almost certainly minimize interpersonal conflict.

This general social equality might not operate whenever particular conditions allowed individual households to gain decisive prestige, status, or material advantage over other households. For example, certain production systems such as the use of domestic animals as movable and renewable sources of food, milk, and traction power made it possible for household heads to manage the labor of women and children in ways that significantly increased production. These systems made accumulation advantageous and allowed more successful households to enjoy a more favorable rate of accumulation. At the same time, heavy reliance on domestic animals increased the risk of misfortune and dependency and tended to shift economic power from women to men, thus amplifying gender inequities. At different stages of the domestic cycle, some households were naturally more likely to be either lenders or dependent borrowers of livestock. This process has been called the Secondary Products Revolution[23] and may be an important pathway to inequality. Archaeologist Peter Bogucki uses the label "transegalitarian" to describe domestic-scale societies in which individual households are competing for status or prestige and aggrandizing individuals are beginning to emerge but there are as yet no rigid rank systems, social classes, or centralized political authority. The existence of elaborate mortuary ceremonialism or competitive feasting suggests the emergence of such societies.[24]

Many anthropologists describe differences in age and gender status in tribal societies as "inequality," and these differences are occasionally described as oppressive and exploitative. For example, such language has been used to describe the apparent dominance of the old men in Australian aboriginal society.[25] However, age and gender inequities that may exist in the tribal world do not deny anyone the opportunity to marry, raise a family, and make a living. We can say that everyone is guaranteed the irreducible minimum. Age differences are of course only temporary, and tribals themselves usually do not consider different gender roles to be oppressive. Two women anthropologists, Phyllis Kaberry and Diane Bell,[26] conducted field studies to investigate the position of aboriginal women in Australia and specifically rejected the charge that women were exploited by the traditional system. In virtually all tribal societies women do tend to work closer to the home and care for children more than do men, and their work is often more routine. Men often do heavier work, and their work can carry them far from home. However, where detailed time-expenditure studies have been carried out[27] they indicate that the total work load appears to be relatively equitably distributed between the sexes.

Conflict and Conflict Resolution

The cultural conditions of tribal societies help reduce the basic causes of violence and disorder, and there are specific mechanisms to reduce the frequency of otherwise unavoidable problems. There are also direct and effective means of handling any trouble that does arise and specific mechanisms to channel conflicts. Serious breaches of tribal norms could result in expulsion from the society, which would mean the loss of all physical and emotional support for the recalcitrant individual. Survival without kins-people is virtually impossible, and an exiled troublemaker would have difficulty being accepted by other groups in a society in which there is no anonymity. Such a drastic sanction rarely needs to be applied, but the threat is always in the background. In many societies the threat of witchcraft accusation might also be an effective means of compelling conformity. Chronic troublemakers might find themselves accused of witchcraft and possibly blamed for a variety of sicknesses and community misfortunes. In extreme cases, accused witches are publicly executed.

In addition to simply moving away, egalitarian tribal societies often employed highly ritualized methods of conflict resolution. In-group interpersonal violence may even have been encouraged by some cultures, but it was usually very carefully regulated. The Yanomamo,[28] for example, recognize several distinct levels of violence in a carefully graded series of increasing intensity. Their disputes might be settled by ritual duels that range from chest pounding (in which two men exchange bare-fist blows to the chest) at the lowest level to spear-throwing duels at the highest. Intermediate duels involve blows to the side and club fighting. Minor injuries and prominent scars may result from these actions, but deaths are uncommon. More pacific ritual forms of conflict resolution in egalitarian societies include Eskimo song duels, in which the disputants publicly insult each other until the loser is laughed down by the audience. Generally, when disputes in these cultures are not settled by the individuals most directly involved, they are resolved by community consensus. The objective is merely to restore order, not to punish. Abstract notions of justice are quite irrelevant in this situation.

Very small, peaceful, domestic-scale societies in the commercial world such as the Hutterites and the islanders of Tristan da Cunha share common elements with the also relatively peaceful contemporary band societies such as the Semai, Siriono, Kalahari Kung, and the Copper Eskimo, suggesting that social scale is a crucial social feature. Peace researcher David Fabbro concluded, "The small size of all these societies is a major contributory factor in their open and basically egalitarian decision-making and social control processes."[29] Fabbro also identified social justice, or the absence of structural violence, as a key feature of these societies, except for gender inequity with the Hutterites. Structural violence exists when social structures such as class divisions, racism, or gender inequity systematically deprive certain social groups of benefits or opportunities to advance their life chances. Thus a more peaceful society would be characterized by relative economic and social equality. The Hutterites and the Tristan da Cunha islanders also demonstrated that small-scale sedentary farming communities could produce and store a surplus and still remain peaceful and egalitarian.

A crucial threshold between relatively peaceful and more conflict-prone tribal societies may be "social substitutability."[30] Social substitutability means that any individual can stand for an entire group, and therefore can be a target for revenge or retribution against the group. This typically occurs when related males live nearby, forming "fraternal interest groups."[31] If someone is killed in any group, individuals in the group view it as an attack against everyone, and this can set off endless cycles of killing. More peaceful tribal societies lack social substitutability, but they are not totally "non-violent." They fight and may even use homicide to settle disputes within the local group, but they are not required to seek vengeance against another group. This is the line between interpersonal and inter-group violence and conflict. Social substitutability assumes the presence of segmented groups in which individuals are obligated to support their own group in opposition to other groups. Tribal societies that are based on overlapping personal, ego-based kindred, or bilateral descent groups may not form discretely bounded membership groups, and thus may reduce the probability of the logic of social substitutability leading to chronic warfare. However, unsegmented groups may have territorially defined groups, and they may defend them against individual intruders. Otherwise, unsegmented groups may view outsiders who speak different languages to be an "out-group," or an "other" to be collectively treated as enemies.

Leadership

There are no rulers in the tribal world, but there are leaders. Headmen have been found in some of the simplest foraging bands, but their authority is severely limited. For example, among the Nambikuara Indians of Brazil, band members delegated primary decision-making responsibility for band subsistence activities, selection of routes and campsites, and interband relations to the band headman.[32] However, he was a leader only as long as his followers consented to his leadership, and he was not to recommend actions that band members would not choose. A chief's success was measured by his ability to see that the band was well fed. He was also expected to excel in generosity, and constant demands were made on him for food and small articles.

Thus, a Nambikuara headman had to be an especially skillful, dedicated, and hardworking individual. He bore a heavy responsibility for band well-being and security, but his position was always tenuous. If his leadership qualities faltered the band might simply disintegrate as disgruntled individuals and households sought out other band leaders with whom to align themselves. A headman was generally allowed a young second wife to ease the burdens of leadership. The only other rewards appear to have been highly personal, and few persons desired the position. Band headmanship in tribal society, therefore, is not the kind of political office found in larger-scale cultures. In fact, anthropologist Claude Lévi-Strauss had a difficult time explaining why anyone would even aspire to such a position in Nambikuara society. He concluded that "there are chiefs because there are, in any human group, men who, unlike most of their companions, enjoy prestige for its own sake, feel a strong appeal to responsibility, and to whom the burden of public affairs brings its own reward."[33] Christopher Boehm[34] called this kind of leadership structure a "reverse dominance hierarchy" because it was highly responsive to the will of the people. The objective was to prevent aggrandizing individuals from asserting exclusionary domination for their self-benefit in ways that would be detrimental to other members of the community.[35]

Anthropologist Richard Lee's description of leadership among the !Kung Bushmen presents a similar picture. He found that the !Kung went to such lengths to prevent the accumulation of power in a leader and were so fiercely egalitarian that it was not always obvious that "headmen" even existed. In fact, when he asked a Bushman whether the !Kung had headmen, the man replied, "Of course we have headmen! . . . Each one of us is headman over himself."[36] Lee concluded that leadership existed but was very diffuse, totally noncoercive, and represented a form of "political reciprocity" much like the reciprocity characteristic of tribal economics.

Internal Order in Politically Centralized Societies

Chiefdoms are the simplest non-egalitarian societies, and many ethnographic examples are known from the Pacific, Africa, and the northwest coast of North America.[37] Chiefdom societies restrict the number of individuals who can occupy important positions within the society but still permit relatively free access to basic natural resources. Social control remains largely a matter of kinship, but true political offices exist, such that chiefs are rulers. Ranking within a chiefdom may be highly elaborated, with a hereditary chief at the top and each corporate descent group ranked both relative to one another and internally. The authority of the chief is defined by the position he (most often a male) occupies, and his personality and special skills are a relatively minor aspect of his qualifications. The office of chief is ritually set apart and reinforced by a variety of sumptuary regulations or taboos, such as the right to eat special foods or to own special articles. Conflicts may become intense as individuals vie for status, and rebellions may occur when particular chiefs overstep the customary bounds of their office; in general, however, the social order problem is qualitatively much simpler, even given ranking, than in societies with full stratification.

Stratified societies, most fully represented by ancient civilizations, kingdoms, and centralized states, have the same potential social order problems as chiefdoms but add the critical element of restricted access to strategic resources. According to Morton Fried's classic definition, "[a] stratified society is one in which members of the same sex and equivalent age status do not have equal access to the basic resources that sustain life."[38] Stratification involves the arrangement of people into classes according to their degree of access to power and resources. There is also a pervasive division of labor by economic specialization such that no one except certain rural peasants can directly provide more than a very small proportion of their basic needs. The ruling elite at the top of the hierarchy can effectively regulate access to and use of both critical natural resources and the technological means of production. Control over water, soil, and air may in this way be denied to large segments of society.

With the development of stratification, for the first time in human history cultural conditions permitted exploitation of one subgroup within a society by another. Exploitation is an emotional and value-laden concept that many social scientists might prefer not to deal with, but in discussing problems of social order it cannot be avoided. Webster's Dictionary defines exploitation as "unfair utilization." The catch here is in the meaning of unfair, because no one would dispute that there is utilization of one class by another in any stratified society. Certainly the members of the ruling class are dependent for their welfare on the lower classes because they draw their labor force and all their food, goods, and services from them. The crucial payoff for the elite is their disproportionate enjoyment of improved life chances and the possibility of significantly greater reproductive success. Elite men are likely to be healthier than non-elite men, and they are likely to have more wives and concubines and, consequently, more numerous and healthier offspring. The evidence for such differential reproductive success is overwhelming; the rulers of all major ancient agrarian civilizations had larger domestic establishments, scaling upward by orders of magnitude corresponding to the scale of society.[39] The fairness of this arrangement may be judged from both an inside and an outside view. This is where Antonio Gramsci's concept of cultural hegemony (see chapter 1) comes into play. If the elite, through their manipulation of the dominant ideology, can convince the commoners of the legitimacy of the system, then no one will feel exploited, even though an outsider, unmystified by culturally shaped beliefs, might label the system exploitation if the commoners are deprived of basic physical necessities while the elite bask in luxury.

Material deprivation can be objectively measured by health status, food supply, clothing, housing, and other indicators and may relate to both a minimal survival level and a culturally defined minimum comfort level. Material deprivation of either sort is absolute deprivation and is encompassed by the popular concept of poverty. Relative deprivation, or the feeling that one is not as "well off" as one would like to be in comparison to the next higher class, may be found wherever there is an inequitable distribution of wealth and power and can occur above the absolute level. Deprivation of some kind seems to be a universal feature of all stratified societies. Some socialist countries have succeeded in easing the absolute deprivation of different classes, but classes exist in these countries nonetheless, along with the potential for disorder.

Anyone viewing a particular stratified society from the outside finds it difficult to understand why the impoverished lower classes so often seem to accept their lot without a struggle. Yet such systems could not exist without the threat of physical coercion and the use of powerful forms of thought control, or cultural hegemony.[40] The use of police force, brutality, and imprisonment in support of the political power, wealth, and property rights of the ruling class is certainly a familiar element in the history of all states. However, in many of the ancient agrarian civilizations, such as those in Egypt, Mesopotamia, Mexico, and Peru, the need for such force was minimized by the great state religions that encouraged the lower classes to accept their positions as part of a divinely established order. An elaborate, esoteric priesthood; awesome pyramids; and complex, dramatic ritual would certainly have intimidated those who might have doubted their place in the divine scheme. In fact, many impoverished peasants may never have considered themselves exploited.

Some researchers have emphasized that the rise of politically centralized, stratified societies was accompanied by the widespread diffusion, or "democratization," of new technologies and "consumer goods" such as metal.

There are also many ways in which potentially despotic political power can be regulated,[41] but it would be misleading to call such societies either egalitarian or democratic. Clearly, a conspicuous element of the politicization process is the disproportionate accumulation of wealth and power at the top. This reality is strong confirmation of the theory that such growth is directed by the elites who most benefit. The politicization process requires increases in social scale[42] and is accompanied by an increased differentiation not only between advantaged and disadvantaged social classes overall but also between urban and rural, and between men and women.[43] The concentration of wealth and power creates difficult problems of legitimation and social order that do not exist in smaller-scale, more egalitarian societies.[44] It is not surprising that chiefdoms and states tend to be short lived. After reviewing the "peaks and valleys" in the growth trajectories of the Mayan, Zapotec, Central Mexican, Andean, Mesopotamian, Egyptian, and Aegean archaic states, archaeologist Joyce Marcus concluded: "As for why the peaks of consolidation inevitably gave way to valleys of dissolution, I suspect it had something to do with the difficulty of maintaining large-scale inegalitarian structures for long periods of time. Large-scale, asymmetrical, and inegalitarian structures were more fragile and unstable than commonly assumed, even though most scholars who work exclusively on states consider such large-scale structures durable."[45]

The recommendation of the National Commission that police forces be strengthened clearly indicates the continuing importance of physical coercion in modern industrial societies such as the United States. The mass media and the institutions of formal education may also be interpreted as forms of thought control that replace the role of state religion in their support of the established order. Anthropologist Marvin Harris[46] suggested that television may be a very important means of minimizing social disorder in highly stratified societies, because it occupies people's minds and provides them with at least vicarious involvement with all levels of the society. A further stabilizing factor, noted earlier, is continuous economic growth, which has helped convince people that they are moving up even though their relative position within the social hierarchy has remained constant.

Cross-Cultural Perspectives on War

A knowledge of how and why primitive peoples made war may shed light on the prospects for war or peace in our own time. (Naroll, "Does Military Deterrence Deter?")[47]

One of the most important perspectives that anthropologists can bring to the study of war and peace is the contrast between tribal and nation-state war. In fact, depending on how it is defined, as we have seen, war may be said to be totally unknown among many of the smallest-scale societies, and even where it does occur in the tribal world there are significant qualitative differences that make tribal war profoundly different from its nation-state counterpart. These points are critical because they bear directly on the central question: Can modern war be prevented? The evidence strongly suggests that war is a variable social and cultural phenomenon, and not genetically determined. War was a prominent feature of large-scale, politically centralized societies in the ancient imperial world, but it may continue only as an anachronism in the contemporary commercial world where trade and wealth accumulation are dominant cultural objectives. Military conquest contributed historically to the economic growth of capitalist nations, but it has now become too destructive to pursue except in very limited ways. War may no longer be inevitable between nations integrated within a decentralized global market economy, although civil war may be a persistent problem when social inequality is significant.

If war is defined broadly as any form of inter-group conflict, then it is a human universal. However, it is striking that the archaeological record contains relatively little unequivocal physical evidence of inter-group violence before about 7,000 years ago. Only a handful of archaeological examples of apparent massacres of a few dozen people at a time have been found in pre-chiefdom societies, but stone projectile points in skeletons and other signs of trauma have often been found, suggesting that interpersonal violence was not uncommon in the early tribal world.[48] From an evolutionary psychology perspective, the determinants of war would be located in the "environment of evolutionary adaptation" (EEA), situated prior to the Neolithic. In theory, natural selection might have predisposed early people to be territorial, to fear outsiders, and to be violent. However, ethnocentrism, xenophobia, and hostility need not go together, and cross-cultural research has shown them not to be correlated with each other.[49] People can believe that their own group is to be preferred above all others without wanting to kill the others. Furthermore, forming alliances with outsiders for marriage and trade, as well as for defense, may be highly adaptive. E. B. Tylor explained the origin of early human exogamy and incest avoidance as the preferred alternative between "marrying-out and being killed out."[50] Some theorists find the roots of human violent behavior in chimpanzee territoriality and inter-band aggression, but bonobos (pygmy chimpanzees) are famously non-violent,[51] and much tribal inter-group conflict seems more concerned with personal revenge than territoriality. Napoleon Chagnon argues that natural selection for human aggression is demonstrated by his finding that some Yanomamo headmen who gained a reputation for aggressiveness had more children than less prominent men.[52] However, this does not explain all Yanomamo inter-group violence, as noted previously.[53]

War is generally considered to be an organized armed conflict between political units in pursuit of a group goal, but in the tribal world individual bands and villages are the largest autonomous political units. When inter-group conflict occurs between tribal villages and bands it may be called "internal war" because it is within the same tribal society,[54] but feuding and raiding is then a more descriptive term than "war," because such actions are so small in scale. In the absence of strong rulers in tribal societies it is difficult for temporary war leaders to organize large, cohesive war parties.

Anthropologist Bronislaw Malinowski was stressing organizational differences when he declared: "[We] do not find . . . any organized clash of armed forces aiming at the enforcement of tribal policy. War does not exist among them."[55] Malinowski was writing during World War II, when French, German, and Soviet rulers commanded armies of 6, 12, and 20 million troops, respectively. An Asháninka big man might motivate 5 to 10 warriors to join him on a raid, but a war party of 200 was a rare event, suggesting that Asháninka war was very different from war fought between nations.

Quincy Wright, unquestionably one of the world's leading authorities on war, used the term in its widest meaning to include violent inter-group conflict or armed aggression in any form, but in his monumental work *A Study of War* he strongly emphasized the qualitative differences between tribal and civilized war. "War in the sense of a legal situation equally permitting groups to expand wealth and power by violence began with civilization . . . . Only among civilized people has war been an institution serving political and economic interests of the community, defined by a body of law which states the circumstances justifying its use, the procedures whereby it is begun and ended, and the methods by which it is conducted."[56]

Certainly, the major conclusion of any evolutionary study of inter-group conflict is that its form is strongly related to the political organization of a given society. As an empirical generalization it can be stated that as a society's political system becomes more centralized its military organization becomes more complex, its weapons and tactics become more effective, and individual engagements become more costly in terms of casualties.[57]

Predictable shifts in the immediate goals for fighting and in the supporting ideology also occur. The rulers of states make war, and war helped create states. In the dynamics of chiefdoms and ancient states warfare often took the form of competition between rival political elites, backed by their supporters or political factions. This violent competition could be both internally directed in civil wars and externally directed in wars of conquest. Thus, a few powerful elite families, individuals, and their descendants were at the center of this competition. Such a chronic "syndrome of competition" is exemplified by patterns of warfare among the Polynesians and the ancient Maya.[58]

The immediate objectives that commonly motivated the leaders of political communities to fight with their neighbors can be grouped into four major categories, following the work of several researchers.[59] These categories are defense, plunder, prestige, and political control. Presumably they reflect considerations that both military decision makers and the combatants have in mind when they go to war. Anthropologists also recognize many other "functions" of war; they do not pretend that these four categories include all the psychological factors that may motivate particular individuals to fight. What is significant about these categories is that they do not occur in different cultures in a random, unpredictable manner; rather, they tend to be distributed in an orderly arrangement that reveals a great deal about the nature of war and its relationship to political organization. There are societies in which no organized fighting occurs for any of these reasons, and such societies may justifiably be described as peaceful.

In general, the motives for war tend to be cumulative so that, for example, a society that goes to war in order to extend political control over a neighbor will probably also fight for defense, plunder, and prestige. However, if people fight for plunder, they may not fight for political control, and those cultures that do not fight for defense do not fight at all. Those cultures showing the most motives for war are politically centralized, usually nation-states.[60]

The nature of the relationship between war and human nature has been debated for many years. Quincy Wright, who directed the University of Chicago's Social Science Research Committee project on the causes of war from 1926 to 1941, took a position that reflected the anthropological opinion of the time: "[It] is meaningless to say that war is inevitable because of the pugnacity of man as an animal. While man has original drives that make war possible, that possibility has only been realized in appropriate social and political conditions."[61]

Prominent anthropologists such as Bronislaw Malinowski[62] and Margaret Mead,[63] who joined the debate during World War II, took much the same position, and this view remains the general consensus among anthropologists today. Humans may indeed possess an innate capacity for aggression, but this capacity must be culturally shaped, however anthropologists may still disagree over how innately peaceful or warlike people are by nature.[64]

The Scale of War and Violence in the Imperial and Commercial Worlds

The rulers of ancient civilizations had power over the lives of so many people that state-sponsored war and violence occurred on a scale that is difficult to comprehend. For example, in AD 1600 two rulers, Akbar the Great of Mughal India and Wan Li, emperor of Ming China, commanded between them some 295 million people, more than half of the world's 556 million people at the time. Chinese and Mongol rulers killed some 64 million people over the two millennia between 221 BC and AD 1900. This is equivalent to 75 percent of the population of the estimated 85 million people in the Neolithic world. Before the Spanish Conquest, the Aztecs were routinely killing tens of thousands annually in ritual sacrifices, perhaps as many as 250,000 in one year. They probably killed millions in wars and rituals during their 273-year reign, in what would now be called state terror. The Spanish of course killed millions more in their conquest of the Aztec, Maya, and Inca empires, and in their subjugation of most tribes and chiefdoms throughout Mesoamerica and South America.

The elite-directed rise of commercially driven nations and empires since AD 1500, along with the corresponding construction of the global economic system by 1815, provided important new incentives for warfare and dramatically increased military sophistication and total casualties. Competition between major powers became periodic struggles for hegemonic power that were often focused on control over territories, colonies, markets, resources, and trade routes for the primary benefit of ruling elites. Some 50 million tribal peoples may have died in the European conquest of the tribal world between 1800 and 1950.[65] This is the equivalent of nearly 60 percent of the Neolithic population destroyed in a mere 150 years. Industrial technology made it possible for governments to kill more than 200 million people worldwide in the twentieth century, including some 25 million combatants and 62 million civilians killed in World War II in just over five years.

The Fiscal-Military State and Military-Industrial Complexes

[T]he armament industry has only one point of view, and that is the commercial . . . it knows no politics, it knows no friends, it knows neither right nor wrong in international relations. (Engelbrecht 1934: 121)[66]

The rise of the commercial world was accompanied by an increase in the scale and scope of armed conflict, in which war became much more destructive and more costly to finance. The very rapid development and proliferation of devastating cannons, warships, and muskets was promoted by an alignment between the English landed elite and the London financial elite who took control of the English state in the Revolution of 1688, created Great Britain in 1707, and turned it into a fiscal-military state.[67] This partnership of public taxation and private wealth produced a culturally unique commercial empire supported by a publicly financed military that became a model that still shapes the contemporary world. The new Parliament of Great Britain issued bonds which were purchased by the wealthy, and the political elite then used the borrowed funds to finance new military hardware produced by the new privately owned factories. The wealthy received profits from armament sales as well as interest payments on the government bonds that they purchased. Often the same people operated as private capitalists and public officials, making decisions that benefited them in both respects.

War became a driving force of social and cultural change that most benefited the great financiers, the armaments manufacturers, and military contractors, but caused hardship, periodic unemployment, higher taxes, and poverty for ordinary people, as well as material shortages and breakdowns in trade networks. This was surely not the only way that the commercial world could have been organized and directed.

America's World War II military mobilization created a permanent "national security state" that enhanced the social power of military, political, and economic elites, and gave military leaders a major role in economic planning.[68] These rulers developed their own "Defense Industrial Base" rather than converting civilian industries to military use only in time of crisis. Individual military officers, politicians, and corporate officials constantly changed their roles by moving through the "Revolving Door" influence network connecting government and business. This is the contemporary "Military-Industrial Complex" that President Eisenhower warned of in his 1961 farewell address:

> [W]e have been compelled to create a permanent armaments industry of vast proportions. . . . This conjunction of an immense military establishment and a large arms industry is new in the American experience. The total influence—economic, political, even spiritual—is felt in every city, every State house, every office of the Federal government. . . . we must not fail to comprehend its grave implications. Our toil, resources and livelihood are all involved; so is the very structure of our society. In the councils of government, we must guard against the acquisition of unwarranted influence, whether sought or unsought, by the militaryindustrial [sic] complex. The potential for the disastrous rise of misplaced power exists and will persist.[69]

Eisenhower's warning seems fully justified and especially relevant in the twenty-first century. After the Cold War ended in 1991 global defense spending initially dropped by one-third, but defense industries quickly consolidated, and regional conflicts and international terrorism soon emerged as the primary national security threats. The American military shifted to higher-tech, more efficient, but even more expensive, weaponry and logistics to quickly move smaller, more effective forces to trouble spots.[70] The hoped for "Peace Dividend" quickly melted away, because defense is still very good business. For example, the price of American weapon systems escalated 10 percent a year between 1950 and 2000.[71] A nuclear aircraft carrier cost $6 billion to build in 2005 and some $500 million per year to maintain and operate. There were ten such ships in the U.S. Navy, with a total purchase price exceeding the GDP of Bangladesh. With more than 368,000 soldiers deployed in 120 countries[72] in 2006 America militarily resembled imperial Rome and the British Empire.

In 2005 total military expenditures for all countries in the world (including defense agencies, armed forces, maintenance and operations, armaments development and procurement, and military aid) exceeded $1 trillion U.S. dollars.[73] American expenditures of $478 billion accounted for nearly 50 percent, which was more than the next fourteen highest-spending countries combined. More than 80 percent of the trillion global defense dollars flowed as revenues to the one hundred largest defense industries, which were predominately American headquartered. The arms business was truly global, but U.S. armaments manufacturers accounted for 63 percent of the world's arms trade in 2004, excluding China.

In 2005 the seven largest American defense corporations General Dynamics, Lockheed Martin, Boeing, Raytheon, Halliburton, Northrop Grumman, and United Technologies supplied much of the country's heavy armaments and logistical support, and received an astounding $230 billion in revenues. The effective owners of these companies were four giant financial corporations headquartered in the United States, Britain, and France, three of which managed total investment funds of more than $1 trillion each.[74] This means that America is a global-scale fiscal-military state dominated by a military-industrial complex.

Deadly Arsenals:
The Nuclear Weapons Threat

Especially deadly weapons such as nuclear, biological, and toxic chemical were stockpiled in large numbers by nations on both sides of the Cold War, primarily by the United States and the former Soviet Union. These weapons have collectively been called "WMD—weapons of mass destruction," but this term is misleading, because these weapons vary greatly in their potential to cause mass casualties and destruction. Chemical and biological weapons are relatively cheap and easy to produce, but they are difficult to use as weapons, and their effects are difficult to predict. Nuclear weapons are difficult and expensive to produce, but they can be unthinkably destructive, and surely constitute the greatest threat to humanity as "WMD." Since the end of the Cold War, the absolute number of nuclear weapons has declined considerably, but the proliferation of nuclear weapons materials to countries or non-government terrorist networks operating outside of the existing international treaties and regulatory regimes is a continuing global threat.[75]

As of 2005 only eight nations had acquired nuclear weapons. Five of these countries—China, France, Russia, the United Kingdom, and the United States—had signed the 1968 Treaty on the Non-Proliferation of Nuclear Weapons, but three nations were still not part of these international controls: India, Israel, and Pakistan. The proliferation of nuclear weapons was accelerated between 1989 and 2000 by the actions of one man, A. Q. Khan, former head of Pakistan's nuclear program, who by operating through a secret international network sold nuclear weapons technology to Iran, Libya, and North Korea.[76] Ninety-five percent of the world's known arsenals of 27,650 nuclear weapons are in Russian and U.S. hands, with 16,000 and 10,300 weapons respectively.[77] None of the six other nuclear powers have more than a few hundred nuclear weapons at most, but of course it only takes a few. The good news is that fewer nations had nuclear weapons in 2005 than previously, because under intense international pressure several countries have abandoned their nuclear programs, including Argentina, Brazil, South Africa, Iraq, Libya, Algeria, and the former Soviet states of Ukraine, Belarus, and Kazakhstan. Diplomatic efforts and international pressure from non-governmental organizations have had very positive effects. Africa is a totally nuclear-weapon-free continent. As of 2005 only five countries had intercontinental ballistic missiles with ranges of 5,500 kilometers or more: China, France, Russia, the United Kingdom, and the United States, but six countries (India, Iran, Israel, North Korea, Pakistan, and Saudi Arabia) had medium-range missiles capable of reaching 1,000 to 3,000 kilometers, and nineteen other countries have short-range missiles with ranges under 1,000 kilometers.

Nuclear weapons held by national governments and their leaders can be brought under international controls, but the possibility that terrorists might acquire and use nuclear weapons, or radiological weapons (radioactive materials, dispersed by conventional weapons), is a very serious international security threat. Terrorists operate through illicit organizations and networks and are difficult to deter, because they are outside of national or international laws, have no national territories, and therefore cannot be threatened with retaliation. Stable national governments that effectively meet the needs of their citizens and cooperate internationally are crucial to deter terrorists and reduce their appeal for potential recruits. This is why the viability of states as organizations is so important.

Failing States and Social Disorder

The modern nation-state as a legitimate government and organized political economy, legally controlling its sovereign territory, and composed of citizens who presumably share a common language and culture or ethnic identity is a cultural form that evolved along with capitalism and the commercial world. However, as national and international corporate business has become a dominant form of social power, the nation-state has widely fallen into disarray. Modern colonial empires, and some very large states, such as the Soviet Union, have largely been replaced by new nation-states, but the authority of governments is being undermined by the vast inequities of social power in much of the world, which are being amplified by market globalization.[78] The very recent problem that these developments have created is spelled out in the following statement by the president of the Fund for Peace:

> Violence is erupting predominantly within societies in which the state—the central locus of authority and power—is disintegrating. These states may be losing political legitimacy in the eyes of their people because of repression, rigged elections, corruption, political exclusion, economic decline or a coup d'état. They may be losing their monopoly on the use of force, confronting private militias, warlords, drug cartels, organized crime, secessionists or armed rebellions. Failing states cannot sustain essential public services, promote equitable economic growth or provide for the public welfare. They do not maintain domestic tranquility or provide for the common defense. They are dysfunctional polities—in large part because they are institutionally incompetent." (Pauline H. Baker, president, The Fund for Peace)[79]

Between 1946 and 2005 there have been no military conflicts between the major powers, and the annual number of armed conflicts and combat deaths has declined significantly (figure 7.2). There were 231 armed conflicts over that period, defined as contested disputes over government or territory in which at least twenty-five people died and a government was a contending party. It is striking that the number of civil wars increased dramatically, peaking in the early 1990s, and then declining.[80] Many of these civil wars were concentrated in post-colonial sub-Saharan Africa where local elites were contending for control. Between 1988 and 2001 there was a sharp decline in genocides, international crises, and all armed conflicts, as well as in conflict-related deaths. Some 10 million people died in all conflicts since World War II, but the trend has been for battle deaths to decline, especially since the last peak in 1982.[81] Troop levels and military expenditures also declined during this period. However, since September 11, 2001, there has been a significant increase in high-casualty terrorist attacks.

Researchers associated with the Fund for Peace (FfP) developed a method of measuring the relative stability of different national governments, recognizing that violence and conflict tend to increase when governments fail to maintain internal order. Their methodology, the Conflict Assessment System Tool (CAST), adds ratings on a 10-point scale for each of 12 indicators of the economic, social, and political effectiveness of each country (table 7.1) to produce a range of possible scores from zero to 120, rating sustainability, or vulnerability to conflict and collapse of particular

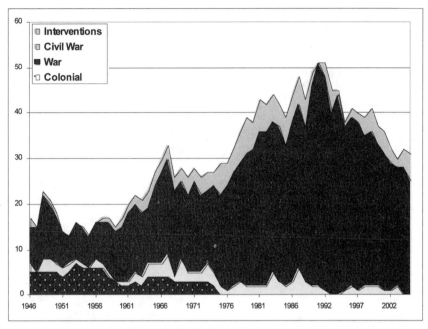

Figure 7.2.   Wars and Civil Wars in the World, 1946–2005.
Source: International Peace Research Institute, Oslo (PRIO), Centre for the Study of Civil War (CSCW). Main Conflict Table. http://new.prio.no/CSCW-Datasets/Data-on-Armed-Conflict/ UppsalaPRIO-Armed-Conflicts-Dataset/UppsalaPRIO-Armed-Conflict-Dataset/.

governments. Their rankings were based on analysis of a vast number of news articles and reports, taking into account the competence of police and corrections, the efficiency of the civil service, the independence of the judicial system, the professionalism and discipline of the military, and the capability of the executive and legislators of each country. The higher the total score, the weaker the state. The 2006 "Failed State Index" ranks 146 states, sorting them into four groups by degree of vulnerability (table 7.2). Norway was the most sustainable with a low score of 17, whereas Iraq was the most vulnerable with a high of 107. The United States ranked 35, placing it in the "Needs Monitoring" category, because of refugee problems, social inequality, demographic problems, and human–rights violations.

The Failed State Index lists only thirteen countries with a total of 255 million people as sustainable states. This is only 4 percent of the world's population living in relative security. More than a billion people in twenty-eight countries are on "Alert" for state failure. These rankings do not mean that all vulnerable states will collapse into civil war. In recent decades sev-

Table 7.1.   Failed State Indicators.

SOCIAL INDICATORS
 1. Mounting Demographic Pressures
 2. Massive Movement of Refugees or Internally Displaced Persons
 3. Legacy of Vengeance-Seeking Group Grievance or Group Paranoia
 4. Chronic and Sustained Human Flight

ECONOMIC INDICATORS
 1. Uneven Economic Development Along Group Lines
 2. Sharp and/or Severe Economic Decline

POLITICAL INDICATORS
 1. Criminalization and/or Deligitimization of the State
 2. Progressive Deterioration of Public Services
 3. Suspension or Arbitrary Application of the Rule of Law and Widespread Violation of Human Rights
 4. Security Apparatus Operates as a "State Within a State"
 5. Rise of Factionalized Elites
 6. Intervention of Other States or External Political Actors

eral states that were considered highly vulnerable have stabilized, including India, Indonesia, and South Africa. Humane leaders and skilled diplomats can choose and have chosen negotiations and power sharing rather than violence and conflict when difficulties arose. The international community, including non-governmental organizations, can help vulnerable states resolve conflicts peacefully through governmental reforms and in some cases by partitioning hopelessly divided states.

Roots of the Security Crisis: Culture, Overpopulation, or Inequality?

With the end of the Cold War strategic planners in wealthy nations began to view social disorder in the impoverished world as the primary threat to global security. They began searching for the basic causes of conflict in much the same way as the National Commission on Violence, discussed

Table 7.2.   Failed State Rankings, 2006.

Status	Score	Nations	People	% Nations	% People
Alert	91–120	28	1,005,864,000	19	16
Warning	61–90	78	4,272,569,000	52	66
Monitoring	31–60	27	909,219,000	18	14
Sustainable	0–30	13	255,184,000	9	4
Totals	120	146	6,442,836,000	98	100

Source: www.fundforpeace.org/programs/fsi/fsindex2006.php

earlier, looked for the causes of domestic disorder within the United States. However, in the case of the global security crisis there has been a clear tendency for analysts to identify overpopulation and resource scarcity as the root problem,[82] rather than inequalities within the structure of the global culture itself. Many observers were quick to attribute contemporary conflicts to "pent-up ethnic hatreds," as Brian Beedham, associate editor for the *Economist*, stated in a survey of the prospects for future wars. He declared, "The world has too many countries where different peoples who do not like each other live within the borders of the same state."[83] This trivializes ethnicity and makes cultural difference a threat rather than a helpful basis for organizing people to confront human problems. Anthropological researchers have shown that many cases of supposed ethnic conflict can be interpreted very differently. For example, even in former Yugoslavia, a much-publicized symbol of ethnic conflict, the real cause of conflict between Serbs and Croats is national-level "competition for power and control of economic wealth" waged between elites who have used ethnic identities to further their own political agendas.[84]

Prominent political scientist Samuel P. Huntington elevated cultural difference as a source of conflict to the level of civilizations, arguing that rather than international conflict between states, there is a "clash of civilizations" in which the antagonists are the great civilizations such as Western (North America and Western Europe), Latin American, African, Islamic, Sinic, Hindu, Orthodox, Buddhist, and Japanese civilizations. This simple model in effect sets the West apart as the driving force of the commercial world, in opposition to the old imperial world, and predicts that conflicts will occur across cultural "fault lines."[85] This focus on civilizations does not deal with the overall well-being of humanity and appears not to be supported by the empirical data on conflicts since 1946.[86]

Prominent Canadian political scientist Thomas Fraser Homer-Dixon initially emphasized population pressure itself as the primary cause of disorder and conflict. He theorized that overpopulated poor countries would be especially vulnerable to environmental pressures that would lower agricultural productivity and cause economic decline, population dislocation, and social disorder. These Malthusian problems would in turn lead to international conflicts, ethnic conflicts, and civil wars that would become security problems for the wealthy nations of the world. However, he later included income gaps between rich and poor countries as important sources of conflict.[87] Global economic structures are certainly part of the dynamic that produces and maintains poverty.

The Financialization Process and the Debt Crisis

> If the goals of official debt managers were to squeeze the debtors dry, to transfer enormous resources from South to North and to wage undeclared war on the poor continents and their people, then their policies have been an unqualified success. If, however, their strategies were intended—as these institutions always claim—to promote development beneficial to all members of society, to preserve the planet's unique environment and gradually to reduce the debt burden itself, then their failure is easily demonstrated. (George 1992, xiii–xiv)[88]

Since the end of the eighteenth century the commercialization process of capital accumulation directed by business enterprise has led to rapid industrialization and generated economic growth for favored groups in the wealthy "core" of European and North American states. A new hierarchy of states emerged in which formerly independent political-scale cultures on the "periphery" were locked by colonialism into unequal economic exchanges with the industrial core.[89] Finance, or money and banking, was the cultural foundation of the commercialization process from its beginning, but when the 1944 Breton Woods Conference established a global monetary system based on the American dollar, financialization itself began to emerge as the dominant cultural process worldwide.[90] Initially, capitalists borrowed to build industrial factories, but increasingly finance has become an autonomous "paper" or electronic economy, only remotely connected to the "real economy" of factories, goods, and human services. On the eve of the American Revolution, tangible assets outnumbered financial assets by almost two to one, but by 2000 America's financial assets outnumbered tangible assets three to one.[91] Even in the early 1990s only 10 percent of the trillions of dollars that daily flow through the world's computerized foreign exchange markets involve actual goods and services.[92] The disconnect between monetary values and the physical world allows petroleum to flow to consuming nations in an unequal social exchange that fuels machines, but dissipates energy as it produces poverty and environmental degradation.[93]

Speculators in what has become a "casino economy" can profit handsomely from tiny shifts in interest rates or spreads in prices between markets because of the staggering scale of the monetary sums involved in the global financial markets. Surprisingly, few individuals participate directly in the financialization process. In 1998 only 19 percent of American families held any stocks, and only 16.5 percent held any mutual funds.[94]

The new global financial order works to benefit the world's High Net Worth Individuals (HNWIs), the 8.7 million people who held $33.3 trillion in financial assets in 2005, giving them an average of $3.8 million to invest.[95] HNWIs are not just millionaires. One needed more than $1 million in investable financial assets to qualify. Financialization is a much more efficient way of transferring wealth from rich to poor than the old colonial systems because the wealthy can let the national governments of poor countries deal with the social control problems that inequality inevitably generates. Money that was temporarily shifted as investments or loans from rich "North" countries in Western Europe and North America to poor countries in the "South" in Latin America, Africa, and Asia to finance their economic development created a gigantic debt and yielded a rich return for investors in the financial community. During the nine years from 1982 through the end of 1990 poor debtor countries in the South transferred $706 billion in interest payments to rich creditor countries in the North and amassed a total payback of a staggering $1.3 trillion—equivalent to more than $1,000 for each of the 600 million people then living in Europe and North America.[96] To put these figures in perspective, all of the financial resources transferred from rich to poor countries from 1982 to 1990 totaled just $927 billion, including all forms of economic assistance, charity, private investment capital, and bank loans. Subtracting the $927 billion in support from the $1.3 trillion in payback yields a balance of $418 billion actually returned to the rich creditor countries. This return is roughly six times the amount (in 1991 dollars) that the United States spent rebuilding Europe after World War II under the Marshall Plan. Susan George, board member of the Amsterdam-based Transnational Institute, called the international debt system an "unprecedented financial assistance to the rich from the poor" and pointed out that the beneficiaries were the elites of the poor countries and wealthy investors in the rich countries.[97]

After nearly a decade of work on the debt issue, researchers at the Transnational Institute concluded that Third World debt was a "central factor in the overall crisis of the third world" and a "major contributing factor" to much of the ecological devastation, especially deforestation, that accelerated worldwide since the late 1960s and 1970s.[98] George pointed out that huge lending programs for massive capital projects, such as dams, highways, power plants, manufacturing facilities, and vast agricultural enterprises, were themselves often highly destructive and unsustainable forms of development that served the immediate interests of national elites. Much of the money actually returned quickly to the banks in core countries either as payments to multinational development corporations or as the personal wealth of corrupt national elites. Furthermore, these development projects displaced and impoverished the small landowners and squatters, many of whom became the "shifted farmers" referred to in chapter 2, who are still being forced to cultivate fragile marginal environments. By the 1980s servicing the debt proved to be an insurmountable problem for many poor countries. The "structural adjustments," or austerity programs, imposed by international financial agencies such as the World Bank and the International Monetary Fund (IMF)—which involved currency devaluations, reduced social welfare programs, and increased resource extraction for export—caused enormous human suffering and dramatically intensified the deterioration of ecosystems. This austerity approach to debt reduction has been called the "Washington Consensus," and it includes the principal features of economic globalization, or neoliberal economic ideology: freedom for investment and international capital flows, and "free trade" in goods, services, and intellectual property.[99] This kind of unrestricted trade favors the wealthy and has been widely criticized for failing to reduce global poverty. One of the most prominent critics of economic globalization has been Joseph Stiglitz, Nobel Prize–winning economist and chief economist at the World Bank from 1997 to 2000,[100] who has more recently advocated "Fair Trade" as an alternative to the Washington Consensus.[101]

In order to meet the structural adjustment goals imposed by the official debt managers, countries must export more than they import to produce a positive balance of payments as a condition for short-term loans to help debtors meet their payments. This approach, called "export-led" economic growth, requires debtor nations to extract as much as possible from their labor force and their natural resources and provides no incentive for sustainable resource management or social equity.

It is probably no accident that Brazil, the country with the largest international debt, was also the top-ranked deforester. In general, countries that were heavy deforesters were also transferring one- to two-thirds of their returns from exports to the wealthy in the form of debt service (payments of interest and principal). Thus, neither the resources themselves nor the income from them benefited the majority of the population. Ironically, many of the giant corporate developments that deforested the Brazilian Amazon actually proved uneconomical, yet they served as profitable tax write-offs for wealthy investors, much like many agribusiness developments in the United States.

The international debt crisis began in 1982 when Mexico, the second-largest debtor nation after Brazil, declared that it was about to default on its debt payments. The International Monetary Fund's structural-adjustment, export-led plan that followed was a prime incentive for the development of the *maquiladora* zone along the border with the United States. Hundreds of foreign manufacturing companies were attracted to the border zone by the promise of a very cheap labor force and lax environmental and worker safety laws. The "winners" in this situation were (1) the Mexican financial elite, (2) the companies that gained a competitive edge in the global "free market," (3) the American banks that received most of the interest payments from the Mexican debt, and (4) the investors who received a hefty return from their holdings in *maquiladora* companies and creditor banks. The "losers" were: (1) the Mexican workers who accepted wages as low as $26 per week and who could not escape their badly polluted environment, (2) the 11.5 million American workers whose jobs disappeared between 1979 and 1984 alone, and (3) those American communities negatively impacted by the influx of desperately poor Mexican immigrants.

Speaking for the Transnational Institute, Susan George was emphatic about assigning responsibility for both the debt crisis and the social and environmental problems that have followed:

> [W]e believe that it is above all the actions of the Northern [Europe and North America] creditor governments, and those of the international institutions [World Bank and IMF] they largely control, which drive the forces behind this destruction. They invented the initial "development" model which has led to ecological disaster. They have used the leverage provided by the debt crisis to perpetuate this model. We have indeed met the enemy and he is not so much "us" as the people and the institutions we have allowed to speak for us. Only informed and active citizens can call them to account.[102]

Export Sugar, Starvation, and Infant Mortality in Brazil

Anthropological research reveals the human side of the global economy's harsh realities as experienced by the world's impoverished majority. Anthropologist Nancy Scheper-Hughes was a Peace Corps health worker near Recife in northeastern Brazil from 1964 through 1966. She returned there between 1982 and 1989 to conduct research on the effects of chronic hunger and infant death on maternal love. Her account of the lives of the residents of a squatter slum in a town she called Bom Jesus is a moving portrayal of how the poor coped with the enormous suffering that accompanied Brazil's economic "miracle."[103]

The economy in this corner of Brazil is based on monocrop sugar production for export and is dominated by the landed aristocracy who own the giant sugar mills and the vast *latifundia* estates. The fifty largest estates range in size from 5,000 to 50,000 acres, dwarfing the largest California agribusinesses described in chapter 5. Since the 1950s, continuous expansion by the large estates at the expense of small holdings and the conversion of all land into sugar production have made it virtually impossible for the underclass, who constitute roughly 80 percent of the population, to raise subsistence crops or even gather firewood. They must purchase all their basic needs. Food prices are high because even beans are imported from the south.

In 1989 those men lucky enough to find seasonal work on the sugar plantations could earn the legal minimum of $10 a week cutting cane, while women were earning $5 a week. Comparing these weekly wages and the $26 Mexican *maquiladora* wages to the $170 legal minimum in the United States at that time makes it clear why American labor is no longer "competitive" in the global economy. The critical factor in Bom Jesus is that the minimum food needs for a household with four children cost $40 a week. Thus, even if both husband and wife had permanent minimum-wage work, they could not provide basic subsistence for their family. In contrast, the severely depressed wage scale made it possible for a Bom Jesus middle-class professional earning just $175 a week to spend $62.50 weekly to feed his household of three family members and five domestic servants.

The sugar barons at the top of the social hierarchy married within their own class in order to protect their wealth. They employed armed security guards twenty-four hours a day and maintained residences on their plantations, in the town of Bom Jesus, and in the city of Recife. Their children might be sent to Europe for school, and they went to the United States for medical attention. A shantytown resident accurately described the elite as follows:

> The rich are the owners of the city. They are the people who don't have to work for a living, who are "excused" from the daily struggle that is life. For the rich, living in their mansions and big houses, nothing is ever wanting. Every wish is satisfied. They are our bosses, our *patroes*. They don't owe anything to anybody. Everybody owes them.[104]

From the viewpoint of the wealthy, there is no real hunger in Brazil. Malnutrition exists because people have poor dietary habits and need to be educated. People are poor because they are unwilling to improve themselves and don't like hard work.

Anthropologist James Scott[105] points out that the weak have many "weapons" for dealing with their exploiters, but they are unlikely to succeed in direct confrontations with the institutions of oppression. The poor of Bom Jesus survived by putting everyone in the family to work, by maintaining a collectivist and egalitarian ethic with kin and within the poor community, and by cultivating their own dependency relations with the wealthy. Even with all these efforts, physical starvation was a chronic problem. Nutritional surveys in the 1980s showed that cane workers averaged only 1,500 calories per day, less than the 1,750 calories the Nazis allowed the residents of the Buchenwald concentration camp during World War II and just 40 percent of the daily U.S. average of 3,700 calories. With some justification the Brazilian northeast could be considered a concentration camp for 30 million people, as some have charged. Two-thirds of rural children showed clinical evidence of under-nutrition, and one-fourth were nutritionally dwarfed.[106] Chronic under-nutrition contributes to overall poor health, low energy, low self-esteem, and high rates of miscarriage and underweight babies. Most important, official figures in 1993 showed that 116 out of 1,000 live births resulted in death within the first year in the Brazilian northeast—double the 1993 national average for Brazil and twelve times the average for the United States—because of starvation.

Not satisfied with the aggregated regional and national infant mortality rates, which she felt were deceptively low, Scheper-Hughes obtained the handwritten birth and death records from the registry books in Bom Jesus, which would more accurately reflect local realities. She also collected full reproductive histories from 100 women. These data revealed that in 1965, shortly after the military took power in Brazil, infants were dying in Bom Jesus at a staggering 493 per 1,000, nearly 50 percent, in their first year of life. By 1987 infant mortality stood at 211 per 1,000, well above any national-level rates in the world. On the average, an older woman had seen 4.7 of her children die.

The women Scheper-Hughes questioned about the general causes of infant mortality correctly blamed social conditions, environmental factors, and poor medical care. As one woman said, "Our children die because we are poor and hungry."[107] However, the poor were also culturally conditioned to attribute the deaths of their own children to "weakness," just as they blamed their own poor health on "nerves." Thus, what was actually a problem generated by the political economy was viewed as a medical problem to be treated with tranquilizers and vitamins from the pharmacy rather than through social change. The medical profession in Bom Jesus supported this "medicalization" of starvation, helping to obscure its roots in the class structure and the global economy. This system was a form of cultural hegemony in which the underclass came to rationalize their own exploitation. Scheper-Hughes was emphatic about the real causes of sickness and death in Bom Jesus:

> I do not want to quibble over words, but what I have been seeing on the Alto de Cruzeiro [the slum in Bom Jesus] for two and a half decades is more than "malnutrition," and it is politically as well as economically caused, although in the absence of overt political strife or war. Adults, it is true, might be described as "chronically undernourished," in a weakened and debilitated state, prone to infections and opportunistic diseases. But it is overt hunger and starvation that one sees in babies and small children, the victims of a "famine" that is endemic, relentless, and political-economic in origin.[108]

The connection between Brazil's high infant mortality rate, as seen in Bom Jesus, and Brazil's position in the global economy is probably not a coincidence. Scheper-Hughes pointed out that Brazil's enormous borrowing to finance its economic "miracle" caused interest on the debt to soar by 1985 to nearly one-third of the government's total expenditures, forcing it to cut expenditures for public health. At the same time wages dropped by one-third, and food costs soared. It is instructive to note that in 1986 Cuba—another Latin American sugar economy but one that had remained isolated from development loans and the global market—showed an infant mortality rate of 13.6 per 1,000 and a life expectancy at birth of seventy-six years, virtually equaling the U.S. figures. Medical anthropologist Paul Farmer[109] describes similar conditions in Haiti as a "pathology of power" and "structural violence," which is a fitting term given their connection with "structural adjustments."

State Terrorism and Investment Risk in Guatemala

> Counterinsurgency violence escalated in geometric proportions. It began with abductions. . . . The escalation of repression gave way to selective massacres . . . repression reached its peak when the massacres were no longer selective but indiscriminate . . . no discrimination was made between civilians and combatants, or between collaborators, sympathizers, and people indifferent or opposed to the insurgency. Distinctions were not made between men and women . . . between young and old, between children and adults. The entire population was seen as "a rotten orange," in the

words of the San Luis officer, and everyone, absolutely everyone, should
be thrown onto the demolishing fire . . . thus the massacres were genoci-
dal. (Falla, *Massacres in the Jungle*, 184)[110]

In a global market economy, prudent investors seeking the highest returns and the lowest risks from their financial capital must consider social
and political conditions wherever they invest. National and international
business interests will likely fear adverse effects whenever oppressed people
demand respect for their basic human rights and press for land reform, social security, higher wages, and improved working conditions. The annual
editions of the *Political Risk Yearbook*[111] rate virtually every country in the
world on its eighteen-month and five-year potential for political turmoil
and give letter grades from A+ to D- for specific risks to international finance, direct investment, and exports, much like Standard & Poor's AAA
to D bond rating system. With the liberalization of global markets in full
swing, the 1994 yearbook gave only a handful of mostly African countries
D grades for "hostility to foreign business" and "serious security concerns"
or for making "foreign business a handy scapegoat in politics." This rating
system clearly placed foreign business interests ahead of the well-being of
local people. Even modest increases in wages that would benefit workers or
the imposition of higher corporate taxes to fund public health and education resulted in a lower rating for security of investment, because such "socialist" policies could threaten international corporate profits and shake
"investor confidence." In a tightly integrated world economy the possibility of adverse changes in the business climate of any country could cause
declines in foreign exchange rates and in the value of government and corporate securities. As international finance capital moves more freely, social
"unrest" in any corner of the world might be felt as a ripple in financial
markets everywhere as worried investors shuffle their assets to safer havens.
The global market produces strong incentives for governments to suppress
disruptive public opinion even as increasing economic inequality makes
public dissatisfaction more likely.

In countries that lack genuine democracy, brutal regimes backed by
well-armed military forces have frequently used internal violence and terror to block social reform and thereby safeguard the interests of the global
financial elite. Linguist Noam Chomsky has persuasively argued that governments have often used labels such as "national security" and "coun-
terinsurgency" to mask human rights violations by military forces against
dissident domestic political groups.[112] Since the end of World War II, the
United States has selectively provided decisive military assistance and de-

velopment aid to many antidemocratic regimes, such as Brazil, under military rule that maintained "favorable attitudes" toward international business. The American government used Cold War fears of Soviet or Cuban communist subversion to justify its support of pro-American Latin American dictatorships.

In a more humane world, truly democratic processes, not political terror, would arbitrate the legitimate interests of competing social groups. Because America is a democracy, its foreign policy can be shaped by public opinion, but it is often difficult for the public to get accurate information on issues involving powerful special interests. The situation in Guatemala is a case in which anthropologists have helped publicly document the community and personal impact of human rights violations committed by a U.S.-supported government in the name of national security. Anthropologists, with their knowledge of the indigenous languages and cultures and their personal contacts stretching over many years, were in a position to see firsthand the realities that official information sources denied.

Guatemala is the largest Central American country. In 1992 over half of its 10 million people were Mayan Indians, speaking twenty different languages and living in rural communities based on subsistence agriculture, migratory wage labor, and production for local markets. During the civil war of the 1970s and 1980s, when leftist guerrilla forces of the Guatemalan Army of the Poor (EGP) and the Organization of the People in Arms (ORPA) began to gain popular support, the Guatemalan army responded by indiscriminately killing tens of thousands of Indians in a scorched-earth campaign of terror. An estimated 440 villages were destroyed. In some cases their residents were systematically murdered; in others they were relocated to strategic hamlets.[113] People were tortured, mutilated, and killed in the most gruesome ways, recalling the holocaust of the original conquest. In 1992, 200,000 Guatemalan refugees were living in Mexico, while many others fled to the United States.

America's interest in Guatemala is easily documented. Guatemala's total external debt in 1992 was $2.7 billion, and roughly one-third of its foreign trade was with the United States. Coffee is its primary export crop. Between 1966 and 1975 the United States provided $16.7 million in military assistance and shipped $23 million worth of military equipment to Guatemala. Also, from 1966 to 1985 the United States gave Guatemala $430 million in grants and credits. The country received an additional $370 million in economic assistance from 1988 to 1991. In 1980 Americans had direct investments of $229 million in Guatemala, but due to continued political "instability" that figure had dropped to $105 million by 1991.[114] In the 1994 *Political Risk Yearbook* Guatemala was predicted to have high short-term risk for "turmoil," defined as "economic disruption due to war, insurrection, demonstrations, or terrorism." Consequently it received a B for direct investment potential and exports because of the risk of "possibly dangerous turmoil or moderate restrictions on business activity" and restrictions on trade and payments. Fortunately for the international finance community, the five-year outlook for Guatemala predicted only moderate turmoil and gave an A- for direct investment, suggesting a "favorable attitude, especially with respect to equity, loan participation, and taxes" and "restraint" in fiscal and labor policy.

The roots of the conflict can be found in the centuries-long political and economic domination by the ladino (non-Indian) elite over the Indian majority. Population growth also played a role, as political scientist Homer-Dixon would predict, because rich agricultural soil is in short supply in the Guatemalan highlands and many Indian farmers are landless, but inequities in the political economy aggravated the problem. In the 1980s, 2 percent of the landholders controlled 70 percent of the land, and 72 percent of the population could not afford a minimum diet.[115] The primary problem was the government's unwillingness to respond to the legitimate grievances of the Indian community. Ladinos have long used their political influence with the government to expropriate Indian land and keep wages low. For example, in 1978 more than 100 Indians were killed by the army for marching on the town hall in Panzos to demand land titles to defend their lands from expropriation by large landholders.[116]

Political violence was also occurring in El Salvador, Brazil, Argentina, Chile, and other Latin American countries at the same time, but what made the Guatemalan case especially noteworthy was that the villages and people destroyed were not anonymous. Places such as Chichicastenango and Huehuetenango are famous in the anthropological literature and are personally known to many anthropologists, including this author. Many of the Indian people who died horrible deaths at the hands of the Guatemalan army had for decades assisted anthropological field researchers who came to know their lives and their families. Outraged by the unspeakable atrocities, eleven anthropologists, a geographer, and a political scientist, all with extensive experience in Guatemala, published their own highly personal accounts of the death squads, disappearances, tortures, and massacres in the book *Harvest of Violence*.[117] They reported that the guerrillas also used political violence, but it was very selective, whereas the army killed indiscriminately. In 1983 and 1984 Ricardo Falla, a Guatemalan anthropologist and Jesuit priest, lived with Indian survivors hiding in the Guatemalan rain forest and interviewed others in the refugee camps in Mexico. He obtained detailed eyewitness accounts of army atrocities against noncombatant men, women, and children. Painstakingly reconstructing specific military operations, he listed the names and ages of 773 civilian victims murdered by the army in the Ixcan region.[118] Myrna Mack, another Guatemalan anthropologist, was killed by the army in 1990.

In 1992 the American Association for the Advancement of Science's Committee on Scientific Freedom and Responsibility sponsored a special training program for human rights workers and government officials in Guatemala. Forensic anthropologist Clyde Snow demonstrated how to properly exhume mass graves, identify victims, and find physical evidence of "extra-judicial executions" and torture. This kind of work will make it much more difficult for anyone to use political terrorism with impunity.

Opulence and Deindustrialization in America

In the United States, just as in the poor countries of the world, economic growth and the globalization of the economy have disproportionately benefited the few while the majority has steadily lost wealth and control over their lives. Various measures of wealth and income distribution suggest that since approximately 1970 changes in American economic policies have worked to redistribute wealth to the richest at the expense of middle- and lower-class households.[119] The most dramatic evidence of this redistribution is the increase in the number of the superrich relative to the poor. Economic growth during the two decades between 1969 and 2003 was reflected in the three orders of magnitude (10 x 10 x 10) increase in the number of millionaires, whereas since 1980 the number of poor also increased.[120] However, in 2003, 35.8 million Americans, 12.5 percent of the population, were living below the official poverty level.[121] This figure included the 17 percent of American children under the age of eighteen who were living in poverty. In 1992, there were only 73 billionaires in the *Forbes 400* annual list of the 400 wealthiest Americans. By 2006 all 400 were billionaires, and the wealthiest individual topped the list with an estimated net worth of $53 billion.[122] Collectively these 400 people were worth $1.25 trillion, which exceeded the total household net worth of Switzerland in 2000.[123] Viewed globally from the bottom up, the wealthiest 400 Americans had more personal wealth than the 2.5 billion people living in the world's 150 poorest countries. The wealthiest American was worth more financially than 675 million people in 81 countries combined. The 2.6 million HNWI Americans constituted 30 percent of the world's

HNWIs in 2005. This tiny proportion of the global population has bene-fited most from economic globalization, whereas even in America, one of the world's richest countries, poverty still abounds.

Net worth, the value of personal assets minus debts, is more highly con-centrated in the United States than income, according to surveys of family finance carried out for the Federal Reserve.[124] In 2004 just 11 million fam-ilies, the top 10 percent of families by net worth, held 69 percent of fam-ily net worth, whereas the bottom 50 percent held only 3 percent. This matters because when net worth is high, it is more likely to be in the form of wealth-producing investable financial assets rather than in just homes and cars. The historic shift of wealth to the top of American society can be at-tributed in part to changes in the income tax laws to favor the wealthy, and is reflected in recent changes in the distribution of income to families (fig-ure 7.3). The middle 20 percent of families received their highest share of

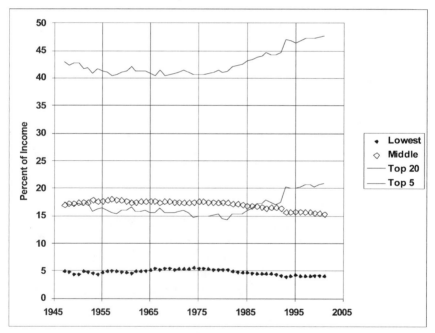

Figure 7.3.   Family Share of U.S. Aggregate Income by Quintile and Top 5 Percent, 1947–2002. Source: Bucks, Brian K., Arthur B. Kennickell, and Kevin B. Moore. 2006. "Recent Changes in U.S. Family Finances: Evidence from the 2001 and 2004 Survey of Consumer Finances." *Federal Reserve Bulletin* 2006 (March 22), A2–A38. Table 3. Family net worth, by selected charac-teristics of families, 1995–2004 surveys.

aggregate family income (18.1 percent) in 1957. This was just below an equitable 20 percent share, and represented real prosperity for the middle class. This middle share fluctuated around 18 percent until 1980, when federal policies shifted dramatically in favor of the wealthiest Americans. Between 1980 and 2001 the middle income share dropped to just 15 percent, and the poorest 20 percent saw their share drop from a high of 5.7 percent in 1974 to 4.2 in 2001. At the same time the share of the top 20 percent soared from 41.1 to 47.7 and the top 5 percent from 14.6 to 21 percent. When income soars beyond the threshold of basic consumption needs, income can be invested to increase wealth, even as wealth increases income. The total effect is that "the rich get richer." This is the power concentrating scale effect of elite-directed economic growth.

Another measure of economic inequality and the overall concentration of growth benefits in the United States is the excessive spread in income between minimum-wage workers and the salaries of top corporate executives. In America as in Brazil, because wages have fallen relative to the cost of living, minimum-wage workers cannot support a household unless both husband and wife are employed. In 1992 the poverty level for a family of three was set at $10,292, well above the minimum annual wage of $8,840. Plato recommended that the highest salary in a community should not exceed five times the lowest. More expansive American authorities suggest that a twenty-fold top-to-bottom salary spread would be reasonable, and that is the range in Japan.[125] However, in 1993 the highest-paid American corporate chief executive officer earned $41.3 million in salary, bonuses, and extra compensation—4,672 times the then-minimum annual wage of $8,840. The average compensation of top executives in 200 of the largest American corporations was $4.1 million in 1993, 463 times the lowest annual wage.[126]

Encouraged by changes in the tax laws and economic policies that favored the rich, the business world allowed excessive salaries that have helped concentrate wealth at the upper levels of American society.[127] From the 1940s through 1964 the highest tax rate stood at 91 percent for the top bracket and thus set a practical ceiling on income. Under the tax "reform" of 1986 the highest incomes were taxed at no more than 28–31 percent. Corporate taxes were also reduced, raising returns to wealthy stockholders, while reductions in the capital gains tax meant that the wealthy could keep more of their "unearned income" from investments. These reductions, combined with increases in Social Security payroll taxes, meant that wage earners paid a larger proportion of their income in total taxes than that paid by the wealthy.

For many reasons the total federal debt quadrupled between 1980 and 1992, making the United States the world's largest debtor nation. The value of the dollar declined in international markets, and a large trade imbalance developed as the United States began to import far more than it exported. Foreign interests began buying up American real estate and businesses.[128] The rising deficit forced up interest rates on borrowing, further increasing investment income for the wealthy 2.2 percent of American households holding government securities. Leveraged buy-outs and mergers further concentrated the ownership and control of corporate assets. Many American corporations kept profits high by firing employees (downsizing); hiring lower-wage, nonunion, or part-time employees; and moving factories overseas. America's heavy industries were increasingly being replaced by highly mobile light manufacturing and service industries in a process that has been called "deindustrialization."[129]

Anthropologist James Toth in 1992 documented the impact of deindustrialization on Carlisle, a small town in Pennsylvania where economic growth occurred in a way that transferred decision-making power over capital and profits from local businesspeople to remote corporate offices. Toth and his researchers found that small businesses, small manufacturing plants, and independent contractors that had formerly provided steady, secure employment for local residents were replaced by electronics firms, shopping malls, banks, and realty agencies that were subsidiaries of conglomerates headquartered elsewhere and that effectively drained the community's capital resources. Toth explains that "as Carlisle loses its isolation and becomes integrated into larger financial, commercial, and labor markets, local economic and government leaders become middlemen and brokers for higher layers of authority located in corporate centers and company headquarters in Pittsburgh, Philadelphia, Baltimore, New York and even outside the country. City government and local business leaders continue to administer to the various needs of the community, but real power has shifted to those living far from Carlisle."[130]

The largest beneficiaries of global financialization, downsizing, and American deindustrialization are those "superconsumer" Americans in the top 0.5 percent of the population who can afford to purchase costly luxuries, such as $21,995 IWC Da Vinci wristwatches, the $189,000 Rolls-Royce Silver Spur III, or a $6 million winter residence on Fisher Island in Florida; those who travel in private jets; and those HNWIs who can take advantage of Citibank's private banking, "integrated wealth management," and "global asset management" programs. The primary concern of these fortunate families is personal security. For example, Fisher Island, a 216-

acre "sanctuary" off the coast of Florida, was described in an advertisement as home to "four hundred of the world's most prominent families" and boasted "perhaps most important of all, an atmosphere of security that allows residents to lead a life of privacy and pleasure."[131] In 1987 the seaside luxury homes, yachts, private racquet clubs, golf course, marinas, shops, and bank on "Fortress Fisher" were protected by a 40-person security force and electronic security systems. The island was accessible only by private ferry to those with security clearances.[132] Such protective measures are not surprising in a country like America, where 12.5 percent of the population live in official poverty, and the bottom half of the population has only 3 percent of the wealth.

Anthropologist Katherine Newman[133] accurately described the 1980s as a period of "declining fortunes" for many middle- and working-class Americans who were "falling from grace." During the decade between 1981 and 1992, 10.6 million adults lost their jobs because of plant closings or force reductions, and most suffered drastic reductions in income when they found lower-wage jobs.[134] This downward mobility affected up to one-third of the American population, many of whom were not previously poor. In 1992 dollars, median income in America declined by 10 percent during the 1980–1993 period, from $35,839 to $32,241. In order to learn how the realities of America's political economy were impacting downwardly mobile Americans, Newman conducted intensive "focused life history" interviews with more than 300 people. She found that many people believed that the American Dream of a steadily improving standard of living was no longer attainable.

Newman found that downsized managers sometimes blamed their fate on powerful external forces, but the dominant culture of capitalist meritocracy provides them little support. Success in the corporate business world ideologically defines the moral worth of the meritorious individual. In this survival-of-the-fittest view, people who lose their jobs deserve their fate. As one former executive declared: "I have to accept my firing. . . . The people who were involved in it are people I respect for the most part. . . . They are successful executives. . . . So I can't blame them for doing what they think is right. I have to say where have I gone wrong."[135]

Anthropologist June Nash[136] found a similar acceptance of job loss by the former workers of a Massachusetts General Electric plant that was moved to Canada in 1986, eliminating 5,000 jobs. Former employees questioned by Nash rejected the notion that General Electric had any responsibility to the community even though it had been its principal employer for over a century. They justified the plant closing by referring to the company imperative to make a profit and did not take the position that organized labor or local governments should have any control over such capital investments. Nash attributes this passivity on the part of displaced workers to the ideological hegemony of the corporate elite. Those holding real power in the world would prefer to continue making decisions in their own immediate best interests. They want ordinary people to believe that their fates are determined by inherently uncontrollable "natural" forces, not by the realities of grossly inequitable wealth and income distributions. Newman explains this as follows: "American culture tends to subtract large forces from our lives—economic trends, historical moments, and even government policies that privilege one group over another—and looks instead to the individual's character traits or values for answers."[137]

Notes

1. Kaplan, Robert D. 1994. "The Coming Anarchy." *Atlantic Monthly* (February) 273(2): 44–76.

2. U.S. National Commission on the Causes and Prevention of Violence. 1969. *Justice: To Establish Justice, to Ensure Domestic Tranquility*. Final Report. Washington, D.C.: U.S. Government Printing Office.

3. U.S. Department of Justice, Bureau of Justice Statistics. 2006. *Uniform Crime Reports*, www.ojp.usdoj.gov/bjs/glance/tables/4meastab.htm

4. U.S. Department of Justice, Bureau of Justice Statistics. 2006. *Uniform Crime Reports*, Homicide Rates from the Vital Statistics of the United States, National Center for Health Statistics.

5. Official Statistics of Norway. 1995. *Statistical Yearbook*. Oslo.

6. U.S. National Commission on the Causes and Prevention of Violence, *Justice*.

7. U.S. National Advisory Commission on Civil Disorders. 1968. Kerner Report. Washington, D.C.: U.S. Government Printing Office.

8. Harris, Fred R. 1998. "The Kerner Report: Thirty Years Later." In *Locked in the Poorhouse: Cities, Race, and Poverty in the United States*, edited by Fred R. Harris and Lynn A. Curds, 7–19. Lanham, MD: Rowman & Littlefield.

9. Eames, Edwin, and Judith G. Goode. 1973. *Urban Poverty in a Cross-Cultural Context*. New York: Free Press.

10. Dentan, Robert K. 1968. *The Semai: A Nonviolent People of Malaya*. New York: Holt, Rinehart & Winston.

11. Keeley, Lawrence H. 1996. *War Before Civilization*. New York and Oxford: Oxford University Press; Knauft, B. 1987. "Reconsidering Violence in Simple Societies." *Current Anthropology* 28: 457–500.

12. Chagnon, Napoleon. 1968. *Yanomamo: The Fierce People*. New York: Holt, Rinehart & Winston; Chagnon, Napoleon. 1988. "Life Histories, Blood Revenge, and Warfare in a Tribal Population." *Science* (February 26) 239: 985–92.

13. Ferguson, R. Brian. 1995. *Yanomami Warfare: A Political History*. Santa Fe, NM: School of American Research Press.

14. Hobbes, Thomas. 1958. *Leviathan*. New York: Liberal Arts. Originally published in 1651, part I, chapter 13.

15. Barclay, Harold. 1982. *People Without Government*. London: Kahn & Averill & Cienfuegos.

16. Turnbull, Colin. 1968. "The Importance of Flux in Two Hunting Societies." In *Man the Hunter*, edited by Richard B. Lee and Irven DeVore, 132–37. Chicago: Aldine, 132–37; Woodburn, James. 1968b. "Stability and Flexibility in Hadza Residential Groupings." In *Man the Hunter*, edited by Richard B. Lee and Irven DeVore, 103–10. Chicago: Aldine.

17. Erdal, David, and Andrew Whiten. 1996. "Egalitarianism and Machiavellian Intelligence in Human Evolution." In *Modelling the Early Human Mind*, edited by Paul Mellars and Kathleen Gibson, 139–50. Cambridge: McDonald Institute for Archaeological Research, University of Cambridge.

18. Fried, Morton. 1967. *The Evolution of Political Society*. New York: Random House, 33.

19. Collier, Jane Fishburne, and Michelle Z. Rosaldo. 1981. "Politics and Gender in Simple Societies." In *Sexual Meanings: The Cultural Construction of Gender and Sexuality*, edited by Sherry B. Orner and Harriet Whitehead, 275–329. Cambridge: Cambridge University Press.

20. Kelly, Raymond C. 1993. *Constructing Inequality: The Fabrication of a Hierarchy of Virtue among the Etoro*. Ann Arbor: University of Michigan Press.

21. Fried, *Evolution of Political Society*, 58.

22. Myers, Fred R. 1982. "Always Ask: Resource Use and Land Ownership Among Pintupi Aborigines of the Australian Western Desert." In *Resource Managers: North American and Australian Hunter-Gatherers*, edited by Nancy M. Williams and Eugene S. Hunn, 173–95. AAAS Selected Symposium No. 67. Boulder, CO: Westview.

23. Bogucki, Peter. 1999. *The Origins of Human Society*. Maiden, MA, and Oxford, U.K.: Blackwell Publishers, 227–30; Sherratt, Andrew G. 1981. "Plough and Pastoralism: Aspects of the Secondary Products Revolution." In *Pattern of the Past: Studies in Honour of David Clarke*, edited by I. Hodder, G. Isaac, and N. Hammond, 261–305. Cambridge: Cambridge University Press.

24. Hayden, Brian. 1995b. "Pathways to Power: Principles for Creating Socioeconomic Inequalities." In *Foundations of Social Inequality*, edited by T. Douglas Price and Gary M. Feinman, 15–86. New York and London: Plenum Press.

25. Bern, John. 1979. "Ideology and Domination: Toward a Reconstruction of Australian Aboriginal Social Formation." *Oceania* 50(2): 118–32.

26. Kaberry, Phyllis M. 1939. *Aboriginal Woman: Sacred and Profane*. London: Routledge; Bell, Diane. 1982. *Aboriginal Women and the Religious Experience*. Young Australian Scholar Lecture Series, no. 3. Bedford Park, South Australia: Australian Association for the Study of Religions, South Australian College of Advanced Education.

27. Johnson, Allen. 1975. "Time Allocation in a Machiguenga Community." *Ethnology* 14(3): 301–10; Johnson, Allen. 1985. "In Search of the Affluent Society." In *Anthropology: Contemporary Perspectives*, edited by David E. K. Hunter and Phillip Whitten, 201–6. Boston: Little, Brown. First published in *Human Nature*, September 1978; Lee, Richard B. 1979. *The !Kung San: Men, Women and Work in a Foraging Society*. Cambridge and New York: Cambridge University Press; Modjeska, Nicholas. 1982. "Production and Inequality: Perspectives from Central New Guinea." In *Inequality in New Guinea Highlands Societies*, edited by Andrew Strathern, 50–108. Cambridge: Cambridge University Press.

28. Chagnon, Napoleon. 1968. *Yanomamo: The Fierce People*. New York: Holt, Rinehart & Winston.

29. Fabbro, David. 1978. "Peaceful Societies: An Introduction." *Journal of Peace Research* 15(1): 67–83, 80.

30. Kelly, Raymond C. 2000. *Warless Societies and the Origin of War*. Ann Arbor: University of Michigan Press, 5–7.

31. Van Velzen, H. U. E. Thoden, and W. Van Wetering. 1960. "Residence, Power Groups and Intra-societal Aggression." *International Archives of Ethnography* 49: 169–200; Otterbein, Keith F. 1968. "Internal War: A Cross-Cultural Study." *American Anthropologist* 70(2): 277–89.

32. Lévi-Strauss, Claude. 1944. "The Social and Psychological Aspects of Chieftainship in a Primitive Tribe: The Nambikuara of Northwestern Matto Grosso." *Transactions of the New York Academy of Sciences* 7: 16–32.

33. Lévi -Strauss, Chieftainship, 16-32.

34. Boehm, Christopher. 1993. "Egalitarian Behavior and Reverse Dominance Hierarchy." *Current Anthropology* 34(3): 227–54.

35. Blanton, Richard E. 1998. "Beyond Centralization: Steps Toward a Theory of Egalitarian Behavior in Archaic States." In *Archaic States*, edited by Gary M. Feinman and Joyce Marcus, 135–72. Santa Fe, NM: School of American Research Press, 151–52.

36. Lee, Richard B. 1981. "Politics, Sexual and Non-sexual, In an Egalitarian Society." In *Social Inequality: Comparative and Developmental Approaches*, edited by Gerald D. Berreman, 83–102. New York: Academic Press.

37. Earle, Timothy, ed. 1991. *Chiefdoms: Power, Economy, and Ideology*. Cambridge: Cambridge University Press; Earle, Timothy. 1997. *How Chiefs Come to Power: The Political Economy in Prehistory*. Stanford, CA: Stanford University Press; Carneiro, Robert L. 1981. "The Chiefdom: Precursor of the State." In *The Transition to Statehood in the New World*, edited by Grant D. Jones and Robert R. Kautz, 37–79. Cambridge: Cambridge University Press; Service, Elman R. 1962. *Primitive Social Organization*. New York: Random House.

38. Fried, *Evolution of Political Society*, 186.

39. Betzig, Laura L. 1986. *Despotism and Differential Reproduction: A Darwinian View of History*. New York: Aldine; Betzig, Laura L. 1993. "Sex, Succession, and

Stratification in the First Six Civilizations: How Powerful Men Reproduced, Passed Power on to Their Sons, and Used Power to Defend Their Wealth, Women, and Children." In *Social Stratification and Socioeconomic Inequality*, vol. 1, *A Comparative Biosocial Analysis*, edited by Lee Ellis, 37–74. Westport, CT, and London: Praeger; Bodley, John H. 2003. *The Power of Scale: A Global History Approach.* Armonk, New York and London: M. E. Sharpe, chapter 4.

40. Harris, Marvin. 1971. *Culture, Man and Nature*. New York: Crowell.

41. Blanton, "Beyond Centralization," 135–72.

42. Feinman, Gary M. 1998. "Scale and Social Organization." In *Archaic States*, edited by Gary M. Feinman and Joyce Marcus, 95–133. Santa Fe, NM: School of American Research Press; Bodley, *Power of Scale*, chapter 4.

43. McCorriston, Joy. 1997. "The Fiber Revolution: Textile Extensification, Alienation, and Social Stratification in Ancient Mesopotamia." *Current Anthropology* 3 8(4): 517–49.

44. Baines, John, and Norman Yoffee. 1998. "Order, Legitimacy, and Wealth in Ancient Egypt and Mesopotamia." In *Archaic States*, edited by Gary M. Feinman and Joyce Marcus, 199–260. Santa Fe, NM: School of American Research Press.

45. Marcus, Joyce. 1998. "The Peaks and Valleys of Ancient States: An Extension of the Dynamic Model." In *Archaic States*, edited by Gary M. Feinman and Joyce Marcus, 59–94. Santa Fe, NM: School of American Research Press, 94.

46. Harris, *Culture, Man and Nature*.

47. Naroll, R. 1966. "Does Military Deterrence Deter?" *Trans-Action* 3(2): 14–20.

48. Thorpe, I. J. N. 2003. "Anthropology, Archaeology, and the Origin of Warfare." *World Archaeology* 35(1): 145–465.

49. Cashdan, Elizabeth 2001. "Ethnocentrism and Xenophobia: A Cross-cultural Study." *Current Anthropology* 42(5): 760–65.

50. Tylor, Edward B. 1889. "On a Method of Investigating the Development of Institutions; Applied to Laws of Marriage and Descent." *Journal of the Royal Anthropological Institute* 18: 245–69.

51. De Waal, F. B. M. 1989. *Peacemaking among Primates*. Cambridge, MA: Harvard University Press.

52. Chagnon, Napoleon. 1988. "Life Histories, Blood Revenge, and Warfare in a Tribal Population." *Science* (February 26) 239: 985–92.

53. Ferguson, R. Brian. 1995. *Yanomami Warfare: A Political History*. Santa Fe, NM: School of American Research Press.

54. Otterbein, "Internal War," 277–89.

55. Malinowski, Bronislaw. 1944. *Freedom and Civilization*. New York: Roy, 277.

56. Wright, Quincy. 1942. *A Study of War*. 2 vols. Chicago: University of Chicago Press, 39.

57. Otterbein, Keith F. 1970. *The Evolution of War: A Cross-Cultural Study*. New Haven, CT: Human Relations Area Files.

58. Webster, David. 1998. "Warfare and Status Rivalry: Lowland Maya and Polynesian Comparisons." In *Archaic States*, edited by Gary M. Feinman and Joyce Marcus, 311–51. Santa Fe, NM: School of American Research Press.

59. Wright, *Evolution of War*, 278–83; Naroll, R. "Does Military Deterrence Deter?" 14–20; Otterbein, *Evolution of War*.

60. Otterbein, *Evolution of War*.

61. Wright, *Study of War*, 5.

62. Malinowski, Bronislaw. 1941. "An Anthropological Analysis of War." *American Journal of Sociology* 46(4): 521–50.

63. Mead, Margaret. 1940. "Warfare Is Only an Invention—Not a Biological Necessity." *Asia* 40: 402–5.

64. Otterbein, Keith F. 1999. "A History of Research on Warfare in Anthropology." *American Anthropologist* 101(4): 794–805. Otterbein, Keith F. 2000. "The Doves Have Been Heard From, Where Are the Hawks?" *American Anthropologist* 102(4): 841–44.

65. Bodley, *Victims of Progress*, 43.

66. Engelbrecht. H. C. 1934. "The World Trend toward Nationalism." *Annals of the American Academy of Political and Social Science*, vol. 174, (July 1934), 121–25.

67. Brewer, John. 1988. *The Sinews of Power: War, Money and the English State, 1688–1783*. New York: Alfred A. Knopf; Bodley, *Power of Scale*, chapter 6; Cain, P. J. and A. G. Hopkins. 1993. *British Imperialism: Innovation and Expansion 1688–1914*. London and New York: London; Cain, P. J. and A. G. Hopkins. 2002. *British Imperialism, 1688–2000*. New York: Longman.

68. Hooks, Gregory. 1991. *Forging the Military-Industrial Complex: World War II's Battle of the Potomac*. Urbana and Chicago: University of Illinois Press.

69. Public Papers of the Presidents. 1960. *Dwight D. Eisenhower*. Washington, D.C.: Federal Register Division, National Archives and Records Service, General Services Administration, 1035–1040.

70. PricewaterhouseCoopers. 2005. *The Defence Industry in the 21st Century*. www.pwc.com/

71. Arena, Mark V., Irv Blickstein, Obaid Younossi, and Clifford A. Grammich. 2006. *Why Has the Cost of Navy Ships Risen?: A Macroscopic Examination of the Trends in U.S. Naval Ship Costs*. Santa Monica, CA: RAND, xiv.

72. Globalsecurity. www.globalsecurity.org/military

73. Stockholm International Peace Research Institute. 2006. *SIPRI Yearbook 2006: Armaments, Disarmament and International Security*. New York: Humanities Press.

74. Mergent Online. www.mergentonline.com/

75. Cirincione, Joseph, Jon Wolfsthal, and Miriam Rajkumar. 2005. *Deadly Arsenals: Nuclear, Biological, and Chemical Threats*. 2nd edition. Washington, D.C.: Carnegie Endowment for International Peace.

76. Albright, David, and Corey Hinderstein. 2005. "Unraveling the A. Q. Khan and Future Proliferation Networks." *The Washington Quarterly* 28(2): 111–28.

77. Cirincione, et al. *Nuclear, Biological, and Chemical Threats*, Table 1.2.

78. Naím, Moisés. 2005. *Illicit: How Smugglers, Traffickers, and Copycats are Hijacking the Global Economy.* New York: Doubleday.

79. The Fund for Peace. www.fundforpeace.org/thefund/president.php

80. Harbom, Lotta, Stina Högbladh, and Peter Wallensteen. 2006. "Armed Conflict and Peace Agreements." *Journal of Peace Research* 43(5): 617–31.

81. Lacina, Bethany, and Nils Petter Gleditsch, 2005. "Monitoring Trends in Global Combat: A New Dataset of Battle Deaths." *European Journal of Population* 21(2–3): 145–66.

82. Homer-Dixon, Thomas F. 1991. "On the Threshold: Environmental Changes as Causes of Acute Conflict." *International Security* 16(2): 76–116.

83. Beedham, Brian. 1993. "The World's Next Wars." In *The World in 1994*, edited by Dudley Fishburn, 13–14. London: The Economist Publications.

84. Olsen, Mary Kay Gilliland. 1993. "Bridge on the Sava: Ethnicity in Eastern Croatia, 1981–1991." *Anthropology of East Europe Review* 11(1-2): 54–62.

85. Huntington, Samuel P. 1993. "The Clash of Civilizations?" *Foreign Affairs* 72(3): 22–49; Huntington, Samuel P. 1996. *The Clash of Civilizations and the Remaking of World Order.* New York: Touchstone, Simon & Schuster.

86. Chiozza, Giacomo. 2002. "Is There a Clash of Civilizations? Evidence from Patterns of International Conflict Involvement, 1946–97." *Journal of Peace Research* 39(6): 711–34.

87. Homer-Dixon, Thomas F. 2006. *The Upside of Down: Catastrophe, Creativity, and the Renewal of Civilization.* Washington, D.C.: Island Press.

88. George, Susan. 1992. *The Debt Boomerang: How Third World Debt Harms Us All.* Boulder, CO: Westview Press.

89. Wallerstein, Immanuel. 1974. *The Modern World-System: Capitalist Agriculture and the Origins of the European World-Economy in the Sixteenth Century.* New York: Academic Press.

90. Phillips, Kevin. 1994. *Arrogant Capital: Washington, Wall Street, and the Frustration of American Politics.* Boston: Little, Brown.

91. Goldsmith, Raymond W. 1985. *Comparative National Balance Sheets: A Study of Twenty Countries, 1688–1978.* Chicago and London: University of Chicago Press; U.S. Bureau of the Census. 1960. *Historical Statistics of the United States, Colonial Times to 1957.* Washington, D.C.: U.S. Government Printing Office. Series F 158–196.

92. Barnet, Richard J., and John Cavanagh. 1994. *Global Dreams: Imperial Corporations and the New World Order.* New York: Simon & Schuster.

93. Hornborg, Alf. 1992. "Machine Fetishism, Value, and the Image of Unlimited Good: Towards a Thermodynamics of Imperialism." *Man* 27(1): 1–18; Hornborg, Alf. 2001. *The Power of the Machine: Global Inequalities of Economy, Technology, and Environment.* Walnut Creek, CA: Altamira Press.

94. Kennickell, Arthur B., Martha Starr-McCluer, and Brian J. Surette. 2000. "Recent Changes in U.S. Family Finances: Results from the 1998 Survey of Consumer Finances." *Federal Reserve Bulletin* 86: 1–29.

95. Capgemini. 2006. *World Wealth Report 2006.* www.us.capgemini.com/worldwealthreport06/default.asp

96. George, *Debt Boomerang.*

97. George, *Debt Boomerang.*

98. George, *Debt Boomerang,* 1–2.

99. George, Susan. 2000. "Corporate-led Globalisation: Succinct Description of What the International Economic System Is, How it Works, and to Whose Benefit." www.tni-archives.org/detail_page.phtml?page=archives_george_corpglob1

100. Stiglitz, Joseph E. 2002. *Globalizations and Its Discontents.* New York: W. W. Norton.

101. Stiglitz, Joseph E., and Andrew Charlton. 2005. *Fair Trade for All: How Trade Can Promote Development.* New York: Oxford University Press.

102. George, *Debt Boomerang,* 31–32.

103. Scheper-Hughes, Nancy. 1992. *Death Without Weeping: The Violence of Everyday Life in Brazil.* Berkeley: University of California Press.

104. Scheper-Hughes, *Death Without Weeping,* 80.

105. Scott, James C. 1985. *Weapons of the Weak.* New Haven, CT: Yale University Press.

106. Scheper-Hughes, *Death Without Weeping,* 153.

107. Scheper-Hughes, *Death Without Weeping,* 313.

108. Scheper-Hughes, *Death Without Weeping,* 146.

109. Farmer, Paul. 2003. *Pathologies of Power: Health, Human Rights, and the New War on the Poor.* Berkeley: University of California Press.

110. Falla, Ricardo. 1994. *Massacres in the Jungle: Ixcan, Guatemala, 1915–1982.* Boulder, CO: Westview.

111. Political Risk Services. 1994. *Political Risk Yearbook.* Syracuse, NY: Political Risk Services.

112. Chomsky, Noam, and Edward S. Herman. 1979. *The Washington Connection and Third World Fascism.* Boston: South End Press; Chomsky, Noam. 1989. *Necessary Illusions: Thought Control in Democratic Societies.* Boston: South End Press; Chomsky, Noam. 1991. *Deterring Democracy.* London and New York: Verso; Chomsky, Noam. 1993. *Year 501: The Conquest Continues.* Boston: South End Press.

113. Falla, *Massacres in the Jungle,* 8.

114. U.S. Department of Commerce. 1994–1995. *Statistical Abstract of the United States.* Various annual editions. Washington, D.C.: U.S. Government Printing Office.

115. Chomsky, *Year 501,* 173.

116. Davis, Shelton H. 1988. "Introduction: Sowing the Seeds of Violence." In *Harvest of Violence: The Maya Indians and the Guatemalan Crisis,* edited by Robert M. Carmack. Norman and London: University of Oklahoma Press; IWGIA. 1978. *Guatemala 1918: The Massacre at Panzos.* Copenhagen: International Work Group for Indigenous Affairs.

117. Carmack, Robert M. 1988. *Harvest of Violence: The Maya Indians and the Guatemalan Crisis*. Norman, OK: University of Oklahoma Press.

118. Falla, *Massacres in the Jungle*.

119. Phillips, Kevin. 1990. *The Politics of Rich and Poor: Wealth and the American Electorate in the Reagan Aftermath*. New York: Random House; Phillips, Kevin. 2002. *Wealth and Democracy: A Political History of the American Rich*. New York: Broadway Books.

120. U.S. Internal Revenue Service (IRS). 2005. *Personal Wealth 2001: Top Wealth Holders with Gross Assets of $675,000 or More, Type of Property by Size of Net Worth*. IRS, Statistics of Income Division.

121. U.S. Census Bureau. *Statistical Abstract of the United States, 2006*. Tables 693, 694.

122. Miller, Matthew, and Tatiana Serafin. 2006. "The 400 Richest Americans." *Fortune Magazine* (October).

123. Calculations based on data in: Davies, James B., Susanna Sandstrom, Anthony Shorrocks, and Edward N. Wolff. 2006. *The World Distribution of Household Wealth*. World Institute for Development Economics Research, Appendix V, Table 1.

124. Bucks, Brian K., Arthur B. Kennickell, and Kevin B. Moore. 2006. "Recent Changes in U.S. Family Finances: Evidence from the 2001 and 2004 Survey of Consumer Finances." *Federal Reserve Bulletin* 2006 (March 22), A2-A38. Table 3. Family net worth, by selected characteristics of families, 1995–2004 surveys.

125. Crystal, Graef S. 1991. *In Search of Excess: The Overcompensation of American Executives*. New York and London: W. W. Norton and Co, 23–24.

126. Dumaine, Brian. 1994. "A Knockout Year for CEO Pay." *Fortune* (July 25): 94.

127. Phillips, *Politics of Rich and Poor*.

128. Phillips, *Politics of Rich and Poor*; Barnet, Richard J., and John Cavanagh. 1994. *Global Dreams: Imperial Corporations and the New World Order*. New York: Simon & Schuster.

129. Bluestone, Barry, and Bennett Harrison. 1982. *The Deindustrializatim of America*. New York: Basic Books; see also *Urban Anthropology* 1985, vol. 14, no. 1–3.

130. Toth, James. 1992. "Doubts About Growth: The Town of Carlisle in Transition." *Urban Anthropology* 21(1): 2–44.

131. *Architectural Digest*. 1994. (February), 99.

132. Flanagan, William G. 1987. "Fortress Fisher." *Forbes* (December): 232–37.

133. Newman, Katherine S. 1988. *Falling from Grace: The Experience of Downward Mobility in the American Middle Class*. New York: Free Press; Newman, Katherine S. 1993. *Declining Fortunes: The Withering of the American Dream*. New York: Basic Books.

134. Newman, *Falling from Grace*; U.S. Department of Commerce, *Statistical Abstract of the United States, 1994–95*.

135. Newman, *Falling from Grace*, 78.

136. Nash, June. 1989. *From Tank Town to High Tech: The Class of Community and Industrial Cycles*. Albany: State University of New York; Nash, June. 1994. "Global Integration and Subsistence Insecurity." *American Anthropologist* 96(1): 7–30.

137. Newman, *Declining Fortunes*, 221.

The Future   8

*Obviously we stand on the threshold of postcivilization. When
we reach solutions to today's problems, the society and culture
that we will have built for the purpose will be of a sort the world
has never seen before. It may be more, or less, civilized than what
we have, but it will not be civilization as we know it.*

—PAUL BOHANNAN, *BEYOND CIVILIZATION*[1]

FOCUSING ON ALL OF THE WORLD'S PROBLEMS at one time can be an
overwhelming and depressing task, but identifying common causes
and seeking solutions from an anthropological perspective can be a
source of new optimism and hope. Indeed, there are common human
causes to our problems as well as common human solutions. Previous chapters necessarily treated the specific problems of environmental deterioration, resource depletion, hunger, overpopulation, poverty, and conflict as if
they were discrete issues, but an anthropological perspective requires us to
look for interconnections between problems. The integrating principle is
that all of these problems are produced by elite-directed growth that concentrates decision making and diffuses costs. The alternative solution is for
democratic development that will diffuse decision making, wealth, social
power, and costs in ways that make everyone accountable for constructing
sustainable local, regional, and global societies. A broader overview is important because the way we conceptualize problems and their causes will
obviously influence the solutions we choose. Judging from humanity's evolutionary history, the future will be shaped by the choices people make, so
we need wise and anthropologically informed decision making. National

and international policymakers and disciplinary theorists have now reached a consensus that "underdevelopment" is the primary world problem and that "sustainable development" is the solution to be worked out in a world dominated by more "free market" capitalism. Certainly "sustainability" is an unassailably desirable goal for the world, but "underdevelopment" is an incomplete diagnosis. Anthropologically based scale and power theory points to alternative explanations for underlying problems and suggests different pathways to a more just and sustainable future. The good news is that alternative power and scale-based solutions to contemporary human problems already exist, and people at all levels of global society are already applying these proven solutions.

Culture process and culture scale have served throughout this book as organizing devices to identify connections between problems and to point the way to solutions. From the scale and power perspective the problem becomes how to construct a global system that will give small-scale community-based societies maximum power and autonomy to thrive. This solution requires national governments and a democratically organized global society that can respond to issues of global concern. The dilemma is that the world's High Net Worth Individuals (HNWIs) are prospering enormously from a social structure and ideology that still maximizes a form of economic growth that undermines the natural environment and does little to reduce poverty and conflict, whereas it is small-scale societies that emphasize community, sustainability, and social equality. The following sections examine different views of the future offered by governments, intergovernmental organizations such as the United Nations, transnational corporations, and non-governmental organizations, and review specific examples of alternative social organizations that address power and scale problems. Special attention will be devoted to existing models and visionary possibilities.

The Dilemma of Scale

Previous editions of this book developed the argument that the world's major problems are different manifestations of a single crisis and that the organization of civilization itself is the most basic problem. Our problems are all extremely complex, interrelated, and in a general sense multi-causal, but many of the most critical are obviously related to scale and concentrated power. Preceding chapters have shown repeatedly that a specific problem was either totally absent or at least not a serious problem in the tribal world of small-scale societies. Many problems did not arise or become critical until the appearance of globally organized commercial societies. Particular problems also often show a peculiar cause-and-effect relationship with advances in social scale and complexity. For example, war, population growth, and technological development are all causes of and results of increases in social scale. Any attempt to single out causes from effects is further complicated by the fact that these particular problems are themselves interrelated.

This multi-causality and complex interrelationship have important implications for any attempt to identify causes and find solutions. In many cases it is apparent that current problem-solving efforts are inadequate because they treat isolated symptoms and avoid basic underlying factors. An example from the medical field illustrates this point. In 1956, T. L. Cleave,[2] then-surgeon-captain in the British Royal Navy, linked together a number of seemingly diverse diseases, including dental decay, peptic ulcers, obesity, diabetes, constipation, and varicose veins, in a single category that he called the "saccharine disease." Using historical data and research on tribal peoples, he argued that all these conditions were caused at least in part by the extensive use of concentrated carbohydrates such as sugar and white flour in commercial societies. A radical change from a diet rich in complex unprocessed carbohydrates, which characterized human food systems for many thousands of years, to diets centered on commercially processed simple and highly refined carbohydrates altered body chemistry and greatly slowed food transit times through the digestive tract by reducing dietary bulk, thereby creating many pathogenic conditions. Previous researchers had simply not conceptualized these problems as interrelated, perhaps because they did not examine populations in which these pathologies seldom occurred and because they did not think of the commercialization of food systems as an underlying cultural cause. More recent researchers have recognized these relationships and now treat the saccharine disease as a lifestyle disease. For example, in 2006 nutrition researchers pointed out that highly advertised sweetened soft drinks account for a high proportion of the increased caloric intake that contributes to obesity in the United States.[3] At higher levels of analysis, it appears that virtually all major world problems are connected to the dominant cultural processes of politicization, commercialization, and financialization that have promoted dangerous increases in the scale of societies, markets, and economies.

Two closely interrelated variables—concentrated social power and institutionalized specialization—are fundamental characteristics of politically centralized cultures, and they were the foundation for the later emergence of commercial culture. Concentration of power and bureaucratic specialization are defining features of political centralization and the market economy, and they contribute to wealth inequality and the frequent conflict between individual and subgroup self-interest on the one hand and societal interest on the other. All of these cultural features, although they are not in themselves crises, tend to promote overpopulation, over-consumption, and other symptoms of the environmental crisis, and they are clearly linked to poverty, war, and crime.

Continued specialization may be a fatal flaw in large-scale societies. Specialists are now busily treating symptoms as causes, and in many cases certain groups even have a special stake in—and indeed may profit by treating—specific symptoms. The defense establishment, for example, "treats" conflict; the police and legal professions "treat" crime; and various health and social work professions "treat" personal crises. The very specialization of these institutions makes it difficult for researchers to perceive connections between deliberately isolated and apparently unrelated symptoms. In many cases, even if a definitive solution were discovered, it would almost certainly be resisted by specialist groups because it might be a clear threat to personal job security. For example, the end of the Cold War caused enormous dislocation for people employed in, or profiting by, the military-industrial complex, and it has had ramifications throughout the global economy. Also, while the discovery of the saccharine disease and its simple cure has led to the addition of "fiber content" to some food labels and the marketing of certain high-fiber processed foods, these minor changes have not eliminated the saccharine disease because concentrated carbohydrates are produced and distributed by a massive food industry, which in turn is merely one expression of extreme stratification and specialization.

It is possible that the extreme forms of social stratification and economic specialization that characterize commercial-scale societies may simply be maladaptive. Sustainable development will require sweeping socio-cultural change perhaps even more dramatic than the change that occurred in Europe and North America during the earlier Industrial Revolution. In fact, economist Robert L. Heilbroner's early 1960s prescription for development change in the "developing" world precisely describes the scope of the change that will be needed in "developed" countries to solve the crises of the entire contemporary world: "Nothing short of a pervasive social transformation will suffice: a wholesale metamorphosis of habits, a wrenching reorientation of values concerning time, status, money, work; an unweaving and reweaving of the fabric of daily existence itself."[4]

This is the sort of transformation that is anticipated in the Global Scenario Group's "Great Transition" report for the Stockholm Environment Institute, which envisions the emergence of a truly sustainable planetary society, "an equitable world of peace, freedom and sustainability," during the twenty-first century.[5] The fundamental requirement for the Great Transition as envisioned by the Global Scenario Group is a profound change in values in which people choose to drastically reorganize their social institutions to emphasize the quality of community, human relationships, individual well-being, and the environment, rather than economic growth driven by increasing consumption of energy and material. This change would solve the problems of scale and concentrated power.

Scale theory offers a liberating approach to contemporary problems because it identifies scale itself as the principal problem. Scale problems are produced by unlimited growth in the size of societies, polities, and economies. Because growth in scale concentrates social power, proportionately fewer people who direct the flow of capital make ever-more-important decisions for ever-larger numbers of people. This means that an increasing majority of people take the role of passive consumers. Consumers may feel that they have a "vote" in the marketplace when they purchase things, but money is undemocratically distributed, and individually their "votes" have a miniscule effect.

When cultural systems, institutions, economies, and societies grow too large, they create human problems that can quickly become unmanageable. The good news is that scale theory also shows that too much growth is neither a natural nor an inevitable outcome of cultural development. The present world with all its problems is not the only possible world. It did not just happen but was created by the decisions of relatively few people who took advantage of historical opportunities in their own self-interest. Thus, if most people do nothing, growth will naturally continue to be an elite-directed process, and elites will continue to make ever-more-colossal mistakes. Earlier political elites produced several "worlds" composed of highly unstable and despotic chiefdoms, kingdoms, city-states, and empires that rose and fell over centuries. Since AD 1500, commercial elites and their political-elite allies have had a virtually free hand in transforming the world, but mercantile capitalism, industrial capitalism, and the latest version of global free-market capitalism have so far failed to work for everyone's benefit and have proved to be unsustainable. Commercial systems in which the interests of investors with great masses of capital are frequently at cross-purposes with the interests of those who must live by selling their labor are inherently difficult to manage. If commercial economies are left undirected, human society, cultures, and people's daily lives will be perpetually transformed by the unpredictable rise and fall of markets and by the persistent chaos of unforeseen waves of change. In the absence of strong democratic countermeasures, elites will "naturally" continue to direct the growth process for their own benefit by default. Tribal societies avoided the problems of runaway growth because they maintained close community control over their leaders and recalled them instantly if they made bad, self-serving, or aggrandizing decisions. It is time for the majority to find cultural solutions that work for all communities and households and that do not rely on perpetual growth in scale. It is possible to imagine a very different, just, humane, and sustainable world constructed from the ground up by democratic decision makers living in human-scale communities.

Imagining the Global Future

> This Commission believes that people can build a future that is more prosperous, more just, and more secure. Our report, *Our Common Future*, is not a prediction of ever increasing environmental decay, poverty, and hardship in an ever more polluted world among ever decreasing resources. We see instead the possibility for a new era of economic growth, one that is based on policies that sustain and expand the environmental resource base. And we believe such growth to be absolutely essential to relieve the great poverty that is deepening in much of the developing world. (World Commission on Environment and Development, 1987)[6]

The consensus adopted by the United Nations and leading governments since 1945 was that more economic growth was the best overall solution to world problems. This emphasis on growth remained dominant in official discourse throughout the second half of the twentieth century. The optimistic growth position, also expressed in the above quote from the UN's Brundtland Commission, is often combined with an emphasis on the need for expanded global trade driven by free-market economic principles, which is the primary means of growing a larger global economy. The persistent priority of economic growth was explicitly reflected in the British government's 1990 environmental strategy, *This Common Inheritance*.[7] Linking the need for continued economic growth in wealthy nations to environmental concerns, the British strategy argued that further growth was needed to pay for pollution abatement and conservation efforts, and to make future industrial production cleaner. More economic growth and increased global trade are also major features of the current recommendations of the UN Millennium Project, which seeks to implement the Millennium Goal of cutting extreme poverty in half by 2015.[8] In this case growth in impoverished countries is offered as the way out of poverty, but it is also linked to continued economic growth in the global system. This stress on continued economic growth is acceptable to many HNWI investors and the transnational corporate elite generally, because it is likely to improve their short-term financial interests. The growth prescription falls short of the far-reaching cultural changes that sustainability actually requires, because it does not view overdevelopment in rich countries as a global problem, does not link overdevelopment to underdevelopment in poor countries, and does not recommend any national or global limits to growth.

By the end of the twentieth century as poverty persisted and environmental problems mounted, it had become increasingly obvious that giving maximum priority to economic growth was perhaps not the best path for the world. Alternative views of the future gradually began to appear. The introduction of the concept of "sustainable development" in 1987 was the first prominent example of a shift in official discourse. It is a hopeful sign that some governments are beginning to question the value of continued economic growth as currently measured. For example, a 2003 report on Britain's progress toward sustainable development called for "social progress which recognizes the needs of everyone" and declared: "sustainable development is more than just economic growth. Growth must be of a higher quality than in the past. It needs to be achieved while reducing pollution and the unsustainable use of resources."[9] This conclusion is supported by the New Economy Foundation's Measure of Domestic Progress (MDP) that, like the Genuine Progress Indicator (GPI) in the United States discussed in chapter 3, stayed flat in Britain between 1950 and 2002 even as GDP tripled.[10] Clearly, beyond a certain point economic growth effectively stops producing significant gains for most people, because of growth's negative side effects.

Since the original Limits to Growth Study appeared in 1972 many new computer simulation models and scenarios have been used to explore possible futures of particular regions and the global system as a whole. These models and the views of the future they produce necessarily reflect different views of the past, and of how human beings and socio-cultural systems work. These various descriptions of possible futures matter because they were influenced by those who funded their production, and because they are being used to shape national and international policy. Those who imagine the future may also shape the future. In order to illustrate the range of future possibilities currently being imagined, this section will examine various examples of futurist scenarios used by UN-related agencies, governments, Shell Oil Corporation, and an independent research network, the Global Scenario Group.

IPCC SRES Scenarios

The Intergovernmental Panel on Climate Change (IPCC), established in 1988 by the United Nations, was a pioneer in futurist work, developing a series of scenarios to explore the impact of human activities on the emission of greenhouse gases (GHGs) and their ongoing effects on global warming to the end of the twenty-first century. These were called SRES scenarios, because they appeared in the *Special Report on Emissions Scenarios*.[11] They were refined in the 1990s, and were a prominent feature of the IPCC's Third Assessment Report[12] issued in 2001, and in the Fourth Assessment Report in 2007. In many respects global warming is the central contemporary human problem, because it will intensify the impact of all other problems of resource degradation, poverty, and conflict. The IPCC's work will play a major role in our collective response.

SRES scenarios exist in some forty variations, but they all assume that population, economy, technology, energy, and land use, especially agriculture, are the impersonal "driving forces" behind GHGs. From an anthropological perspective it is important to remember that these five forces are socio-cultural variables, not forces of nature. Human decision making creates them, and humans can choose to change these forces. IPCC researchers apply SRES scenarios either to the world as a whole, or to particular regions. They grouped them into four "scenario families" representing different global futures called A1, A2, B1, and B2. A's emphasize policy choices favoring economic growth, and B's emphasize social equity and environmental protection; 1's and 2's reflect predominance of either global or regional decision making, respectively. A1 is a world that maximizes market globalization, but there are important variations, focused primarily on different choices in technology. For example, A1FI is fossil fuel intensive; A1B draws on all energy sources, and A1T is high tech, non–fossil fuel intensive. B2 is a socially just and environmentally friendly future world where development is locally and regionally directed. According to SRES projections run in 2000, A1T (maximum growth, globally directed, with high tech, non–fossil fuel energy sources) and B1 (priority to social equity and environment, locally directed) produce the lowest total carbon emissions from 1990 to 2100, whereas A1FI (fossil fuel–intensive global growth) produces the highest emissions, roughly double the B1 total. Atmospheric carbon dioxide is now much higher than it has ever been over the past 650,000 years.[13] These projections show the absurdity of unlimited growth.

The SRES scenarios show global population reaching 8.7 to 10.4 billion, then dropping to some 7 billion by 2100, but GDP soars from $21 trillion in 1990 to $235 or $550 trillion by 2100. It is difficult to imagine such GDP levels ever being reached if the ecological footprint findings are correct that the world had already exceeded global bio-capacity before 1990. However, these high growth projections do reflect prevailing beliefs about the necessity for global economic growth still held by many world leaders and dominant member nation governments in the United Nations. SRES scenarios are thus conservative projections that do not seriously challenge the current dominance of pro-economic growth ideology. The stress on impersonal "driving forces" rather than decision makers and decision-making processes makes more economic growth, globalization, and high technology appear to be obvious and inevitable solutions to global warming.

American Intelligence Community Futures

In the mid-1990s the United States National Intelligence Council (NIC) looked ahead fifteen years to produce an American view of what the world might look like in 2010. This was followed by *Global Trends 2015*,[14] co-sponsored by the NIC, the State Department, and the Central Intelligence Agency (CIA), with assistance from non-governmental futurists. This project was initiated in 1999 and issued in 2000, on the eve of the George W. Bush presidency. The NIC is an advisory body that develops estimates of possible future outcomes of policies and events to guide the federal government's strategic planning. The NIC draws methods and data from academic and business experts, as well as from the American Intelligence Community (IC), which includes the U.S. military, the CIA, Homeland Security, the Department of Energy, and several other federal agencies. NIC reports go to the director of National Intelligence, who reports to the president, and they could have major effects on the world, given America's predominant role as an economic and military power. The NIC studies are strikingly short-ranged in comparison with the IPCC's futurist scenarios, but this may make them more influential as policy shapers.

The NIC *Global Trends 2015* report added governance, conflict, and the United States itself to the earlier SRES list of driving forces. The report makes economic globalization a "powerful driver" and explicitly acknowledges the impact of "U.S. hegemony" as a "key driver of the international systems" with impacts on the foreign and domestic policies of many countries in the world. The report declared, "U.S. global economic, technological, military, and diplomatic influence will be unparalleled among nations as well as regional and international organizations in 2015." The United States is treated as both the leading promoter and beneficiary of economic globalization, and "achieving broad and sustained high levels of global growth" is seen as crucial for a positive future. Although economic globalization and U.S. policy are treated as central concerns, global warming is described as an increasing concern, raising the possibility of rapid changes, grave danger, and enormous costs as a challenge to the international community. Shortages of oil or natural gas are not considered to be a concern, in part because the time frame is so short.

Global Trends 2015 developed four scenarios, all of which focused on the effects of economic globalization and a possible decline of American influence in the world: (1) Inclusive Globalization, (2) Pernicious Globalization, (3) Regional Competition, and (4) Post-Polar World. In Inclusive Globalization the majority of the world's people benefit from economic globalization, and only a few are left behind. Wealth is spread widely, new technology solves environmental problems, and government functions are replaced by "public-private" partnerships. Pernicious Globalization imagines global elites doing well, but the majority of people do not benefit. Governments are ineffective, illicit activities and conflicts increase, and WMD are used internally. Under Regional Competition Europe, East Asia, and the Americas prosper economically, leaving sub-Saharan Africa, the Middle East, and Central and South Asia to fall into regional and internal conflict. The Post-Polar World shows the United States withdrawing from Europe and Asia, and regional conflicts developing in Asia. Inclusive Globalization appears to be the best future, which is not surprising, because it would also produce the apparent stability and prosperity that would garner the best return on investment for HNWIs.

The NIC issued its fifteen-year forecast for 2020, *Mapping the Global Future*,[15] in 2004. This report was developed under the new political regime of the George W. Bush presidency after the terrorist attacks on the World Trade Center and Pentagon, and at the beginning of the American invasion and occupation of Iraq in 2003. The 2020 forecast is remarkably different from the 2015 scenarios. In the 2020 NIC report global warming is naturalized and minimized as "climate-change," and it is treated as a public relations problem for the United States and a matter for public debate. It becomes an ethical issue that will challenge American global authority. The sense of urgency expressed on global warming in *Global 2015* is replaced by an emphasis on doubt and uncertainty. Globalization is the big certainty, and it is described as a "largely irreversible" and a ubiquitous "mega-trend" force. For 2020, uncertainties are raised about the access of international oil companies to major oil fields in the face of increased demand. Politicized Islam and radical Islamic ideology, and extremist (terrorist) groups are viewed as a challenge to global governance. Insecurity will increase, and the UN may slide into "obsolescence." The 2020 scenarios were explicitly influenced by Shell Oil's futurist work, and considered four possible futures: (1) Davos World in which economic growth is led by China and India, (2) Pax Americana in which the United States remains the predominant global power, (3) A New Caliphate in which radical Islam attempts but fails to re-assert a pan-Islamic political dominance, and (4) Cycle of Fear where concerns over security and counter-terrorism radically transform America and other countries (table 8.1).

Unfortunately the American 2020 New Caliphate scenario, which is a metaphor for the American "Global War on Terrorism," effectively displaces the scenarios that the European Union, the IPCC, the UNEP, and the Global Scenarios Group consider to be the most promising futures. Furthermore, from the American government's 2020 view, political movements by indigenous peoples and other disadvantaged groups aimed at promoting human rights and improving local and regional economic autonomy are treated as examples of disruptive "Identity Politics" which would threaten American interests in economic globalization and global governance. Indigenous tribal groups are considered "ethno-religionists" and in that sense are lumped together with Muslim radicals. This apparent rejection of futures that would give human well-being and the environment priority over commerce shows how strongly commercial elites direct American society and culture.

Shell Oil's Perspective on the Future

A global business perspective on the future is represented by scenarios published by Royal Dutch Shell PLC, headquartered in the Netherlands. Shell is a transnational group of companies and the world's third-largest publicly traded corporation, according to *Fortune Magazine*'s 2006 *Global 500*.[16] Shell's revenues were nearly $307 billion, and it had operations in 140 countries. Shell has been producing global scenarios focused on the global business environment since the 1970s, and it is not surprising that the NIC consulted Shell's futurists for its own work. Shell's 2025 scenarios were issued in 2005,[17] shortly after the attack on the World Trade Center and the almost simultaneous December 2001 bankruptcy and subsequent collapse of Enron, the fifth-largest American corporation, because of criminal corporate misbehavior.[18] Shell provides an influential business view of the future from the second-largest oil company in the world. Thirteen of Shell's directors also sat on the boards of directors of

Table 8.1. Representative Global Future Scenarios, Government, Intergovernmental Organizations, Business, and Civil Society.

Government		Intergovernmental		Business	Civil Society
USA	EU	IPCC	UNEP	Shell	Tellus
Project 2020	TERRA-2000	SRES	GEO-3	Global 2025	GSG
Davos World	A WTO World	A1 Global Growth	Markets First Centric	Market Forces	Market
Cycle of Fear	B Security Regimes	A2 Regional Growth	Security First	State Centric	Barbarization
New Caliphate	C Ecosocial	B2 Regional Environmental	Sustainability First	Socio-Centric Transitions	Great
Pax Americana	D Resource Dictatorship	B1 Global Environment	Policy First	State Centric	Policy Reform

Sources: NIC, 2004; Cave, 2003; Nakicenovic and Swart, 2000.

twenty other global corporations in 2005, giving them management decision making over a combined $1.1 trillion dollars in revenues, which was nearly the GDP of the Russian Federation.

The Shell scenarios identify just three forces shaping the future business environment, which it calls market-centric, society-centric, and state-centric, each force aiming at efficiency, social cohesion or social justice, and security, respectively. These forces represent decision making by just three often-opposing sets of human agents: business elites and investors, ordinary people and non-governmental organizations, and government leaders. Shell describes the interaction between these agents as a three-cornered dilemma, which it calls the "Trilemma Triangle," because the objectives of each actor tend to be mutually exclusive. Presumably no more than two of these forces can win, and one must lose. This means the future will necessarily involve trade-offs. There are only three 2025 Shell scenarios: (1) Open Doors in which business elites and society win, government loses; (2) Low Trust Globalization, in which business and government win, society loses; and (3) Flags, in which government and society win, business loses. Shell rejects as "utopian" the possibility that one point of the triangle could dominate, whether business, society, or government. Shell's Trilemma masks the dilemma of scale while also disregarding the large socio-cultural transformations that will be required to produce a truly sustainable planetary society. The reality of course is that the supremacy of society was precisely what defined the tribal world, and social supremacy was human supremacy achieved by suppressing personal aggrandizers. Tribal societies also succeeded because they did not require hierarchies and large-scale production and distribution systems to enhance individual power. Whenever possible tribal people have resisted the growth of hierarchies, whether military, political, or commercial, because hierarchies are inherently dehumanizing. As hierarchies expand they become metaphorical machines transforming subordinated people into automatons.

For Shell, Open Doors is obviously the most desirable future, because Shell expects it to result in the greatest economic prosperity. Under Open Doors business regulates itself voluntarily, and non-governmental organizations represent civil society. However, given the concentration of economic power in the present global system, it seems clear that if government were to be relegated to a subordinate position and business regulation became voluntary, local communities and societies would lose decision-making power. Even now non-governmental organizations are highly dependent on wealthy donors and very large corporations for funding.

Shell's 2025 scenario warns ominously of three "discontinuities" that may adversely shape the future: (1) the dependence of further economic growth on energy consumption, (2) concerns over the long-term supply of energy, and (3) the risk of "catastrophic climate change" and how this is connected to carbon emissions and carbon markets. This acknowledgment that the Open Doors scenario may not produce sustainable development is amazing from a company that benefited enormously from fossil fuel–based globalization.

Sustainable Global Futures

The elite-directed imperial and commercial worlds produced mixed benefits and have proven to be very costly to human well-being and the environment. Scale and power theory proposes that elite-directed growth is responsible for the sustainability crisis in the contemporary commercial world, and in view of the failure of elite-directed growth to deliver on its promises, serious alternatives are in order. The corollary to the theory of elite-directed growth is that democratically directed growth disperses both power and costs. Democratic decision making may prove better able to maintain household and human well-being, rather than simply increasing the flow of energy and materials, or expanding population. Constructing democratic decision-making structures in a society approaching 10 billion people will require new social forms that mimic the advantages of very small-scale societies. Twenty-first-century people can take advantage of new information technologies, vast accumulations of knowledge, and new social networks, organizations, and institutions to produce democratically directed development that will transform the contemporary world into a sustainable world where benefits are widely dispersed and equitably shared rather than concentrated; human well-being is fostered; and natural resources are protected and restored for the benefit of future generations.

TERRA-2000 and Information Society

At the beginning of the new millennium many international efforts were under way to reevaluate the prospects for the global future as planners continued to grapple with the problem of making economic growth and development actually sustainable. For example, in 1998–2002 the European Commission, executive branch of the European Union, funded a research project called TERRA-2000 to explore how new computer technologies could make it possible to simultaneously promote economic growth, social equity, and sustainable development. The research was carried out by a network of research institutes from all over the world, including the RAND Corporation, which had also contributed to the *NIC 2020 Project*. *TERRA-2000* used the *International Futures* (IF) computer modeling system that began in the 1970s as an effort to improve on the Limits to Growth model, and was in its fourth generation by 2000.[19]

TERRA-2000 assumed that computerization of the global economy by the universal adoption of Information and Communication Technologies (ICTs) would be a transformative event, producing an "Information Society" (IS) and a "Global Networked Knowledge Society" (GNK) in the twenty-first century. This would have the potential of reducing conflict because people would be linked by a maze of allegiances cross-cutting other identities. Such a transformative outcome could mimic on a global level the overall social effects of marriage alliances, exchange networks, small-scale social groups, and the low consumption affluence of the tribal world. Information technology makes it possible for people to form widely dispersed social networks, share information, and make decisions that bypass rulers at the top of sprawling hierarchies. This could make democracy work at a global level, and has truly revolutionary potential for transforming the commercial world by decentralizing decision-making power and by making it possible to equitably distribute social power and the benefits of economic prosperity. There would also be important environmental benefits. If the Information Society remains democratic it could eventually be as transformative as the politicization process that created the imperial world, or as the invention of capitalism and the commercial world. *TERRA-2000* researchers summarized the potential of the Information Society as follows: "The new technologies of the Information Society (ISTs) seem likely to offer scope to enable economic growth, and to allow a more equitable distribution of wealth, without necessarily increasing consumption, pollution and energy use."[20]

However, the Information Society is not just about technology. The application of previous technologies such as steam engines, electricity, and internal combustion engines did transform societies, but not always in humane and sustainable ways, because these technologies and social transformations were directed by an elite few who made use of public funds but did not always have broad popular support. Elites used these earlier technologies to create very large-scale business enterprises that allowed a few to gain vast economic power and concentrate decision making. The hope is that new information technologies will facilitate more democratic decision making. They may also make it possible to "dematerialize" production and distribution processes, increasing efficiency, and thereby reducing energy and material requirements. More importantly, in a more democratic society the benefits of any efficiencies gained could more easily be broadly shared.

The Information Society can also involve more extreme forms of dematerialization, which are sometimes called "immaterialization." This means replacing material goods with immaterial services, allowing GNP to grow at a much lower unit cost because energy flows and physical consumption would be reduced. Knowledge can be freely shared, especially when patent and copyright restrictions are reduced. Immaterialization is the essence of tribal society where, as we have seen, both material culture and consumption are minimized. The "good life" in the tribal world is defined by social relationships, and the emphasis is on individual and household well-being, which futurist researchers are now measuring as "happiness" or satisfaction with life.

Thus, in an Information Society the economy could actually continue to grow even as material costs declined, but such an outcome would not occur naturally, and probably not without resistance from elites entrenched in the old society and culture. New political structures would be needed. This sort of growth would in reality be more social and cultural than purely economic, even though it would be measured as "economic" growth in national accounts. Growth would be in intangible wealth, not in factories, cars, and buildings. All of these promising outcomes depend on people having full access to computer networks and digital information, as well as education and knowledge. These social distribution issues will necessarily be shaped by democratic processes to create new public policies and new institutional structures.

It seems clear that in the absence of supportive public decision making, even the best information technology will not automatically produce a sustainable global society. *TERRA-2000* considered four different future scenarios (A, B, C, and D) for the twenty-first century involving logical combinations of social equity and economic growth at a global level (table 8.2).

Scenario A is a future dominated by the existing World Trade Organization and free-market economics, giving maximum economic growth priority over environmental concerns. As long as energy remains cheap there will be little market incentive for dematerializing growth. The natural tendency for growth to concentrate social power makes it difficult to achieve social equity when growth is maximized in the absence of major countervailing social policy. This causes wealth and income gaps to widen

Table 8.2.   Four *TERRA-2000* Scenarios for the Twenty-first Century: Social Equity and Economic Growth (Cave 2003).

	Social Equity	No Social Equity
No Growth Limits	A. WTO World No Growth Limits Social Equity	B. Security Regime No Growth Limits No Social Equity
Growth Limits	C. Eco-Social EU Social Market Strict, but Fair Enviro-Rules Social Equity	D. Resource Dictatorship Growth Limits Enforced Asymmetrically No Social Equity

throughout the world in spite of token efforts at poverty reduction. The world's most influential leaders seemed to have been following this path in the year 2000 because it appeared to be in their immediate best interests, but computer simulations suggest that this path will quickly produce unacceptable social and environmental costs for the majority.

Scenario B also maximizes economic growth but makes little attempt at social equity, causing wealth to be concentrated in the already wealthiest countries. This compounds global environmental problems by dividing the world into rich and poor regions, generating conflict and terrorism, and forcing rich countries to protect themselves with military force and elaborate national security measures. Scenario D limits growth in poor countries to protect the environment for the benefit of the already rich, but by imposing social inequity it creates a dangerous and unstable world that would certainly not be sustainable.

Scenario C is the Eco-Social model already being followed by the European Union and a few other countries as a matter of high-priority public policy. It seeks to limit growth to protect the environment, and to distribute benefits to maximize social equity. This approach requires a knowledgeable citizenry, as well as highly democratic and participatory governments in which social power is decentralized and widely dispersed. According to *TERRA-2000* simulations it is the only scenario that has the potential to be sustainable over the twenty-first century. These conditions would also be ideal for a flourishing Information Society.

UN *GEO-3* Global Futures

The United Nations Environment Program (UNEP) published *Global Environment Outlook 3 (GEO-3)*[21] in 2003. It presents an unusually grim view of the near future up to 2031, drawing on scenarios and simulations originally produced by the Global Scenario Group (GSG) in cooperation with the Stockholm Environment Institute (SEI) beginning in 1995. The *GEO-3* report considered four alternative futures which they called Markets First, Security First, Sustainability First, and Policy First, each corresponding closely to the *TERRA-2000* A, B, C, D scenarios (table 8.1). Even though *GEO-3* used somewhat different computer programs and modeling techniques, the results were similar to *TERRA-2000*, showing that only the Sustainability First or the Eco-Social scenarios produced generally acceptable futures. The *GEO-3* scenarios are also very similar to those presented in the Millennium Ecosystem Assessment Synthesis, which labels four alternative scenarios: Global Orchestration, Order from Strength, Adapting Mosaic, and Techno-Garden.[22] Thus, multiple modeling pathways lead to the same sustainable alternative. This hopeful future was described as follows: "Sustainability First pictures a world in which a new development paradigm emerges in response to the challenge of sustainability, supported by new, more equitable values and institutions."[23]

The Great Transition Initiative

Envision an equitable future of material sufficiency for all, where the quality of human knowledge, creativity, and self-realization, not the quantity of goods and services, signals development. (*The Great Transition Initiative*, Tellus Institute)[24]

Organizations such as the Global Scenario Group (GSG) and the Stockholm Environment Institute (SEI) are hubs in a vast international network connecting researchers, funders, and client organizations worldwide. This decentralized network is part of the evolving Information Society (IS) discussed earlier, and the ideas produced by the individual researchers in the network have become crucial tools for solving global problems. Their findings and recommendations will need to reach political decision makers who will be able to respond effectively. The GSG is a network of twenty-one researchers from nineteen countries representing all parts of the world. In addition to the SEI, their major support came from prominent non-governmental organizations and philanthropic foundations including the Rockefeller Foundation, the Japan-based Nippon Foundation, and the Global Industrial and Social Progress Research Institute (GISPRI) as well as the UN Environment Programme. These GSG funders and clients are truly global. The directors and trustees of GISPRI represent a cross-section of the directors of Japan's major commercial corporations. The SEI is headquartered in Stockholm, Sweden, but also has offices in Thailand, the United Kingdom, the United States, and Estonia.

The Boston-based Tellus Institute, founded by futurist Paul Raskin, who also founded and co-coordinates the GSG, has been at the forefront of sustainable development efforts. As an independent civil society organization, Tellus has been able to envision alternative futures with dramatic social and culture transformations in governments, intergovernmental organizations in the business world, and in global society. One of the institute's most important activities is *The Great Transition Initiative* (GTI) and related activities that consider how business corporations, global politics, and institutions, communities, and economic systems could be redesigned to more effectively promote human well-being and protect the environment in a newly evolving planetary civilization. For example, the GTI uses special series of GSG scenarios that offers a clearer view of future worlds than the scenarios used by the IPCC or the UN Environment Programme's *GEO-3* work. Initially the Great Transition was one of four global scenarios along with Market Forces, Barbarization, and Policy Reform.[25] The Great Transition broadly corresponded with the most socially and environmentally sensitive worlds previously discussed (table 8.1). The GTI distinguishes three broad worlds: (1) the Conventional World, the current economic growth-maximizing path, represented by both Market Forces and Policy Reform, because both endorse economic growth as the primary objective; (2) Barbarization, in which the Conventional World fails; and (3) the Great Transition, in which people make the radical changes required to create a sustainable planetary society. This seems very compatible with earlier proposals advocating political decentralization, "down-scaling" of markets, and reduced use of energy and materials.[26] The Great Transition future assumes that people will change their values,[27] but it allows for considerable diversity. There are two major variants of the Great Transition, describing alternative socio-cultural types that could co-exist: Eco-communalism and New Sustainability. Eco-communalism is represented by peoples who reject economic globalization, choosing instead to maximize local community and regional autonomy. This is the alternative that many indigenous peoples and existing tribal societies appear to favor, and it corresponds closely with the bioregional approaches. Eco-communalism would be very compatible with the humanistic environmentally aware global society envisioned for the New Sustainability scenario. New Sustainability blends elements of *TERRA-2000*'s Eco-Social alternative C, IPCC's SRES B1 and B2 scenarios, and the UNEP's Sustainability First. It also contains important elements of the society-centric alternative that Shell rejects as impossible.

Transforming the Corporation

> [A]t the turn of the twenty-first century, the corporation is arguably the most powerful social institution. . . . The co-existence of surging corporate scale, wealth and influence with persistent and widespread global poverty and a compromised biosphere raises the question: if corporations are so powerful and, as many claim, contributing so much to global wealth creation, why do billions of people remain mired in poverty and why do the earth's vital signs continue to deteriorate? (White 2006: 1)[28]

The *Great Transition Initiative* includes a specific focus on the need to transform business corporations in order to achieve the Great Transition. In a world in which the 500 largest companies have revenues equal to 43 percent of global GDP in 2005, as noted in chapter 1, as few as 3,000 people are making crucial decisions over the allocation of capital resources that affect the lives of billions of people, as well as the future of the planet.[29] It does indeed seem reasonable to suggest that corporate business institutions need to be culturally transformed so that they can function more effectively in a sustainable world system that makes human well-being more important than the accumulation of financial wealth. Corporations are human cultural constructions, and scale distortions of this magnitude have resulted from government policies granting immortality to corporations and setting few effective limits to their power. In a democratically organized world people could change the cultural rules that shape corporations and the distribution of the wealth that corporations produce.

The scale of corporations and the power of their owners and directors at the beginning of the twenty-first century is almost incomprehensible, but it can be illustrated by the example of ExxonMobil, in 2006 the world's largest corporation. Its revenues at the end of the year were over $370 billion. Exxon fully owned 105 other companies headquartered in 25 countries, and was a part owner of 36 other companies in 8 more countries. Ten of its directors also directed 21 other large companies with combined revenues of $529 billion more.[30] This means that these ten individuals controlled companies producing total revenues of $900 billion, which was more than the GDP of Brazil, and which exceeded the combined GDP of 112 poor countries with 908 million people. When just 10 people control this much economic power in the midst of so much poverty it suggests a world that is obscenely out of balance. In theory ExxonMobil's shareholders control the company, but only according to the number of shares held, and in reality few shareholders actually vote. In 2007, there were only 614,599 registered ExxonMobil shareholders holding 5.8 billion shares, which at current share value of $69.91 per share, was then worth $407.7 billion. The top owner was Barclay's Global, a trillion-dollar investment bank headquartered in London. It held 239 million ExxonMobil shares, worth $16 billion, but even that very large amount was a mere 4 percent. The 25 largest owners held a total of 28 percent of the shares, but except for one billionaire individual, the top owners were all financial institutions such as banks, retirement funds, and mutual funds, the largest of which managed over a trillion dollars in shares in many companies on behalf of many other investors. This means that most shareholders simply delegated ultimate decision-making power to a handful of virtually anonymous corporate directors. Shareholders often are only temporary owners, seeking short-term profits on price fluctuations. Such extreme delegation of authority would be unimaginable in a small-scale society, but this impersonality does help explain why global resources, human and natural, are being squandered.

The obvious cultural solutions to such disempowering forms of giant corporate organization are readily available, and include the S corporation in the United States, and various forms of employee-owned businesses. The owners of S corporations must be individuals, not other corporations, institutions, or business partnerships, and there can be no more than 100 owners. This effectively makes owners a face-to-face group. Some relatively large corporate businesses are privately held. This means their shares are not publicly traded, and there might be only a few individual owners. For example, Menasha Corporation is a manufacturing company headquartered in Wisconsin that had $1 billion in revenues in 2003. It had 3,500 employees, but only 140 owners—all descendants of one man who founded the company in 1849. The Colville Tribe in eastern Washington State has some 9,000 enrolled members and a 1.4-million-acre reservation.[31] The Colvilles own and manage a credit union and 14 tribal businesses in gaming, tourism, construction, and wood products. They employ 1,000 people and generate some $120 million in revenues. Such small companies can be very responsive to the interests of all of their owners, because decision making, costs, and benefits are broadly shared.

Farmers have a long history of cooperative production and marketing organizations. For example in the Pacific Northwest states of Idaho, Oregon, and Washington some 700 dairy farmers own Westfarm Foods, headquartered in Seattle. Westfarm was originally the Northwest Dairymen's Association, founded in 1918. These farmer-owners pool their milk, and in 2006 produced some $1.5 billion in revenues from dairy products marketed under the Darigold brand and processed in 11 plants, employing 1,200 workers.

CROPP (Cooperative Regions of Organic Producer Pools), a similar co-op in Wisconsin founded in 1988, is owned by 801 independent farmers in 24 states and Canada.[32] They market organic dairy products under the Organic Valley brand, producing revenues of $242 million in 2004.

The Mondragón Cooperatives

The Mondragón cooperative system centered in the Basque region of northern Spain is one of the most famous examples of how corporate commercial businesses can be intentionally organized to put community and employees and long-term sustainability ahead of short-term profits. The Mondragón cooperatives were founded in 1955 and by 2005 had grown to some 63,500 member shareowners, producing revenues of $15 billion.[33] Known as MCC (Mondragón Corporación Cooperativa), in 2005 the Mondragón cooperatives were a network of 108 cooperatives, 138 subsidiary companies—all primarily worker owned—and 18 support organizations, including training and research centers. All of these were organized in three functional groups: financial (banking), industrial (manufacturing), and distribution (retail markets), under a democratically elected congress with a general council and standing committees. The distribution group operates hundreds of supermarkets, shops, and restaurants under the EROSKI brand in Spain and France. MCC manufactures a wide variety of high-tech components, equipment, tools, and household appliances. It is the seventh-largest business corporation in Spain, and operates 57 subsidiaries in 16 countries, demonstrating that industrial production can be organized democratically and in a way that diffuses, rather than concentrates, decision-making power as well as wages, benefits, and profits. Worker management and ownership, democratic decision making, and scale limits on number of employees in individual cooperatives and companies are central MCC "human and participatory" organizational principles. The salary scale is structured so that the entry-level worker earns a livable wage of $16,480 (U.S. dollars) per year, and the highest rank receives a maximum of $98,880, which is just six times higher than the minimum. Workers buy shares in their companies and receive an annual share of the dividends. The success of the Mondragón system is clearly shown by the fact that the Basque districts of Spain have some of the highest GDPs and household incomes in the country.[34]

In comparison, the American corporation ConAgra, 434th-largest in the 2005 Fortune Global 500[35] with $15.5 billion in revenues, was approximately the same size as MCC by revenues, but it was organized like

ExxonMobil, the world's largest publicly traded corporation. ConAgra's ownership system concentrated benefits and decision making, contributing to the wealth of a few very large owners and managers, but provided only wages to the company's 33,000 employees. ConAgra's 30,000 shareholders were less than half the 63,500 worker-owners of MCC, but 495 of ConAgra's owners were institutions holding a total of 61 percent. The three largest institutional owners were mutual funds—Old Mutual, Capital Group, and State Street—owning 21 percent. Eighteen ConAgra managers owned 7 percent. Most ConAgra stock held directly by individual owners would have conveyed little benefit or control.

Bhutan's Middle Path

> We need to ask how the dramatic changes propelling us into the 21st century will affect prospects for happiness? How will shrinkage of biological and cultural diversities affect the individual and collective potential for happiness. Will the particular scientific world-view of contemporary education and curricula undercut in the next century the basis for the culturally rich and value-full basis of daily life? . . . How will global capitalism and competitive international trade make people more vulnerable to unhappiness and uncertainty of their lives? (Thinley, *Gross National Happiness*)[36]

Bhutan is a Buddhist kingdom in the Himalayan Mountains between India and Tibet. It has intentionally remained on the margins of, but not totally isolated from, the commercial world until very recently. Bhutan's rulers accepted British protection in 1865, and they have wisely managed to remain a peaceful buffer state between India and China. Because it has remained so marginal to the global export market, and because the kingdom imposed strict environmental protections, Bhutan's natural resources are largely intact, making it an exceptional showpiece of biodiversity in South Asia. In 2007 the kingdom was moving toward full democracy with a draft constitution and a national referendum planned. The head of state is a hereditary monarch, who since 1998 has served at the will of the National Assembly. Estimates place the population at 810,000 to 2.3 million, and the PPP economy was just $2.9 billion, for a per capita of only $1,400.[37] The exchange rate economy was only $840 million, reflecting the country's continuing isolation and its predominately rural, agrarian economy. In 1995 Bhutan's largest city had only 35,000 people. There were only 20 other urban places, and 85 percent of the population was rural, largely pursuing subsistence farming and pastoralism. By most international measures, the

Table 8.3.   GDP/Capita, Globalization, and Development Indexes for Six Countries.

Country	GDP/capita	GI	HDI	GEM	ESI	HPI	Population
Bhutan	$1,272	—	0.53	—	53.5	61.1	2,279,723
China	$4,990	54	0.75	—	38.6	56.0	1,288,400,000
Norway	$37,300	14	0.96	0.92	73.4	39.2	4,600,000
Panama	$6,310	24	0.80	0.56	57.7	63.5	3,000,000
United States	$37,500	4	0.94	0.79	53.0	28.8	291,000,000
Uruguay	$7,980	—	0.84	0.50	71.8	49.3	3,400,000

GDP/capita in PPP dollars, 2006 or most recent.
GI = Globalization Index ranking (A.T. Kearney).
HDI = Human Development Index 2005 (UNDP).
GEM = Gender Equity Measure (UNDP).
ESI = Environmental Sustainability Index 2005 (Yale Center for Environmental Law & Policy).
HPI = Happy Planet Index, 2006.
Marks, Nic, and Saamah Abdallah, Andrew Simms, and Sam Thompson. 2006. *The Happy Planet Index: An Index of Human Well-Being and Environmental Impact.* London: New Economics Foundation. www.neweconomics.org/gen/z_sys_PublicationDetail.aspx?PID=225

country would be considered underdeveloped and its people poor, but what is striking about Bhutan is that it ranks number 13 out of 178 countries on the *Happy Planet Index*[38] due to its high life satisfaction rating, moderate life expectancy, and very low ecological footprint. The country is doing very well at protecting the environment and making sure that people are happy, but health and education could be improved to bring the country in line with UN development standards (table 8.3).

The government of Bhutan formed a National Environment Commission (NEC) in 1990 and formally adopted a "Middle Path" for sustainable development.[39] The Middle Path calls for increased agricultural self-sufficiency, political decentralization, and modest development of hydropower to support mineral-based industries, but this is a very cautious approach. The *National Environment Strategy*, which implements the Middle Path, is explicitly differentiated from the Western concept of development, which is thought to emphasize "waste and excess," unsustainable growth, competitive consumption, and imported manufactured goods. Instead, the Middle Path promotes Buddhist and tribal values of placing community above individual, and stresses communal enrichment by acquisition of knowledge, with the goal of overcoming the "delusions arising from ignorance, aggression, and the desire for consumption and acquisition." Development is aimed at modest increases in material living standards to improve health and education, while at the same time preventing unsustainable population growth and urbanization. This path to sustainable development is represented by the goal of "Gross National Happiness" and the Buddhist concept of respect for all life, together with karma—the belief that what one does today affects the future. This is also supported by tribal beliefs that mountains, rivers, rocks, and soil are the domains of spirit beings.

In 1998, Lyonpo Jigmi Y. Thinley, chairman of the Council of Ministers, following the lead of King Jigme Singye Wangchuck, addressed a UN Millennium development conference in Seoul, describing Bhutan's adoption of the "Gross National Happiness" (GNH) as its development goal.[40] In his address, Minister Thinley boldly stated: "His Majesty has proclaimed that the ultimate purpose of government is to promote the happiness of the people. His Majesty has said, 'Gross National Happiness is more important than Gross National Product', and has given happiness precedence over economic prosperity." Thinley recommended that happiness be incorporated in the UN's Human Development Index (HDI), but only the New Economics Foundation's *Happy Planet Index* has incorporated happiness into a development index. Following Thinley's address the government of Bhutan promptly organized a conference on Gross National Happiness, and its National Planning Commission adopted its *Bhutan 2020: A Vision for Peace, Prosperity and Happiness*.[41] Bhutan's circumstances are unique, but they offer a model for transformative development change for the "developed" world.

Toward a Sustainable Planetary Society

The best hope for the future is that people will create a sustainable planetary society in response to the contemporary crisis of environmental degradation, poverty, and social protest. Elsewhere I have argued that this transformation is already under way, and will hopefully be complete by 2050. It will be brought about by popularly based non-violent political action to redistribute social power and decentralize decision making in order to promote human economic and social rights, freedom, social equity, and sustainability.[42] In this transformation global corporations would lose much of their immortality, omniscience, and omnipotence, just as monarchs lost their divinity at the beginning of the Commercial Age. Totalitarian, plutocratic, and aristocratic political systems would be replaced by genuinely democratic systems. This new socio-cultural future emerges as a clear consensus of the futurist scenarios discussed above, and can appropriately be called the "Eco-Social World" following the terminology used by *TERRA-2000*. In the Eco-Social World social power would be decentralized, local economies would have priority over the global, knowledge and information would be more important than machine technology, and the dominant ideology would be humanist. Many of the technological details of this new socio-cultural world appear in existing futurist scenarios, and are outlined in books such as Lester Brown's *Plan B*.[43] Much more than new technology, or the design and construction of "ecocities,"[44] will be required. Power will need to be decentralized and redistributed, and total flows of energy and materials will need to be reduced.[45]

Scaling Down: The Small Nations Alternative

> Thus we see that a small-state world would not only solve the problems of social brutality and war: it would solve the equally terrible problems of oppression and tyranny. It would solve all problems arising from power. (Kohr, *Breakdown of Nations*)[46]

The most promising approaches to the future are those proposals by various anthropologists, ecologists, economists, and social activists for truly sustainable and humane cultural systems based on local communities, ecosystems, regions, and nationalities. In effect they would adapt the proven achievements of domestic-scale societies to the world of market commerce and industrial technology. All of these approaches assume that most world problems are problems of scale. Global markets and multinational corporations are simply too large and too focused on profit making to operate in the human interest. The alternative is to scale down the organization of cultural systems to make them responsive to human needs.

In 1957, in an obscure book titled *The Breakdown of Nations*, economist Leopold Kohr modestly proposed a "new and unified political philosophy" based on a "theory of size."[47] This new theory contained the solution to all the world's problems, Kohr argued. According to Kohr, the basic problem underlying all forms of "social misery" was "bigness"—nations had become too large. Large nations simply could not prevent their power from becoming internally oppressive, and they could not prevent devastating wars. Kohr identified precisely the problems in state organization that emerge when states are contrasted with domestic-scale tribal societies, even though he did not have a clear picture of what tribal societies were like. Kohr argued persuasively that a world divided into a global system of small nations of relatively equal power would be safer and more humane. His conclusions were so profound and were applied to so many diverse world problems that he was virtually ignored. The original edition of his book was published in England, and only five hundred copies reached the United States. The book was soon out of print and has now virtually disappeared. The work did inspire fellow economist E. F. Schumacher to write *Small Is Beautiful*,[48] a work stressing the advantages of small-scale solutions and "appropriate technology" for economic problems. As I will show here, many others have followed a similar scale-based approach to contemporary human problems.

Kohr's proposal implies that world problems will not be solved by the United Nations or by deregulating international trade. Solutions require maximum cultural diversity. They must be worked out independently in each country and region of the world, preferably without regard to external economic or political interests and pressures. A world of small nations would, of course, still contain nations, and each nation would presumably still be stratified and hierarchical, but the nations could in theory be more responsive to the needs of their people. Furthermore, like tribes, they would be dependent on their own resources and would have an immediate interest in taking care of them. There would be room for great diversity in the kinds of solutions that might be developed to solve problems, with local culture being related to local environments. This is not to say that a small-nation world would be a Utopia or totally free from war. There would still be internal conflicts and perhaps local wars, but both would be easier to contain and much less destructive than global wars of the sort fought twice in the twentieth century.

Kohr pointed out that the kind of small states that he envisioned already existed, as represented by local cultural and linguistic groupings. These "nations" simply needed to be granted political autonomy. He suggested that the large nations could break themselves down into appropriately sized small nations by providing local "nationalities" with equal voting power within a federal system that could then dissolve itself. Anthropologist Sol Tax made a strikingly similar proposal in 1977, suggesting that the world be divided into 10,000 relatively self-sufficient, politically autonomous "localities" averaging 500,000 people each.[49] These local territories were to be connected by an egalitarian global communication network that sounds very much like the Internet computer network and would be very compatible with the *TERRA-2000* Eco-Social World.

Recent history suggests that the breakup of great powers can be accomplished swiftly by a highly centralized government, given the example of the former Soviet Union, which dissolved itself on December 26, 1991. However, the sudden transition from socialism to capitalism was carried out in a way that concentrated enormous economic power in private hands, causing great social distress, widespread poverty, and disorder. Russia's transition to capitalism was so chaotic that by 2007 it was estimated that fifty-three Russian billionaires were suddenly worth $282 billion dollars, and just thirty-six men had gained ownership of one-fourth of the economy.[50]

The United States,
Happy Planets, and Billionaires

This section compares the United States with other countries on a variety of measures to explore the possibilities for national-level socio-cultural changes that could better enhance sustainability. This discussion draws on several sources of cross-national data, including the online *International Futures* computer modeling system, which provides multiple databases for all contemporary national societies in the world, along with software tools for comparative analysis.[51] Cross-national analysis can identify thresholds at which growth produces human benefits, but beyond which negative costs may begin to accumulate. Such analysis is crucial, because as we have seen in previous chapters, larger societies and economies are likely to be less sustainable than smaller societies, and they may be less effective at producing human well-being. Smaller-scale societies and cultural systems may be crucial models for creating a sustainable future for the United States and the world.

International Futures data clearly shows that there is little relationship between the size of a society and life expectancy, or reported happiness levels, although larger societies do tend to have larger economies. Not surprisingly, although economic growth can produce very large national economies, it does not by itself produce health and happiness. In seven countries with economies of a trillion dollars or higher—China, Japan, India, Germany, France, Italy, and Russia—the proportion of people who reported being very happy with their lives ranged from a low of 6 percent in Russia to a high of only 31 percent in France. In four countries—Nigeria, Tanzania, Venezuela, and Puerto Rico—the "very happy" percentages ranged from 53 to 67 percent, although their economies were comparatively small ($21 to $139 billion).

There is a small tendency for larger societies to have lower per capita GDPs, and very small countries to have very high per capita GDPs. In 2003 the tiny Falkland Islands society, with fewer than 3,000 people, had an average GDP of $25,278 in U.S. Purchasing Power Parity (PPP) dollars, and Bermuda, with 65,773 people, had the world's highest per capita GDP of $68,417.[52] Raising per capita GDP only appears to improve quality of life up to a certain point. Japan achieved the highest average life expectancy in the world (eighty-two years), with a per capita GDP of just $27,111. At a lower GDP extreme, Bosnia and Herzegovina enjoyed a life expectancy of seventy-four years with a per capita income of just $1,042. Every society with a GDP of $10,000 or higher had life expectancies of seventy years or more, and nearly two-thirds of the 32 countries with per capita GDPs of between $5,000 and $10,000 had life expectancies of seventy years or higher, well above the average of sixty-five years for 181 countries. These figures are striking, because average global GDP per capita was $8,760 in 2004,[53] which would thus appear to be sufficient to comfortably provide everyone in the world with a life expectancy of seventy years or more if equitably distributed. From this perspective, the United States, with a PPP per capita GDP of $39,710, was far over the minimum needed to provide high life expectancy. Distribution is the crucial variable. There is a tendency for life expectancy to decline and mortality to increase as income inequality increases, even in countries that would be considered rich.[54] Inequality is unhealthy because it increases stress, whether or not absolute deprivation occurs.

The *International Futures* data showed that more than two-thirds of Nigerians reported being very happy, which was the highest proportion for 64 countries, even though their per capita GDP was just $1,050—second lowest of the sample. Only a third of the population of Luxembourg reported being very happy, although Luxembourg was the highest ($62,298) GDP per capita country in the happiness sample. The United States (GDP per capita $37,562) was only slightly higher, with less than half, or just under 40 percent, very happy. Fewer than 20 percent reported being very happy in fifteen relatively high, $10,000-plus GDP per capita countries. Again, how income is distributed, and what it is used for, makes the difference.

The persistence of economic growth-centered development ideology is supported by simple correlations between expanding economies and commonly recognized measures of human well-being, but such associations are misleading. For example, at first glance, economic growth appears to be beneficial when countries are ranked by the United Nations' "Human Development Index"(HDI),[55] in comparison with the "Globalization Index" designed by A. T. Kearney Inc.,[56] a business management consulting company. There is a general trend for the HDI to improve as globalization increases, but there are important exceptions. The Kearney Globalization Index ranks each country based on its international activities on four dimensions: economic integration (trade and investment), personal contact (international travel, remittances, phone calls), technology (Internet users), and political engagement (international organizations, treaties, foreign aid). In 2005 Singapore was ranked number one as the most globalized country in the world; the United States ranked number four, and Iran was number sixty-two at the bottom.[57] Not surprisingly, many high per capita GDP European countries were grouped tightly at the top of the HDI, but less-globalized countries showed wide variation in their HDI rankings. For example, Argentina, which ranked number foury-seven on globalization, was higher in HDI than the Czech Republic, which ranked fifteen for globalization.

Human development and globalization are complex phenomena, and simple correlations do not by themselves prove that one variable causes another, or that the most important variables are included. The Human Development Index was designed to reflect life expectancy, knowledge, and standard of living, all of which are important human values, but many other factors also matter. The HDI has many variants but it most commonly combines life expectancy at birth, adult literacy rate, school enrollment, and GDP per capita in a single index number. For example, Norway had the top HDI ranking (0.963), reflecting a life expectancy of 79.4 years, a literacy rate of 99 percent, and a per capita GDP of $37,670. Niger had the lowest HDI (0.281), with a life expectancy of 44.4 years, an adult literacy rate of 14.4 percent, and a per capita GDP of only $835. These are all important, readily measured variables, but they are often indirect and incomplete measures of human well-being because they leave out other variables such as political and economic participation in decision making, wealth and income distribution, and power over economic resources. These latter variables are explicitly included in the UN's "Gender Empowerment Measure" (GEM), a variant of the HDI, which emphasizes equity between female and male, but it is less often cited. A gender focus is important, but it also overlooks group- and community-level human rights. In 2003 Norway rated at the top of both the HDI (0.963) and the GEM (0.928) indexes, but it ranked only fourteenth for globalization. The United States was in tenth place on the HDI (0.944), and twelfth on the GEM (0.793).

The most obvious shortcoming of both the HDI and the Globalization Index is that they ignore environmental sustainability. This problem was addressed by the "Environmental Sustainability Index 2005" (ESI) produced by the Yale Center for Environmental Law and Policy and the Center for International Earth Science Information Network (CIESIN) at Columbia University for the World Economic Forum and the European Commission.[58] The ESI is a very comprehensive and highly empirical quantitative measure that shows how a given country is presently managing the environment, and what its future trajectory is likely to be. It explicitly combines social and environmental variables grouped in five components: (1) The existing quality of the environment, including biodiversity, land, and water; (2) Efforts to reduce environmental stresses, such as lowering population growth, pollution, and the ecological footprint; (3) Efforts to reduce human vulnerability, by improving nutrition and public health, and reducing exposure to environmental hazards; (4) Social and institutional capacity to set and enforce environmental standards, and the technical basis to manage resources and improve efficiency; and (5) Global stewardship, especially international cooperation to reduce global warming and manage cross-national environmental issues. The ESI draws on a vast database to quantify 76 variables, and averages 21 equally weighted indicators to yield a single index calculated for 146 countries. Scores range from a high of 75.1 (Finland), suggesting the most environmentally sustainable country, to 29.2 (North Korea), the least sustainable country.

The ESI rankings of 146 countries reveal a weak trend for environmental sustainability to decline as societies grow larger, but the many exceptions make it clear that population is not the most crucial variable. However, there may be important population scale thresholds, because the top five ESI countries—Finland, Norway, Uruguay, Sweden, and Iceland—all have populations smaller than 10 million people, and all score above 70. This may be a scale effect of political processes. Effective environmental regulations may depend on effective democratic decision making, which is more likely to take place in smaller societies. No country with more than 100 million people rates higher than 62.2 (Brazil) for environmental sustainability because corruption can be more easily observed and controlled in smaller societies. Very large economies are also not helpful. The economies of the five most sustainable countries range from $8 billion to $240 billion, but none of the 10 countries with trillion-dollar economies rate higher than Brazil (62.2). The United States (ESI 52.9) has a $10 trillion economy, but it ranks 45 out of 146, relatively far down on the scale for environmental sustainability, just above Burma (Myanmar, ESI 52.8). China, which has the world's second-largest economy ($6.4 trillion), ranks near the bottom (133) for sustainability (ESI 38.6). There is a weak trend for environmental sustainability to improve as per capita GDP rises, but Uruguay ranks third for sustainability with a per capita GDP of just $7,980. The highest per capita GDP ($49,717) country, the United Arab Emirates, ranks 110 for environment (ESI 44.6). Twenty-eight countries with half a billion people rank higher on environmental sustainability than the United States, and they do so with per capita GDPs that are half or less than the U.S. figure of $37,500. These figures suggest that GDP is greatly overrated as a determinant of environmental quality.

One crucial growth trend is for scale increases in a country's per capita GDP to correlate strongly with scale increases in carbon dioxide emissions per capita (figure 8.1). This correlation points to a link between economic growth and global warming and environmental degradation. The causal

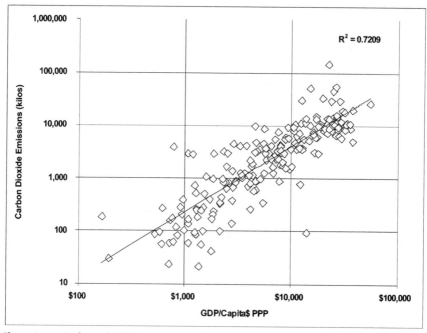

Figure 8.1.   Carbon Dioxide Emission/Capita and GDP/Capita for 195 Countries, 2004.
U.S. Department of Energy, Energy Information Agency. 2006. International Energy Annual 2004. Table E1.p Energy Intensity: Total Primary Energy Consumption per Dollar of Gross Domestic Product using Purchasing Power Parities, 1980–2004. (August 23).

connection is that growing very large economies and high per capita GDPs is currently a very energy-intensive process that has been highly dependent on burning fossil fuels. Ever-increasing flows of material and energy are necessary to support larger markets and greater consumption. The high carbon emissions that support very high per capita GDPs ($10,000 plus) multiplied by a very large population cause catastrophic global warming. Carbon dioxide is of course the primary greenhouse gas, and its primary source is burning fossil fuels.

The good news demonstrated by the previous examples is that growing gigantic energy-intensive economies with very high GDPs per capita is not the only path to prosperity. In reality, only part of the world and a small number of influential decision makers are responsible for much of the damage to global sustainability. Much of this has occurred in the past fifty years. Just thirty-five high-impact countries among the seventy-two with per capita GDPs over $10,000 and carbon dioxide emissions of over 10,000 kilograms per capita accounted for nearly 60 percent of global carbon dioxide emissions in 2004, yet they constituted only 20 percent of global population. A handful of financial elites were probably among the prime directors and beneficiaries of this unsustainable global economic growth, because more than 90 percent of the world's billionaires lived in these thirty-five countries. The connection between the production of billionaires and economic growth is apparent in the strong correlation between billionaire wealth and very large national economies. In 2004, all but seven of the world's 691 billionaires were residents of countries with GDPs of over $100 billion, and more than 80 percent were located in eight countries with economies of over $1 trillion. These eight countries accounted for 44 percent of global carbon emissions. This is not to suggest that billionaires directly and intentionally cause global warming, but they certainly benefit from the energy-intensive economic growth development pathway. They might also resist efforts to change directions. The real problem with trillionaire national economies is that because scale naturally tends to concentrate power, unlimited growth allows a very small investor class to emerge whose members will have a collective interest in promoting ever more growth, and they will be in a position to shape public perceptions and public policies to support their personal short-term interests. At the same time, because of their great wealth they are insulated from many of the costs of growth.

The Environmental Sustainability Index only deals with society as it relates to the institutional capacity to protect the environment, but a more subjective measure of both environmental sustainability and human well-being points to a less-energy-intensive and more-sustainable development pathway for the human future. The *Happy Planet Index* (HPI) produced by the New Economics Foundation (NEF) measures how well 178 different countries support "a good life for their citizens, whilst respecting the environmental resource limits upon which all our lives depend."[59] This index ignores the economy, and instead is concerned with broadly measured human well-being as the ultimate purpose of society and our economic activities. From this perspective people and society come before the economy. The HPI takes into account life expectancy, ecological footprint, and the subjective well-being, or "life satisfaction," that people report, which is presumed to be related to people's physical and mental well-being. There is little overall relationship between size of society, economy, or GDP per capita and country rankings on the *Happy Planet Index*. Five countries with 47 million people had the best rankings, combining high ratings for "happy life years" with very low ecological footprints. Three of these, Saint Lucia, Saint Vincent, and Vanuatu, were very small island countries with under

250,000 people, with economies of under $1 billion and per capita GDPs well under $10,000.

Transforming America

The political choices and cultural changes that Americans are now making to create a sustainable national society will have an enormous impact on the global future. At the beginning of the twenty-first century, the United States, with less than 5 percent of world population, was unquestionably the dominant global power. America's economy was the world's largest. In 2004 American carbon dioxide emissions were also the greatest in the world, accounting for nearly 22 percent of the global total. Americans also consumed 22 percent of the world's primary energy,[60] produced more than one-fourth of global GDP, held a third of world household wealth,[61] and were responsible for more than half of all military expenditures in the world.[62] American corporations accounted for more than a third of all revenues in the 2006 *Global Fortune 500* list of the world's largest publicly traded corporations,[63] and the total shareholder value of U.S. corporations was 44 percent of the value of all the companies listed on the world's stock markets in 2004.[64] The 2007 Forbes list of 946 global billionaires counted 415 Americans with $1.3 trillion, or 44 percent of the world's billionaire wealth.

Scale and power theory suggests that downscaling and redistributing American social power would dramatically reduce the human costs of American society and American impact on the global environment. Americans could reorganize their society and change their culture in ways that would also improve the quality of their own lives.

The United States has successfully grown the world's largest economy, and its per capita wealth and income imply that its people are enormously prosperous. However, social power has become so concentrated, and the costs of America's economy are so high, that it would be a mistake to imagine that American-style economic growth is the world's only route to human well-being. Since 1950 global political and economic elites have mobilized enormous resources to promote global economic growth following the American model. This effort has been successful, because the global economy has increased sevenfold, staying well ahead of population growth, and per capita global GDP has nearly tripled.[65] Nevertheless, as we have seen, overall human well-being has declined on many measures, and growth has pushed the environment to the edge of catastrophe.

If global problems are primarily scale and power problems, the obvious solution is for the presently most powerful and most unsustainable countries, and especially the United States, to take the lead in redeveloping themselves by implementing policies that will redistribute wealth and income, install effective minimum living standards, and institute drastically less-energy-intensive development processes. Markets in energy, food, and consumer goods will need to shrink in order to reduce production, processing, and transportation costs. The big question becomes, is it politically possible for a country as large as the United States to voluntarily carry out such a transformation?

The magnitude of the potential savings in energy and dollars that might accompany this necessary socio-cultural transformation can be estimated by several measures. For example, the Genuine Progress Indicator suggests that perhaps as much as 60 percent of the American GDP in 2002 was wasted in social and environmental costs.[66] This can be compared with the estimate that 56 percent of the country's energy flow was wasted in 2005 in thermodynamically inefficient processes.[67] Half of the thermodynamic loss was in the fossil fuels used in thermal electric power generation and in transmission. The rest of the loss was in the transportation sector. Any cultural changes that reduced thermal electric production and long-distance transmission, and transportation requirements would be a huge energy savings. Other potential savings do not involve energetic or technological inefficiencies. Combined American expenditures on national security, including the Defense Department ($495 billion) and domestic advertising ($271 billion) in 2005 nearly equaled the $827 billion spent on all forms of education in the 2003–2004 academic year.[68] A substantial part of the $654 billion spent on transporting, warehousing, and manufacturing chemical products, food, and beverages can be attributed to national-scale marketing.[69] How much of these costs are scale-related processing and distribution costs rather than primary production is indicated by the fact that in 2004 only 20 percent of consumer expenditures on food went to the farmer (as noted in chapter 5). Only 15 percent of the foodstuffs and animal feed by weight in the American food system is actually consumed by people.[70] Any shifts toward vegetarian diets and local, rather than national and global food provisioning, and toward less processing would be a savings. Consuming less processed food would produce immediate savings on health care, which cost $626 billion in 2004. Water is so heavy that carbonated soft drinks, alcohol, fruit drinks, and bottled water made up nearly 40 percent of the weight of all inflows of food and beverages into an American city in

1997.[71] Consuming locally produced, rather than nationally advertised, transported, and warehoused, beverages would be an enormous savings. These cultural changes in diet would stimulate local producers, creating employment, and they might dramatically lower the consumption of corn syrup, which is implicated in obesity and diabetes.

There are ways to improve the distribution of household wealth and income in the country, such as taxing wealth, unearned income, and very large estates to discourage the cross-generation accumulation of vast personal fortunes; distributing a substantial share of national wealth to everyone at certain ages; using progressive income taxes to create income ceilings; and universal basic incomes, or guaranteed annual income distributed equally. Most of these measures are already in effect in different countries, or they have existed historically in the United States, or they have been proposed.

Unless American Christians suddenly became more charitable, peaceful, and environmentally aware, or everyone suddenly converted to Buddhism, the necessary changes in cultural values are most likely to come about as a result of a major financial collapse, political crisis, global warming–related environmental disasters, or because of steady increases in energy costs. It is possible to imagine the federal government ceding greater autonomy to the states following a constitutional convention. Citizens might choose to restructure along more democratic lines in order to balance the interests of cities, regions, states, employers, employees, and other social groups in response to crisis.

A balance among domestic-, political-, and commercial-scale cultural institutions would undoubtedly offer the most satisfying future for all people and would have the best chance of being sustainable. Implementing such change will require a reordering of cultural processes. The process of humanization that originally produced humanity and the tribal world must be given priority over politicization. Political power in turn must regulate the commercialization and financialization processes. The primary obstacle to such change will not be the concentrated political and economic power of governments and transnational corporations as such but rather the ability of elites to control the cultural symbols that motivate human beliefs and behavior for their own interests. Political and economic democracy will help limit this power, thus making sustainable development possible. The rapidly evolving decentralized global communications and information networks could help strengthen the autonomy of domestic-scale cultures and communities, if these technologies are not totally dominated by giant, for-profit corporate businesses and are accessible to everyone.

Notes

1. Bohannan, Paul. 1971. "Beyond Civilization." *Natural History* 80(2): 50–67.

2. Cleave, T. L. 1974. *The Saccharine Disease*. Bristol, England: Wright.

3. Popkin, Barry M., L. Armstrong, G. M. Bray, B. Caballero, B. Frei, and W. C. Willett. 2006. "A New Proposed Guidance System for Beverage Consumption in the United States." *American Journal of Clinical Nutrition* 83: 529–42.

4. Heilbroner, Robert L. 1963. *The Great Ascent: The Struggle for Economic Development in Our Time*. New York: Harper & Row Torchbooks, 53.

5. Raskin, Paul, Tariq Banuri, Gilberto Gallopín, Pablo Gutman, Al Hammond, Robert Kates, and Rob Swart. 2002. *Great Transition: The Promise and Lure of the Times Ahead*. Global Scenario Group. Boston: Stockholm Environment Institute, Tellus Institute, x.

6. WCED (World Commission on Environment and Development). 1987. *Our Common Future*. Oxford: Oxford University Press, i.

7. United Kingdom, Department of the Environment. 1990. *This Common Inheritance: Britain's Environmental Strategy*. (September). House of Commons Cm. 1200, 8.

8. United Nations, Millennium Project. 2005. *Investing in Development: A Practical Plan to Achieve the Millennium Development Goals*. London: Earthscan; Sachs, Jeffrey D. 2005. *The End of Poverty: Economic Possibilities of Our Time*. New York: Penguin.

9. United Kingdom, Department for Environment, Food and Rural Affairs. 2004. *Achieving a Better Quality of Life: Review of Progress Towards Sustainable Development*. Government Annual Report 2003. London: Defra Publications, 15, 77.

10. New Economics Foundation. 2004. *Chasing Progress: Beyond Measuring Economic Growth*. London, 2, Figure. www.neweconomics.org/

11. Nakicenovic, Nebojsa, and Robert Swart, ed. 2000. *Special Report on Emissions Scenarios: A Special Report of Working Group III of the Intergovernmental Panel on Climate Change*. Cambridge and New York: Cambridge University Press.

12. IPCC (Intergovernmental Panel on Climate Change). 2001. *Climate Change 2001: Synthesis Report. Contribution of Work Groups I, II, and III to the Third Assessment*. Report of the Intergovernmental Panel on Climate Change. Edited by R. T. Watson. Cambridge and New York: Cambridge University Press.

13. IPCC. 2007. *Climate Change 2007: The Physical Science Basis, Summary for Policymakers. Contribution of Working Group I to the Fourth Assessment Report of the Intergovernmental Pattern on Climate Change*. www.ipcc.ch/WG1_SPM_17Apr07.pdf

14. NIC (National Intelligence Council). 2000. *Global Trends 2015: A Dialogue About the Future With Nongovernment Experts*. NIC 2000-02. infowar.net/cia/publications/globaltrends2015/

15. NIC. 2004. Mapping the Global Future: Report of the National Intelligence Council's 2020 Project. NIC 2004-13. www.dni.gov/nic/NIC_2020_project.html

16. *Fortune Magazine*. 2006. "Fortune Global 500." (July 24).

17. Shell International. 2005. *Shell Global Scenarios to 2025: Executive Summary and Excerpts*. Shell International Limited.

18. McLean, Bethany, and Peter Elkind. 2004. *The Smartest Guys in the Room: The Amazing Rise and Scandalous Fall of Enron*. New York: Penguin.

19. Hughes, Barry B. and Evan E. Hillebrand. 2006. *Exploring and Shaping International Futures*. Boulder, CO: Paradigm Publishers. www.du.edu/~bhughes/ifsoverview.htm

20. Cave, Jonathan. 2003. *Towards a Sustainable Information Society*. TERRA 2000 IST-2000-26332, iii.

21. UNEP (United Nations Environment Programme). 2002. *Global Environment Outlook 3: Past, Present and Future Perspectives*. London: Earthscan.

22. Millennium Ecosystem Assessment. 2005. *Ecosystems and Human Well-being: Synthesis*. Washington, D.C.: Island Press.

23. UNEP, *Global Environment Outlook 3*, 231.

24. Tellus Institute. 2005. *Great Transition Initiative: Visions and Pathways for a Hopeful Future*. GTI Brochure. www.gtinitiative.org/default.asp?action=42

25. Raskin, *The Great Transition*.

26. Goldsmith, Edward, et al. 1972. *Blueprint for Survival*. Boston: Houghton Mifflin; Kohr, Leopold. 1977. *The Overdeveloped Nations: The Diseconomies of Scale*. New York: Schocken Books; Kohr, Leopold. 1978 [1957]. *The Breakdown of Nations*. New York: Dutton; Sale, Kirkpatrick. 1980. *Human Scale*. New York: Coward, McCann & Geoghegan; Sale, Kirkpatrick. 1985. *Dwellers in the Land: The Bioregional Vision*. San Francisco: Sierra Club Books; Sale, Kirkpatrick. 1996a. "Principles of Bioregionalism." In *The Case Against the Global Economy and for a Turn Toward the Local*, edited by Jerry Mander and Edward Goldsmith, 471–84. San Francisco: Sierra Club Books.

27. The values change approach is also prominent in a related book with a similar title: Korten, David C. 2006. *The Great Turning: From Empire to Earth Community*. San Francisco, CA: Berrett-Koehler; Bloomfield, CT: Kumarian Press.

28. White, Allen L. 2006. *Transforming the Corporation*. GTI Paper Series, Frontiers of a Great Transition 5. Boston: Tellus Institute, 1.

29. Assuming 500 corporations with an average of 12 directors each, and each director serves on two corporate boards (500 companies x 12 = 6,000 directors / 2 = 3,000 directors). Overlapping board memberships are ignored.

30. Ownership and financial data for ExxonMobil was obtained from corporate annual reports, and SEC filings were compiled and summarized by Mergent-Online (March 2007). www.mergentonline.com/

31. Colville Tribe. www.colvilletribes.com/

32. CROPP (Cooperative Regions of Organic Producer Pools). www.organicvalley.coop/trade/index.html

33. MCC (Mondragón Corporación Cooperativa). 2006. *2005 Annual Report*. www.mcc.es/

34. Eurostat. 2007. *Europe in figures: Eurostat yearbook 2006–2007*. ec.europa.eu/eurostat

35. *Fortune Magazine*, 2005. "Fortune Global 500," (July 25).

36. Thinley, Lyonpo Jigmi Y. 2004. "Values and Development: 'Gross National Happiness.'" In *Gross National Happiness and Development. Proceedings of the First International Seminar on Operationalization of Gross National Happiness*, edited by Karma Ura and Karma Galay, 12–23. Thimphu, Bhutan: The Centre for Bhutan Studies, 14. www.bhutanstudies.org.bt

37. U.S. Central Intelligence Agency (CIA). 2007. *The World Factbook*. www.cia .gov/cia/publications/factbook/geos/bt.html (updated April 17, 2007).

38. Marks, Nic, and Saamah Abdallah, Andrew Simms, and Sam Thompson. 2006. *The Happy Planet Index: An Index of Human Well-Being and Environmental Impact*. London: New Economics Foundation. www.neweconomics.org/gen/z_sys_ PublicationDetail.aspx?PID=225

39. Bhutan, National Environment Commission. 1998. *The Middle Path: National Environment Strategy for Bhutan*. Royal Government of Bhutan.

40. Thinley, *Gross National Happiness*, 12–23.

41. Bhutan, Planning Commission. 1999. *Bhutan 2020: A Vision for Peace, Prosperity and Happiness*. Royal Government of Bhutan.

42. Bodley, John H. 2005. *Cultural Anthropology: Tribes, States, and the Global System*. New York: McGraw-Hill, 510–12, table 15.2.

43. Brown, Lester R. 2006. Plan B 2.0: *Rescuing a Planet under Stress and a Civilization in Trouble*. New York: W. W. Norton. www.earth-policy.org/Books/PB2/ index.htm.

44. Register, Richard. 2006. *Ecocities: Rebuilding Cities in Balance with Nature*. Gabriola Island, B.C.: New Society Publisher.

45. Odum, Howard T., and Elisabeth C. Odum. 2001. *A Prosperous Way Down: Principles and Policies*. Boulder, CO: University Press of Colorado.

46. Kohr, *The Breakdown of Nations*.

47. Kohr, *Breakdown of Nations*, xviii.

48. Schumacher, E. F. 1973. *Small Is Beautiful: Economics As If People Mattered*. New York: Harper and Row.

49. Tax, Sol. 1977. "Anthropology for the World of the Future: Thirteen Professions and Three Proposals." *Current Anthropology* 36(3): 225–34.

50. Wingfield-Hayes, Rupert. 2007. "Moscow's suburb for billionaires." BBC News. (April 21); Kroll, Luisa, and Allison Fass. 2007. "The World's Billionaires." *Forbes Magazine* (March 8).

51. Hughes and Hillebrand, *International Futures*. Data is usually "most recent" available in 2006. The *International Futures* computer software and databases can be accessed online at www.du.edu/~bhughes/ifswelcome.html

52. World Bank. 2006. *World Development Report 2006. Equity and Development*. New York: Oxford University Press, table 1. Key indicators of development expressed in Purchasing Power Parity (PPP) dollars, to adjust for international differences in cost of living.

53. Expressed as Gross National Income (GNI) in PPP dollars.

54. Wilkinson, Richard G. 1996. *Unhealthy Societies: The Afflictions of Inequality.* London and New York: Routledge; Bezruchka, Stephen. 2001. "Societal Hierarchy and the Health Olympics." *Canadian Medical Association Journal* 164(12): 1701–703.

55. United Nations Development Program (UNDP). 2005. *Human Development Report 2005: International cooperation at a crossroads.* hdr.undp.org/reports/global/2005/

56. A.T. Kearney, Inc. 2004. "Measuring Globalization: Economic Reversals, Forward Momentum." *Foreign Policy* (March/April).

57. *Foreign Policy.* 2005. "Measuring Globalization." (May/June).

58. Esty, Daniel C., Marc Levy, Tanja Srebotnjak, and Alexander de Sherbinin. 2005. *2005 Environmental Sustainability Index: Benchmarking National Environmental Stewardship.* New Haven: Yale Center for Environmental Law & Policy. www.yale.edu/esi/

59. Marks, et al. *The Happy Planet Index,* 1.

60. U.S. Department of Energy, Energy Information Administration. 2006. *Annual Energy Review 2005.* report no. DOE/EIA-0384(2005), table 11.19 World carbon dioxide emissions from energy consumption, 1995–2004. U.S. Department of Energy, Energy Information Administration. 2006. *International Energy Annual.* table E.1 World total primary energy consumption, 1980–2004. www.eia.doe.gov/iea/wecbtu.html

61. See table 4.1.

62. Stockholm International Peace Research Institute. 2006. *SIPRI Yearbook 2006: Armaments, Disarmament and International Security.* New York: Humanities Press.

63. *Fortune Magazine,* "Global 500 2006"; *Fortune Magazine.* 2006. "Fortune 500" (April 17).

64. World Bank. 2005. *World Development Indicators, 2005.* Table 5.4 Stock Markets.

65. Maddison, Angus. 2003. *The World Economy: Historical Statistics.* OECD: Development Centre Studies. Paris.

66. Venetoulis, Jason, and Cliff Cobb. 2004. *The Genuine Progress Indicator 1950–2002 (2004 Update).* Oakland, CA: Redefining Progress.

67. Whitesides, George M., and George W. Crabtree. 2007. "Don't Forget Long-Term Fundamental Research in Energy." *Science* 315: 796–98.

68. U.S. Department of Education, National Center for Education Statistics. 2005. *Revenues and Expenditures for Public Elementary and Secondary Education: School Year 2002–2003* (NCES 2005-353), Current Expenditures per Student.

69. U.S. Department of Commerce, Bureau of the Census. 2007. *Statistical Abstract of the United States.* Various annual editions. Washington, D.C.: U.S. Government Printing Office.

70. Heller, Martin C., and Gregory A. Keoleian. 2000. "Life Cycle-based Sustainability Indicators for Assessment of the U.S. Food System." report no.

CSS00-04 Center for Sustainable Systems. University of Michigan. Ann Arbor, MI.

71. Garvin, Lewis, Natalie Henry, and Melissa Vernon. 2000. *Community Materials Flow Analysis: A Case Study of Ann Arbor, Michigan*. Center for Sustainable Systems, University of Michigan. report no. CSS00-02.

Bibliography

Advertising Age. 1992–1993. Chicago: Crain Communications, Inc.

———. 2006. "Special Report: 100 Leading National Advertisers." Supplement (June 26).

Albright, David, and Corey Hinderstein. 2005. "Unraveling the A.Q. Khan and Future Proliferation Networks." *Washington Quarterly* 28(2): 111–28.

Alexander, Richard D. 1990. *How Did Humans Evolve?: Reflections on the Uniquely Unique Species.* Ann Arbor: Museum of Zoology, the University of Michigan Special Publication No. 1.

Alkire, William H. 1978. *Coral Islanders.* Arlington Heights: AHM.

Alliance for Democracy. 2007. "About the Alliance for Democracy." www .thealliancefordemocracy.org/about.html (April).

———. 2007. *CAIS: Modeling a Democratic Society.* www.thealliancefordemocracy .org/html/eng/1699-AA.shtml (April).

Alvarado, Anita L. 1970. "Determinants of Population Stability in the Havasupai Indians." *American Journal of Physical Anthropology* 33(1): 9–14.

Alvard, Michael S. 1993. "Testing the 'Ecologically Noble Savage' Hypothesis: Interspecific Prey Choice by Piro Hunters of Amazonian Peru." *Human Ecology* 21(4): 355–87.

———. 1995. "Intraspecific Prey Choice by Amazonian Hunters." *Current Anthropology* 36(5): 789–818.

———. 1998. "Evolutionary Ecology and Resource Conservation." *Evolutionary Anthropology* 7(2): 62–74.

American Forests. 1998. *Regional Ecosystem Analysis, Puget Sound Metropolitan Area.* www.amfor.org

Anthropology Resource Center. 1978. *Native Americans and Energy Development.* Cambridge, MA: ARC.

Applbaum, Kalman. 1998. "The Sweetness of Salvation: Consumer Marketing and the Liberal-Bourgeois Theory of Needs." *Current Anthropology* 19(3): 323–49.

Architectural Digest. 1994. (February).

Arena, Mark V., Irv Blickstein, Obaid Younossi, and Clifford A. Grammich. 2006. *Why Has the Cost of Navy Ships Risen?: A Macroscopic Examination of the Trends in U.S. Naval Ship Costs*. Santa Monica, CA: RAND, xiv.

Arms Trade News. 1993. (November).

Asimov, Isaac. 1971. "The End." *Penthouse*, January.

A. T. Kearney, Inc. 2004. "Measuring Globalization: Economic Reversals, Forward Momentum." *Foreign Policy* (March/April).

Bailey, Robert C., G. Head, M. Jenike, B. Owen, R. Rechtman, and E. Zechenter. 1989. "Hunting and Gathering in Tropical Rain Forest: Is It Possible?" *American Anthropologist* 91: 59–82.

Baillie, Jonathan, and Brian Groombridge, eds. 1996. *1996 IUCN Red List of Threatened Animals*. Gland, Switzerland: World Conservation Union (IUCN).

Baines, John, and Norman Yoffee. 1998. "Order, Legitimacy, and Wealth in Ancient Egypt and Mesopotamia." In *Archaic States*, edited by Gary M. Feinman and Joyce Marcus, 199–260. Santa Fe, NM: School of American Research Press.

Barclay, Harold. 1982. *People Without Government*. London: Kahn & Averill & Cienfuegos.

Barlett, Peggy F. 1987. "Industrial Agriculture in Evolutionary Perspective." *Cultural Anthropology* 2: 137–54.

———. 1989. "Industrial Agriculture." In *Economic Anthropology*, edited by Stuart Planner, 253–91. Stanford, CA: Stanford University Press.

Barnet, Richard J., and John Cavanagh. 1994. *Global Dreams: Imperial Corporations and the New World Order*. New York: Simon and Schuster.

Barnett, Harold, and Chandler Morse. 1963. *Scarcity and Growth: The Economics of Natural Resource Availability*. Baltimore: Johns Hopkins University Press.

Barney, Gerald O., ed. 1977–1980. *The Global 2000 Report to the President of the United States*. 3 vols. New York: Pergamon.

Barnosky, Anthony D., Paul L. Koch, Robert S. Feranec, Scott L. Wing, and Alan B. Shabel. 2004. "Assessing the Causes of Late Pleistocene Extinctions on the Continents." *Science* 306 (1 Oct): 70–75.

Bartlett, H. H. 1956. "Fire, Primitive Agriculture, and Grazing in the Tropics." In *Man's Role in Changing the Face of the Earth*, edited by William L. Thomas Jr., 692–720. Chicago: University of Chicago Press.

Barton, J. 1980. *Transportation and Fuel Requirements in the Food and Fiber System*. USDA, Agricultural Economic Report No. 444. Economic, Statistics, and Cooperative Service.

Basso, Keith. 1972. "Ice and Travel Among the Fort Norman Slaves: Folk Taxonomies and Cultural Rules." *Language in Society* 1 (1972): 31–49.

Bayliss-Smith, Tim. 1974. "Constraints on Population Growth: The Case of the Polynesian Outlier Atolls in the Precontact Period." *Human Ecology* 2(4): 259–95.

Beard, Charles A., and Mary R. Beard. 1934. *The Rise of American Civilization*. New York: Macmillan.

Beckerman, Stephen. 1983. "Does the Swidden Ape the Jungle?" *Human Ecology* 11(1): 1–12.

Beedham, Brian. 1993. "The World's Next Wars." In *The World in 1994*, edited by Dudley Fishburn, 13–14. London: The Economist Publications.

Bell, Diane. *1982. Aboriginal Women and the Religious Experience*. Young Australian Scholar Lecture Series, no. 3. Bedford Park, South Australia: Australian Association for the Study of Religions, South Australian College of Advanced Education.

Benedict, Ruth. 1959. *Patterns of Culture*. New York: Mentor. Originally published in 1934.

Bentley, Gillian R., Tony Goldberg, and Grazyna Jasienska. 1993. "The Fertility of Agricultural and Non-Agricultural Traditional Societies." *Population Studies* 47: 269–81.

Bern, John. 1979. "Ideology and Domination: Toward a Reconstruction of Australian Aboriginal Social Formation." *Oceania* 50(2): 118–32.

Berry, Christopher J. 1994. *The Idea of Luxury: A Conceptual and Historical Investigation*. Cambridge, England: Cambridge University Press.

Berry, Wendell. 1977. *The Unsettling of America: Culture and Agriculture*. San Francisco: Sierra Club Books.

Betzig, Laura L. 1986. *Despotism and Differential Reproduction: A Darwinian View of History*. New York: Aldine.

———. 1993. "Sex, Succession, and Stratification in the First Six Civilizations: How Powerful Men Reproduced, Passed Power on to Their Sons, and Used Power to Defend Their Wealth, Women, and Children." In *Social Stratification and Socioeconomic Inequality*, vol. 1, *A Comparative Biosocial Analysis*, edited by Lee Ellis, 37–74. Westport, CT, and London: Praeger.

BFF (Best Food Forward). 2002. *City Limits: A resource flow and ecological footprint analysis of Greater London*. www.citylimitslondon.com

Bhagwati, Jagdish. 1993. "The Case for Free Trade." *Scientific American* 269(5): 42–49.

Bhutan, National Environment Commission. 1998. *The Middle Path: National Environment Strategy for Butan*. Royal Government of Bhutan.

Bhutan, Planning Commission. 1999. *Bhutan 2020: A Vision for Peace, Prosperity and Happiness*. Royal Government of Bhutan.

Bird-David, Nurit. 1992. "Beyond 'The Original Affluent Society': A Culturalist Reformulation." *Current Anthropology* 33(l): 25–47.

Birdsell, J. B. 1953. "Some Environmental and Cultural Factors Influencing the Structure of Australian Aboriginal Populations." *American Naturalist* 87 (834): 171–207.

———. 1971. "Ecology, Spacing Mechanisms, and Adaptive Behavior in Aboriginal Land Tenure." In *Land Tenure in the Pacific*, edited by Ron Crocombe, 334–61. Melbourne: Oxford University Press.

———. 1979. "Ecological Influences on Australian Aboriginal Social Organization." In *Primate Ecology and Human Origins: Ecological Influences on Social Organization*, edited by Invin S. Bernstein and Euclid O. Smith, 117–51. New York: Garland STPM.

Blanton, Richard E. 1998. "Beyond Centralization: Steps Toward a Theory of Egalitarian Behavior in Archaic States." In *Archaic States*, edited by Gary M. Feinman and Joyce Marcus, 135–72. Santa Fe, NM: School of American Research Press.

Bluestone, Barry, and Bennett Harrison. 1982. *The Deindustrializatim of America*. New York: Basic Books.

Boas, Franz. 1928. *Anthropology and Modern Life*. New York: Norton.

Bodley, John H. 1975. *Victims of Progress*. Menlo Park, CA: Cummings.

———. 1981. "Inequality: An Energetics Approach." In *Social Inequality: Comparative and Developmental Approaches*, edited by Gerald D. Berreman, 183–97. New York: Academic.

———. 1988. *Tribal Peoples and Development Issues: A Global Overview*. Mountain View, CA: Mayfield Publishing.

———. 1999a. "Socioeconomic Growth, Culture Scale, and Household Well-Being: A Test of the Power-Elite Hypothesis." *Current Anthropology* 40(5): 595–620.

———. 1999b. *Victims of Progress*. 4th ed. Mountain View, CA: Mayfield Publishing.

———. 2000. *Cultural Anthropology: Tribes, States, and the Global System*. 3rd ed. Mountain View, CA: Mayfield Publishing.

———. 2001. "Growth, Scale, and Power in Washington State." *Human Organization* 60(4): 367–79.

———. 2003. *The Power of Scale: A Global History Approach*. Armonk, New York and London: M. E. Sharpe.

———. 2005a. "The Rich Tribal World: Scale and Power Perspectives on Cultural Valuation," paper presented at the Annual Meeting of the Society for Applied Anthropology, Santa Fe, New Mexico.

———. 2005b. *Cultural Anthropology: Tribes, States, and the Global System*. New York: McGraw-Hill.

Boehm, Christopher. 1993. "Egalitarian Behavior and Reverse Dominance Hierarchy." *Current Anthropology* 34(3): 227–54.

Boehma, Addeke H. 1970. "A World Agricultural Plan." *Scientific American* 223(2): 54–69.

Bogucki, Peter. 1999. *The Origins of Human Society*. Maiden, MA, and Oxford, U.K.: Blackwell Publishers.

Bogue, Donald T. 1969. *Principles of Demography*. New York: Wiley.

Bohannan, Paul. 1971. "Beyond Civilization." *Natural History* 80(2): 50–67.

Bongaarts, John. 1994. "Can the Growing Human Population Feed Itself?" *Scientific American* 270(3): 36–42.

Bookchin, Murray. 1991. *The Ecology of Freedom: The Emergence and Dissolution of Hierarchy*. Montreal and New York: Black Rose Books.

Borgstrom, Georg. 1965. *The Hungry Planet*. New York: Macmillan
———. 1967. *The Hungry Planet*. New York: Macmillan.
Boserup, Ester. 1965. *The Conditions of Economic Growth*. Chicago: Aldine.
Boulding, Kenneth. 1966. "The Economics of the Coming Spaceship Earth." In *Environmental Quality in a Growing Economy: Essays from the Sixth Resources for the Future Forum*, edited by Henry Jarrett, 3–14. Baltimore: Johns Hopkins University Press.
Bowdler, S. 1977. "The Coastal Colonization of Australia." In *Sunda and Sahul: Prehistoric Studies in Southeast Asia, Melanesia and Australia*, edited by J. Allen, J. Golson, and R. Jones, 205–46. London: Academic Press.
Boyd, Robert, and Peter J. Richerson. 1985. *Culture and the Evolutionary Process*. Chicago and London: University of Chicago Press.
Braudel, Fernand. 1977. *Afterthoughts on Material Civilization and Capitalism*. Baltimore and London: Johns Hopkins University Press.
———. 1982. *The Wheels of Commerce: Civilization and Capitalism, 15th–18th Century*. New York: Harper & Row.
———. 1992. *Civilisation Materielle, Economic et Capitalisme* (Civilization and Capitalism, 15th–18th Century). Berkeley: University of California Press.
Braun, Denny. 1991. *The Rich Get Richer: The Rise of Income Inequality in the United States and the World*. Chicago: Nelson-Hall.
Briody, Dan. 2003. *The Iron Triangle: Inside the Secret World of the Carlyle Group*. Hoboken, NJ: John Wiley.
Brooks, David J. 1993. *U.S. Forests in a Global Context*. USDA Technical Report RM-228. Fort Collins, CO: U.S. Department of Agriculture, Forest Service, Rocky Mountain Forest and Range Experiment Station.
Brown, Harrison. 1954. *The Challenge of Man's Future*. New York: Viking.
———. 1956. "Technological Denudation." In *Man's Role in Changing the Face of the Earth*, edited by William L. Thomas Jr., 1023–32. Chicago: University of Chicago Press.
Brown, Lester R. 1963. *Man, Land and Food*. U.S. Department of Agriculture, FAE Report No. 11. Washington, D.C.: U.S. Government Printing Office.
———. 1994. "Facing Food Insecurity." In *State of the World, 1994*, edited by Lester R. Brown et al., 177–97. New York and London: W. W. Norton and Co.
———. 2000. "Challenges of the New Century." In *State of the World 2000: A Worldwatch Institute Report on Progress Toward a Sustainable Society*, edited by Lester R. Brown, Christopher Flavin, Hilary French, and Linda Starke, 1–21. New York and London: W. W. Norton and Co.
———. 2006. Plan B 2.0: *Rescuing a Planet under Stress and a Civilization in Trouble*. New York: W. W. Norton. www.earth-policy.org/Books/PB2/index.htm
Brown, Lester R., and Christopher Flavin. 1999. "A New Economy for a New Century." In *State of the World 1999: A Worldwatch Institute Report on Progress Toward a Sustainable Society*, edited by Lester R. Brown, Christopher Flavin, Hilary French, and Linda Starke, 3–21. New York and London: W. W. Norton and Co.

Brown, Lester R., Michael Renner, Christopher Flavin, et al. 1998. *Vital Signs 1998: The Environmental Trends That Are Shaping Our Future.* Washington, D.C.: Worldwatch Institute.

Brown, Paula, and H. C. Brookfield. 1963. *Struggle for Land.* Melbourne: Oxford University Press.

Bucks, Brian K., Arthur B. Kennickell, and Kevin B. Moore. 2006. "Recent Changes in U.S. Family Finances: Evidence from the 2001 and 2004 Survey of Consumer Finances." *Federal Reserve Bulletin* 2006 (March 22).

Budiansky, Stephen. 1993. "The Doomsday Myths." *U.S. News and World Report* 115(23): 81–91.

Burch, Ernest S., and Linda J. Ellanna, eds. 1994. *Key Issues in Hunter-Gatherer Research.* Oxford: Berg.

Buzby, Jean C., and Hodan A. Farah. 2006. "Findings: Americans Switch From Fresh to Frozen Potatoes." *Amber Waves* 4(3): 5.

Cain, P. J., and A. G. Hopkins. 1993. *British Imperialism: Innovation and Expansion 1688–1914.* London and New York: London.

———. 2002. *British Imperialism, 1688–2000.* New York: Longman.

Cairncross, Frances. 1993. *Costing the Earth: The Challenge for Governments, the Opportunities for Business.* Boston, MA: Harvard Business Press.

Califano, Dave. 1998. "The Battle for Assets." *Worth* 7(11): 106.

Campbell, Alastair H. 1965. "Elementary Food Production by the Australian Aborigines." *Mankind* (6): 206–11.

Capgemini. 2006. *World Wealth Report 2006.* www.us.capgemini.com/worldwealth report06/default.asp

Capps, Oral, Jr., Annette Clauson, Joanne Guthrie, Grant Pittman, and Matthew Stockton. 2005. *Contributions of Nonalcoholic Beverages to the U.S. Diet.* USDA, Economic Research Service, Economic Research Report Number 1. www.ers .usda.gov/publications/err1/err1.pdf

Carlyle Group, The. www.carlyle.com

Carmack, Robert M. 1988. *Harvest of Violence: The Maya Indians and the Guatemalan Crisis.* Norman, OK: University of Oklahoma Press.

Carneiro, Robert L. 1960. "Slash-and-Burn Agriculture: A Closer Look at Its Implications for Settlement Patterns." In *Men and Cultures*, edited by A. F. C. Wallace, 229–34. Philadelphia: University of Pennsylvania Press.

———. 1968. "The Transition from Hunting to Horticulture in the Amazon Basin." *Proceedings of the Eighth International Congress of Anthropological and Ethnological Sciences*, 244–48. Tokyo: ICAES.

———. 1970. "A Theory of the Origin of the State." *Science* 169(3947): 733–38.

———. 1978. "The Knowledge and Use of Rain Forest Trees by the Kuikuru Indians of Central Brazil." *Anthropological Papers* (University of Michigan Museum of Anthropology) 67: 201–16.

———. 1981. "The Chiefdom: Precursor of the State." In *The Transition to Statehood in the New World*, edited by Grant D. Jones and Robert R. Kautz, 37–79. Cambridge: Cambridge University Press.

Carneiro, Robert L., and D. F. Hilse. 1966. "On Determining the Probable Rate of Population Growth During the Neolithic." *American Anthropologist* 68(1): 177–81.

Carrier, James G., and Josiah McC. Heyman. 1997. "Consumption and Political Economy." *Journal of the Royal Anthropological Institute* (N.S.) 3: 355–73.

Carruthers, Bruce G. 1996. *City of Capital: Politics and Markets in the English Financial Revolution*. Princeton, NJ: Princeton University Press.

Cashdan, Elizabeth. 2001. "Ethnocentrism and Xenophobia: A Cross-cultural Study." *Current Anthropology* 42(5): 760–5.

Casimir, Michael J., R. P. Winter, and Bernt Glatzer. 1980. "Nomadism and Remote Sensing: Animal Husbandry and the Sagebrush Community in a Nomad Winter Area in Western Afghanistan." *Journal of Arid Environments* 3(1980): 231–54.

Catton, William. 1980. *Overshoot: The Ecological Basis of Revolutionary Change*. Chicago: University of Illinois Press.

Caulfield, Mina Davis. 1981. "Equality, Sex, and Mode of Production." In *Social Inequality: Comparative and Developmental Approaches*, edited by Gerald D. Berreman, 201–19. New York: Academic.

Cavalli-Sforza, L. L., and M. W. Feldman. 1981. *Cultural Transmission and Evolution: A Quantitative Approach*. Princeton, NJ: Princeton University Press.

Cave, Jonathan. 2003. *Towards a Sustainable Information Society*. TERRA-2000 IST-2000-26332.

Center for Responsive Politics, The. Opensecrets. www.opensecrets.org/index.asp

Chagnon, Napoleon. 1968. *Yanomamo: The Fierce People*. New York: Holt, Rinehart & Winston.

———. 1988. "Life Histories, Blood Revenge, and Warfare in a Tribal Population." *Science* (26 February) 239: 985–92.

Chandler, Alfred D., Jr. 1977. *The Visible Hand: The Managerial Revolution in American Business*. Cambridge, MS, and London: Belknap Press of Harvard University Press.

Chandler, David G. 1966. *The Campaigns of Napoleon*. New York: Macmillan.

Chaudhuri, K. N. 1965. *The English East India Company: The Study of an Early Joint-Stock Company 1600–1640*. London: Frank Cass & Co.

Chayanov, A. V. 1966. *The Theory of Peasant Economy*. Homewood, IL: Richard D. Irwin, for the American Economic Association.

Chew, Sing C. 2001. *World Ecological Degradation: Accumulation, Urbanization, and Deforestation 3000 B.C–A.D. 2000*, New York: Altamira Press.

Chewtow, Marian R. 2001. "The IPAT Equation and Its Variants: Changing Views of Technology and Environmental Impact." *Journal of Industrial Ecology* 4(4): 13–29.

Chiozza, Giacomo. 2002. "Is There a Clash of Civilizations? Evidence from Patterns of International Conflict Involvement, 1946–97." *Journal of Peace Research* 39(6): 711–34.

Chomsky, Noam. 1989. *Necessary Illusions: Thought Control in Democratic Societies*. Boston: South End Press.

———. 1991. *Deterring Democracy*. London and New York: Verso.

———. 1993. *Year 501: The Conquest Continues*. Boston: South End Press.

Chomsky, Noam, and Edward S. Herman. 1979. *The Washington Connection and Third World Fascism*. Boston: South End Press.

Christensen, Kaare, Anne Maria Herskind, and James W. Vaupel. 2006. "Why Danes Are Smug: Comparative Study of Life Satisfaction in the European Union." *BMJ* (*British Medical Journal*) 333 (23–30 December): 1289–91.

Cirincione, Joseph, Jon Wolfsthal, and Miriam Rajkumar. 2005. *Deadly Arsenals: Nuclear, Biological, and Chemical Threats*. 2nd ed. Washington, D.C.: Carnegie Endowment for International Peace.

Clanton, Gene. 1991. *Populism: The Humane Preference in America, 1890–1900*. Boston: Twayne Publishers.

Clark, Colin. 1958. "World Population." *Nature* 181 (3 May): 1235–36.

———. 1968. *Population Growth and Land Use*. London: Macmillan.

———. 1977. *Population Growth and Land Use*. 2nd ed. London: Macmillan.

Clark, J. G. D. 1952. *Prehistoric Europe: The Economic Base*. New York: Philosophical Library.

Cleave, T. L. 1974. *The Saccharine Disease*. Bristol, England: Wright.

Coale, Ansley J. 1974. "The History of the Human Population." *Scientific American* 231(3): 40–51.

Cohen, Joel E. 1995. *How Many People Can the Earth Support?* New York. W. W. Norton.

Cohen, Mark Nathan. 1977. *The Food Crisis in Prehistory: Overpopulation and the Origins of Agriculture*. New Haven, CT: Yale University Press.

———, ed. 1982. "Paleopathology at the Origins of Agriculture." Conference on Paleopathology and Socioeconomic Change at the Origins of Agriculture, State University of New York College at Plattsburgh.

———. 1989. *Health and the Rise of Civilization*. New Haven, CT: Yale University Press.

Cohen, Yehudi, ed. 1974. *Man in Adaptation*. 2nd ed. Chicago: Aldine.

Cole, H. S. D., ed. 1973. *Models of Doom*. New York: Universe.

Collier, Jane Fishburne, and Michelle Z. Rosaldo. 1981. "Politics and Gender in Simple Societies." In *Sexual Meanings: The Cultural Construction of Gender and Sexuality*, edited by Sherry B. Orner and Harriet Whitehead, 275–329. Cambridge, MA: Cambridge University Press.

Colquhoun, Patrick. 1815. *A Treatise on the Wealth, Power, and Resources of the British Empire*. London: Joseph Mawman.

Colson, Elizabeth. 1979. "In Good Years and in Bad: Food Strategies of Self-Reliant Societies." *Journal of Anthropological Research* 35 (1): 18–29.

Colville Tribe. www.colvilletribes.com (August 2005).

Commoner, Barry. 1971. *The Closing Circle*. New York: Knopf.

Communities Directory: A Guide to Cooperative Living. 2nd ed. 1996. Rutledge, MO: Fellowship for International Community.

Comp, T. Allan, ed. 1989. *Blueprint for the Environment: A Plan for Federal Action.* Salt Lake City: Howe Brothers.

Conklin, Harold C. 1954. "An Ethnoecological Approach to Shifting Agriculture." *Transactions of the New York Academy of Sciences,* 2nd ser., 17(2): 133–42.

Cook, Earl. 1971. "The Flow of Energy in an Industrial Society." *Scientific American* 224(3): 134–44.

Cooke, G. W. 1970. "The Carrying Capacity of the Land in the Year 2000." In *The Optimum Population for Britain,* edited by L. R. Taylor, 15–42. London: Academic.

Coon, Carleton S. 1971. *The Hunting Peoples.* Boston: Little, Brown.

Costanza, Robert, et al. 1997. "The Value of the World's Ecosystem Services and Natural Capital." *Nature* 387 (15 May): 253–60.

Coughenour, M. B., J. E. Ellis, D. M. Swift, D. L. Coppock, K. Galvin, J. T. McCabe, and T. C. Hart. 1985. "Energy Extraction and Use in a Nomadic Pastoral Ecosystem." *Science* 230(4726): 619–25.

Cowgill, George L. 1975. "Population Pressure as a Non-Explanation." *In American Antiquity* 40(2): 127–31, part 2, memoir 30.

Cowlishaw, Gillian. 1978. "Infanticide in Aboriginal Australia." *Oceania* 48(4): 262–83.

Craft, Cassady. 2002. "The Arms Trade and the Incidence of Political Violence in Sub-Saharan Africa, 1967–97." *Journal of Peace Research* 39(2): 693–710.

CROPP (Cooperative Regions of Organic Producer Pools). www.organicvalley .coop/trade/index.html (November 2006).

Crosby, Alfred W. 1972. *The Columbian Exchange: Biological and Cultural Consequences of 1492.* Westport, CT: Greenwood Publishing Co.

———. 1986. *Biological Imperialism: The Biological Expansion of Europe, 900–1900.* Cambridge: Cambridge University Press.

Crystal, Graef S. 1991. *In Search of Excess: The Overcompensation of American Executives.* New York and London: W. W. Norton and Co.

Culbert, T. Patrick. 1974. *The Lost Civilization: The Story of the Classic Maya.* New York: Harper & Row.

Dakeyne, R. B. 1967. "Conflicting Interests on Bougainville." *Pacific Viewpoint* 8(2): 186–7.

Dalton, George. 1961. "Economic Theory and Primitive Society." *American Anthropologist* 63(l): 1–25.

———. 1965. "Primitive Money." *American Anthropologist* 67(l): 44–65.

———. 1967. *Economic Development and Social Change: The Modernization of Village Communities.* Garden City, NY: Natural History.

———. 1971. *Economic Anthropology: Essays on Tribal and Peasant Economies.* New York: Basic Books.

Daly, Herman E. 1993. "The Perils of Free Trade." *Scientific American* 269(5): 50–57.

Daly, Herman E., and John B. Cobb. 1989. *For the Common Good: Redirecting the Economy Toward Community, the Environment, and a Sustainable Future.* Boston: Beacon Press.

Dasmann, Raymond. 1976. "Future Primitive: Ecosystem People Versus Biosphere People." *Convolution Quarterly* 1 (Fall): 26–31.

Davies, James B., Susanna Sandstrom, Anthony Shorrocks, and Edward N. Wolff. 2006. *The World Distribution of Household Wealth.* World Institute for Development Economics Research.

Davis, Shelton H. 1988. "Introduction: Sowing the Seeds of Violence." In *Harvest of Violence: The Maya Indians and the Guatemalan Crisis*, edited by Robert M. Carmack. Norman and London: University of Oklahoma Press.

Deevy, Edward S. 1960. "The Human Population." *Scientific American* 203(3): 195–204.

Demarest, Arthur A. 1993. "The Violent Saga of a Maya Kingdom." *National Geographic* 183(2): 94–111.

Demeny, Paul. 1990. "Population." *The Earth As Transformed by Human Action: Global and Regional Changes in the Biosphere Over the Past 300 Years*, edited by B. L. Turner et al., 41–54. Cambridge: Cambridge University Press.

Dentan, Robert K. 1968. *The Semai: A Nonviolent People of Malaya.* New York: Holt, Rinehart & Winston.

de Soysa, Indra. 2002. "Paradise Is a Bazaar? Greed, Creed, and Governance in Civil War, 1989–99." *Journal of Peace Research* 39(4): 395–416.

De Waal, F. B. M. 1989. *Peacemaking among Primates.* Cambridge, MA: Harvard University Press.

DeWalt, Billie R. 1988. "The Cultural Ecology of Development: Ten Precepts for Survival." *Agriculture and Human Values* 5(1–2): 112–23.

Dewhurst, J. Frederic, and Associates. 1947. *America's Needs and Resources: A Twentieth Century Fund Survey Which Includes Estimates for 1950 and 1960.* New York: Twentieth Century Fund.

———. 1955. *America's Needs and Resources: A New Survey.* New York: Twentieth Century Fund.

De Wit, C. T. 1967. "Photosynthesis: Its Relationship to Overpopulation." In *Harvesting the Sun: Photosynthesis in Plant Life*, edited by Anthony San Pietro, Frances A. Greer, and Thomas J. Army, 315–20. New York: Academic Press.

Diamond, Jared 2005. *Collapse: How Societies Choose to Fail or Succeed.* New York: Viking.

Diamond, Stanley. 1968. "The Search for the Primitive." In *The Concept of the Primitive*, edited by Ashley Montagu, 96–147. New York: Free Press.

———. 1974. *In Search of the Primitive.* New Brunswick, NJ: Transaction.

Divale, W. I., and Marvin Harris. 1976. "Population, Warfare, and the Male Supremacist Complex." *American Anthropologist* 78(3): 521–38.

Dole, Gertrude. 1978. "The Use of Manioc Among the Kuikuru: Some Implications." *Anthropological Papers* (Ann Arbor: University of Michigan Museum of Anthropology) 67: 217–47.

Domhoff, G. William. 1996. *State Autonomy or Class Dominance?: Case Studies on Policy Making in America.* New York: Aldine de Gruyter.

Dowling, John H. 1979. "The Goodfellows vs. the Dalton Gang: The Assumptions of *Economic Anthropology." Journal of Anthropological Research* 35(3): 292–308.

Drewnowski, Adam, and Barry M. Popkin. 1997. "The Nutrition Transition: New Trends in the Global Diet." *Nutrition Review* 55(2): 31–43.

Dumaine, Brian. 1994. "A Knockout Year for CEO Pay." *Fortune* (25 July): 94.

Dumond, Don E. 1972. "Population Growth and Political Centralization." In *Population Growth: Anthropological Implications*, edited by Brian Spooner, 286–310. Cambridge, MA: MIT Press.

Dunbar, R. I. M. 1993. "Coevolution of Neocortical Size, Group Size and Language in Humans." *Behavioral and Brain Sciences* 16(4): 681–735.

Durham, William H. 1979. *Scarcity and Survival in Central America: Ecological Origins of the Soccer War*. Stanford, CA: Stanford University Press.

———. 1991. *Coevolution: Genes, Culture, and Human Diversity*. Stanford, CA: Stanford University Press.

———. 1995. "Political Ecology and Environmental Destruction in Latin America." In *The Social Causes of Environmental Destruction in Latin America*, edited by Michael Painter and William H. Durham, 249–64. Ann Arbor: University of Michigan Press.

Dye, Thomas R. 1983. *Who's Running America?: The Reagan Years*. Englewood Cliffs, NJ: Prentice-Hall.

Eames, Edwin, and Judith G. Goode. 1973. *Urban Poverty in a Cross-Cultural Context*. New York: Free Press.

Earle, Timothy, ed. 1991. *Chiefdoms: Power, Economy, and Ideology*. Cambridge: Cambridge University Press.

———. 1997. *How Chiefs Come to Power: The Political Economy in Prehistory*. Stanford, CA: Stanford University Press.

———. 2002. *Bronze Age Economics: The Beginnings of Political Economies*. Boulder, CO: Westview Press.

Economics Working Group. 1999. *General Agreement on a New Economy (GANE)*. Working Draft 11. Washington, D.C.: Economics Working Group/Project of the Tides Foundation, www.greenecon.org

Edwards, Mike. 1994. "Chernobyl: Living with the Monster." *National Geographic* 183(2): 100–15.

Ehrlich, Paul. 1968. *The Population Bomb*. New York: Ballantine.

———. 1969. "Eco-Catastrophe." *Ramparts* 8:24–28.

———. 1992. "Environmental Deterioration, Biodiversity and the Preservation of Civilization: The Ninth World Conservation Lecture." *The Environmentalist* 12(1): 9–14.

Ehrlich, Paul, and Anne Ehrlich. 1972. *Population, Resources, Environment*. San Francisco: W. H. Freeman.

———. 1974. *The End of Affluence*. New York: Ballantine.

———. 1990. *The Population Explosion*. New York: Simon and Schuster.

———. 2004. *One with Ninevah: Politics, Consumption, and the Human Future.* Washington, D.C.: Island Press, Shearwater Books.

Ehrlich, Paul, and Richard L. Harriman. 1971. *How to Be a Survivor: A Plan to Save Spaceship Earth.* New York: Ballantine.

Ehrlich, Paul R., and John P. Holdren. 1971. "Impact of Population Growth." *Science* 171(3977): 1212–17.

Emsley, John. 2001. *Nature's Building Blocks: An A-Z Guide to the Elements.* Oxford: Oxford University Press.

Engelbrecht, H. C. 1934. "The World Trend toward Nationalism." *Annals of the American Academy of Political and Social Science* 174 (July 1934): 121–25.

Engelbrecht, H. C., and F. C. Hanighen. 1934. *Merchants of Death: A Study of the International Armament Industry.* New York: Dodd, Mead.

Engels, Donald W. 1978. *Alexander the Great and the Logistics of the Macedonian Army.* Berkeley: University of California Press.

Erdal, David, and Andrew Whiten. 1996. "Egalitarianism and Machiavellian Intelligence in Human Evolution." In *Modelling the Early Human Mind,* edited by Paul Mellars and Kathleen Gibson, 139–50. Cambridge: McDonald Institute for Archaeological Research, University of Cambridge.

Estes, Ralph. 1996. *Tyranny of the Bottom Line: Why Corporations Make Good People Do Bad Things.* San Francisco: Berrett-Kohler Publishers.

Esty, Daniel C., Marc Levy, Tanja Srebotnjak, and Alexander de Sherbinin. 2005. *2005 Environmental Sustainability Index: Benchmarking National Environmental Stewardship.* New Haven: Yale Center for Environmental Law & Policy. www.yale.edu/esi/.

Eurostat. 2007. *Europe in Figures: Eurostat Yearbook 2006–2007.* European Commission.

Ewen, Stuart. 1976. *Captains of Consciousness: Advertising and the Social Roots of the Consumer Culture.* New York: McGraw-Hill.

Fabbro, David. 1978. "Peaceful Societies: An Introduction." *Journal of Peace Research* 15(1): 67–83.

Fabun, Don. 1970. *Food: An Energy Exchange System.* Beverly Hills, CA: Glencoe.

Fairchild, Hoxie Neale. 1928. *The Noble Savage: A Study in Romantic Naturalism.* New York: Columbia University Press.

Falla, Ricardo. 1994. *Massacres in the Jungle: Ixcan, Guatemala, 1915–1982.* Boulder, CO: Westview.

FAO, Food and Agriculture Organization of the United Nations. 1963. *Third World Food Survey.* Freedom from Hunger Basic Study No. 11. Rome.

———. 1987. *The Fifth World Food Survey.* Rome.

———. 1992. *The State of Food and Agriculture.* Rome.

———. 1993. *The State of Food and Agriculture 1993.* Rome.

———. 1999. *The State of Food Insecurity in the World 1999.* Rome.

———. 2004. *The State of the World Fisheries and Aquaculture 2004.* Rome. Food and Agriculture Organization of the United Nations. ftp://ftp.fao.org/docrep/fao/007/y5600e/y5600e00.pdf

———. 2006. *The State of Food Insecurity in the World 2006: Eradicating World Hunger— Taking Stock Ten Years after the World Food Summit*. Rome: UNFAO. www.fao.org/ docrep/009/a0750e/a0750e00.htm

———. 2007. *FAOSTAT*. FAO Statistics Division. faostat.fao.org/default.aspx.

Farmer, Paul. 2003. *Pathologies of Power: Health, Human Rights, and the New War on the Poor*. Berkeley: University of California Press.

Farrell, Betty G. 1993. *Elite Families: Class and Power in Nineteenth-Century Boston*. Albany: State University of New York.

Fearnside, Philip M. 2005. "Deforestation in Brazilian Amazonia: History, Rates, and Consequences." *Conservation Biology* 19(3): 680–8.

———. 2006. "Tropical Deforestation and Global Warming." *Science* 312(5777): 1137.

Fei, Hsiao-t'ung, and Chih-i Chang. 1945. *Earthbound China: A Study of Rural Economy in Yunnan*. Chicago: University of Chicago Press.

Feinman, Gary M. 1998. "Scale and Social Organization." In *Archaic States*, edited by Gary M. Feinman and Joyce Marcus, 95–133. Santa Fe, NM: School of American Research Press.

Ferguson, R. Brian. 1995. *Yanomami Warfare: A Political History*. Santa Fe, NM: School of American Research Press.

Feshbach, Murray, and Alfred Friendly Jr. 1992. *Ecocide in the USSR: Health and Nature under Siege*. New York: Basic Books.

Firth, Raymond. 1957. *We the Tikopia*. New York: Barnes and Noble.

Fischer, David Hackett. 1996. *The Great Wave: Price Revolutions and the Rhythm of History*. New York and Oxford: Oxford University Press.

Flanagan, William G. 1987. "Fortress Fisher." *Forbes* (December): 232–37.

Flannery, Kent V. 1969. "Origins and Ecological Effects of Early Domestication in Iran and the Near East." In *The Domestication and Exploitation of Plants and Animals*, edited by Peter J. Ucko and G. W. Dimbleby, 73–100. London: Duckworth.

Fleisher, Mark S. 1995. *Beggars and Thieves: Lives of Urban Street Criminals*. Madison: University of Wisconsin Press.

Fletcher, Roland. 1995. *The Limits of Settlement Growth: A Theoretical Outline*. Cambridge: Cambridge University Press.

Forbes Magazine. "Forbes 400 2001. " (September 27, 2001) www.forbes.com/2001/ 09/27/400.html

Foreign Policy. 2005. "Measuring Globalization" (May/June).

Fortune Magazine. 2005. "Fortune Global 500" (July 25).

———. 2006. "Fortune 500" (April 17).

———. 2006. "Fortune Global 500" (July 24).

Foster, George. 1969. *Applied Anthropology*. Boston: Little, Brown.

Fox, James. 1994. "Security." *Forbes FYI* (September 26): 13–14.

Fox, Richard Wightman, and T. J. Jackson Lears, eds. 1983. *The Culture of Consumption: Critical Essays in American History, 1880–1980*. New York: Pantheon Books.

Freeman, M. M. R. 1971. "A Social and Ecological Analysis of Systematic Female Infanticide." *American Anthropologist* 73(5): 1011–18.

Frenzel, Burkhard, ed. 1992. *Evaluation of Land Surfaces Cleared from Forests by Prehistoric Man in Early Neolithic Times and the Time of Migrating Germanic Tribes.* Stuttgart: G. Fischer.

Freydberg, Nicholas, and Willis A. Gortner. 1982. *The Food Additives Book.* Toronto: Bantam.

Fried, Morton. 1967. *The Evolution of Political Society.* New York: Random House.

Friedman, Jonathan. 1974. "Marxism, Structuralism and Vulgar Materialism." *Man* 9(3): 444–69.

———. 1979. "Hegelian Ecology: Between Rousseau and the World Spirit." In *Social and Ecological Systems*, edited by P. C. Burnham and R. F. Ellen, 253–70. ASA Monograph No. 18. London: Academic.

Friedman, Lawrence M. 1964. "The Dynastic Trust." *Yale Law Journal* 73: 547–92.

Friedman, Milton. 1970. "The Social Responsibility of Business." *New York Times Magazine* (September 13): 122–26.

Fund for Peace, The. 2007. www.fundforpeace.org/thefund/president.php (February).

Gardner, Gary, and Brian Halweil. 2000. "Nourishing the Underfed and Overfed." In *State of the World 2000: A Worldwatch Institute Report on Progress Toward a Sustainable Society*, edited by Lester R. Brown, Christopher Flavin, Hilary French, and Linda Starke, 59–78. New York and London: W. W. Norton and Co.

Garvin, Lewis, Natalie Henry, and Melissa Vernon. 2000. *Community Materials Flow Analysis: A Case Study of Ann Arbor, Michigan.* Center for Sustainable Systems, University of Michigan. Report No. CSS00-02.

Geertz, Clifford. 1963. *Agricultural Involution: The Process of Ecological Change in Indonesia.* Berkeley: University of California Press.

Gemini Consulting. 1998. *World Wealth Report 1998.* New York: Gemini Consulting Limited.

George, Susan. 1977. *How the Other Half Dies: The Real Reasons for World Hunger.* Montclair, NJ: Allanheld, Osmum & Co.

———. 1992. *The Debt Boomerang: How Third World Debt Harms Us All.* Boulder, CO: Westview Press.

———. 2000. "Corporate-led Globalisation: Succinct Description of What the International Economic System Is, How It Works, and to Whose Benefit." www .tni-archives.org/detail_page.phtml?page=archives_george_corpglob1

Globalsecurity. 2007. www.globalsecurity.org/military

Goldschmidt, Walter. 1978. *As You Sow: Three Studies in the Social Consequences of Agribusiness.* Montclair, NJ: Allanheld, Osmum & Co.

Goldsmith, Edward, et al. 1972. *Blueprint for Survival.* Boston: Houghton Mifflin.

Goldsmith, Raymond W. 1985. *Comparative National Balance Sheets: A Study of Twenty Countries, 1688–1978.* Chicago and London: University of Chicago Press.

Goldstein, Joshua S. 1988. *Long Cycles: Prosperity and War in the Modern Age*. New Haven and London: Yale University Press.

Goodland, Robert. 1982. *Tribal Peoples and Economic Development: Human Ecological Considerations*. Washington, D.C.: World Bank.

Gould, Richard A. 1971. "Uses and Effects of Fire Among the Western Desert Aborigines of Australia." *Mankind* 8(1): 14–24.

———. 1981. "Comparative Ecology of Food-Sharing in Australia and Northwest California." In *Omnivorous Primates: Gathering and Hunting in Human Evolution*, edited by Robert S. O. Harding and Geza Teleki, 422–54. New York: Columbia University Press.

Gould, Stephen Jay. 1996. *Full House: The Spread of Excellence from Plato to Darwin*. New York: Harmony Books.

Goulet, Denis. 1971. *The Cruel Choice: A New Concept in the Theory of Development*. New York: Atheneum.

Gras, Norman S. B. 1915. *The Evolution of the English Corn Market: From the Twelfth to the Eighteenth Century*. Cambridge: Harvard University Press.

Grayson, Donald K. 1984. "Explaining Pleistocene Extinctions: Thoughts on the Structure of a Debate." In *Quaternary Extinctions*, edited by P. S. Martin and R. G. Klein, 807–23. Tucson: University of Arizona Press.

———. 1991. "Late Pleistocene Mammalian Extinctions in North America: Taxonomy, Chronology, and Explanations." *Journal of World Prehistory* 5: 193–231.

Grayson, Donald K., and David J. Meltzer. 2002. "Clovis Hunting and Large Mammal Extinction: A Critical Review of the Evidence." *Journal of World Prehistory* 16(4):313-59.

———. 2003. "A Requiem for North American Overkill." *Journal of Archaeological Science* 30: 585–93.

Great Britain. *Britain 1982: An Official Handbook*. London: Her Majesty's Stationery Office.

Great Britain, Ministry of Agriculture. 1990. *Agricultural Statistics United Kingdom 1988*. London: HMSO.

Greenberg, Ilan. 2006. "As a Sea Rises, So Do Hopes for Fish, Jobs and Riches." *New York Times*. (April 6).

Greenpeace International. www.exxonsecrets.org (2006).

Greider, William. 1987. *Secrets of the Temple: How the Federal Reserve Runs the Country*. New York: Simon and Schuster.

———. 2000. "Business Creates Eco-Side!" Review of *Natural Capitalism*, by Paul Hawken, Amory Lovins, and L. Hunter Lovins. *The Nation* 270(8): 26–28.

Gross, Daniel R., and Barbara A. Underwood. "Technological Change and Caloric Costs: Sisal Agriculture 1971." *American Anthropologist* 73(2): 725–40.

Gunderson, Lance H., and C. S. Hilling, ed. 2002. *Panarchy: Understanding Transformations in Human and Natural Systems*. Washington, D.C.: Island Press.

Gunn, Christopher, and Hazel Dayton Gunn. 1991. *Reclaiming Capital: Democratic Initiatives and Community Development*. Ithaca and London: Cornell University Press.

Gustafson, A. E, C. H. Guise, W. J. Hamilton Jr., and H. Ries. 1939. *Conservation in the United States*. Ithaca, NY: Comstock.

Gutkind, E. A. 1956. "Our World from the Air: Conflict and Adaptation." In *Man's Role in Changing the Face of the Earth*, edited by William L. Thomas Jr., 1–44. Chicago: University of Chicago Press.

Hagood, Mel A. 1972. "Which Irrigation System?" *Proceedings of the 11th Annual Washington Potato Conference and Trade Fair*, 83–86. Washington Potato Conference, Moses Lake, Washington.

Hall, Peter Dobkin. 1982. *The Organization of American Culture, 1700–1900: Private Institutions, Elites, and the Origins of American Nationality*. New York: New York University Press.

Hallam, S. 1975. *Fire and Hearth*. Canberra: Australian Institute of Aboriginal Studies.

Hallpike, C. R. 1979. *The Foundations of Primitive Thought*. Oxford: Clarendon.

Hancock, David. 1995. *Citizens of the World: London Merchants and the Integration of the British Atlantic Community, 1735–1785*. Cambridge: Cambridge University Press.

Harbom, Lotta, Stina Högbladh, and Peter Wallensteen. 2006. "Armed Conflict and Peace Agreements." *Journal of Peace Research* 43(5): 617–31.

Hardin, Garrett. 1968. "The Tragedy of the Commons." *Science* 162(3859): 1243–48.

———. 1991. "The Tragedy of the Unmanaged Commons: Population and the Disguises of Providence." In *Commons Without Tragedy*, edited by Robert V Andelson, 162–85. London: Shepheard-Walwyn.

Harris, David R. 1972. "The Origins of Agriculture in the Tropics." *American Scientist* 60(2): 180–93.

———. 1989. "An Evolutionary Continuum of People-Plant Interaction." In *Foraging and Farming: The Evolution of Plant Exploitation*, edited by D. R. Harris and G. C. Hillman, 11–26. London: Unwin Hyman.

Harris, Fred R. 1998. "The Kerner Report Thirty Years Later." In *Locked in the Poorhouse: Cities, Race, and Poverty in the United States*, edited by Fred R. Harris and Lynn A. Curds, 7–19. Lanham, MD: Rowman & Littlefield.

Harris, Marvin. 1971. *Culture, Man and Nature*. New York: Crowell.

———. 1975. *Culture, People and Nature*. New York: Crowell.

Harris, Marvin, and Eric B. Ross. 1987. *Death, Sex, and Fertility: Population Regulation in Preindustrial and Developing Societies*. New York: Columbia University Press.

Hartmann, Betsy, and James Boyce. 1982. *Needless Hunger: Voices from a Bangladesh Village*. San Francisco: Institute for Food and Development Policy.

Hassan, Fekri A. 1981. *Demographic Archaeology*. New York: Academic Press.

Hawken, Paul. 1993. *The Ecology of Commerce: A Declaration of Sustainability*. New York: HarperCollins.

Hawken, Paul, Amory B. Lovins, and L. Hunter Lovins. 1999. *Natural Capitalism: Creating the Next Industrial Revolution*. Boston: Little, Brown.

Hayden, Brian. 1975. "The Carrying Capacity Dilemma: An Alternate Approach." *American Antiquity* 40(2): 11–19, Memoir 30.

———. 1981a. "Research and Development in the Stone Age: Technological Transitions Among Hunter-Gatherers." *Current Anthropology* 22(5): 519–48.

———. 1981b. "Subsistence and Ecological Adaptations of Modern Hunter/ Gatherers." In *Omnivorous Primates: Gathering and Hunting in Human Evolution*, edited by Robert S. Harding and Geza Teleki, 344–421. New York: Columbia University Press.

———. 1990. "Nimrods, Piscators, Pluckers, and Planters: The Emergence of Food Production." *Journal of Anthropological Archaeology* 9(1): 31–69.

———. 1995a. "A New Overview of Domestication." In *Last Hunters, First Farmers: New Perspectives on the Prehistoric Transition to Agriculture*, edited by T. D. Price and A. B. Gebauer, 273–99. Santa Fe, NM: School of American Research Press.

———. 1995b. "Pathways to Power: Principles for Creating Socioeconomic Inequalities." In *Foundations of Social Inequality*, edited by T. Douglas Price and Gary M. Feinman, 15–86. New York and London: Plenum Press.

Hazell, Peter B. R. 1994. "Rice in India." *National Geographic Research & Exploration* 10(2): 172–83.

Headland, Thomas N. 1990. "Time Allocation, Demography, and Original Affluence in a Philippine Negrito Hunter-Gatherer Society." In *Sixth International Conference on Hunting and Gathering Societies: Precirculated Papers and Abstracts* 1: 427–39. Fairbanks: University of Alaska.

———. 1997. "Revisionism in Ecological Anthropology." *Current Anthropology* 38(4): 605–30.

Hecker, Howard M. 1982. "Domestication Revisited: Its Implications for Faunal Analysis." *Journal of Field Archaeology* 9: 217–36.

Heilbroner, Robert L. 1963. *The Great Ascent: The Struggle for Economic Development in Our Time.* New York: Harper & Row Torchbooks.

———. 1974. *An Inquiry into the Human Prospect.* New York: Norton.

Heller, Martin C., and Gregory A. Keoleian. 2000. *Life Cycle-based Sustainability Indicators for Assessment of the U.S. Food System.* Report No CSS00-04 Center for Sustainable Systems. Ann Arbor: University of Michigan.

Hemming, John. 1978. *Red Gold: The Conquest of the Brazilian Indians.* Cambridge: Harvard University Press.

Henry, Jules. 1963. *Culture Against Man.* New York: Random House.

Herskovits, Melville J. 1952. *Economic Anthropology.* New York: Knopf.

Hewlett, Barry. 1991. "Demography and Childcare in Preindustrial Societies." *Journal of Anthropological Research* 47(1): 1–37.

Hewlett, Barry S., and L. L. Cavalli-Sforza. 1986. "Cultural Transmission Among Aka Pygmies." *American Anthropologist* 88: 922–34.

Hobbes, Thomas. 1958. *Leviathan.* New York: Liberal Arts. Originally published in 1651.

Hölldobler, Bert, and Edward O. Wilson. 1990. *The Ants*. Cambridge, MA: Belknap Press of Harvard University Press.

Homer-Dixon, Thomas F. 1991. "On the Threshold: Environmental Changes as Causes of Acute Conflict." *International Security* 16(2): 76–116.

———. 2006. *The Upside of Down: Catastrophe, Creativity, and the Renewal of Civilization*. Washington, D.C.: Island Press.

Hooks, Gregory. 1991. *Forging the Military-Industrial Complex: World War II's Battle of the Potomac*. Urbana and Chicago: University of Illinois Press.

Hooper, Wilfrid. 1915. "The Tudor Sumptuary Laws." *English Historical Review* 30(119): 433–49.

Hornborg, Alf. 1992. "Machine Fetishism, Value, and the Image of Unlimited Good: Towards a Thermodynamics of Imperialism." *Man* 27(1): 1–18.

———. 2001. *The Power of the Machine: Global Inequalities of Economy, Technology, and Environment*. Walnut Creek, CA: Altamira Press.

Horton, D. R. 1984. "Red Kangaroos: Last of the Australian Megafauna." In *Quaternary Extinctions: A Prehistoric Revolution*, edited by Paul S. Martin and Richard G. Klein, 639–80. Tucson: University of Arizona Press.

Hubbert, M. King. 1969. "Energy Resources." *In Resources and Man*. National Academy of Sciences, 157–242. San Francisco: W. H. Freeman.

Huey, John. 1993. "The World's Best Brand." *Fortune* (May 31): 44–54.

Hughes, Barry B., and Evan E. Hillebrand. 2006. *Exploring and Shaping International Futures*. Boulder, CO: Paradigm Publishers. www.du.edu/~bhughes/ifsoverview.htm

Hulett, H. R. 1970. "Optimum World Population." *BioScience* 20(3): 160–61.

Humphrey, Nicholas K. 1976. "The Social Function of Intellect." In *Growing Points in Ethology*, edited by P. P. G. Bateson and R. A. Hinde, 303–17. Based on a conference sponsored by St. John's College and King's College, Cambridge. Cambridge and New York: Cambridge University Press.

Hunn, E. 1982. "Mobility as a Factor Limiting Resource Use in the Columbia Plateau of North America." In *Resource Managers: North American and Australian Hunter-Gatherers*, edited by N. Williams and E. Hunn, 17–43. Boulder, CO: Westview Press.

Hunt, Terry L. 2006. "Rethinking the Fall of Easter Island: New Evidence Points to an Alternative Explanation for a Civilization's Collapse." *American Scientist* 94(5): 412–19.

Hunt, Terry L., and Carl P. Lipo. 2006. "Late Colonization of Easter Island." *Science* 311(5767): 1603–6.

Hunter, Beatrice Tram. 1982. *Food Additives and Federal Policy: The Mirage of Safety*. Brattleboro, VT: Greene.

Huntington, Samuel P. 1993. "The Clash of Civilizations?" *Foreign Affairs* 1993 72(3): 22–49.

———. 1996. *The Clash of Civilizations and the Remaking of World Order*. New York: Touchstone, Simon and Schuster.

Imhoff, Marc L., Lahouari Bounoua, Taylor Ricketts, Colby Loucks, Robert Harriss, and William T. Lawrence. 2004. "Global Patterns in Human Consumption of Net Primary Production." *Nature* 429 (June 24): 870–73.

Instiuto Nacional de Pesquisas Espacias (INPE). 2002. "Monitoring of the Brazilian Amazonian Forest by Satellite 2000–2001." www.inpe.br/

IPCC (Intergovernmental Panel on Climate Change). 1991. *Climate Change: The IPCC Response Strategies.* Washington, D.C., and Covelo, CA: Island Press.

———. 2001. *Climate Change 2001: Synthesis Report. Contribution of Work Groups I, II, and III to the Third Assessment.* Report of the Intergovernmental Panel on Climate Change. Edited by R. T. Watson. Cambridge and New York: Cambridge University Press.

———. 2007. *Climate Change 2007: The Physical Science Basis, Summary for Policymakers. Contribution of Working Group I to the Fourth Assessment Report of the Intergovernmental Pattern on Climate Change.* www.ipcc.ch/WG1_SPM_17Apr07.pdf

IUCN (International Union for the Conservation of Nature). 2006. Red List of Threatened Species. www.iucnredlist.org/

IWGIA. 1978. *Guatemala 1918: The Massacre at Panzos.* Copenhagen: International Work Group for Indigenous Affairs.

Jacobsen, Thorkild, and Robert M. Adams. 1958. "Salt and Silt in Ancient Mesopotamian Agriculture." *Science* 128(3334): 1251–58.

Jannuzi, F. Tomasson, and James T. Peach. 1977. *Report on the Hierarchy of Interests in Land in Bangladesh.* Washington, D.C.: Agency for International Development, September 1977.

Jhally, Sut. 1997. Advertising & the End of the World. Transcript. Northhampton, MA: Media Education Foundation. www.mediaed.org/handouts/pdfs/AEW.pdf

Johnson, Allen. 1975. "Time Allocation in a Machiguenga Community." *Ethnology* 14(3): 301–10.

———. 1985. "In Search of the Affluent Society." In *Anthropology: Contemporary Perspectives*, edited by David E. K. Hunter and Phillip Whitten, 201–6. Boston: Little, Brown. First published in *Human Nature*, September 1978.

———. 2003. *Families of the Forest: The Matsigenka Indians of the Peruvian Amazon.* Berkeley: University of California Press.

Johnson, Allen, and Clifford A. Behrens. 1982. "Nutritional Criteria in Machiguenga Food Production Decisions: A Linear-Programming Analysis." *Human Ecology* 10(2): 167–89.

Jones, Nicola. 2003. "South Aral gone in 15 Years." *New Scientist* 179(2404): 9.

Kaberry, Phyllis M. 1939. *Aboriginal Woman: Sacred and Profane.* London: Routledge.

Kaplan, Robert D. 1994. "The Coming Anarchy." *Atlantic Monthly* (February) 273(2): 44–76.

Kardong, Kenneth V. 1998. *Vertebrates: Comparative Anatomy, Function, Evolution.* 2nd ed. Boston: WCB McGraw-Hill.

Keeley, Lawrence H. 1996. *War Before Civilization*. New York and Oxford: Oxford University Press.

Keenleyside, H. L. 1950. "Critical Mineral Shortages." In *Proceedings of the United Nations Scientific Conference on the Conservation and Utilization of Resources*, August 17–September 6, 1949, 38–46. Lake Success, NY: United Nations.

Kelly, Raymond C. 1968. "Demographic Pressure and Descent Group Structure in the New Guinea Highlands." *Oceania* 38(l): 36–63.

———. 1993. *Constructing Inequality: The Fabrication of a Hierarchy of Virtue among the Etoro*. Ann Arbor: University of Michigan Press.

———. 2000. *Warless Societies and the Origin of War*. Ann Arbor: University of Michigan Press.

Kennedy, Paul M. 1993. *Preparing for the Twenty-First Century*. New York: Random House.

Kennickell, Arthur B., Martha Starr-McCluer, and Brian J. Surette. 2000. "Recent Changes in U.S. Family Finances: Results from the 1998 Survey of Consumer Finances." *Federal Reserve Bulletin* 86: 1–29.

Kermode, G. O. 1972. "Food Additives." *Scientific American* 226(3): 15–21.

King, Gregory. 1936. *Two Tracts: (a) Natural and Political Observations and Conclusions upon the State and Condition of England and (b) Of the Naval Trade of England Ao. 1688 and the National Profit Then Arising Thereby*, edited by George E. Barnett. Baltimore: Johns Hopkins University Press. Originally published in 1696.

Kintisch, Eli. 2006. "Climate Change: Along the Road From Kyoto Global Greenhouse Gas Emissions Keep Rising." *Science* 311(5758): 1702–3.

Kirch, Patrick Vinton, and D. E. Yen. 1982. *Tikopia: The Prehistory and Ecology of a Polynesian Outlier*. Bernice P. Bishop Museum Bulletin 238. Honolulu: Bishop Museum Press.

Klein, Richard G. 1979. "Stone Age Exploitation of Animals in Southern Africa." *American Scientist* 67(2): 151–60.

———. 1981. "Stone Age Predation on Small African Bovids." *South African Archaeological Bulletin* 36(1981): 55–65.

———. 1984. "Mammalian Extinctions and Stone Age People in Africa." In *Quaternary Extinctions: A Prehistoric Revolution*, edited by Paul S. Martin and Richard G. Klein, 354–403. Tucson: University of Arizona Press.

Knauft, B. 1987. "Reconsidering Violence in Simple Societies." *Current Anthropology* 28: 457–500.

Knudson, Bob. 1972. "Time Management—It Pays." *Proceedings of the 11th Annual Washington Potato Conference and Trade Fair*, 71–76. Washington Potato Conference, Moses Lake, Washington.

Knudson, Kenneth E. 1970. "Resource Fluctuation, Productivity, and Social Organization on Micronesian Coral Islands." Doctoral dissertation, University of Oregon.

Kohr, Leopold. 1978. *The Breakdown of Nations*. New York: Dutton. Originally published in 1957.

Komlos, John. 1989. *Nutrition and Economic Development in the Eighteenth-Century Habsburg Monarchy: An Anthropometric History*. Princeton, NJ: Princeton University Press.

Korten, David C. 2006. *The Great Turning: From Empire to Earth Community*. San Francisco: Berrett-Koehler; Bloomfield, CT: Kumarian Press.

Krantz, Grover S. 1976. "On the Nonmigration of Hunting Peoples." *Northwest Anthropological Research Notes* 10(2): 209–16.

Krebs, A. V. 1992. *The Corporate Reapers: The Book of Agribusiness*. Washington, D.C.: Essential Books.

Krech, Shepard, III. 1999. *The Ecological Indian: Myth and History*. New York: W. W. Norton and Co.

Kroll, Luisa, and Lea Goldman. 2005. "The World's Billionaires." *Forbes Magazine* (March 10). www.forbes.com/2005/03/09/bill05land.html

Kroll, Luisa, and Allison Fass. 2007. "The World's Billionaires." *Forbes Magazine*. (March 8).

Kunstadter, Peter. 1971. "Natality, Mortality and Migration in Upland and Lowland Populations in Northwestern Thailand." In *Culture and Population*, edited by Steven Polgar, 46–60. Cambridge, MA: Schenkman.

Lacina, Bethany, and Nils Petter Gleditsch. 2005. "Monitoring Trends in Global Combat: A New Dataset of Battle Deaths." *European Journal of Population* 21(2–3): 145–66.

Lancaster, P. A., et al. 1982. "Traditional Cassava-Based Foods: Survey of Processing Techniques." *Economic Botany* 36(1): 12–45.

Landsberg, Hans H. 1964. *Natural Resources in America's Future: A Look Ahead to the Year 2000*. Baltimore: Johns Hopkins University Press.

Landsberg, Hans H., Leonard L. Fischman, and Joseph L. Fisher. 1963. *Resources in America's Future: Patterns of Requirements and Availabilities 1960–2000*. Baltimore: Johns Hopkins University Press.

Lappé, Frances Moore, and Joseph Collins. 1977. *Food First: Beyond the Myth of Scarcity*. Boston: Houghton Mifflin.

Lathrap, Don W. 1970. *The Upper Amazon*. New York: Praeger.

———. 1977. "Our Father the Cayman, Our Mother the Gourd: Spinden Revisited, or a Unitary Theory for the Emergence of Agriculture in the New World." In *Origins of Agriculture*, edited by Charles A. Reed, 713–51. The Hague: Mouton.

Lee, Richard B. 1968. "What Hunters Do for a Living, or How to Make Out on Scarce Resources." In *Man the Hunter*, edited by Richard B. Lee and Irven De Vore, 30–48. Chicago: Aldine.

———. 1969. "!Kung Bushman Subsistence: An Input-Output Analysis." *Contributions to Anthropology: Ecological Essays*. National Museums of Canada Bulletin 230, 73–94.

———. 1979. *The !Kung San: Men, Women, and Work in a Foraging Society*. Cambridge and New York: Cambridge University Press.

———. 1981. "Politics, Sexual and Non-sexual, in an Egalitarian Society." In *Social Inequality: Comparative and Developmental Approaches*, edited by Gerald D. Berreman, 83–102. New York: Academic Press.

———. 1982. "Politics, Sexual and Non-sexual, in an Egalitarian Society." In *Politics and History in Band Societies*, edited by Eleanor Leacock and Richard Lee, 37–59. Cambridge University Press.

Lee, Richard B., and Irven De Vore. 1968. *Man the Hunter.* Chicago: Aldine.

Leeuw, Sander E. van der. 1997. *ARCHAEOMEDES: A DG-XII Research Programme to Understand the Natural and Anthropogenic Causes of Land Degradation and Desertification in the Mediterranean Basin.* Paris: University of Paris.

Leeuw, Sander E. van der, and J. McGlade, eds. 1997. *Archaeology: Time and Structured Transformation.* London: Routledge.

Levin, M. G., and L. P. Potapov. 1964. *The Peoples of Siberia.* Chicago: University of Chicago Press.

Levintanus, Arkady. 1993. "On the Fall of the Aral Sea." *Environments* 22(1): 89–94.

Levi-Strauss, Claude. 1944. "The Social and Psychological Aspects of Chieftainship in a Primitive Tribe: The Nambikuara of Northwestern Matto Grosso." *Transactions of the New York Academy of Sciences* 7:16–32.

———. 1966. *The Savage Mind.* Chicago: University of Chicago Press.

Lewis, Henry T. 1982. *A Time for Burning.* Edmonton, Alberta: Boreal Institute for Northern Studies, Occasional Publications 17.

List, Georg Friedrich. 1922. *The National System of Political Economy.* London: Longmans, Green and Co. Originally published in 1837.

Loh, Jonathan, and Mathis Wackernagel. 2004. *Living Planet Report 2004.* Gland, Switzerland: WWF-World Wide Fund for Nature.

Lomborg, Bjørn, ed. 2004. *Global Crises, Global Solutions.* Cambridge and New York: Cambridge University Press.

———. 2001. *The Skeptical Environmentalist: Measuring the Real State of the World.* Cambridge and New York: Cambridge University Press.

Lourandos, Harry. 1985. "Intensification and Australian Prehistory." In *Prehistoric Hunter-Gatherers: The Emergence of Cultural Complexity*, edited by T. Douglas Price and James A. Brown, 385–423. New York: Academic Press.

———. 1987. "Pleistocene Australia: Peopling a Continent." In *The Pleistocene Old World: Regional Perspectives*, edited by Olga Soffer, 147–65. New York: Plenum Press.

Lovelock, James. 2006. *The Revenge of Gaia: Earth's Climate Crisis and the Fate of Humanity.* New York: Basic Books.

Lovering, T. S. 1968. "Non-Fuel Mineral Resources in the Next Century." *Texas Quarterly* (Summer): 127–47.

Luten, Daniel B. 1974. "United States Requirements." In *Energy, the Environment, and Human Health*, edited by A. Finkel, 17–33. Acton, MA: Publishing Sciences Group, Inc.

MacCannell, Dean, and Jerry White. 1984. "The Social Costs of Large-Scale Agriculture: The Prospects of Land Reform in California." In *Land Reform, American Style*, edited by Charles C. Geisler and Frank J. Popper, 35–54. Totawa, NJ: Rowman & Allanheld.

MacNeish, Richard S. 1971. "Speculation About How and Why Food Production and Village Life Developed in the Tehuacan Valley, Mexico." *Archaeology* 24(4): 307–15.

Madden, J. Patrick. 1967. *Economics of Size in Farming: Theory, Analytic Procedures, and a Review of Selected Studies*. Economic Research Service, USDA. Agricultural Economic Report 107.

Maddison, Angus. 2003. *The World Economy: Historical Statistics*. OECD: Development Centre Studies, Paris.

Mager, Nathan H. 1987. *The Kondratieff Waves*. New York: Praeger.

Malinowski, Bronislaw. 1941. "An Anthropological Analysis of War." *American Journal of Sociology* 46(4): 521–50.

———. 1944. *Freedom and Civilization*. New York: Roy.

Malthus, Thomas R. 1895. *An Essay on the Principle of Population*. Parallel chapters from the 1st and 2nd eds. New York: Macmillan. Originally published in 1798, 2nd ed. originally published in 1807.

Mamdani, Mahmood. 1973. *The Myth of Population Control: Family, Caste, and Class in an Indian Village*. New York: Monthly Review Press.

Mander, Jerry. 1996. "The Rules of Corporate Behavior." In *The Case Against the Global Economy and for a Turn Toward the Local*, edited by Jerry Mander and Edward Goldsmith, 309–22. San Francisco: Sierra Club Books.

Mander, Jerry, and Edward Goldsmith, eds. 1996. *The Case Against the Global Economy and for a Turn Toward the Local*. San Francisco: Sierra Club Books.

Manning, Richard. 2004. "The Oil We Eat: Following the Food Chain Back to Iraq." *Harper's Magazine*. (February).

———. 2004. *Against the Grain: How Agriculture Has Hijacked Civilization*. New York: North Point Press.

Mansel, Philip. 1987. *The Eagle in Splendor: Napoleon I and His Court*. London: George Philip.

Mansfield, Edward D. 1994. *Power, Trade, and War*. Princeton, NJ: Princeton University Press.

Marcus, George E., with Peter Dobkin Hall. 1992. *Lives in Trust: The Fortunes of Dynastic Families in Late Twentieth-Century America*. Boulder, CO: Westview Press.

Marcus, Joyce. 1998. "The Peaks and Valleys of Ancient States: An Extension of the Dynamic Model." In *Archaic States*, edited by Gary M. Feinman and Joyce Marcus, 59–94. Santa Fe, NM: School of American Research Press.

Marks, Nic, and Saamah Abdallah, Andrew Simms, and Sam Thompson. 2006. *The Happy Planet Index: An Index of Human Well-Being and Environmental Impact*. London: New Economics Foundation. www.neweconomics.org/gen/z_sys_PublicationDetail.aspx?PID=225

Marple, Gary A., and Harry B. Wissman, eds. 1968. *Grocery Manufacturing in the United States*. New York: Praeger.

Marsh, George P. 1864. *Man and Nature*. New York: Scribner's.

Marshall, Peter, ed. 1986. *The Anarchist Writings of William Godwin*. London: Freedom Press.

Marshall, Yvonne. 2006. "Introduction: Adopting a Sedentary Lifeway." *World Archaeology* 38(2): 153–163.

Martin, Paul S. 1967. "Prehistoric Overkill." In *Pleistocene Extinctions: The Search for a Cause*, edited by P. S. Martin and H. E. Wright Jr., 75–120. Proceedings of the 7th Congress of the International Association for Quaternary Research. New Haven: Yale University Press.

———. 1984. "Prehistoric Overkill: The Global Model." In *Quaternary Extinctions: A Prehistoric Revolution*, edited by Paul S. Martin and Richard G. Klein, 553–73. Tucson: University of Arizona Press.

Mather, Alexander. 2000. "South-North Challenges in Global Forestry." In *World Forests from Deforestation to Transition?* edited by Matti Palo and Heidi Vanhanen, 25–40. Dordrecht: Kluwer Academic.

Mathias, Peter, and Patrick K. O'Brien. 1976. "Taxation in Britain and France, 1715–1810." *Journal of European Economic History* 5: 601–50.

Matthews, Anne. 1992. *Where the Buffalo Roam*. New York: Grove Weidenfeld.

Mayhew, Bruce H. 1973. "System Size and Ruling Elites." *American Sociological Review* 38: 468–75.

Mayhew, Bruce H., and Paul T. Schollaert. 1980a. "Social Morphology of Pareto's Economic Elite." *Social Forces* 59(l): 25–43.

———. 1980b. "The Concentration of Wealth: A Sociological Model." *Sociological Focus* 13(1): 1–35.

Mazur, Allan, and Eugene Rosa. 1974. "Energy and Life Style." *Science* 186(4164): 607–10.

MCC (Mondragón Corporación Cooperativa). 2006. *2005 Annual Report*. www.mcc.es/

McCabe, J. Terrence. 1990. "Turkana Pastoralism: A Case Against the Tragedy of the Commons." *Human Ecology* 18: 81–103.

———. 2004. *Cattle Bring Us to Our Enemies: Turkana Ecology, Politics, and Raiding in a Disequilibrium System*. Ann Arbor: University of Michigan Press.

McCarthy, F. D., and Margaret McArthur. 1960. "The Food Quest and Time Factor in Aboriginal Economic Life." In *Records of the American-Australian Scientific Expedition to Arnhem Land*, edited by C. P. Mountford. Vol. 2, *Anthropology and Nutrition*, 145–94. Melbourne: Melbourne University Press.

McCay, Bonnie J., and James M. Acheson, eds. 1987. *The Question of the Commons: The Culture and Ecology of Communal Resources*. Tucson: University of Arizona Press.

McConnell, Grant. 1953. *The Decline of Agrarian Democracy*. Berkeley and Los Angeles: University of California Press.

McCorriston, Joy. 1997. "The Fiber Revolution: Textile Extensification, Alienation, and Social Stratification in Ancient Mesopotamia." *Current Anthropology* 38(4): 517–49.

McCracken, Grant. 1988. *Culture and Consumption: New Approaches to the Symbolic Character of Consumer Goods and Activities*. Bloomington and Indianapolis: Indiana University Press.

McDonald, David. 1977. "Food Taboos: A Primitive Environmental Protection Agency (South America)." *Anthropos* 72: 734–48.

McEvedy, Colin, and Richard Jones. 1978. *Atlas of World Population History*. Middlesex, England, and New York: Penguin Books.

McGlade, James. n.d. *ARCHAEOMEDES II. Proyecto Emporda: Human Ecodynamics and Land Use Conflict: Monitoring Degradation-Sensitive Environments in the Emporda North-East Spain*, www.ucl.ac.uk/archaeology/research/profiles/mcglade/archgld.htm.

McKendrick, Neil. 1982a. "The Commercialization of Fashion." In *The Birth of a Consumer Society: The Commercialization of Eighteenth-Century England*, edited by Neil McKendrick, John Brewer, and J. H. Plumb, 34–99. Bloomington: Indiana University Press.

———. 1982b. "The Consumer Revolution of Eighteenth-Century England." In *The Birth of a Consumer Society: The Commercialization of Eighteenth-Century England*, edited by Neil McKendrick, John Brewer, and J. H. Plumb, 9–33. Bloomington: Indiana University Press.

McKendrick, Neil, John Brewer, and J. H. Plumb, eds. 1982. *The Birth of a Consumer Society: The Commercialization of Eighteenth-Century England*. Bloomington: Indiana University Press.

McLean, Bethany, and Peter Elkind. 2004. *The Smartest Guys in the Room: The Amazing Rise and Scandalous Fall of Enron*. New York: Penguin.

McMahon, T. A., and. T. Bonner. 1983. *On Size and Life*. New York: Scientific American Library.

Mead, Margaret. 1940. "Warfare Is Only an Invention—Not a Biological Necessity." *Asia* 40: 402–5.

Meadows, Donella H., Dennis L. Meadows, and Jorgen Randers. 1992. *Beyond the Limits: Confronting Global Collapse, Envisioning a Sustainable Future*. Post Mills, VT: Chelsea Green Publishing Co.

Meadows, Donella H., Dennis L. Meadows, Jorgen Randers, and William W. Behrens III. 1972. *The Limits to Growth*. New York: Universe.

Meadows, Donella, Jorgen Randers, and Dennis Meadows. 2004. *Limits to Growth: The 30-Year Update*. White River Jct., VT: Chelsea Green Publishing.

Meggers, Betty J. 1971. *Amazonia: Man and Culture in a Counterfeit Paradise*. Chicago: Aldine.

———. 1995. "Judging the Future by the Past: The Impact of Environmental Instability on Prehistoric Amazonian Populations." In *Indigenous Peoples and the Future of Amazonia: An Ecological Anthropology of an Endangered World*, edited by Leslie E. Sponsel, 15–43. Tucson and London: University of Arizona Press.

Mellars, Paul. 1976. "Fire Ecology, Animal Populations and Man: A Study of Some Ecological Relationships in Prehistory." *Proceedings of the Prehistoric Society* 42: 15–45.

Mergent-Online (March 2007). www.mergentonline.com/

Millennium Ecosystem Assessment. 2005. *Ecosystems and Human Well-being: Synthesis.* Washington, D.C.: Island Press.

Millennium Ecosystem Assessment. 2005. *Living Beyond Our Means: Natural Assets and Human Well-Being. Statement from the Board.* Technical Volume. Washington, D.C.: Island Press. www.maweb.org/en/Products.BoardStatement.aspx

Miller, Daniel. 1987. *Material Culture and Mass Consumption.* Oxford and New York: Basil Blackwell Inc.

Miller, Matthew, and Tatiana Serafin. 2006. "The 400 Richest Americans." *Forbes Magazine.* (October). www.forbes.com/lists/2006/54/biz_06rich400_The-400-Richest-Americans_land.html

Mills, C. Wright. 1963. "A Diagnosis of Our Moral Uneasiness." In *Power, Politics, and People,* edited by I. H. Horowitz. New York: Ballantine.

Mining Magazine. 1971. "Bougainville Project Nearing Completion." *Mining Magazine* 124(5): 377–81.

Modjeska, Nicholas. 1982. "Production and Inequality: Perspectives from Central New Guinea." In *Inequality in New Guinea Highlands Societies,* edited by Andrew Strathern, 50–108. Cambridge: Cambridge University Press.

Montagu, Ashley. 1972. "Sociogenic Brain Damage." *American Anthropologist* 74(5): 1045–61.

Moore, Andrew M. T. 1983. "The First Farmers in the Levant." In *The Hilly Flanks and Beyond: Essays on the Prehistory of Southwestern Asia,* 91–111. Studies in Ancient Oriental Civilization No. 36. Chicago: The Oriental Institute of the University of Chicago.

Moore, Andrew M. T., G. C. Hillman, and A. J. Legge. 2000. *Village on the Euphrates: From Foraging to Farming at Abu Hureyra.* New York: Oxford University Press.

Moran, Emilio. 1993. *Through Amazonian Eyes: The Human Ecology of Amazonian Populations.* Iowa City: University of Iowa Press.

Morgan, Dan. 1979. *Merchants of Grain.* New York: Viking Press.

Morgan, Lewis Henry. 1877. *Ancient Society.* New York: Holt.

Morris, David M. 1979. *Measuring the Condition of the World's Poor: The Physical Quality of Life Index.* New York: Pergamon.

Morrison, Roy. 1991. *We Build the Road as We Travel.* Philadelphia: New Society Publishers.

Morton, Douglas C. et al. 2006. "Cropland expansion changes deforestation dynamics in the southern Brazilian Amazon." Proceedings of the National Academy of Science 103(39): 14637–41.

Moseley, Michael Edward. 1975. *The Maritime Foundations of Andean Civilization.* Menlo Park, CA: Cummings.

Mouawad, Jad. 2006. "For Leading Exxon to Its Riches, $144,573 a Day." *New York Times* (April 15, 2006), Business/Financial Desk.

Myers, Fred R. 1982. "Always Ask: Resource Use and Land Ownership Among Pintupi Aborigines of the Australian Western Desert." In *Resource Managers: North American and Australian Hunter-Gatherers*, edited by Nancy M. Williams and Eugene S. Hunn, 173–95. AAAS Selected Symposium No. 67. Boulder, CO: Westview.

Myers, Norman. 1980. *Conversion of Tropical Moist Forests: A Report Prepared by Norman Myers for the Committee on Research Priorities in Tropical Biology of the National Research Council.* Washington, D.C.: National Academy of Sciences.

———. 1992. *The Primary Source: Tropical Forests and Our Future.* New York: Norton.

Naím, Moisés. 2005. *Illicit: How Smugglers, Traffickers, and Copycats are Hijacking the Global Economy.* New York: Doubleday.

Naisbitt, John. 1994. *Global Paradox: The Bigger the World Economy, the More Powerful Its Smallest Players.* New York: William Morrow.

Naisbitt, John, and Patricia Aburdene. 1990. *Megatrends 2000.* New York: William Morrow.

Nakicenovic, Nebojsa, and Robert Swart, ed.. 2000. *Special Report on Emissions Scenarios: A Special Report of Working Group III of the Intergovernmental Panel on Climate Change.* Cambridge and New York: Cambridge University Press.

Naroll, R. 1966. "Does Military Deterrence Deter?" *Trans-Action* 3(2): 14–20.

Nash, June. 1989. *From Tank Town to High Tech: The Class of Community and Industrial Cycles.* Albany: State University of New York.

———. 1994. "Global Integration and Subsistence Insecurity." *American Anthropologist* 96(1): 7–30.

Nash, Manning. 1966. *Primitive and Peasant Economic Systems.* San Francisco: Chandler.

NASS (National Agricultural Statistics Service) Farm Labor, August 16, 2002. usda.mannlib.cornell.edu/MannUsda/homepage.do

National Academy of Sciences. 1969. *Resources and Man.* San Francisco: W. H. Freeman.

National Research Council, Committee on Mineral Resources and the Environment. 1975. *Mineral Resources and the Environment.* Washington, D.C.: National Academy of Sciences.

Neel, James V. 1968. "Some Aspects of Differential Fertility in Two American Indian Tribes." *Proceedings of the Eighth International Congress of Anthropological and Ethnological Sciences* 1(1968): 356–61. Tokyo: ICAES.

———. 1970. "Lessons from a Primitive People." *Science* 170(3960): 815–21.

Nelson, Richard K. 1969. *Hunters of the Northern Ice.* Chicago: University of Chicago Press.

Netting, Robert McC. 1993. *Smallholders, Householders: Farm Families and the Ecology of Intensive, Sustainable Agriculture.* Stanford, CA: Stanford University Press.

New Economics Foundation. 2004. *Chasing Progress: Beyond Measuring Economic Growth.* London, 2, Figure. www.neweconomics.org/

Newman, Katherine S. 1988. *Falling from Grace: The Experience of Downward Mobility in the American Middle Class.* New York: Free Press.

———. 1993. *Declining Fortunes: The Withering of the American Dream.* New York: Basic Books.

NIC (National Intelligence Council). 2000. *Global Trends 2015: A Dialogue about the Future With Nongovernment Experts.* NIC 2000-02. infowar.net/cia/publications/globaltrends2015/

———. 2004. *Mapping the Global Future: Report of the National Intelligence Council's 2020 Project.* NIC 2004-13. www.dni.gov/nic/NIC_2020_project.html

Nicklin, Flip. 1984. "Krill: Untapped Bounty from the Sea?" *National Geographic* 165(5): 626–43.

Noble, David F. 1993. *Progress Without People: In Defense of Luddism.* Chicago: Charles H. Kerr.

Noble, David Grant (Editor). 2004. *In Search of Chaco: New Approaches to an Archaeological Enigma.* Santa Fe, NM: School of American Research Press.

Nordhaus, William D. 1974. "Resources as a Constraint on Growth." *American Economic Review* 64: 22–26.

Nougier, Louis-Rene. 1954. "Essai sur le peuplement prehistorique de la France." *Population* (Paris) 9: 241–73.

Nulty, Leslie. 1972. *The Green Revolution in West Pakistan.* New York: Praeger.

O'Brien, Patrick K. 1988a. "The Cost and Benefits of British Imperialism 1864–1914." *Past & Present (Great Britain)* 120: 163–200.

———. 1988b. "The Political Economy of British Taxation, 1660–1815." *Economic History Review (Great Britain)* 41(1): 1–32.

Odum, Howard T. 1971. *Environment, Power, and Society.* New York: Wiley, Inter-Science.

Odum, Howard T., and Elisabeth C. Odum. 2001. *A Prosperous Way Down: Principles and Policies.* Boulder: University Press of Colorado.

Office of the United Nations High Commissioner for Human Rights. United Nations Millennium Declaration. General Assembly resolution 55/2 of September 8, 2000. www.ohchr.org/english/law/millennium.htm

Official Statistics of Norway. 1995. *Statistical Yearbook.* Oslo.

Oliver, Douglas L. 1973. *Bougainville: A Personal History.* Honolulu: University of Hawaii Press.

Olsen, Mary Kay Gilliland. 1993. "Bridge on the Sava: Ethnicity in Eastern Croatia, 1981–1991." *Anthropology of East Europe Review* 11 (1–2): 54–62.

Olson, Jerry S. 1985. "Cenozoic Fluctuations in Biotic Parts of the Global Carbon Cycle." In *The Carbon Cycle and Atmospheric CO2: Natural Variations Archean to Present*, edited by E. T. Sundquist and W. S. Broecker, 377–96. Geophysical Monograph 32. Washington, D.C.: American Geophysical Union.

Ostrom, E. 1990. *Governing the Commons: The Evolution of Institutions for Collective Action*. Cambridge: Cambridge University Press.

Otterbein, Keith F. 1968. "Internal War: A Cross-Cultural Study." *American Anthropologist* 70(2): 277–89.

———. 1970. *The Evolution of War: A Cross-Cultural Study*. New Haven, CT: Human Relations Area Files.

———. 1999. "A History of Research on Warfare in Anthropology." *American Anthropologist* 101(4): 794–805.

———. 2000. "The Doves Have Been Heard From, Where Are the Hawks?" *American Anthropologist* 102(4): 841–44.

Paddock, William, and Paul Paddock. 1967. *Famine—1975!* Boston: Little, Brown.

Payne, Roger. 1968. "Among Wild Whales." *New York Zoological Society Newsletter*, November, 1–6.

Pearce, David W., and Jeremy J. Warford. 1993. *World Without End: Economics, Environment, and Sustainable Development*. New York: Published for the World Bank by Oxford University Press.

Peoples, James G. 1982. "Individual or Group Advantage? A Reinterpretation of the Maring Ritual Cycle." *Current Anthropology* 23(3): 291–310.

Pessen, Edward. 1973. *Riches, Class, and Power Before the Civil War*. Lexington, MA: Heath and Company.

Peters, C. M., A. H. Gentry, and R. Mendelsohn. 1989. "Valuation of an Amazonian Rain Forest." *Nature* 339 (June 29).

Phillips, Kevin. 1990. *The Politics of Rich and Poor: Wealth and the American Electorate in the Reagan Aftermath*. New York: Random House.

———. 1994. *Arrogant Capital: Washington, Wall Street, and the Frustration of American Politics*. Boston: Little, Brown.

———. 2002. *Wealth and Democracy: A Political History of the American Rich*. New York: Broadway Books.

Pimm, Stuart L., et al. 1995. "The Future of Biodiversity." *Science* 269(5222): 347–50.

Platt, John. 1969. "What We Must Do." *Science* 166(3909): 1115–21.

Polgar, Steven. 1972. "Population History and Population Policies from an Anthropological Perspective." *Current Anthropology* (132): 203–11.

Political Risk Services. 1994. *Political Risk Yearbook*. Syracuse, NY: Political Risk Services.

Politis, Gustavo G., Jose L. Prado, and Roelf P. Beukens. 1995. "The Human Impact in Pleistocene-Holocene Extinctions in South America: The Pampean Case." *In Ancient People and Landscapes*, edited by E. Johnson, 187–205. Lubbock: Museum of Texas Tech University.

Pollan, Michael. 2006. *The Omnivore's Dilemma: A Natural History of Four Meals.* New York: Penguin Press.

Popkin, Barry M. 1998. "The Nutrition Transition and Its Health Implications in Lower-Income Countries." *Public Health Nutrition* 1(1): 5–21.

Popkin, Barry M., L. Armstrong, G. M. Bray, B. Caballero, B. Frei, and W. C. Willett. 2006. "A New Proposed Guidance System for Beverage Consumption in the United States." *American Journal of Clinical Nutrition* 83: 529–42.

Popper, Deborah Eppstein, and Frank J. Popper. 1987. "The Great Plains: From Dust to Dust." *Planning* 53(12): 12–18.

Porter, Bernard. 1968. *Critics of Empire.* London: Macmillan.

Powell, Douglas S., Joanne L. Faulkner, David R. Darr, Zhiliang Zhu, and Douglas W. MacCleery. 1993. *Forest Resources of the United States, 1992.* Rocky Mountain Forest and Range Experiment Station, General Technical Report RM-234. Fort Collins, CO: USDA, Forest Service.

Power, Thomas Michael. 1988. *The Economic Pursuit of Quality.* Armonk, NY: M. E. Sharpe.

PricewaterhouseCoopers. 2005. *The Defence Industry in the 21st Century.* www.pwc.com

Public Papers of the Presidents. 1960. *Dwight D. Eisenhower.* Washington, D.C.: Federal Register Division, National Archives and Records Service, General Services Administration, 1035–1040.

Quilter, Jeffrey, and Terry Stocker. 1983. "Subsistence Economies and the Origins of Andean Complex Societies." *American Anthropologist* 85(3): 545–62.

Rabb, Theodore K. 1967. *Enterprise and Empire: Merchant and Gentry Investment in the Expansion of England, 1515–1630.* Cambridge, MA: Harvard University Press.

Radin, Paul. 1971. *The World of Primitive Man.* New York: Dutton.

Rambo, A. Terry. 1985. *Primitive Polluters: Semang Impact on the Malaysian Tropical Rain Forest Ecosystem.* Anthropological Papers No. 76. Ann Arbor: Museum of Anthropology, University of Michigan.

Rappaport, Roy A. 1968. *Pigs for the Ancestors: Ritual in the Ecology of a New Guinea People.* New Haven: Yale University Press.

———. 1971. "The Flow of Energy in an Agricultural Society." *Scientific American* 224(3): 117–32.

———. 1977. "Maladaptation in Social Systems." In *The Evolution of Social Systems,* edited by J. Friedman and M. J. Rowlands, 49–71. London: Duckworth.

———. 1979. *Ecology, Meaning, and Religion.* Richmond, CA: North Atlantic.

Raskin, Paul, Tariq Banuri, Gilberto Gallopín, Pablo Gutman, Al Hammond, Robert Kates, and Rob Swart. 2002. *Great Transition: The Promise and Lure of the Times Ahead.* Global Scenario Group. Boston: Stockholm Environment Institute, Tellus Institute.

Rathje, William L., and Cullen Murphy. 1992. *Rubbish: The Archaeology of Garbage.* New York: HarperCollins Publishers.

Raup, David M. 1991. "A Kill Curve for Phanerozoic Marine Species." *Paleobiology* 17(1): 37.

Ravenstein, E. G. 1891. "Lands of the Globe Still Available for European Settlement." *Proceedings of the Royal Geographical Society* 13: 27–35.

Redfield, Robert. 1947. "The Folk Society." *American Journal of Sociology* 52(4): 293–308.

———. 1953. *The Primitive World and Its Transformations*. Ithaca, NY: Cornell University Press.

Redford, K. 1991. "The Ecologically Noble Savage." *Orion* 9: 24–29.

Rees, William E., and Mathis Wackernagel. 1994. "Ecological Footprints and Appropriated Carrying Capacity: Measuring the Natural Capital Requirements of the Human Economy." In *Investing in Natural Capital: The Ecological Economics Approach to Sustainability*, edited by AnnMari Jansson, Monica Hammer, Carl Folke, and Robert Costanza, 362–390. Washington, D.C.: Island Press.

Register, Richard. 2006. *Ecocities: Rebuilding Cities in Balance with Nature*. Gabriola Island, B.C.: New Society Publisher.

Reichel-Dolmatoff, Gerardo. 1971. *Amazonian Cosmos: The Sexual and Religious Symbolism of the Tukano Indians*. Chicago: University of Chicago Press.

Reisner, Marc. 1986. *Cadillac Desert: The American West and Its Disappearing Water*. New York: Viking Penguin.

Ribeiro, Darcy. 1968. *The Civilizational Process*. Washington, D.C.: Smithsonian Institution Press.

Richards, Paul W. 1973. "The Tropical Rain Forest." *Scientific American* 229(6): 58–67.

Riches, David. 1974. "The Netsilik Eskimo: A Special Case of Selective Female Infanticide." *Ethnology* 13(4): 351–61.

Robbins, Richard H. 1999. *Global Problems and the Culture of Capitalism*. Boston: Allyn and Bacon.

Robey, Bryant, Shea O. Rutstein, and Leo Morris. 1993. "The Fertility Decline in Developing Countries." *Scientific American* 269(6): 60–67.

Rojas, Jose Dualok. 1994. "UNCED: Ethics & Development from the Indigenous Point of View." United Nations Environment Programme (UNEP).

Rojstaczer, Stuart, Shannon M. Sterline, and Nathan J. Moore. 2001. "Human Appropriation of Photosynthesis Products." *Science* 294(5551): 2549–52.

Ross, Eric. 1998. *The Malthus Factor: Poverty, Politics and Population in Capitalist Development*. New York: Zed Books.

Roy, William G. 1983. "Interlocking Directorates and the Corporate Revolution." *Social Science History* 7(2): 143–64.

Rummel, R. J. 1997. *Death by Government*. New Brunswick, NJ: Transaction.

Ruttan, Lore M., and Monique Borgerhoff Mulder. 1999. "Are East African Pastoralists Truly Conservationists?" *Current Anthropology* 40(5): 621–52.

Ryan, Peter, ed. 1972. "Bougainville Copper Project." In *Encyclopedia of Papua New Guinea* 1: 92–102. Melbourne: Melbourne University Press.

Sachs, Jeffrey D. 2005. *The End of Poverty: Economic Possibilities of Our Time*. New York: Penguin.

Sahlins, Marshall. 1960. "Evolution: Specific and General." In *Evolution and Culture*, edited by Marshall Sahlins and Elman R. Service, 12–44. Ann Arbor: University of Michigan Press.

———. 1961. "The Segmentary Lineage: An Organization of Predatory Expansion." *American Anthropologist* 63(2), 322–45.

———. 1968. "Notes on the Original Affluent Society." In *Man the Hunter*, edited by Richard B. Lee and Irven DeVore, 85–89. Chicago: Aldine.

———. 1972. *Stone Age Economics*. Chicago: Aldine.

———. 1996. "The Sadness of Sweetness: The Native Anthropology of Western Cosmology." *Current Anthropology* 37(3): 395–428.

Sahlins, Marshall, and Elman R. Service, eds. 1960. *Evolution and Culture*. Ann Arbor: University of Michigan Press.

Sale, Kirkpatrick. 1980. *Human Scale*. New York: Coward, McCann & Geoghegan.

———. 1985. *Dwellers in the Land: The Bioregional Vision*. San Francisco: Sierra Club Books.

———. 1996a. "Principles of Bioregionalism." In *The Case Against the Global Economy and for a Turn Toward the Local*, edited by Jerry Mander and Edward Goldsmith, 471–84. San Francisco: Sierra Club Books.

———. 1996b. *Rebels Against the Future: The Luddites and Their War on the Industrial Revolution: Lessons for the Computer Age*. Reading, MA: Addison-Wesley.

Sampat, Payal. 2000. "Groundwater." *World Watch* (January/February): 10–22.

Samuels, Michael. 1982. "Popreg 1: A Simulation of Population Regulation Among the Maring of New Guinea." *Human Ecology* 10(2): 78–84.

Sapir, Edward. 1964. "Culture, Genuine and Spurious." In *Culture, Language and Personality*, edited by David G. Mandelbaum, 78–119. Berkeley and Los Angeles: University of California Press. Originally published in 1924.

Saucier, Jean-Francois. 1972. "Correlates of the Long Postpartum Taboo: A Cross-Cultural Study." *Current Anthropology* 13(2): 38–49.

Schele, Linda, and David Freidel. 1990. *A Forest of Kings: The Untold Story of the Ancient Maya*. New York: William Morrow & Co.

Scheper-Hughes, Nancy. 1992. *Death Without Weeping: The Violence of Everyday Life in Brazil*. Berkeley: University of California Press.

Schneider, David. 1955. "Abortion and Depopulation on a Pacific Island: Yap." In *Health, Culture, and Community*, edited by B. D. Paul, 211–35. New York: Russell Sage Foundation.

Schrire, C., and W. L. Steiger. 1974. "A Matter of Life and Death: An Investigation into the Practice of Female Infanticide in the Arctic." *Man* 9(2): 161–84.

Schumacher, E. F. 1973. *Small Is Beautiful: Economics As If People Mattered*. New York: Harper & Row.

Scott, James C. 1976. *The Moral Economy of the Peasant: Subsistence and Rebellion in Southeast Asia*. New Haven, CT: Yale University Press.

———. 1985. *Weapons of the Weak*. New Haven, CT: Yale University Press.

Sen, Amartya. 1981. *Poverty and Famines: An Essay on Entitlement and Deprivation.* Oxford: Clarendon Press.

Sengel, Randal A. 1973. "Comments." *Current Anthropology* 14(5): 540–42.

Service, Elman R. 1962. *Primitive Social Organization.* New York: Random House.

Seward, Desmond. 1986. *Napoleon's Family.* New York: Viking.

Sewell, Tom. 1992. *The World Grain Trade.* New York: Woodhead-Faulkner.

Shaler, Nathaniel S. 1905. *Man and the Earth.* New York: Duffield.

Shammas, Carole. 1990. *The Pre-industrial Consumer in England and America.* Oxford: Oxford University Press.

———. 1993. "Changes in English and Anglo-American Consumption from 1550 to 1800." In *Consumption and the World of Goods,* edited by John Brewer and Roy Porter, 177–205. London and New York: Routledge.

Shantzis, Steven B., and William W. Behrens III. 1973. "Population Control Mechanisms in a Primitive Agricultural Society." In *Toward Global Equilibrium,* edited by D. H. Meadows and D. L. Meadows, 257–88. Cambridge, MA: Wright-Allen.

Sharpley, A. N., T. Daniel, T. Sims, J. Lemunyon, R. Stevens, and R. Parry. 1999. *Agricultural Phosphorus and Eutrophication.* United States Department of Agriculture, Agricultural Research Service. ARS-149.

Shell International. 2005. *Shell Global Scenarios to 2025: Executive Summary and Excerpts.* Shell International Limited.

Sherratt, Andrew G. 1981. "Plough and Pastoralism: Aspects of the Secondary Products Revolution." In *Pattern of the Past: Studies in Honour of David Clarke,* edited by I. Hodder, G. Isaac, and N. Hammond, 261–305. Cambridge: Cambridge University Press.

Simmons, Matthew R. 2000. *Revisiting the Limits to Growth: Could the Club of Rome Have Been Correct, After All? An Energy White Paper.* Simmons & Company International. www.simmonsco-intl.com/research

Simon, David R. 1999. *Elite Deviance.* 6th ed. Boston: Allyn and Bacon.

Simon, Herbert A. 1957. *Models of Man: Social and Rational.* New York: John Wiley.

Simon, Julian. 1981. *The Ultimate Resource.* Princeton, NJ: Princeton University Press.

Sklair, Leslie. 1991. *Sociology of the Global System.* Baltimore, MD: Johns Hopkins University Press.

Smil, Vaclav. 2002. *The Earth's Biosphere: Evolution, Dynamics, and Change.* Cambridge, MA: The MIT Press.

———. 2005. *Creating the Twentieth Century: Technical Innovations of 1867–1914 and Their Lasting Impact.* Oxford and New York: Oxford University Press.

Smith, Adam. 1776. *An Inquiry into the Nature and Causes of the Wealth of Nations.* London: Strahan & Cadell.

———. 1976. *The Theory of Moral Sentiments.* Indianapolis, IN: Liberty Classics. Originally published in 1759.

Smith, E. A., and S. A. Smith. 1994. "Inuit Sex-Ratio Variation: Population Control, Ethnographic Error, or Parental Manipulation?" *Current Anthropology* 35: 595–614.

Smith, Eric Alden. 1983. "Anthropological Applications of Optimal Foraging Theory: A Critical Review." *Current Anthropology* 24: 625–51.

———. 1991. "The Current State of Hunter-Gatherer Studies." *Current Anthropology* 32: 72–75.

Smith, Philip E. 1972. *The Consequences of Food Production*. Module in Anthropology No. 21. Reading, MA: Addison-Wesley.

Sofer, Cyril. 1965. "Buying and Selling: A Study in the Sociology of Distribution." *Sociological Review* (July): 183–209.

Solow, Robert M. 1974. "The Economics of Resources or the Resources of Economics." *American Economic Review* 64(2): 1–14.

Soltow, Lee. 1975. *Men and Wealth in the United States, 1850–1870*. New Haven and London: Yale University Press.

Somer, Adrian. 1976. "Attempt at an Assessment of the World's Tropical Moist Forests." *Unasylva* 28 (112–13): 5–23.

Sorokin, Pitirim. 1962. *Social and Cultural Dynamics*. vol. 3. *Fluctuation of Social Relationships, War, and Revolution*. New York: The Bedminister Press, 306–31.

Spaulding, Willard M., Jr., and Ronald D. Ogden. 1968. *Effects of Surface Mining on the Fish and Wildlife Resources of the United States*. Bureau of Sport Fisheries and Wildlife Resources. Publication 68. Washington, D.C.: U.S. Government Printing Office.

Spoehr, Alexander. 1956. "Cultural Differences in the Interpretation of Natural Resources." In *Man's Role in Changing the Face of the Earth*, edited by William L. Thomas Jr., 93–102. Chicago: University of Chicago Press.

Spooner, Brian. 1973. *The Cultural Ecology of Pastoral Nomads*. Module in Anthropology No. 45. Reading, MA: Addison-Wesley.

SRES Home (Special Report on Emissions Scenarios). sres.ciesin.org/final_data .html

Steingarten, Jeffrey. 1997. *The Man Who Ate Everything and Other Gastronomic Feats, Disputes, and Pleasurable Pursuits*. New York: Random House, Vintage Books.

Steinhart, John S., and Carol E. Steinhart. 1974. "Energy Use in the U.S. Food System." *Science* 184(4134): 307–16.

Stiglitz, Joseph E. 2002. *Globalizations and Its Discontents*. New York: W. W. Norton.

Stiglitz, Joseph E., and Andrew Charlton. 2005. *Fair Trade for All: How Trade Can Promote Development*. New York: Oxford University Press.

Stockholm International Peace Research Institute (SIPRI). Stockholm International Peace Research Institute. 2006. *SIPRI Yearbook 2006: Armaments, Disarmament and International Security*. New York: Humanities Press.

———. 2007. *Facts on International Relations and Security Trends* (FIRST), International Relations and Security Network (ISN). first.sipri.org/

Stone, Lawrence. 1965. *The Crisis of the Aristocracy 1558–1641*. London: Oxford University Press.

———. 1973. *Family and Fortune: Studies in Aristocratic Finance in the Sixteenth and Seventeenth Centuries*. Oxford: Oxford University Press.

Stork, Nigel. 1997. "Measuring Global Biodiversity and Its Decline." In *Biodiversity II: Understanding and Protecting Our Biological Resources*, edited by Marjorie L. Reaka-Kudla, Don E. Wilson, and Edward O. Wilson. Washington, D.C.: Joseph Henry Press.

Story, Mary, and Simone French. 2004. "Food Advertising and Marketing Directed at Children and Adolescents in the U.S." *International Journal of Behavioral Nutrition and Physical Activity* 1(3).

Stover, Leon N., and Takeko Kawai Stover. 1976. *China: An Anthropological Perspective*. Pacific Palisades, CA: Goodyear Publishing Co.

Stuart, David E. 2000. *Anasazi America: Seventeen Centuries on the Road from Center Place*. Albuquerque, NM: University of New Mexico Press.

Stull, Donald D., and Michael J. Broadway. 2004. *Slaughterhouse Blues: The Meat and Poultry Industry in North America*. Belmont, CA: Wadsworth/Thomson Learning.

Sussman, Robert W. 1972. "Child Transport, Family Size, and Increase in Human Population During the Neolithic." *Current Anthropology* 13(2): 258–59.

Suttles, Wayne. 1960. "Affinal Ties, Subsistence, and Prestige Among the Coast Salish." *American Anthropologist* 62: 296–305.

Taagepera, Rein. 1978a. "Size and Duration of Empires: Systematics of Size." *Social Science Research* 7: 108–27.

———. 1978b. "Size and Duration of Empires: Growth-Decline Curves, 3000 to 600 B.C." *Social Science Research* 7: 180–96.

———. 1997. "Expansion and Contraction Patterns of Large Polities: Context for Russia." *International Studies Quarterly* 41: 475–504.

Tainter, Joseph A. 2006. "Archaeology of Overshoot and Collapse." *Annual Review of Anthropology*, 2006, 35(1): 59–74.

Talberth, John, Karen Wolowicz, Jason Venetoulis, Michel Gelobter, Paul Boyle, and Bill Mott. 2006. *The Ecological Fishprint of Nations: Measuring Humanity's Impact on Marine Ecosystems*. Oakland, CA: Redefining Progress. www.rprogress.org/newprograms/sustIndi/fishprint/index.shtml

Talburt, William E., and Ora Smith. 1967. *Potato Processing*. Westport, CT: Avi.

Tax, Sol. 1977. "Anthropology for the World of the Future: Thirteen Professions and Three Proposals." *Current Anthropology* 36(3): 225–34.

Tellus Institute. 2005. *Great Transition Initiative: Visions and Pathways for a Hopeful Future*. GTI Brochure. www.gtinitiative.org/default.asp?action=42

Thinley, Lyonpo Jigmi Y. 2004. "Values and Development: 'Gross National Happiness.'" In *Gross National Happiness and Development. Proceedings of the First International Seminar on Operationalization of Gross National Happiness*, edited by Karma Ura and Karma Galay, 12–23. Thimphu, Bhutan: The Centre for Bhutan Studies, 14. www.bhutanstudies.org.bt

Thorpe, I. J. N. 2003. "Anthropology, Archaeology, and the Origin of Warfare." *World Archaeology* 35(1): 145–65.

Thu, Kendall M., and E. Paul Durrenberger, eds. 1998. *Pigs, Profits, and Rural Communities*. Albany: State University of New York Press.

Toffler, Alvin. 1971. *Future Shock*. New York: Bantam.

Tokar, Brian. 1987. *The Green Alternative: Creating an Ecological Future*. San Pedro, CA: R. & E. Miles.

Toth, James. 1992. "Doubts About Growth: The Town of Carlisle in Transition." *Urban Anthropology* 21(l): 2–44.

Trowell, Hugh C. 1954. "Kwashiorkor." *Scientific American* 191(6): 46–50.

Turnbull, Colin. 1968. "The Importance of Flux in Two Hunting Societies." In *Man the Hunter*, edited by Richard B. Lee and Irven DeVore, 132–37. Chicago: Aldine.

Turner, B. L., II, William C. Clark, Robert W. Kates, John F. Richards, Jessica T. Mathews, and William B. Meyer. 1990. *The Earth as Transformed by Human Action: Global and Regional Changes in the Biosphere over the Past 300 years*. Cambridge: Cambridge University Press.

Tuxill, John. 1997. "Primate Diversity Dwindling Worldwide." In *Vital Signs 1991: The Environmental Trends That Are Shaping Our Future*, edited by Lester R. Brown, Michael Renner, Christopher Flavin, and Linda Starke, 100–101. New York and London: W. W. Norton and Co.

———. 1999. "Appreciating the Benefits of Plant Biodiversity." In *State of the World 1999: A Worldwatch Institute Report on Progress Toward a Sustainable Society*, edited by Lester R. Brown, Christopher Flavin, Hilary French, and Linda Starke, 96–114. New York and London: W. W. Norton and Co.

Tuxill, John, and Chris Bright. 1998. "Losing Strands in the Web of Life." In *State of the World 1998: A Worldwatch Institute Report on Progress Toward a Sustainable Society*, edited by Lester R. Brown, Christopher Flavin, Hilary French, and Linda Starke, 41–58. New York and London: W. W. Norton and Co.

Tylor, Edward B. 1889. "On a Method of Investigating the Development of Institutions; Applied to Laws of Marriage and Descent." *Journal of the Royal Anthropological Institute* 18: 245–69.

UNCE (United Nations Economic Commission for Europe). The Statistical Yearbook of the Economic Commission for Europe 2005. www.unece.org/stats/trends2005/Sources/110_Average annual population growth rate.pdf

Underwood, Jane H. 1973. "The Demography of a Myth: Abortion in Yap." *Human Biology in Oceania* 2: 115–27.

Union of Concerned Scientists. 1992. *World Scientists' Warning to Humanity*. First issued on November 18, 1992. www.ucsusa.org/ucs/about/1992-world-scientists-warning-to-humanity.html

United Kingdom, Department of the Environment. 1990. *This Common Inheritance: Britain's Environmental Strategy*. (September). House of Commons Cm. 1200.

United Kingdom, Department for Environment, Food and Rural Affairs. 2004. *Achieving a Better Quality of Life: Review of Progress Towards Sustainable Development*. Government Annual Report 2003. London: Defra Publications.

United Nations. 2005. *The Millennium Development Goals Report*. New York. United Nations Department of Public Information.

United Nations, Department of Economic and Social Affairs. 1992. *Agenda 21*. Division for Sustainable Development. www.un.org/esa/sustdev/documents/agenda21/index.htm (April 2007).

UNDP. United Nations Development Programme. 2005. *Human Development Report 2005: International Cooperation at a Crossroads. Aid, Trade and Security in an Unequal World*. New York: UNDP. hdr.undp.org/

UNEP. United Nations Environment Program. 1992. *Rio Declaration on Environment and Development*. www.unep.org/Documents.Multilingual/Default.asp?DocumentID=78&ArticleID=1163 (April 2007).

———. 2002. *Global Environment Outlook 3: Past, Present and Future Perspectives*. London: Earthscan.

United Nations, Food and Agriculture Organization. 2006. *Global Forest Resources Assessment 2005: Progress Towards Sustainable Forest Management*. FAO Forestry Paper 147. www.fao.org/forestry/site/32039/en

United Nations, Millennium Project. 2005. *Investing in Development: A Practical Plan to Achieve the Millennium Development Goals*. London: Earthscan.

United Nations Secretariat, Department of Economic and Social Affairs, Population Division. 2004. *World Population Prospects: The 2004 Revision and World Urbanization Prospects*. esa.un.org/unpp

United Nations, Trusteeship Council. 1968. "Report of the United Nations Visiting Mission to the Trust Territory of New Guinea, 1968." *Trusteeship Council Official Records: Thirty-fifth Session* (May 27–June 19, 1968). Supplement No. 2. New York.

———. 1971. "Report of the United Nations Visiting Mission to the Trust Territory of New Guinea, 1971." *Trusteeship Council Official Records: Thirty-eighth Session* (May 25–June 18, 1971). Supplement No. 2. New York.

U.S. Bureau of the Census. 1960. *Historical Statistics of the United States Colonial Times to 1957*. Washington, D.C.: U.S. Government Printing Office.

———. 1983. *Statistical Abstract of the United States: 1984*, 104th ed. Washington, D.C.: U.S. Government Printing Office.

U.S. Central Intelligence Agency (CIA). The World Factbook 2007. www.cia.gov/cia/publications/factbook/index.html

U.S. Department of Agriculture. 1992. *Agricultural Statistics*. Washington, D.C.: U.S. Government Printing Office.

———. 2000. "Annual Spotlight on the U.S. Food System, 2000." *FoodReview* 23(3).

———. 2002 *Census of Agriculture*, vol. 1, chapter 1: U.S. National Level Data. Table 41. www.nass.usda.gov/census/census02/volume1/us/index1.htm

U.S. Department of Agriculture (USDA), Economic Research Service. 2002. *The U.S. Food Marketing System, 2002*. Agricultural Economic Report No. 811.

———. 2006. *U.S. Food Supply: Nutrients and Other Food Components, 1909 to 2004. Nutrient Availability Spreadsheet* (March 3).

———. 2007. *Food Price Spreads*, table 1—Marketing bill and farm value components of consumer expenditures for domestically produced farm foods. www .ers.usda.gov/Briefing/FoodPriceSpreads/bill/table1.htm

———. 2007. *Potato Statistics* (91011), table 52—Utilization of U.S. potatoes, 1959–2001.

U.S. Department of Agriculture (USDA), Grain Inspection, Packers and Stockyards Administration. 2006. *Assessment of the Cattle, Hog, and Poultry Industries. 2005 Report*. archive.gipsa.usda.gov/pubs/05assessment.pdf

U.S. Department of Commerce, Bureau of the Census. 1969a. *Census of Agriculture*. vol. 1, pt. 46, *Area Reports*, [state of] Washington. Washington, D.C.: U.S. Government Printing Office.

———. 1969b. *Census of Agriculture*, vol. 5, pt. 4, *Sugar Crops, Potatoes, Other Specified Crops*. Washington, D.C.: U.S. Government Printing Office.

———. 1984. *1982 Census of Agriculture*. vol. 1, pt. 5, *Geographic Area Series*. California. Washington, D.C.: U.S. Government Printing Office.

———. 1983–2007. *Statistical Abstract of the United States*. Various annual editions. Washington, D.C.: U.S. Government Printing Office.

U.S. Department of Education, National Center for Education Statistics. 2005. *Revenues and Expenditures for Public Elementary and Secondary Education: School Year 2002-2003* (NCES 2005-353), nces.ed.gov/ccd/pubs/npefs03/findings.asp#3

U.S. Department of Energy, Energy Information Administration. 2006. *Annual Energy Review 2005*. Report No. DOE/EIA-0384 (2005).

———. 2006. International Energy Annual. Table E.1 World total primary energy consumption, 1980–2004. www.eia.doe.gov/iea/wecbtu.html

———. 2006. International Energy Annual 2004. Table E1.p Energy Intensity: Total Primary Energy Consumption per Dollar of Gross Domestic Product Using Purchasing Power Parities, 1980–2004. (August 23).

———. 2007. *Monthly Energy Review*. (January).

U.S. Department of the Interior, Bureau of Land Management. 1974. *Draft Environmental Impact Statement: Proposed Federal Coal Leasing Program*. 2 vols. Washington, D.C.: U.S. Government Printing Office.

U.S. Department of Justice, Bureau of Justice Statistics. 2006. *Uniform Crime Reports*, www.ojp.usdoj.gov/bjs/glance/tables/4meastab.htm

U.S. Internal Revenue Service, (IRS). 2005. *Personal Wealth 2001: Top Wealth Holders with Gross Assets of $675,000 or More, Type of Property by Size of Net Worth*. IRS, Statistics of Income Division.

U.S. National Advisory Commission on Civil Disorders. 1968. Kerner Report. Washington, D.C.: U.S. Government Printing Office.

U.S. National Commission on the Causes and Prevention of Violence. 1969. *Justice: To Establish Justice, to Ensure Domestic Tranquility.* Final Report. Washington, D.C.: U.S. Government Printing Office.

U.S. President's Materials Policy Commission. 1952. *Resources for Freedom.* Paley Commission Report. Washington, D.C.: U.S. Government Printing Office.

U.S. President's Science Advisory Committee. 1967. *The World Food Problem: A Report of the Panel on the World Food Supply.* 3 vols. Washington, D.C.: U.S. Government Printing Office.

Van der Veen, Marijke. 2005. "Gardens and Fields: The Intensity and Scale of Food Production." *World Archaeology* 37(2): 157–63.

Vanek, Joann. 1974. "Time Spent in Housework." *Scientific American* 23(15): 116–20.

Van Velzen, H. U. E. Thoden, and W. Van Wetering. 1960. "Residence, Power Groups and Intra-societal Aggression." *International Archives of Ethnography* 49: 169–200.

Veblen, Thorstein. 1912. *The Theory of the Leisure Class: An Economic Study of Institutions.* New York: Macmillan Company.

Venetoulis, Jason, and Cliff Cobb. 2004. *The Genuine Progress Indicator 1950–2002 (2004 Update).* Oakland, CA: Redefining Progress. www.rprogress.org/projects/gpi/

Vickers, William. 1988. "Game Depletion Hypothesis of Amazonian Adaptation: Data from a Native Community." *Science* 239: 1521–22.

———. 1991. "Hunting Yields and Game Composition over Ten Years in Amazon Indian Territory." In *Neotropical Wildlife Use and Conservation,* edited by J. Robinson and K. Redford, 53–81. Chicago: University of Chicago Press.

Vitousek, Peter M., Paul R. Ehrlich, Anne H. Ehrlich, and Pamela A. Matson. 1986. "Human Appropriation of the Products of Photosynthesis." *BioScience* 36(6): 368–73.

Wackernagel, M., and W. E. Rees. 1996. *Our Ecological Footprint: Reducing Human Impact on the Earth.* Gabriola Island, B.C.: New Society Publishers.

Wackernagel, Mathis, Niels B. Schulz, Diana Deumling, Alejandro Callejas Linares, Martin Jenkins, Valerie Chad Monfreda, Jonathan Loh, Norman Myers, Richard Norgaard, and Jørgen Randers. 2002. "Tracking the Ecological Overshoot of the Human Economy." *Proceedings of the National Academy of Science* 99(14): 9266–71.

Wackernagel, Mathis, and Judith Silverstein. 2000. "Big Things First: Focusing on the Scale Imperative with the Ecological Footprint." *Ecological Economics* 32: 391–94.

Wagley, Charles. 1951. "Cultural Influences on Population." *Revista do Museu Paulista* 5: 95–104.

Walker, B. H., et al. 1981. "Stability of Semi-Arid Savanna Grazing Systems." *Journal of Ecology* 69: 473–98.

Wallace, Scott. 2007. "Last of the Amazon." *National Geographic* 211(1): 40–71.

Wallerstein, Immanuel. 1974. *The Modern World-System: Capitalist Agriculture and the Origins of the European World-Economy in the Sixteenth Century.* New York: Academic Press.

———. 1990. "Culture as the Ideological Battleground of the Modern World-System." *Theory, Culture, and Society* 7:31–55.

Walter, Edward. 1981. *The Immorality of Limiting Growth.* Albany: State University of New York Press.

Warner, Marina. 1972. *The Dragon Empress: The Life and Times of Tz'U-His Empress Dowager of China 1835–1908.* New York: Macmillan.

Warren-Rhodes, Kimberley, and Albert Koeing. 2001. "Ecosystem Appropriation by Hong Kong and Its Implication for Sustainable Development." *Ecological Economics* 39(3): 347–59.

Washington Potato Commission. 1962. *Proceedings of the Annual Washington Potato Conference and Trade Fair.* Moses Lake, WA: Washington Potato Commission.

Watson, Patty Jo. 1995. "Explaining the Transition to Agriculture." In *Last Hunters, First Farmers: New Perspectives on the Prehistoric Transition to Agriculture,* edited by T. D. Price and A. B. Gebauer, 3–37. Santa Fe, NM: School of American Research Press.

WCED (World Commission on Environment and Development). 1987. *Our Common Future.* Oxford: Oxford University Press.

Weaver, Richard M. 1984. *Ideas Have Consequences.* Chicago and London: University of Chicago Press. Originally published in 1948.

Weber, Max. 1930. *The Protestant Ethic and the Spirit of Capitalism.* London: George Allen & Unwin.

Webster, David. 1981. "Late Pleistocene Extinction and Human Predation: A Critical Overview." In *Omnivorous Primates: Gathering and Hunting in Human Evolution,* edited by Robert S. Harding and Geza Teleki, 556–95. New York: Columbia University Press.

———. 1998. "Warfare and Status Rivalry: Lowland Maya and Polynesian Comparisons." In *Archaic States,* edited by Gary M. Feinman and Joyce Marcus, 311–51. Santa Fe, NM: School of American Research Press.

Weeratunge, Nireka. 2000. "Nature, Harmony, and the *Kaliyugaya*: Global/Local Discourses on the Human-Environment Relationship." *Current Anthropology* 41(2): 249–68.

Weiss, K. M. 1973. "Demographic Models for Anthropology." *American Antiquity* 38(2), pt. 2, Memoir 27.

Western, David, and Virginia Finch. 1986. "Cattle and Pastoralism: Survival and Production in Arid Lands." *Human Ecology* 14(1): 77–94.

Western Wood Products Association. 2002. *Lumber Track.* (Oct. 2002). www.wwpa.org/econpubs.htm

White, Allen L. 2006. *Transforming the Corporation.* GTI Paper Series, Frontiers of a Great Transition 5. Boston: Tellus Institute, 1.

White, Leslie A. 1949. *The Science of Culture.* New York: Grove.

———. 1959. *The Evolution of Culture*. New York: McGraw-Hill.

White, Lynn, Jr. 1967. "The Historical Roots of Our Ecological Crisis." *Science* 155(3767): 1203–7.

Whitesides, George M., and George W. Crabtree. 2007. "Don't Forget Long-Term Fundamental Research in Energy." *Science* 315: 796–98.

Whiting, John M. 1969. "Effects of Climate on Certain Cultural Practices." In *Environment and Cultural Behavior: Ecological Studies in Cultural Anthropology*, edited by A. P. Vayda, 416–55. New York: Natural History Press.

WHO, World Health Organization. 2003. *Diet, Nutrition and the Prevention of Chronic Diseases*. Report of a Joint WHO/FAO Expert Consultation. WHO Technical Report Series 916. Geneva: WHO.

Whyte, William Foote, and Kathleen King Whyte. 1988. *Making Mondragn: The Growth and Dynamics of the Worker Cooperative Complex*. Ithaca, NY: ILR Press.

Wiebe, Keith. 2006. "Global Resources and Productivity." In *Agricultural Resources and Environmental Indicators*, edited by Keith Wiebe and Noel Gollehon, 81–88. Economic Information Bulletin 16. USDA Economic Research Service.

Wilkinson, Richard G. 1996. *Unhealthy Societies: The Afflictions of Inequality*. London and New York: Routledge.

Willey, Gordon R., and Demitric B. Shimkin. 1971. "The Collapse of Classic Maya Civilization in the Southern Lowlands: A Symposium Summary Statement." *Southwestern Journal of Anthropology* 27(10): 1–18.

Williams, Michael. 1990. *Americans and Their Forests: A Historical Geography*. New York: Cambridge University Press.

Wills, John E., Jr. 1993. "European Consumption and Asian Production in the Seventeenth and Eighteenth Centuries." In *Consumption and the World of Goods*, edited by John Brewer and Roy Porter, 133–47. London and New York: Routledge.

Wilson, Edward O. 2002. *The Future of Life*. New York: Alfred A. Knopf.

Wilson, William Julius, James M. Quane, and Bruce H. Rankin. 1998. "The New Urban Poverty: Consequences of the Economic and Social Decline of Inner-City Neighborhoods." In *Locked in the Poorhouse: Cities, Race, and Poverty in the United States*, edited by Fred R. Harris and Lynn A. Curtis, 57–78. Lanham, MD: Rowman & Littlefield.

Wingfield-Hayes, Rupert. 2007. "Moscow's Suburb for Billionaires." BBC News. (April 21).

Winterhalder, B., W. Baillargeon, F. Cappelletto, I. Daniel, and C. Prescott. 1988. "The Population Ecology of Hunter-Gatherers and Their Prey." *Journal of Anthropological Archaeology* 7: 289–328.

Winterhalder, B., and F. A. Smith, eds. 1981. *Hunter-Gatherer Foraging Strategies: Ethnographic and Archaeological Analyses*. Chicago: University of Chicago Press.

Wolf, Eric R. 1957. "Closed Corporate Peasant Communities in Mesoamerica and Central Java." *Southwest Journal of Anthropology* 13(1): 1–18.

———. 1982. *Europe and the People Without History*. Berkeley: University of California Press.

Woodburn, James. 1968a. "An Introduction to Hadza Ecology." In *Man the Hunter*, edited by Richard B. Lee and Irven DeVore, 49–55. Chicago: Aldine.

———. 1968b. "Stability and Flexibility in Hadza Residential Groupings." In *Man the Hunter*, edited by Richard B. Lee and Irven DeVore, 103–10. Chicago: Aldine.

World Almanac. 1993. *The World Almanac and Book of Facts 1994*. Mahwah, NJ: Funk and Wagnalls.

———. 1999. *The World Almanac and Book of Facts 2000*. Mahwah, NJ: World Almanac Books.

———. 2004. *The World Almanac and Book of Facts 2004*. New York: World Almanac Books.

World Bank. 1983. *World Development Report 1983*. New York: Oxford University Press.

———. 1994. *World Development Report 1994: Infrastructure for Development*. New York: Oxford University Press.

———. 1999. *Entering the 21st Century: World Development Report 1999/2000*. New York: Oxford University Press.

———. 2005. *World Development Indicators, 2005*. New York: Oxford University Press.

———. 2006. *World Development Indicators*, devdata.worldbank.org/data-query/

———. 2006. *World Development Report 2006. Equity and Development*. New York: Oxford University Press.

Worm, Boris, et al. 2006. "Impacts of Biodiversity Loss on Ocean Ecosystem Services." *Science* 314 (November 3): 787–90.

Wright, David Hamilton. 1990. "Human Impacts on Energy Flow Through Natural Ecosystems, and Implications for Species Endangerment." *Ambio* 19(4): 189–94.

Wright, Quincy. 1942. *A Study of War*. 2 vols. Chicago: University of Chicago Press.

Wrigley, E. A. 1994. "The Classical Economists, the Stationary State, and the Industrial Revolution." In *Was the Industrial Revolution Necessary?* edited by Graeme Snooks, 27–42. London and New York: Routledge.

WWF International. 2006. *Living Planet Report 2006*. World Wildlife Fund. www.panda.org/news_facts/publications/living_planet_report/index.cfm

Yde, Jens. 1965. "Material Culture of the Waiwai. Narionalmuseets Skrifter." *Etnografisk Roekke* 10. Copenhagen: National Museum.

Yengoyan, Aram A. 1981. "Infanticide and Birth Order: An Empirical Analysis of Preferential Female Infanticide Among Australian Aboriginal Populations." In *The Perception of Evolution: Essays Honoring Joseph B. Birdsell*, edited by Larry L. Mai, Eugenia Shanklin, and R. W. Sussman, *Anthropology UCLA* 7: 255–73.

York, Richard, Eugene A. Rosa, Thomas Dietz. 2003. "STIRPAT, IPAT and Im-
    PACT: Analytic Tools for Unpacking the Driving Forces of Environmental Im-
    pacts." *Ecological Economics* 46: 351–65.
Young, Vernon R., and Nevin S. Scrimshaw. 1971. "The Physiology of Starva-
    tion." *Scientific American* 225(4): 14–21.
Zipf, George Kingsley. 1949. *Human Behavior and the Principle of Least Effort: An In-
    troduction to Human Ecology*. Cambridge, MA: Addison-Wesley. Reprint 1965,
    New York and London: Hafner Publishing Co.
Zubrow, Ezra B. 1975. *Prehistoric Carrying Capacity*. Menlo Park, CA: Cummings.

Index

About the Author

John H. Bodley is a cultural anthropologist and Regents Professor at Washington State University, where he has taught since 1970. His Ph.D. is from the University of Oregon. His research interests include indigenous peoples, cultural ecology, and contemporary issues. He conducted field research with the Ashaninka, Conibo, and Shipibo indigenous groups in the Peruvian Amazon throughout his early career. He has visited other indigenous groups in Alaska, Australia, British Columbia, Dominica, Ecuador, Guatemala, Mexico, and the Philippines. He has held visiting academic appointments at the University of Alaska, Fairbanks, and the University of Uppsala, Sweden, and was a visiting researcher at the International Work Group for Indigenous Affairs in Copenhagen. In 1986, he served on the Tasaday Commission for the University of the Philippines Department of Anthropology in Manila, and was a member of the advisory subcommittee for the human rights section of the American Association for the Advancement of Science's Committee on Scientific Freedom and Responsibility.